Lecture Notes in Computer Science 4637

Commenced Publication in 1973
Founding and Former Series Editors:
Gerhard Goos, Juris Hartmanis, and Jan van Leeuwen

Christopher Kruegel   Richard Lippmann
Andrew Clark (Eds.)

Recent Advances in Intrusion Detection

10th International Symposium, RAID 2007
Gold Coast, Australia, September 5-7, 2007
Proceedings

 Springer

Volume Editors

Christopher Kruegel
Secure Systems Lab
Technical University of Vienna
1040 Vienna, Austria
E-mail: chris@seclab.tuwien.ac.at

Richard Lippmann
Lincoln Laboratory
Massachusetts Institute of Technology
Lexington, MA 02420-9108, USA
E-mail: lippmann@ll.mit.edu

Andrew Clark
Information Security Institute
Queensland University of Technology
Brisbane, QLD 4001, Australia
E-mail: a.clark@qut.edu.au

Library of Congress Control Number: 2007932747

CR Subject Classification (1998): K.6.5, K.4, E.3, C.2, D.4.6

LNCS Sublibrary: SL 4 – Security and Cryptology

ISSN   0302-9743
ISBN-10   3-540-74319-7 Springer Berlin Heidelberg New York
ISBN-13   978-3-540-74319-4 Springer Berlin Heidelberg New York

Springer is a part of Springer Science+Business Media

springer.com

© Springer-Verlag Berlin Heidelberg 2007
Printed in Germany

Typesetting: Camera-ready by author, data conversion by Scientific Publishing Services, Chennai, India
Printed on acid-free paper   SPIN: 12110704   06/3180   5 4 3 2 1 0

Preface

On behalf of the Program Committee, it is our pleasure to present the proceedings of the 10th Symposium on Recent Advances in Intrusion Detection (RAID 2007), which took place in Queensland, Australia, September 5–7, 2007. As in every year since 1998, the symposium brought together leading researchers and practitioners from academia, government, and industry to discuss intrusion detection research and practice.

This year, the RAID Program Committee received 101 paper submissions from all over the world. All submissions were carefully reviewed by at least three members of the Program Committee and judged on the basis of scientific novelty, importance to the field, and technical quality. The final selection took place at the Program Committee meeting held in Oakland, USA, May 22–23, 2007. Sixteen full papers and one short paper were selected for presentation and publication in the conference proceedings, placing RAID among the most competitive conferences in the area of computer security.

A successful symposium is the result of the joint effort of many people. In particular, we would like to thank all the authors who submitted papers, whether accepted or not. We also thank the Program Committee members and additional reviewers for their hard work in evaluating submissions. In addition, we want to thank the General Chair, George Mohay, for handling the conference arrangements, Rei Safavi-Naini for publicizing the conference, Andrew Clark for putting together the conference proceedings, and Ming-Yuh Huang for finding sponsor support.

Finally, we extend our thanks to Northwest Security Institute, SAP, and CERT at the Software Engineering Institute, Carnegie Mellon University for their sponsorship and support.

September 2007

Christopher Kruegel
Richard Lippmann
Andrew Clark

Organization

RAID 2007 was organized by the Information Security Institute, Queensland University of Technology, Brisbane, Australia.

Conference Chairs

General Chair	George Mohay (Queensland University of Technology, Australia)
Program Chair	Christopher Kruegel (Technical University of Vienna, Austria)
Program Co-chair	Richard Lippmann (Massachusetts Institute of Technology, USA)
Publication Chair	Andrew Clark (Queensland University of Technology, Australia)
Publicity Chair	Rei Safavi-Naini (University of Calgary, Canada)
Sponsorship Chair	Ming-Yuh Huang (The Boeing Company, USA)

Program Committee

Michael Behringer	Cisco Systems Inc., France
Sungdeok Cha	Korea Advanced Institute of Science and Technology, Korea
Andrew Clark	Queensland University of Technology, Australia
Marc Dacier	Institut Eurécom, France
Hervé Debar	France Telecom R&D, France
Ulrich Flegel	University of Dortmund, Germany
Jonathon Giffin	Georgia Institute of Technology, USA
Thorsten Holz	University of Mannheim, Germany
Farnam Jahanian	University of Michigan and Arbor Networks, USA
Richard A. Kemmerer	University of California, Santa Barbara, USA
Kwok-Yan Lam	Tsinghua University, China
Wenke Lee	Georgia Institute of Technology, USA
Richard Lippmann	MIT Lincoln Laboratory, USA
Raffael Marty	ArcSight Inc., USA
Roy Maxion	Carnegie Mellon University, USA
Ludovic Mé	Supélec, France
George Mohay	Queensland University of Technology, Australia
Aloysius Mok	University of Texas, Austin, USA
Benjamin Morin	Supélec, France
Rei Safavi-Naini	University of Calgary, Canada
Vern Paxson	International Computer Science Institute and Lawrence Berkeley National Laboratory, USA

Robin Sommer   International Computer Science Institute and
                             Lawrence Berkeley National Laboratory, USA
Dawn Song   Carnegie Mellon University, USA
Salvatore Stolfo   Columbia University, USA
Toshihiro Tabata   Okayama University, Japan
Vijay Varadharajan   Macquarie University, Australia
Giovanni Vigna   University of California, Santa Barbara, USA
Jianying Zhou   Institute for Infocomm Research, Singapore

Steering Committee

Marc Dacier (Chair)   Institut Eurécom, France
Hervé Debar   France Telecom R&D, France
Deborah Frincke   Pacific Northwest National Lab, USA
Ming-Yuh Huang   The Boeing Company, USA
Erland Jonsson   Chalmers University, Sweden
Wenke Lee   Georgia Institute of Technology, USA
Ludovic Mé   Supélec, France
Alfonso Valdes   SRI International, USA
Giovanni Vigna   University of California, Santa Barbara, USA
Andreas Wespi   IBM Research, Switzerland
Felix Wu   University of California, Davis, USA
Diego Zamboni   IBM Research, Switzerland

Local Organizing Committee

Matt Bradford   Queensland University of Technology, Australia
Andrew Clark   Queensland University of Technology, Australia
Elizabeth Hansford   Queensland University of Technology, Australia
James Mackie   Queensland University of Technology, Australia
George Mohay   Queensland University of Technology, Australia
Julien Vayssiére   SAP Research, Brisbane, Australia
Jacob Zimmermann   Queensland University of Technology, Australia

Additional Reviewers

Hirotake Abe   Simon Chung   Markus Hagenbuchner
Michael Bailey   Siu-Leung Chung   Jeffrey Horton
Venkat Balakrishnan   Evan Cooke   Yiyuan Huang
Gregory Banks   Malcolm Corney   Grégoire Jacob
Michael Becher   Scott Fluhrer   Frank Kargl
John Bethencourt   Felix Freiling   Kevin Killourhy
David Brumley   Debin Gao   Kee-Eung Kim
Martim Carbone   Meng Ge   Sang-Rok Kim

Christian Kreibich
Junsup Lee
Minsoo Lee
Corrado Leita
Francois Lesueur
Zhuowei Li
Liang Lu
Michael Meier
Z. Morley Mao
Koichi Mouri

James Newsome
Yoshihiro Oyama
Jon Oberheide
Sorot Panichprecha
James Riordan
Sebastian Schmerl
Jeong-Seok Seo
Wook Shin
Takahiro Shinagawa
Sushant Sinha

Hongwei Sun
Rafael Timoteo de
  Sousa Jr
Eric Totel
Uday Tupakula
Jouni Viinikka
Heng Yin
Stefano Zanero
Jacob Zimmermann

Table of Contents

Host-Based Intrusion Detection

Anomaly-Based Intrusion Detection

Network-Based Intrusion Detection and Response

Insider Detection and Alert Correlation

Malicious Code Analysis

Evasion

Malicious Code Defense

Exploiting Execution Context
for the Detection of Anomalous System Calls

Darren Mutz, William Robertson, Giovanni Vigna, and Richard Kemmerer

Computer Security Group
Department of Computer Science
University of California, Santa Barbara
{dhm,wkr,vigna,kemm}@cs.ucsb.edu

Abstract. Attacks against privileged applications can be detected by
analyzing the stream of system calls issued during process execution.
In the last few years, several approaches have been proposed to detect
anomalous system calls. These approaches are mostly based on modeling
acceptable system call sequences. Unfortunately, the techniques proposed
so far are either vulnerable to certain evasion attacks or are too expensive
to be practical. This paper presents a novel approach to the analysis of
system calls that uses a composition of dynamic analysis and learning
techniques to characterize anomalous system call invocations in terms
of both the invocation context and the parameters passed to the system
calls. Our technique provides a more precise detection model with respect
to solutions proposed previously, and, in addition, it is able to detect
data modification attacks, which cannot be detected using only system
call sequence analysis.

Keywords: Intrusion Detection, System Call Argument Analysis, Execution Context.

1 Introduction

A recent thrust of intrusion detection research has considered model-based detection of attacks at the application level. Model-based systems operate by comparing the observed behavior of an application to *models* of normal behavior,
which may be derived automatically via static analysis [8,23] or learned by analyzing the run-time behavior of applications [3,5,12,18,15]. In each case, attacks
are detected when observed behavior diverges in some respect from the normal
behavior captured by the model. In contrast to misuse-based approaches, where
the analysis identifies attacks against applications using patterns of known malicious actions, model-based schemes have the advantage of being able to detect
novel attacks, since attacks are not explicitly represented by the system. We
note that this advantage typically comes at the cost of performance, precision,
and explanatory capability, three properties that misuse-based approaches often
achieve very well.

Most model-based intrusion detection systems monitor the sequence of system calls issued by an application, possibly taking into account some execution
state. For example, the system described in [3] monitors pairs of system calls

C. Kruegel, R. Lippmann, and A. Clark (Eds.): RAID 2007, LNCS 4637, pp. 1–20, 2007.

```
1    void write_user_data(void)
2    {
3      FILE *fp;
4      char user_filename[256];
5      char user_data[256];
6
7      gets(user_filename);
8
9      if (privileged_file(user_filename)) {
10        fprintf(stderr, "Illegal filename. Exiting.\n");
11        exit(1);
12     }
13     else {
14        gets(user_data);      // overflow into user_filename
15
16        fp = fopen(user_filename, "w");
17
18        if (fp) {
19          fprintf(fp, "%s", user_data);
20          fclose(fp);
21        }
22     }
23   }
```

Fig. 1. Sample data modification attack

and records the application's stack configuration (that is, part of the history of function invocations). During the detection phase, the system checks if the observed pairs of system calls (and their associated stack configuration) match pairs recorded during the learning period. The systems described in [8] and [23] check call sequences against automata-based models derived from the application's source code or binary representation, and identify sequences that could not have been generated by the model.

Some of the shortcomings of sequence-based approaches were discussed in [2], where the problems of *incomplete sensitivity* and *incomplete sets of events* were introduced. Incomplete sensitivity affects models derived from static analysis. Due to the limitations of static analysis techniques, these models may accept impossible sequences of system calls (for example because branch predicates are not considered).

The problem of incomplete sets of events is more general, and it affects all approaches based on system call sequences. This problem stems from the fact that, in these systems, the manifestation of an attack must be characterized in terms of anomalies in the order in which system calls are executed. Changes in the ordering of system call invocations occur, for example, because foreign code is injected into the application (such as through a buffer overflow) or because the order in which instructions are executed is modified. Therefore, by modeling system call sequences, these approaches implicitly restrict themselves to only detecting attacks that modify the execution order as expressed by the application's code or by the execution histories observed during a training period. Unfortunately, an attacker can successfully compromise an application's goals by modifying the application's *data* without introducing anomalous paths in the application's execution.

Consider, for example, the procedure write_user_data in Figure 1. Here, an overflow of the variable user_data at line 14 allows an attacker to overwrite the value contained in user_filename, which the application assumes was checked by the procedure invoked at line 9. Therefore, the attacker can leverage the overflow to append data of her choice to any file the application has access to. Note that the execution of this data modification attack does not affect the type or ordering of the system calls issued by the application.

To detect data modification attacks, models must include some representation of valid or normal program state. For example, prior work in [11] and [12] uses learning models to characterize "normal" system call argument values and to demonstrate that changes to program state as a result of an attack often manifest themselves as changes to the argument values of system calls. The assumption underlying this approach is that the goal of the attacker is to leverage the privileges of an application to change some security-relevant state in the underlying system (e.g., write chosen values to a file, execute a specific application, or change the permissions of a security-critical file). This type of activity may be readily observed as suspicious system call argument values.

One limitation of the argument modeling approach in [11], [12], and [15] is that models of normal argument values are built for each system call. That is, one set of models is created for open, another set for execve, and so on. As a result, a model captures the full range of argument values observed during all phases of the execution of an application. A better approach would be to train the models in a way that is specific to individual phases of a program's execution. For example, the arguments used during a program's initialization phase are likely to differ from those used during a production phase or termination phase. This can be achieved by differentiating program behavior using the *calling context* of a procedure – that is, the configuration of the application's call stack when a procedure is invoked. Similar techniques have been explored in the programming languages literature. Examples include improving profiling by considering a procedure's calling context [1], analyzing pointer variables more accurately [9], and improving lifetime predictions of dynamically allocated memory [16]. A common observation in these approaches is that the calling context of a procedure is often a powerful predictor of how the procedure and its data interact.

In this paper, we first propose and evaluate a metric for determining to what extent argument values are unique to a particular call stack for a given application. Our study, presented in Section 2, shows that this is predominantly the case, indicating that the argument modeling approach of [12] can be made more precise if models are built for each calling context in which a system call is issued by an application. Armed with this knowledge, we then introduce and evaluate a model-based detection system that builds separate argument models for each call stack in which an application issues a system call. Our experiments demonstrate that the trained models effectively generalize from the training data, performing well during a subsequent detection period.

This paper makes the following primary contributions:

- It analyzes the relationship between system call arguments and different calling contexts, and it introduces a novel metric to quantify the degree to which argument values exhibit uniqueness across contexts.
- It demonstrates that the application's call stack can be leveraged to add context to the argument values that appear at the system call interface. It

also demonstrates that the increased sensitivity of context-specific argument models results in better detection performance.

- It defines a technique to detect data modification attacks, which are not detected by previously proposed approaches based on system call sequences.
- It presents an extensive real-world evaluation encompassing over 44 million system call invocations collected over 64 days from 10 hosts.

The remainder of the paper is structured as follows. In Section 2 we introduce and apply a metric to characterize the degree to which system call argument values are unique to calling contexts in which system calls are issued. Then, in Section 3, we present our detection approach, which builds argument models that are specific to each calling context. Section 4 reports the results of evaluating the system empirically. Section 5 covers related work on system call-based anomaly detection. Finally, Section 6 draws conclusions and outlines future work.

2   System Call Argument and Calling Context Analysis

The effectiveness of system call analysis that includes call stack information is directly related to the number of contexts in which a given argument value associated with the invocations of a particular system call occurs. More specifically, if argument values appear in many contexts, essentially randomly, context-specific learning models are likely to offer no benefit. Furthermore, if each observed argument value appears (possibly multiple times) in only one context, we would expect system call argument analysis that includes call stack information to outperform context-insensitive models. In this section, we propose a metric to express the degree of context-uniqueness of argument values. We then use this metric to determine which applications are likely to be amenable to system call analysis that takes into account stack-specific behavior.

Before introducing our context-uniqueness metric, we need to define some notation. Let $S = \{s_1, s_2, \ldots\}$ be the set of monitored system calls, and let $A^{s_i} = \langle A_1^{s_i}, \ldots, A_n^{s_i} \rangle$ be the vector of formal arguments for system call s_i. Consistent with [6], we define the calling context of a system call invocation as the sequence of return addresses $C = \langle r_1, \ldots, r_l \rangle$ stored on the application's call stack at the time the system call invocation occurs. Each invocation s_{ij} of s_i has a concrete vector of values for A^{s_i} defined as $a^{s_{ij}} = \langle a_1^{s_{ij}}, \ldots, a_n^{s_{ij}} \rangle$, and two argument vectors $a^{s_{ij}}$ and $a^{s_{ij'}}$ are considered distinct if any of their subvalues $a_l^{s_{ij}}$ and $a_l^{s_{ij'}}$ differ.

We are interested in the set of argument vectors appearing in the invocation of a system call in a particular context. For this, we introduce the notion of an *argument set*. An argument set for a system call s_i in a context C is the set of all argument vectors $a^{s_{ij}}$ observed for the chosen system call when it is issued in the calling context C. This is denoted by $AS(C, s_i)$. The argument set for s_i across the entire application (i.e., ignoring the calling context) is denoted by $AS(*, s_i)$. We observe that if the set $AS(*, s_i)$ is partitioned by the subsets $\{AS(C_1, s_i), AS(C_2, s_i), \ldots\}$, then each recorded argument vector a^{s_i} occurs in only one calling context.

One potential route in the development of this metric would be to adapt cluster quality measures from the machine learning literature. Unfortunately, computing the distance between two argument vectors $a^{s_{ij}}$ and $a^{s_{ij}'}$ is problematic. For example, integer arguments that exhibit numeric similarity are often dissimilar in their semantic meaning. This occurs in cases where an integer argument is the logical OR of a collection of boolean flags. Computing string similarity also presents difficulties. For example, two filesystem paths may have large common substrings or a small Hamming distance, but correspond to files that have a very different meaning to the users of the system. For these reasons, we build our metric using argument vector equality only.

With this in mind, we would like to determine the number of contexts where each distinct argument vector is used. To measure this we define the *actual partitioning* value $AP(s_i)$, which is the sum over all recorded concrete argument vectors of the number of argument sets where each $a^{s_{ij}}$ appears during the period of monitoring. That is,

$$AP(s_i) = \sum_{j=1}^{K} \sum_{m=1}^{L} | \{a^{s_{ij}}\} \cap AS(C_m, s_i) | \qquad (1)$$

where K is the number of distinct argument vector values recorded, and L is the number of distinct stack configurations observed during the monitoring period.

For our context-uniqueness metric, we would like to compare the actual partitioning value to both the optimal partitioning and the worst case partitioning values. For the optimal case, each argument vector should appear in as few contexts as possible. There are two cases to consider. In the case where the number of distinct argument vectors is greater or equal to the number of calling contexts ($K \geq L$), each argument value appears in only one context in the optimal partition of $AS(*, s_i)$. For the case when $K < L$, some argument vectors must appear in more than one context[1]. The optimal partitioning, in this case, is for each concrete argument vector to appear in L/K argument sets. Both cases can be expressed by specifying the number of argument sets where each argument vector is to appear as $max(L/K, 1)$.

We can now define the optimal partitioning value and the worst case partitioning value. Since there are K distinct argument vector values, the *optimal partitioning* value $OP(s_i)$ is defined as:

$$OP(s_i) = K * max(L/K, 1) = max(L, K) \qquad (2)$$

To define the worst case, we need to know how many instances of each of the K distinct argument vectors $a^{s_{ij}} \in AS(*, s_i)$ were recorded during the monitoring period. We define the counter $cnt_{a^{s_{ij}}}$ as the number of times that a particular argument vector $a^{s_{ij}}$ occurs in the recorded invocations. The worst case partitioning is determined by distributing each of the K argument vectors in $AS(*, s_i)$ over as many contexts as possible. Although $a^{s_{ij}}$ can appear a maximum of $cnt_{a^{s_{ij}}}$ times, there are only L distinct contexts. Therefore, $a^{s_{ij}}$ appears

---

[1] If each distinct value appeared in only one context, then there would be contexts with no argument vectors.

in $min(cnt_{a^{s_{ij}}}, L)$ argument sets in the worst case partitioning. Thus, the *worst case partitioning* value WP is defined as:

$$WP(s_i) = \sum_{j=1}^{K} min(cnt_{a^{s_{ij}}}, L) \tag{3}$$

Now that we have the actual partitioning value, the optimal partitioning value, and the worst case partitioning value, we can define a measure of the partition quality $Q(s_i)$ for a system call s_i. $Q(s_i)$ is defined as the ratio of the difference between the actual and optimal partitioning to the difference between the worst case and optimal partitioning:

$$Q(s_i) = \frac{AP(s_i) - OP(s_i)}{WP(s_i) - OP(s_i)}$$

Since the actual partitioning $AP(s_i)$ must fall between $WP(s_i)$ and $OP(s_i)$, $Q(s_i)$ takes on values in the interval $[0, 1]$ with 0 being the highest quality partitioning (i.e., no difference from the optimal case) and 1 being the worst (i.e., no difference from the worst case partitioning). In the special case where there is no difference between $WP(s_i)$ and $OP(s_i)$, we define $Q(s_i)$ to be 1.

Table 1. Observed argument sets for a fictional system call `foo(char *pathname)` in three different calling contexts, C_1, C_2, and C_3

Context	Observed argument set
C_1	$AS(C_1, s_{foo}) = \{$"/tmp/a", "/tmp/b", "/tmp/c"$\}$
C_2	$AS(C_2, s_{foo}) = \{$"/tmp/a"$\}$
C_3	$AS(C_3, s_{foo}) = \{$"/tmp/a"$\}$

Consider the example shown in Table 1, which gives observed argument values for a fictional system call `foo(char *pathname)` for $L = 3$ different calling contexts, C_1, C_2, and C_3. Further, suppose that each argument appears 3 times during the period of monitoring, that is, $cnt_{a^{s_{(foo)j}}} = 3$ for each of the three $s_{(foo)j}$. Since the concrete argument vector $\langle$"/tmp/a"$\rangle$ appears in all three contexts and the argument vectors $\langle$"/tmp/b"$\rangle$ and $\langle$"/tmp/c"$\rangle$ appear in one context each, the actual partitioning $AP(s_{foo})$ is:

$$AP(s_{foo}) = (1 + 1 + 1) + (1 + 0 + 0) + (1 + 0 + 0) = 5 \tag{4}$$

Because $L = K = 3$, the optimal partitioning for s_{foo} is

$$OP(s_{foo}) = max(3, 3) = 3 \tag{5}$$

and the worst case partitioning for s_{foo} is

$$WP(s_{foo}) = min(3, 3) + min(3, 3) + min(3, 3) = 9 \tag{6}$$

Combining the actual, optimal, and worst case partitioning, we have the following measure of the overall quality of the partitioning for s_{foo}:

$$Q(s_{foo}) = \frac{5 - 3}{9 - 3} = 1/3 \tag{7}$$

To evaluate our quality metric, we selected 9 root-owned services and periodic (cron) applications running in a production setting on 10 servers in an undergraduate computer science lab. The 9 audited programs were chosen from a larger pool of processes that run with root privileges in the following way. First, no interactive command line executables were evaluated since they appear sporadically and generate a relatively small number of audit records. For similar reasons, 8 periodic and daemon processes were removed from the study because they did not appear frequently enough in the audit set to produce a meaningful evaluation. Second, script language interpreters (e.g., Perl and Python) were removed since programs implemented in those languages execute with a virtualized call stack. Next, 6 processes associated with the X11 windowing system were eliminated because their role in the system is primarily to facilitate graphical interaction with the user. Finally, 5 programs associated with the package management and compilation subsystem were eliminated because they have a peripheral role with respect to the security of the system.

Table 2 shows the mean and standard deviation of Q values across 36 security-critical system calls issued by each of the 9 programs over a 10-day period. Section 3.1 specifies the monitored system calls and provides further justification for their inclusion in the study. Table 2 tabulates the average (μ) and standard deviation (σ) of Q across each of the 36 system calls (denoted $Q(s_*)$). The data shows that the values of Q recorded for a collection of real applications in a production setting are optimal in 3 of 9 cases, and are never greater than 0.169. This suggests that including call stack information in system call argument analysis is likely to produce models that outperform those that do not consider execution context.

Table 2. Mean and standard deviation of Q over all system calls for the nine applications in the study

Application	$Q(s_*)$ μ	$Q(s_*)$ σ
cfenvd	0.038	0.066
cfexecd	0.107	0.191
crond	0.000	0.000
cupsd	0.085	0.159
idmapd	0.000	0.000
sendmail	0.093	0.194
slocate	0.169	0.379
sshd	0.168	0.218
ypbind	0.000	0.000
Overall	0.063	0.209

3   System Design

The empirical evaluation of context-sensitivity in the previous section showed that system call arguments are often uniquely associated with specific calling context in real-world applications. Therefore, we developed an intrusion detection system that takes advantage of this property. Our approach uses a collection of context-specific learning models that operate in three distinct phases. The first two phases consist of a *training phase* and a *threshold learning phase*, during which learning is performed on attack-free audit data. In the training phase, models gather examples of normal system call arguments. At the end of this phase, detection models are generated for use in the two subsequent phases. Following the training phase is the threshold learning phase, where thresholds are computed for the finalized models by measuring their response to attack-free data. In the final *detection phase*, the trained models and thresholds are used together to classify events as normal or anomalous.

In the following, we describe feature selection and the context-specific modeling approach in Section 3.1. Then, in Sections 3.2 through 3.4, we describe the three phases of system operation. Finally, Section 3.5 provides details about the audit collection infrastructure.

3.1   Feature Selection and the Context-Specific Modeling Approach

Experience shows that evidence of attacks often appears in the argument values of system calls. Sometimes this may be due to "collateral damage" to local (stack) variables when overwriting a return address. In these cases, damaged variables are then used in system call invocations before the procedure returns. In other cases, the attack is leveraging the privileges of the application to perform actions that are not normally performed by the victim program. In many instances, these differences can be identified by argument models.

To determine the set of system calls to use for our analysis, we studied the 243 system calls implemented in the version 2.6.10 of the Linux kernel to determine which additional calls represent avenues to leveraging or increasing the privilege of applications. This study identified 36 system calls, shown in Table 3, that we found should be monitored to detect attempts to compromise the security of a host. Note that in our system only arguments that have intrinsic semantic meaning are modeled. Integer arguments corresponding to file descriptors and memory addresses, for example, are ignored, since their values are not meaningful across runs of an application. Additionally, these values rarely contain any semantic information about the operation being performed.

In order to leverage the context information provided by the application's call stack at the time a system call is invoked, we instantiate detection models for each calling context encountered during the training phase. We rely on audit records that are composed of two parts: (a) the system call s_i that was invoked, along with its arguments $a^{s_{ij}} = \langle a_1^{s_{ij}}, \ldots, a_n^{s_{ij}} \rangle$, and (b) the sequence of return addresses gathered from the application's call stack when the system call was invoked. These addresses form the system call's context $C = \langle r_1, \ldots, r_l \rangle$. In all three phases (training, thresholding, and detection), the pair $\langle C, s_i \rangle$ is used as a lookup key in a data structure that maintains the collection of context-specific models and thresholds.

Table 3. The 36 system calls monitored by the system

open	creat	link	unlink
execve	mknod	chmod	mount
umount	rename	mkdir	rmdir
umount2	symlink	truncate	uselib
ftruncate	fchmod	ioperm	iopl
ipc	mprotect	create_module	prctl
capset	lchown	setreuid	setregid
fchown	setresuid	setresgid	chown
setuid	setgid	setfsuid	setfsgid

3.2 Training Phase

The first phase of system operation is training, during which the audit records received by the audit daemon are used as examples of normal behavior to train context-specific argument models. This approach improves upon prior work ([12]), which did not consider execution context, but instead applied the same argument model instantiations to all invocations of a particular system call issued by an application.

We now describe the individual argument models used to characterize normal values for system call arguments. The models are described in substantial detail in our previous work; the reader is referred to [12] and [14] for information beyond the brief descriptions provided here.

The following three models are applied to string arguments:

- *String Length:* The goal of the string length model is to approximate the actual (but unknown) distribution of the lengths of string arguments and to detect instances that significantly deviate from the observed normal behavior. Usually, system call string arguments represent canonical file names that point to an entry in the file system. These arguments are commonly used when files are accessed (**open**, **stat**) or executed (**execve**), and their lengths rarely exceed a hundred characters. However, when malicious input is passed to programs, this input often occurs in an argument of a system call with a length of several hundred bytes. The detection of significant deviations is based on the Chebyshev inequality.
- *String Character Distribution:* The string character distribution model captures the concept of a normal string argument by looking at its character distribution. The approach is based on the observation that strings have a regular structure, are often human-readable, and almost always contain only printable characters. In the case of attacks that send binary data, a completely different character distribution can be observed. This is also true for attacks that send many repetitions of a single character (e.g., the nop-sledge of a buffer overflow attack). The detection of deviating arguments is performed using a statistical test (Pearson χ^2-test) that determines the probability that the character distribution of a system call argument fits the normal distribution established during the training phase.
- *String Structural Inference:* Often, the manifestation of an exploit is immediately visible in system call arguments as unusually long strings or strings that

contain repetitions of non-printable characters. There are situations, however, when an attacker is able to craft her attack in a manner that makes its manifestation appear more regular. For example, non-printable characters can be replaced by groups of printable characters. In such situations, we need a more detailed model of the system call argument. Such a model can be acquired by analyzing the argument's structure. For the purposes of this model, the structure of an argument is the regular grammar that describes all of its normal, legitimate values. The process of inferring the grammar from training data is based on a Markov model and a probabilistic state-merging procedure. The details are presented in [21] and [22].

The fourth model can be used for all types of system call arguments:

− *Token Finder:* The purpose of the token finder model is to determine whether the values of a certain system call argument are drawn from a limited set of possible alternatives (i.e., they are elements or tokens of an enumeration). An application often passes identical values such as flags or handles to certain system call arguments. When an attack changes the normal flow of execution and branches into maliciously injected code, these constraints are often violated. The decision whether to identify the set as an enumeration or a collection of random identifiers can be made utilizing a simple statistical test, such as the non-parametric Kolmogorov-Smirnov variant, as suggested in [13].

In prior work ([12]), models were instantiated for each system call (e.g., open, execve). As we noted, in this paper models have been replicated for each calling context C. In this way, when the audit daemon is operating in the training phase, aggregate model instances are trained on the observed argument set $AS(C, s_i)$.

3.3   Threshold Learning Phase

In our design, an *aggregate model* is used to associate a set of models with each system call. The task of an aggregate model is to combine the outputs of all models that are associated with a system call into a single anomaly score that is used to assess whether the entire system call is normal or not. As in [12], we sum the negative logarithm of the individual model outputs to produce one score, which is then compared to a threshold (described below) to determine whether or not an alert should be generated for the system call.

At the start of the threshold-learning phase, training ceases and all models instantiated by the system are switched to detection mode. Each event in the (attack-free) threshold learning set is then assigned an anomaly score by the aggregate model specific to its system call s_i and context C. The threshold for the aggregate model associated with the pair (C, s_i) is computed by adding 20% to the maximum anomaly score generated by the aggregate model over the threshold training set.

Using a context-specific characterization allows thresholds to be independent of one another, permitting some thresholds to be "loose" and others to be "tight". For example, in one context where there are a large number of training examples, models might characterize the context's features virtually flawlessly implying a very tight threshold for that context. In another context that appears far less frequently in the training set, the instantiated models may have a more coarse approximation of the feature values, resulting in a relatively loose threshold.

3.4 Detection Phase

When an audit record is received during the detection phase, the system first checks if the context and system call pairing associated with it (that is, $\langle C, s \rangle$) has been observed during the training period. If the pairing was not recorded during the training phase, the system issues an alert. For pairings that were observed during the training phase, the system uses the values for C and s to look up the aggregate model that was created during training, uses the model to evaluate the argument values contained in the audit record, and issues an alert if the resulting score exceeds the threshold associated with $\langle C, s \rangle$.

3.5 Auditing Subsystem

This section provides details of the implementation used for the evaluation of the system. The system described in this paper is composed of two modules: a kernel-resident audit module that records system call invocations and the application calling context in which they appear, and a user-space audit daemon that develops models of system call argument values using machine learning techniques. The two components communicate via an entry in the proc filesystem.

Both the learning and detection phases require a stream of system call invocation events. System call event auditing is accomplished using an implementation based on the Snare audit module, which is an existing loadable kernel module written for the Linux operating system by Intersect Alliance [20]. This module intercepts system calls through the use of system call interposition, which is realized by overwriting the kernel's table of function pointers to system calls with pointers to wrapper functions. These wrapper functions generate an audit record prior to calling the original system call and before returning its result. To realize the goals of this project, several significant changes were made to the Snare module:

> **User stack unwinding.** When audited system calls are invoked, in addition to recording the arguments to the system call, the user's memory space is probed iteratively to unwind the frames stored on the user application's stack. This process is very similar to the one followed by a debugger as it recovers the stack frames from the memory of a running application.
>
> Virtual addresses encountered on the user's stack are matched against the memory-mapped address ranges maintained in the process control block. When a matching address range is found, the stack address is normalized by subtracting the starting address of the memory-mapped region, and the module records the normalized address along with the i-node of the file containing the memory mapped code. In this way, address consistency is maintained across runs of an application, or in the face of dynamic loading and unloading of code by the application.

Signaling of user audit daemon replaced with support for blocking reads. The original version of the Snare audit module delivered a signal to the audit daemon each time an event was generated. This created performance problems during periods of high load, which were often accompanied by a high volume of audit data. Our version uses a kernel wait queue, which avoids signal storms during periods of heavy load.

4   Empirical Validation

The purpose of this empirical study is to investigate the impact of considering the calling context of system calls on the detection capability of the system. The evaluation consists of three parts. Section 4.1 compares context-specific models to context-insensitive models with respect to the generation of false positives. Next, Section 4.2 addresses the question of whether context-specific models offer an improvement in precision over context-insensitive models. Section 4.3 evaluates the ability of the system to detect real attacks launched against two monitored applications. Finally, Section 4.4 quantifies the computational overhead of context-sensitive monitoring.

4.1   Comparing Context-Sensitive and Context-Insensitive Argument Models

Since models trained specific to particular calling contexts occurring in an application have a smaller, more restrictive set of training examples, they potentially suffer from the drawback of being too sensitive to variations in argument values observed during the detection phase. Therefore, it is critical to determine their false positive rate relative to context-insensitive argument models.

In order to quantify the rate of false positives observed in practice in each case, we collected audit data on root-owned daemons and periodic (cron) applications running on 10 hosts in an undergraduate computer science instructional laboratory over a period of 64 days. During the recorded period, each of the hosts were accessed regularly by approximately 100 unique users (administrators and undergraduate users) who interacted with the system in local X11 sessions in

Table 4. False positive rates for models that do not consider calling context

Application	Total Events	False Positives	False Positive Rate
cfenvd	11,918,468	0	$0.00 \times 10^{+00}$
cfexecd	457,812	4,407	9.63×10^{-03}
crond	1,265,345	0	$0.00 \times 10^{+00}$
cupsd	291,022	1,942	6.67×10^{-03}
idmapd	57,316	2,962	5.17×10^{-02}
sendmail	5,514,158	1,559	2.97×10^{-04}
slocate	11,914,501	155	1.30×10^{-05}
sshd	13,347,164	1,931	1.45×10^{-04}
ypbind	30,268	0	$0.00 \times 10^{+00}$
Overall	44,796,054	12,956	2.89×10^{-04}

Table 5. False positive rates using context-sensitive models

Application	Total Events	Unknown Context Alarms	Model Violation Alarms	Overall FP Rate
cfenvd	11,918,468	21	0	1.76×10^{-06}
cfexecd	457,812	1,007	31	2.27×10^{-03}
crond	1,265,345	0	0	$0.00 \times 10^{+00}$
cupsd	291,022	6	252	8.87×10^{-04}
idmapd	57,316	0	0	$0.00 \times 10^{+00}$
sendmail	5,514,158	1,122	154	2.31×10^{-04}
slocate	11,914,501	0	183	1.54×10^{-05}
sshd	13,347,164	379	1,705	1.56×10^{-04}
ypbind	30,268	0	0	$0.00 \times 10^{+00}$
Overall	44,796,054	2,535	2,325	1.09×10^{-04}

addition to remote logins. The recorded audit data was checked for known attacks and is, to the authors' knowledge, free of attacks. We also tracked publicly released vulnerabilities on security mailing lists and noted no vulnerabilities in the monitored software. In all cases, the system was trained and evaluated using data collected at each host. In the interest of conciseness, however, detection performance is reported in aggregated form (i.e., measurements are combined from all 10 hosts used in the study).

Of the 64 days of recorded audit data, the first 39 days were used for training the argument models. Thresholds were computed using the following 7 days of audit data, and detection was performed on the final 18 days. The false positives produced by the system for context-insensitive models (i.e., models that ignore calling context) are shown in Table 4, and Table 5 summarizes the false positive rates for context-sensitive models. Separate figures are given for alarms generated for unknown contexts (i.e., contexts that were not seen during the training phase) as well as for alarms generated from anomalous model scores.

From the tabulated data, it is clear that the overall false positive rates of context-sensitive models outperform context-insensitive models by a factor of about 2.7. Further inspection of the 1,007 unknown context alarms for the cfexecd application revealed that they were repeated instances of alarms for 40 contexts that did not appear in the training data. Additionally, all 1,122 unknown context alarms issued for the sendmail application, and 348 of 379 of the alarms issued for sshd each occurred on a single day. This suggests that it would be straightforward for an administrator to add these contexts to the known set and eliminate future instances of those alarms. Taken together, unknown context and model violation alarms represent an average of 34 alarms per application per day. This is a relatively manageable number, and post-processing tools could likely improve this figure by summarizing duplicate alarms [17].

Table 5 shows a large number of model violation alarms (1,705) for the sshd application. Further analysis showed that 652 (more than 38%) of those violations were triggered by models for the setresuid system call. These anomalous calls were the result of users that had not been observed during the training period logging into the system. In an academic computer network, this level of irregular user behavior can be expected. However, on more sensitive networks, these alarms could be valuable indicators of misuse or misconfiguration of login policies.

4.2 Cross-Comparison of Context-Specific Models

Section 2 proposed the metric Q for quantifying the degree to which argument values are unique across the various execution contexts in which a particular system call occurs. The experiment described in this section is intended to further validate the context-specific detection approach. The experiment performs cross-comparison of context-sensitive models for system calls s_i on events drawn from all contexts C in which s_i occurs. Whereas Q measured the extent to which the observed argument sets (ASs) are disjoint, this experiment is designed to measure the extent to which learned context-specific models are able to capture these differences.

To show this, the models are trained for each context exactly as described in Section 4.1, but each system call is evaluated not only on the model for its native context, but on all non-native models as well. If context-specific models capture context-specific features, we would expect events to be classified as normal in their native context and as anomalous in all other contexts.

Table 6. Cross-comparison of context-sensitive models. Rate of false positives for events in native and non-native contexts are shown.

Application	Native FP rate	Non-native FP rate
cfenvd	$0.000 \times 10^{+00}$	0.967
cfexecd	6.771×10^{-05}	0.877
crond	$0.000 \times 10^{+00}$	1.000
cupsd	8.660×10^{-04}	0.947
idmapd	$0.000 \times 10^{+00}$	1.000
sendmail	2.793×10^{-05}	0.933
slocate	1.536×10^{-05}	0.974
sshd	1.277×10^{-04}	0.855
ypbind	$0.000 \times 10^{+00}$	1.000
Average	1.105×10^{-04}	0.950

Table 6 shows that context-sensitive models are, in the vast majority of cases, able to correctly classify events as belonging or not belonging to the context for which the model was trained. This evidence supports three conclusions. First, the calling context of system calls is a strong predictor of the subclass of argument values observed at the system call interface for a number of applications in a real-world, operational setting. Second, learning models are able to capture this differentiated behavior. Finally, the results suggest that context-specific models capture a more restricted range of behavior than context-insensitive models. This implies that context-sensitive models restrict the number of options that an attacker has to influence the arguments of system calls while avoiding detection.

4.3   Measuring the Detection Capability of Call Stack-Specific Argument Models

Source code and binary audits were performed for the 9 services and application used in our study, but no vulnerabilities were found. Therefore, in order to measure the attack detection capability of call stack-specific argument models, we tested the system using attacks on a proprietary setuid application as well as on an Apache web server. Following is a description of the attacks and the corresponding detection performance of the system.

Proprietary setuid Application. An experiment was conducted on a setuid root application installed on the 10 audit hosts used in this study. The program in question is a proprietary setuid root application written to allow students to submit homework assignments to a class account for grading. While this program is not a daemon or periodic job, an analysis of its binary revealed an exploitable stack overflow vulnerability in a request logging function. This vulnerability was used to test the detection capability of our system. The attack on this program required circumventing the exec-shield, stack randomization, and heap randomization protection mechanisms deployed on the monitored hosts. The attack involved overwriting two stack variables: the current function's return address and the frame pointer. This caused the program to jump to an indirect jump instruction through the modified frame pointer, transferring control to an exploit payload previously injected in a buffer on the heap. This was necessary in order to overcome the exec-shield and randomization protection mechanisms. The results and analysis of the context-sensitive detection system's sensitivity to exploit payloads is discussed below.

Rootshell Exploit. The first exploit payload executed against the vulnerable program was a simple shell execution with root privileges. Because the execve system call was invoked from a context not previously observed during the training period, the context-sensitive detection system was able to distinguish the system call invocation as anomalous and report an alert. The detection system configured in context-insensitive mode, however, did not detect the execve call as anomalous. This stems from the fact that both a file archiving utility and a compression utility are spawned during the normal execution of the assignment submission program, and thus the context-insensitive argument models on their own were not sensitive enough to detect an anomaly based on the execve target alone. A final observation of this scenario is that a sequence-based system call IDS would have detected a deviation from the normal sequence of system calls, and would have raised an alert.

Data Modification Exploit. The second exploit payload executed against the assignment submission program was a variation of a data modification attack. The objective of this exploit was to manipulate the logging of an assignment submission such that the submitter and timestamp could be subverted with attacker-supplied values. To accomplish this, the exploit payload first called mprotect from a legitimate, in-sequence context to mark the code segments of the process read/write. Since the stack was modified to hold a legitimate sequence of return addresses prior to calling mprotect, the program continued executing native application code upon returning. In order to regain control for the second part of the attack, a system library function pointer was overwritten in the procedure linkage table (PLT). This type of attack is described in detail in [10]. Changing the memory protection bits on the code segment of the program allowed the statically defined format string that is used in the invocation to fprintf to be overwritten. In this way, the attacker's format string was used in place of the legitimate one when the transaction was logged by the program.

A sequence-based system call IDS would not have detected an anomaly, as no invalid or out-of-sequence system calls were invoked. In addition, the context-insensitive argument models were not tight enough to detect an aberration in the parameters to the system call mprotect. The context-sensitive detection system, however, was able to detect the anomalous argument due to the more precise argument modeling that included system call context.

Detecting Attacks Against OpenSSL. The final demonstration of the attack detection capability of the system involved testing an off-the-shelf exploit for the Apache web server running with a vulnerable version of OpenSSL, which is a popular implementation of the Secure Sockets Layer (SSL) and Transport Layer Security (TLS) protocols. This version of OpenSSL is vulnerable to a remote client master key overflow, allowing an attacker to potentially execute arbitrary code in any network service that utilizes the library.

As before, context-sensitive and context-insensitive model instances were trained against traces of normal HTTP client behavior. The models were then applied to a trace of an attack against OpenSSL. As before, the stack specific models correctly identified the attack, in this case from an anomalous execve of "/bin/sh." The context-insensitive models, however, did not consider this system call to be sufficiently anomalous to raise an alarm. We speculate that since the training data included benign invocations of CGI scripts, which necessarily involve issuing an execve for an external script execution, the context-insensitive models were not able to differentiate between benign and malicious invocations of the system call. This is because only one profile was constructed from the training set for execve, which supports our claim that the detection capability of argument models is measurably enhanced by instantiating models specific to each call stack context.

4.4   Performance Overhead of Stack Unwinding

To evaluate the performance overhead of unwinding the call stacks of user processes, we constructed a benchmark application. The benchmark invokes a system call after creating a parameterized number of frames on the callstack. In each run of the benchmark, 100 groups of 100 such invocations are made and the average time to complete 100 invocations is returned. In Figure 2 we compare the benchmark running times of an identical system in three configurations: no auditing whatsoever, simple system call auditing (no stack unwinding), and system call auditing with stack unwinding. The benchmark execution time is given for a variety of stack depths.

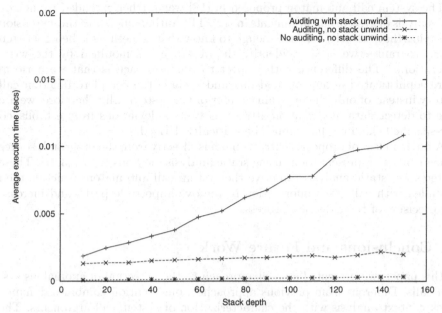

Fig. 2. Comparison of average execution time of system call invocation benchmark

The figure shows that there is significant overhead associated with unwinding user call stacks while auditing. However, the overheads are roughly similar to simple auditing for stack depths less than 40 (i.e., within a factor of two). We also note that the benchmark is designed to expose differences in the audit times, and differs from normal applications in that it does essentially no other processing aside from rapidly invoking system calls.

5   Related Work

Research on model-based detection using system call invocation models originated with [4], which analyzes fixed-length sequences of system calls, without considering arguments or return values. The model of legitimate program behavior is built by observing normal system call sequences in attack-free application runs. Alternative data models for the characterization of system call sequences were proposed in [25] and [26].

These detection techniques could be easily evaded by mimicry attacks, in which an exploit is crafted to produce a legitimate sequence of system calls while performing malicious actions [24]. The introduction of gray-box and white-box approaches, which use additional information such as the stack context and information derived through static analysis techniques, have considerably raised the bar for this kind of attack [18,3,5]. Nevertheless, these approaches do not provide effective modeling of system call arguments, giving the attacker a considerable amount of freedom in crafting an exploit that evades detection. Therefore, black-box, learning-based models that take into account the arguments of system calls were introduced to further limit the ability of an attacker to perform mimicry attacks [12,15].

The system call automaton proposed in [18] was further extended to include the analysis of system call arguments in [19]. The authors motivate this extension by saying that "clearly, it is not enough to know that something is being written by a program – we need to identify the object being modified by the write [operation]." The difference with respect to our approach is that we perform more sophisticated argument modeling and include the complete function call history instead of only the program counter of the system call. Therefore, we are able to detect data modification attacks as well as deviations from established site-specific behaviors that cannot be statically derived.

A further class of proposals extracts models directly from the program's source code or binary representations using static analysis methods [23,7,8,3,27]. These systems use static analysis to derive the system call automaton, which is then extended with call stack information to remove impossible paths and increase the precision of the detection process.

6   Conclusions and Future Work

In this paper, we presented a novel approach to the detection of anomalous system calls. Different from previous approaches, our solution combines dynamic stack context analysis with the characterization of system call arguments. The resulting context-sensitive system call model is effective against data modification attacks, which do not modify the sequence of system calls executed by vulnerable applications. It also improves upon the false positive rates of models that only operate on argument values and ignore context information.

We have also introduced a metric that quantifies the degree to which system call arguments are unique to particular execution contexts. Applying this metric to a number of programs deployed in a production setting showed that the set of argument values is optimally or nearly optimally partitioned by the argument sets associated with individual stack configurations. Future work will explore the utility of applying this metric to other intrusion detection domains.

The use of system call argument modeling is orthogonal with respect to analysis techniques that characterize system call sequences. In future work, we will explore how the two approaches can be composed to achieve even more precise detection and better resilience to mimicry attacks[2].

References

1. Ammons, G., Ball, T., Larus, J.R.: Exploiting hardware performance counters with flow and context sensitive profiling. In: Proceedings of the Conference on Programming Language Design and Implementation (PLDI'97) (1997)
2. Feng, H., Giffin, J., Huang, Y., Jha, S., Lee, W., Miller, B.: Formalizing sensitivity in static analysis for intrusion detection. In: Proceedings of the IEEE Symposium on Security and Privacy, May 2004, IEEE Computer Society Press, Los Alamitos (2004)

[2] This research was supported by the Army Research Office, under agreement DAAD19-01-1-0484, and by the National Science Foundation, under grants CCR-0238492 and CCR-0524853.

3. Feng, H., Kolesnikov, O., Fogla, P., Lee, W., Gong, W.: Anomaly detection using call stack information. In: Proceedings of the IEEE Symposium on Security and Privacy, May 2003, IEEE Computer Society Press, Los Alamitos (2003)
4. Forrest, S.: A Sense of Self for UNIX Processes. In: Proceedings of the IEEE Symposium on Security and Privacy, Oakland, CA, May 1996, pp. 120–128. IEEE Computer Society Press, Los Alamitos (1996)
5. Gao, D., Reiter, M., Song, D.: Gray-Box Extraction of Execution Graphs for Anomaly Detection. In: Proceedings of ACM CCS, Washington, DC, USA, October 2004, pp. 318–329. ACM Press, New York (2004)
6. Gao, D., Reiter, M., Song, D.: On Gray-Box Program Tracking for Anomaly Detection. In: Proceedings of the 13th USENIX Security Symposium, San Diego, CA, USA (August 2004)
7. Giffin, J., Jha, S., Miller, B.: Detecting Manipulated Remote Call Streams. In: Proceedings of the 11th USENIX Security Symposium, pp. 61–79 (2002)
8. Giffin, J., Jha, S., Miller, B.: Efficient context-sensitive intrusion detection. In: Proceedings of the 11th Network and Distributed System Security Symposium, San Diego, California (February 2004)
9. Hind, M., Burke, M., Carini, P., Choi, J.-D.: Interprocedural pointer alias analysis. ACM Transactions on Programming Languages 21(4) (July 1999)
10. Kruegel, C., Kirda, E., Mutz, D., Robertson, W., Vigna, G.: Automating mimicry attacks using static binary analysis. In: Proceedings of the 14th USENIX Security Symposium (July 2005)
11. Kruegel, C., Mutz, D., Robertson, W., Valeur, F.: Bayesian Event Classification for Intrusion Detection. In: Omondi, A.R., Sedukhin, S. (eds.) ACSAC 2003. LNCS, vol. 2823, Springer, Heidelberg (2003)
12. Kruegel, C., Mutz, D., Valeur, F., Vigna, G.: On the Detection of Anomalous System Call Arguments. In: Snekkenes, E., Gollmann, D. (eds.) ESORICS 2003. LNCS, vol. 2808, pp. 326–343. Springer, Heidelberg (2003)
13. Lee, S., Low, W., Wong, P.: Learning Fingerprints for a Database Intrusion Detection System. In: Gollmann, D., Karjoth, G., Waidner, M. (eds.) ESORICS 2002. LNCS, vol. 2502, Springer, Heidelberg (2002)
14. Mutz, D.: Context-sensitive Multi-model Anomaly Detection. Ph.d. thesis, UCSB (June 2006)
15. Mutz, D., Valeur, F., Kruegel, C., Vigna, G.: Anomalous System Call Detection. ACM Transactions on Information and System Security 9(1), 61–93 (2006)
16. Nystrom, E., Kim, H., Hwu, W.: Importance of heap specialization in pointer analysis. In: Proceedings of Program Analysis for Software Tools and Engineering (2004)
17. Robertson, W., Vigna, G., Kruegel, C., Kemmerer, R.: Using Generalization and Characterization Techniques in the Anomaly-based Detection of Web Attacks. In: Proceeding of NDSS, San Diego, CA (February 2006)
18. Sekar, R., Bendre, M., Dhurjati, D., Bollineni, P.: A fast automaton-based method for detecting anomalous program behaviors. In: Proceedings of the IEEE Symposium on Security and Privacy, May 2001, IEEE Computer Society Press, Los Alamitos (2001)
19. Sekar, R., Venkatakrishnan, V., Basu, S., Du Varney, B.S.D.: Model-carrying code: A practical approach for safe execution of untrusted applications. In: Proceedings of the 19th ACM Symposium on Operating Systems Principles, ACM Press, New York (2003)
20. SNARE - System iNtrusion Analysis and Reporting Environment, http://www.intersectalliance.com/projects/Snare

21. Stolcke, A., Omohundro, S.: Hidden Markov Model Induction by Bayesian Model Merging. Advances in Neural Information Processing Systems (1993)
22. Stolcke, A., Omohundro, S.: Inducing probabilistic grammars by bayesian model merging. In: Proceedings of the International Conference on Grammatical Inference (1994)
23. Wagner, D., Dean, D.: Intrusion Detection via Static Analysis. In: Proceedings of the IEEE Symposium on Security and Privacy, Oakland, CA, May 2001, IEEE Press, Los Alamitos (2001)
24. Wagner, D., Soto, P.: Mimicry Attacks on Host-Based Intrusion Detection Systems. In: Proceedings of ACM CCS, Washington DC, USA, November 2002, ACM Press, New York (2002)
25. Warrender, C., Forrest, S., Pearlmutter, B.: Detecting intrusions using system calls: Alternative data models. In: Proceedings of the IEEE Symposium on Security and Privacy, pp. 133–145. IEEE Computer Society Press, Los Alamitos (1999)
26. Wespi, A., Dacier, M., Debar, H.: Intrusion Detection Using Variable-Length Audit Trail Patterns. In: Debar, H., Mé, L., Wu, S.F. (eds.) RAID 2000. LNCS, vol. 1907, Springer, Heidelberg (2000)
27. Xu, H., Du, W., Chapin, S.: Context Sensitive Anomaly Monitoring of Process Control Flow to Detect Mimicry Attacks and Impossible Paths. In: Jonsson, E., Valdes, A., Almgren, M. (eds.) RAID 2004. LNCS, vol. 3224, Springer, Heidelberg (2004)

Understanding Precision in Host Based Intrusion Detection
Formal Analysis and Practical Models

Monirul Sharif, Kapil Singh, Jonathon Giffin, and Wenke Lee

School of Computer Science, Georgia Institute of Technology
{msharif,ksingh,giffin,wenke}@cc.gatech.edu

Abstract. Many host-based anomaly detection systems monitor process execution at the granularity of system calls. Other recently proposed schemes instead verify the destinations of control-flow transfers to prevent the execution of attack code. This paper formally analyzes and compares real systems based on these two anomaly detection philosophies in terms of their attack detection capabilities, and proves and disproves several intuitions. We prove that for any system-call sequence model, under the same (static or dynamic) program analysis technique, there always exists a more precise control-flow sequence based model. While hybrid approaches combining system calls and control flows intuitively seem advantageous, especially when binary analysis constructs incomplete models, we prove that they have no fundamental advantage over simpler control-flow models. Finally, we utilize the ideas in our framework to make external monitoring feasible at the precise control-flow level. Our experiments show that external control-flow monitoring imposes performance overhead comparable to previous system call based approaches while detecting synthetic and real world attacks as effectively as an inlined monitor.

Keywords: Anomaly detection, Formal analysis, Program models.

1 Introduction

Over the years, researchers have developed an abundance of host-based intrusion detection systems, utilizing a variety of mechanisms. Most systems, e.g. [11,29,9,10,17,16, 12,27], model an application's normal system call usage and use run-time monitoring to detect attacks that cause behavior deviating from the model. While useful attacks typically require system calls, they provide only a coarse view of a process' execution. The existence of mimicry attacks [32,21] that cloak an attack by generating valid sequences demonstrates that attackers may exploit this coarse view. System-call based detectors have another drawback in that they detect attacks well after execution is diverted—at best at the next system call invocation. Monitors verifying system call usage are often implemented as an external process, which eases implementation, debugging, and data protection.

Recently proposed schemes take an alternative approach that detects attacks when they divert control flow. CFI [5], a static analysis based system, efficiently verifies dynamically computed control-flow targets in the program. It guarantees [6] that the execution path will be restricted to the statically generated control flow graph (CFG) of the program, and it can thus detect and stop attacks involving illegal control transfers. In

C. Kruegel, R. Lippmann, and A. Clark (Eds.): RAID 2007, LNCS 4637, pp. 21–41, 2007.

contrast to external monitors verifying a process' system call use, CFI inlines its checks into the existing code of a program. While inlining complicates monitor development, debugging, and application to arbitrary binary code, it offers exceptional performance when verifying fine-grained control flow operations.

Speculation about these systems' designs leads to several intuitive conclusions:

- Control-flow based models can provide better attack detection than system-call based models.
- A hybrid model combining control-flow operations and system-call operations better detects attacks than a control-flow based model alone, particularly in the event that static program analysis incompletely identifies control-flows requiring verification code.
- An external monitor cannot efficiently verify control-flow operations.

In this paper, we formally *prove* the first intuition, *disprove* the second, and provide *experimental evidence against* the third. Our goal is to provide clarity to host-based intrusion detection systems research.

In order to understand the strengths and weaknesses or limitations of these anomaly detection schemes, we provide a formal framework to analyze their *precision* in terms of how close they can model a program's normal execution. We first show that for any given system-call sequence based model derived from any program analysis technique (static vs dynamic), *there always exists a more precise control-flow sequence based model*. Such a control-flow based model can precisely match the normal execution behavior of the program from which it was derived, considerably limiting mimicry attacks that plagued system-call based intrusion detectors.

Control-flow sequence based intrusion detectors require the identification of security-critical control flows in a program. A system using static program analysis to identify such control flows may incompletely analyze the program's code due to undecidable problems in static analysis [25]. As a result, a program may contain unchecked control flows. System-call sequence based intrusion detectors face no such shortcoming, as they can completely mediate the system call interface without complete program analysis. Intuitively, we expect hybrid systems combining control flow verification with system call verification, such as PAID [23] to provide better security than control-flow based systems alone. If an attacker breaks out of control-flow checks due to a missed control flow, they can still be detected by the system call checks. Using our framework, we prove that *even if static analysis is incomplete, hybrid models are not more precise than control-flow models*. With appropriate control-flow checks in place, system call checks are redundant and could be removed for model simplification and improved performance.

Finally, we provide experimental evidence against the intuition that efficient enforcement of fine-grained control-flow models can only occur with an inlined monitor. For a fair comparison between the performance overhead of system call and control-flow based approaches, we have implemented an efficient external control-flow based IDS. Using principles developed in our analysis of system-call and control-flow based systems, we apply program transformation to reduce the number of control-flows events exposed to the monitor and improve performance without sacrificing precision. The performance overhead introduced by our detection system, ranging from 1% to 23%, is comparable to previous external system call monitoring. The results also show that our external control-flow monitor can detect a wide range of synthetic and real attacks.

Our current formal framework considers the sequence in which control flows and system calls are executed. As future work, our analysis will incorporate the notion of data in order to cover approaches that can detect data-only attacks such as program variable or system-call argument manipulation.

2 Related Work

The search for defensive techniques that can detect application-level attacks has led to a rich research area. We consider examples of host-based anomaly detection systems that characterize normal program execution with a language of allowed event sequences. System calls predominantly form the basis of these events, although recent work has developed new models based upon finer-grained control-flow information. Since a primary aim of this paper is to provide illumination of the differences among these model types, we also review previous work in formal analysis of sequence-based models.

Numerous prior systems detect application-level attacks by observing process execution at the granularity of system calls [9, 14, 15, 20, 26, 30, 31, 16, 13, 27]. Rather than directly detecting the execution of malicious code, these tools attempt to detect attacks through the secondary effect of the malicious code or inputs upon the system call sequences executed by the process. By allowing attack code to execute, these secondary detectors provide attackers with opportunities to evade detection. Mimicry attacks [32,28,18] succeed by appearing normal to a system-call sequence based detector. System call models have grown in complexity to address mimicry attacks, but remain vulnerable because they allow invalid control flows to execute [21]. We note that our paper does not consider non-sequence aspects of system call models, such as characterizations of expected argument values [7,22].

Control-flow based techniques [5, 34] detect various code execution attacks by verifying destinations of control-flow transfers. Abadi et al. [5] developed Control Flow Integrity (CFI), a recent implementation of control-flow verification. CFI constrains allowed process execution to a model of valid control-flow transfers defined by the program's static control-flow graph (CFG). CFI uses binary rewriting to place instructions immediately before dynamically computed control-flow instructions for inlined verification of the destination of the transfer. An attacker cannot escape the inlined checks [6] because the static source code analysis or hinted binary analysis can completely identify the set of control transfer points in the program. In this paper, we generalize the idea of CFI to any control-flow based model, including models constructed from training, containing path sensitivity or resulting from incomplete binary analysis.

Given two different classes of sequence-based models, those using system calls and those using control flows, we aim to reason about their attack detection ability. Formal analysis has been previously applied to host-based intrusion detection. Wagner and Dean developed a precision metric called average branching factor (ABF) [31], but this metric is specific to system-call models and cannot be adapted to models of control flow. Chen and Wagner [8] and Giffin et al. [18] use model-checking to find allowed sequences of events in system-call models that execute attack behavior. As with ABF, those tools cannot be adapted to also reason about control-flow models. Gao et al. [12] provided a systematic way of comparing various system call models by organizing them in three axes of design space. This establishes a relation between dynamically and statically constructed system call models, but provides no mechanism to compare system call models with control-flow models. Our formalization not only provides the means to directly compare system-call models with control-flow models, but also provides insight into what effects the precision of control-flow models.

Although the primary intent of this paper is to provide a comparative analysis of system-call and control-flow based models, we additionally consider environments where a hybrid model containing both sets of events may be advantageous. Xu et al. [33] insert waypoints into program code, but these waypoints are not used to verify all computed transfers. PAID [23] inserts notify system calls before indirect function calls so that the monitor can correctly follow indirect control flows. Recent improvements [24] apply this technique to binaries and also incorporate return address checking. We show that hybrid approaches do not provide fundamentally more attack detection capability than control-flow based approaches even in the case of incomplete program analysis.

We also implement an external monitoring based control-flow intrusion detection. We generate the events visible to an external monitor via insertion of null system calls or software interrupts. The Dyck model [17] uses similar code instrumentation techniques. However, the monitor enforcing a Dyck model uses null call events to improve efficiency, not security. In this paper, we use a mechanism similar to null calls for secure exposure of a process' control-flow behavior.

3   Formal Framework for Analyzing Precision

The intrusion detection capability of an IDS is limited by the set of program generated *events* visible to it for modeling and monitoring. In order to compare the attack detection capabilities, it is worthwhile to analyze the relative abilities of recent approaches in terms of how *precisely* they can represent the underlying *normal* behavior of the program they try to enforce. Although our framework enables formal analysis of models comprising any event, we focus on system calls and control-flow transfers. We develop definitions so that they can be applied to both statically and dynamically generated models. We present a *control-flow sequence* based IDS model, which is more precise than any system call sequence based model representing the same valid program execution behavior. This model can precisely represent a program's execution, but requires the exposure of all control-flow events in a program. In Section 4, simplified derivations of this model is used to analyze the precision of practical control-flow based approaches.

Section 3.1 begins with an abstract model of program execution from which we derive all sequence-based models used for intrusion detection. Section 3.2 defines our approach of comparing the precision of different models. We derive system-call based models in Section 3.3 and show that it imprecisely characterizes valid program execution. In Section 3.4, we derive control-flow based models that precisely describe valid execution and consider mimicry attacks in Section 3.5.

3.1   Abstract Model of Execution Sequences

Our abstract model considers the sequence in which code is executed. The smallest unit of executed code is a machine instruction, which can be uniquely identified by its address in memory. Therefore, an execution sequence can be represented as a sequence of addresses from where instructions are executed. Without loss of generality, we consider a coarser *basic block* unit of execution. A basic block is an ordered set of instructions that are executed in sequence as a unit; execution enters only at the start of the block

```
main:                    placeholder:
B1:    if (…)            B6:    jmp (*fptr)()
B2:        fptr = open
       else              open:
B3:        fptr = reopen B7:    syscall_1
                                return
B4:    placeholder()     reopen:
B5:    syscall_3         B8:    syscall_2
       return                   return
```

E_v (Static Analysis)

e_1:	B1	B2	B4	B6	B7	B5
e_2:	B1	B2	B4	B6	B8	B5
e_3:	B1	B3	B4	B6	B7	B5
e_4:	B1	B3	B4	B6	B8	B5

E_v (Dynamic Analysis)

e_5:	B1	B2	B4	B6	B7	B5
e_6:	B1	B3	B4	B6	B8	B5

Fig. 1. An example program to illustrate control flow and system call based models. The vulnerable function has not been shown.

Fig. 2. The language of valid execution sequences E_v as constructed by a static or dynamic analyzer

and exits only at the end. The address of the first instruction uniquely identifies a basic block in memory. Basic blocks can also be used to represent high-level statements, making our analysis applicable in the context of both source code and binaries.

Our abstract models of execution are built on sequences of basic blocks executed by a running program. For a program Pr, let B_v denote the complete set of basic blocks in Pr that can be executed during some valid execution. We use the term *valid* and *normal* interchangeably throughout the paper because from the point of view of an anomaly detector, anything that is deemed normal is considered valid. Figure 1 lists an example program and the basic blocks in its set B_v. Let B_f be the set of all basic blocks that may be feasibly executed in any run of the program. Note that feasible execution differs from valid execution and includes blocks belonging to the program, unknown blocks containing code maliciously introduced into Pr's address space, and blocks generated by disassembling from the middle of instructions belonging to the program. Clearly $B_v \subseteq B_f$. We next present the abstract models of valid and feasible execution, which are languages over the sets of program points B_v and B_f, respectively.

The Language of Valid Execution. The language of valid execution $E_v \subseteq B_v{}^*$ contains all sequences of basic blocks from B_v that denote valid execution behavior of Pr. The actual sequences contained in E_v depend upon the algorithms used to compute a program's valid behavior; our framework is general and suitable for any algorithm able to generate E_v. For example, static and dynamic analysis each produce differing characterizations of valid behavior E_v. In the domain of static analysis, different approaches produce models having different sensitivities to program behavior [9]. Dynamic analysis approaches may consider paths that seem valid from the program's static view as invalid. Our framework derives control-flow and system-call sequences from any given E_v. Therefore, our method of comparing precision is orthogonal to the choice of method used to generate abstract model of valid execution E_v.

Figure 2 shows two different languages E_v constructed from typical static analysis and dynamic analysis of the example program. The shaded boxes highlight where the sequences differ. Note that the example program has correlated execution between the direction of the if branch in main and the target of the indirect jump at B7. The E_v constructed from context sensitive static analysis has four possible execution sequences and fails to characterize the correlated execution. However, the dynamically constructed model contains only two sequences because the correlation occurring actual execution carries over to the observed execution sequences.

The Language of Feasible Execution. The language $E_f \subseteq B_f^*$ represents all feasible execution sequences of code in B_f that Pr's execution can generate. Again, feasible execution need not be valid execution.

The language E_f contains both valid executions and also executions that occur due to an attack. In the example program, any block may appear after blocks B6, B7, and B8 in sequences of E_f because it may be possible for an attacker to change the targets of the control transfers found in those blocks to any address in memory.

The effectiveness of any IDS can be improved by restricting the set of feasible execution paths. Non-writable code (NWC), a standard assumption in almost all systems, restricts feasible execution by disallowing executions that directly modify program code. Non-executable data (NXD) restricts E_f so that executions containing code injection attacks would no longer be feasible behavior. For practical use, the system-call based systems of Section 3.3 require neither NWC nor NXD, but the control-flow based systems in Section 3.4 require at least NWC. Throughout the paper, we assume the usage of NWC.

3.2   Approach of Comparing Precision

We now define how the precision of IDS models can be compared in our framework. For any IDS that models a particular set of events X generated by a program, we can generate the language of valid sequences of such events from the execution language E_v. We will use the notation E_v^X to denote the language containing any sequence of basic blocks that generate a valid sequence of such events. Therefore, any feasible execution of the program that will be considered valid by the IDS is in $E_f \cap E_v^X$. An execution $e \in E_f$ is detected as an anomaly when $e \notin E_v^X$. We will use the following definition for comparing precision of various approaches (illustrated in Figure 3):

Definition 1. *Given the sequence of basic blocks considered valid by two IDSs modeling event categories X and Y from valid executions in E_v are E_v^X and E_v^Y respectively, the former is more precise than the latter if $E_v^X \subseteq E_v^Y$, but not vice versa while keeping $E_v \subseteq E_v^X$ and $E_v \subseteq E_v^Y$.*

From the definition above, IDS modeling X can detect any anomaly detected by the IDS modeling Y. This is because for any feasible execution $e \in E_f$, if $e \notin E_v^Y$ then $e \notin E_v^X$ also. However, more attacks are detectable by the IDS modeling the events X, which are executions in $E_f \cap (E_v^Y - E_v^X)$.

3.3   System Call Sequence Based Intrusion Detection

Our approach for formalizing the precision of system call sequence based schemes is to first derive the language of system call sequences homomorphic to E_v, and then use the inverse homomorphism to identify the language of actual execution behavior allowed by a system call model, which we denote as E_v^S. Let Σ_S be the set of symbols containing all system calls. Without loss of generality, we assume that a basic block contains at most one system call because a block can be subdivided into multiple blocks to meet the requirement. Let $\sigma \lhd b$ hold if basic block b contains system call σ. Define the homomorphism $h_s : B_f^* \to \Sigma_S^*$ as follows. For any $b \in B_f$,

$$h_s(b) = \begin{cases} \sigma, & \text{if } \sigma \lhd b; \\ \epsilon, & \text{otherwise.} \end{cases}$$

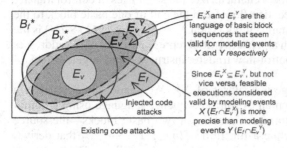

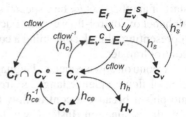

Fig. 3. Illustration of the comparison of precision of two different approaches modeling different types of events.

Fig. 4. Relations among various languages in our proofs. Edges indicate functional or homomorphic relationships.

The language S_v of all system call sequences produced by any valid execution of Pr is then $S_v = h_s(E_v)$. The language containing sequence of basic blocks producing valid system call sequences E_v^S can be found using the inverse homomorphism $h_s^{-1} : \Sigma_S^* \to B_f^*$ on S_v. It produces the language E_v^S that is less restrictive than E_v:

$$E_v^S = h_s^{-1}(S_v) = \{e \in B_f^* : h_s(e) \in S_v\}$$

The imprecision of system call sequence based approaches can be realized in our framework from $E_v \subseteq E_v^S$. Figure 4 illustrates this relationship along with other languages presented throughout the paper. Using the homomorphism, $e \in E_v \implies s = h_s(e) \in S_v \implies e \in E_v^S$. The contrapositive states that if an executing program generates a system call sequence $s \notin S_v$, then s is generated by a program execution $e \notin E_v$. An invalid system call sequence implies invalid execution. However, the converse is not true; an invalid execution does not imply an invalid system call sequence. This imprecision allows any feasible execution in $E_v^S \cap E_f \supseteq E_v$ to be considered valid. Mimicry attacks [32, 21] that utilize invalid execution exploit this imprecision.

Our framework can be used to derive the known results of Gao et al. [12] indicating that a system call's program counter [27] and calling context [10] improve the precision of system call models by producing a more restrictive E_v^S. However, unless an execution sequence generates a unique system call sequence, E_v^S can never be as precise as E_v. Using control-flow sequences, we can capture the association between consecutively executed basic blocks in order to uniquely represent executions.

3.4 Control-Flow Sequence Based Intrusion Detection

In order to be able analyze the precision of any control-flow based model, in this section we present a *control-flow sequence* based IDS model, which for now, assumes the exposure of all control-flow transfers in a program. We prove that given E_v, we can always derive a control-flow sequence model that provides detection as precise as E_v. This provides an important theoretical result: *for any system-call sequence based model derived using any program analysis approach, there always exists a more precise control-flow based model.*

A control-flow sequence based model characterizes the sequences of control transfer instructions or events that move execution flow from the end of one basic block to the start of another. Let b_S be a special start symbol. Then $\Sigma_C = ((B_f \cup \{b_S\}) \times B_f)$ is the alphabet of control-flow events. Each alphabet symbol represents a pair of the addresses representing a block containing a control-flow transfer instruction and targeted block of control transfer.

A control-flow sequence language is a subset of Σ_C^*. We cannot directly derive a control-flow sequence language from an execution sequence language using a homomorphism because a control-flow transfer depends on two basic blocks—the source and the destination. Instead, we define a function $cflow : B_f^* \rightarrow \Sigma_C^*$ that derives the control-flow sequence from an execution sequence string as follows. For any string $e = b_1 b_2 b_3 ... b_{k-1} b_k \in B_f^*$,

$$cflow(e) = (b_S, b_1)(b_1, b_2)(b_2, b_3)...(b_{k-1}, b_k)$$

In a minor overloading of notation, we also denote the application of $cflow$ to every sentence in a language as $cflow(L) = \{cflow(e) : e \in L\}$. Then, we can derive the language $L_C \subseteq \Sigma_C^*$.

Any language representing a sequence of basic blocks is homomorphic to a language of control-flow sequences:

Theorem 1. *For any language $L \subseteq B_f^*$ there exists a control-flow sequence language $L_C \subseteq \Sigma_C^*$ and a homomorphism $h_c : \Sigma_C^* \rightarrow B_f^*$ such that $L = h_c(L_C)$.*

Proof. Our proof is by construction. We first construct a control-flow sequence language L_C using $L_C = cflow(L)$. We now define the homomorphism $h_c : \Sigma_C^* \rightarrow B_f^*$ as follows:

$$h_c((b_1, b_2)) = b_2$$

The homomorphism h_c is constructed in such a way that we can use it on a control-flow sequence $c = cflow(e)$ derived from some execution sequence $e \in L$, and get the execution string e back, i.e. $e = h_c(c)$. Therefore, $L = h_c(L_C)$.   □

We use $cflow$ to derive control-flow sequence languages from E_v and E_f. The language $C_v = cflow(E_v)$ contains only valid control-flow sequences, and $C_f = cflow(E_f)$ contains feasible sequences. Figure 4 illustrates the relations.

This control-flow sequence model precisely characterizes execution. Let E_v^C denote the language of all basic block sequences that can generate valid control-flow sequences, giving $E_v^C = cflow^{-1}(C_v)$. We are going to show that $E_v = E_v^C$. From the definition, $E_v \subseteq cflow^{-1}(C_v)$. Our approach is to show that $cflow^{-1}(C_v)$ is contained in E_v. We first prove that every execution sequence generates a unique control-flow sequence by showing that $cflow$ is one-to-one.

Theorem 2. *Let $e_1, e_2 \in B_f^*$. Then $e_1 \neq e_2 \implies cflow(e_1) \neq cflow(e_2)$.*

Proof. Assume that $cflow(e_1) = cflow(e_2)$. Let $c_1 = cflow(e_1)$. Then $e_1 = h_c(c_1) = h_c(cflow(e_1))$. Similarly, $e_2 = h_c(c_2)$. Since $c_1 = c_2$, $e_1 = e_2$, which is a contradiction. Therefore, $cflow(e_1) \neq cflow(e_2)$.   □

From Theorem 2, it is clear that $cflow$ is injective, and $\forall c \in C_v : \exists e = cflow^{-1}(c) = h_c(c) \in E_v$. Hence, $cflow^{-1}(C_v) \subseteq E_v$. Therefore, $cflow^{-1}(C_v) = h_c(C_v) = E_v$.

An execution sequence is therefore an anomaly if and only if its control-flow sequence is an anomaly.

Corollary 1. *For any system call sequence model S_v derived from a valid/normal execution E_v, there always exists a more precise control-flow sequence model C_v : $E_v^C \subseteq E_v^S$, but not vice versa where $E_v^C = cflow^{-1}(C_v) = E_v$ and $E_v^S = h_s^{-1}(S_v)$.*

Therefore, any attack that can be detected by a system call sequence language S_v can be detected using the control-flow sequence language C_v, along with more attacks as described in the next section.

3.5 Mimicry Attacks

A mimicry attack [32] is a variant of an attack that achieves the same goal, but can evade detection by an IDS. Better model precision limits opportunities of possible mimicry attacks. For the models of this paper, we set a broad definition of mimicry attacks:

Definition 2. *Given a malicious sequence of events required for an attack, a mimicry attack $\mathcal{A} \in E_f$ is a feasible execution that can achieve the same malicious goal and $\mathcal{A} \in E_v^X$ for E_v^X being the basic block sequence language considered valid by an IDS modeling events X.*

Mimicry attacks on system call based IDS have the freedom of generating feasible executions outside of E_v but in E_v^S to evade detection [21]. Since the control-flow sequence based model is as precise as E_v, any such mimicry attack for which $\mathcal{A} \notin E_v$ can be detected. However, any mimicry attack that switches between valid execution paths, or modifies data only without altering paths cannot be detected. *This is a fundamental limitation of any approach based on execution sequences without data.*

4 Applying Formalisms to Real Intrusion Detection

Our control-flow sequence based model provides the foundation to analyze any control-flow based approach. As presented, the model requires complete exposure and complete history of all control-flow events of a program. Practical control-flow based approaches usually cannot satisfy this requirement due to undecidability problems in program analysis and performance cost. In this section, we simplify our model to analyze the precision of control-flow approaches based on the exposed and covered control-flow events.

CFI [5] only checks the targets of dynamically computed control-transfer instructions, yet it was proven [6] to keep the execution of a program in the statically computed CFG. However, models extracted using dynamic analysis and path sensitive models [34] may need static branches to be exposed for monitoring. Moreover, a control-flow event may be valid or invalid depending on the occurrence of a prior control flow. Hence, the control-flow events that need to be exposed for verification depend on the valid execution model that is being enforced.

We provide a generic framework to derive a simplified yet precise control-flow model that only requires the exposure of a subset of control-flow events. Using this framework, we analyze the precision of CFI in comparison to the system call based models. Our framework also provides insight into derivation strategies for precise dynamically constructed control-flow models. Our goals are different than that of Abadi et al. [6], which proved that the stateless checks provided by CFI were sufficient to constrain program control flow to the static CFG.

4.1   Retaining Precision While Simplifying Models

We simplify control-flow sequence models by deriving a simpler language from C_v. We remove control-flow events from C_v that do not help a monitor identify an invalid sequence. If a feasible control-flow event can cause an anomaly or its appearance correlates with another anomalous control-flow event, then it cannot be discarded. We call such events *essential* control-flow events. Any control-flow event emanating from a block that has no essential control-flow events can be discarded without affecting the precision of the model.

Figure 5 illustrates the statically and dynamically constructed control-flow sequence language C_v of the program presented in Figure 1. Invalid but feasible control-flow events emanating from the basic blocks of the program are shown using dotted arrows. Notice that for both models, basic blocks $B6, B7$ and $B8$ have invalid but feasible control-flow events. Each control-flow transfer instruction in these blocks uses a dynamically computed target, and can feasibly point anywhere in memory to generate invalid sequences. Additionally, in the C_v constructed from dynamic analysis, the JUMP instruction at block $B6$ is correlated with the branch in $B1$. The control-flow event occurring at $B1$ is required to validate the event at $B6$. These control-flow events have to be visible to the model and cannot be removed.

We first define *essential* control-flow events as any of the following:

1. *Anomaly Generating Control-flow Event* (AG). An AG event is the first control-flow event in a sequence to turn a valid sequence into an invalid, but feasible sequence. A control-flow event c is an AG if $\exists \tilde{u}, \tilde{v}, \tilde{w} \in \Sigma_C^*, \forall \tilde{x} \in \Sigma_C^* : \tilde{u}\tilde{v} \in C_v \wedge \tilde{u}c\tilde{x} \notin C_v \wedge \tilde{u}c\tilde{w} \in C_f$ (refer to Figure 6). If c never appears in any valid control-flow sequence, then we call it an *independent* anomaly generator (IAG), which is always anomalous regardless of the events appearing before it. Otherwise, we call c a *dependent* anomaly generator (DAG), which is invalid based upon some previous control-flow events in the sequence. A typical example of an IAG is a feasible control-flow transfer into injected code. In addition, it can be an invalid control-transfer to existing code, such as the event $(B6, B5)$ in Figure 5. Examples of DAG events are function returns that may be sometimes valid and sometimes invalid based on the call site.

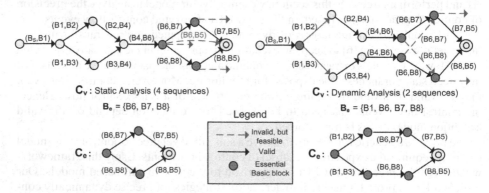

Fig. 5. Simplification of the control-flow sequence language C_v derived from the execution languages given in Figure 2 (The languages are shown by finite state automata)

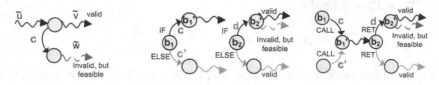

Fig. 6. Illustration of an AG control-flow event c

Fig. 7. The two cases where c is an AC event correlated with the DAG event d

2. *Anomaly Correlating Control-flow Event* (AC). A control-flow event c is an AC event if its appearance is correlated with a dependent anomaly generator (DAG) event d. Examples are function calls instructions or static branches. More precisely, in order for c to be an AC of d (assume that $c = (b_1, b'_1)$ and $d = (b_2, b'_2)$ here), two conditions must be satisfied. First, in all valid control-flow sequences following the event c, the next control-flow event emanating from b_2 must be d. Second, if c' is another event sharing either the source (e.g. conditional branches) or destination block with c (e.g. function CALL instruction), following c', if d is the next event emanating from b_2, it generates an invalid sequences. We show two types of correlation that broadly encapsulates all possible cases in Figure 7. In the dynamic analysis case of Figure 5, $(B1, B2)$ is an AC event correlating with the DAG $(B6, B7)$. If $(B1, B3)$ appears instead of $(B1, B2)$, $(B6, B7)$ generates an invalid control-flow sequence. In case a DAG has multiple AC events, the first one is selected. Our definition can be extended to handle complex cases that involve recursion by incorporating the notion of a stack, and correlating a DAG event with an AC event on top of the stack.

The set of *essential basic blocks* $B_e \subseteq B_v$ contains blocks having at least one outgoing essential control-flow event. The basic blocks in the set B_e are the only ones whose control-flow events need to be exposed for verification. As a result, when a program executes, sequences of control-flow events will be generated from these blocks only.

In Figure 5, the statically constructed C_v has the essential basic blocks $B_e = \{B6, B7, B8\}$ because independent anomaly generating control-flow events exist from them. In the dynamic analysis case, the control-flow events $(B6, B7)$ and $(B6, B8)$ are dependent anomaly generators because they are sometimes valid and sometimes invalid. Since the appearance of $(B1, B2)$ and $(B1, B3)$ correlate to the validity of $(B6, B7)$ and $(B6, B8)$ respectively, they are anomaly correlating control-flow events. Therefore, $B_e = \{B1, B6, B7, B8\}$. Notice that even though block $B1$ contains a branch with static target addresses, it must be visible to the monitor.

Our simplification generalizes to any control-flow model. Unlike CFI, which only considers dynamically computed control-transfer instructions, the set B_e may include control-transfer instructions with static targets if they become an anomaly generating or correlating event. For example, a model enforcing correlated branching would verify the static branches that were correlated. B_e may exclude computed control flows if analysis reveals that an attacker cannot control the destination. For example, an indirect jump reading from a read-only jump table may be safely left unverified.

We define a smaller alphabet $\Sigma_{CE} = B_e \times B_f$ containing only the exposed control-flow events. The simplified subsequence language is derived using the homomorphism

$h_{ce} : \Sigma_C^* \to \Sigma_{CE}^*$, defined as:

$$h_{ce}((b_1, b_2)) = \begin{cases} (b_1, b_2), & b_1 \in B_e; \\ \epsilon, & \text{otherwise} \end{cases}$$

The simplified model is now $C_e = h_{ce}(C_v)$, which is a language of subsequences of strings in C_v. Again, refer to Figure 5 for the derived C_e of the running example. The model appears to be less precise than the full control-flow model C_v. The inverse homomorphism h_{ce}^{-1} applied to C_e yields $C_v^e \supseteq C_v$. However, this imprecision does not contain any feasible anomalous control-flow sequence:

Theorem 3. *If $C_v^e = h_{ce}^{-1}(h_{ce}(C_v))$, then $C_v^e \cap C_f = C_v$.*

Proof. We first prove that $C_v \subseteq C_v^e \cap C_f$, and then prove $C_v^e \cap C_f \subseteq C_v$. The first part of the proof is straightforward. By definition, $C_v \subseteq C_f$ and $C_v \subseteq C_v^e$. Therefore, $C_v \subseteq C_v^e \cap C_f$.

For the second part of the proof, we show that if $c \in C_v^e \cap C_f$, then $c \in C_v$. The proof is by induction on the length of the string c. Since $c \in C_f$, by definition $c = (b_S, b_1)(b_1, b_2)...(b_{l-1}, b_l)$ with $\forall i : b_i \in B_f$. Let $c_s \in \Sigma_{CE}^*$ be the subsequence of control-flow events in c emanating from basic blocks in B_e, i.e. $c_s = h_{ce}(c)$. Since $c \in C_v^e, \exists c' \in C_v : h_{ce}(c') = c_s = h_{ce}(c)$.

For the induction base case, we show that some string in C_v begins with (b_S, b_1). If $b_S \notin B_e$, then (b_S, b_1) cannot be an essential control-flow event. This means that no anomalous sequence can begin with b_S. Therefore, some sequence in C_v begins with b_S. On the other hand, if $b_S \in B_e$, then (b_S, b_1) is in the subsequence c_s and should be the first event in the subsequence. Since $\exists c' \in C_v : h(c') = c_s$ and control-flow events emanating from b_S can only be found at the beginning of a string, c' begins with (b_S, b_1).

For the induction step, we assume that the $(k-1)$ length prefix of c is also a prefix of some string $c' \in C_v$. We have to prove it for the k length prefix. In other words, assuming that $(b_S, b_1)(b_1, b_2) ... (b_{k-2}, b_{k-1})$ is a prefix of a valid control-flow sequence, we have to show that the next event (b_{k-1}, b_k) does not induce an anomaly or create a prefix of a sequence outside C_v. First, for $b_{k-1} \notin B_e$, it is obvious from the definition of B_e that no control-flow event emanating from b_{k-1} can create an anomalous sequence. Therefore, the k-length prefix of c has to be the prefix of some sequence in C_v. Suppose $b_{k-1} \in B_e$. This means that (b_{k-1}, b_k) is in the subsequence c_s. The k-length prefix can be invalid only if (b_{k-1}, b_k) is an anomaly generating event. If it is, then we can first reject the possibility that it may be an independent anomaly generator because it cannot be contained in any subsequence of strings in C_v. Therefore, it should be a dependent anomaly generator event. Even in this case, we can prove that it will not create an anomalous prefix of length k. For (b_{k-1}, b_k) to create an anomalous prefix, some anomaly correlating control-flow events should be missing or not in valid order in the $k - 1$ length prefix. If that was the case, then the subsequence of essential control-flow events generated by the $k - 1$ prefix cannot be the prefix of any subsequence generated by strings in C_v. That contradicts $c \in C_v^e$. Therefore, some string in C_v should have the k length prefix of c. $\square$

Hence, exposing events from B_e and checking with the simplified subsequence model C_e is necessary and sufficient to detect anomalies with the same precision as the comprehensive sequence language C_v with all control-flow events exposed.

Corollary 2. *Checking exposed events from the essential set B_e with the simplified subsequence language C_e is as precise as checking all events with the comprehensive model C_v, which is equivalent to the precision of E_v.*

If basic blocks in B_e are missed, control-flow models become imprecise. The relative precision depend on the covered basic blocks. Models with more exposed control-flow events are more precise.

Corollary 3. *For the same valid and feasible executions of a program, if two control-flow based approaches expose control-flow events from set of basic blocks B_X and B_Y respectively, where $B_e \supseteq B_X \supseteq B_Y$, then the former is at least as precise as the latter, i.e. $E_v \subseteq E_v^X \subseteq E_v^Y$ (basic block sequences considered valid by them are E_v^X and E_v^Y).*

Next, we can state another result that helps reduce the size of the essential basic block set. Restricting feasible execution of a program reduces the set of essential basic blocks without loss of precision:

Corollary 4. *For any program with valid execution language E_v, feasible execution E_f and essential basic blocks B_e, if the feasible execution is constrained such that $E'_f \subseteq E_f$, then the new essential basic block set is $B'_e \subseteq B_e$.*

4.2 Comparing Precision of Practical Systems

Using our framework, we now analyze the precision of several recent host based intrusion detection systems. We first consider models built via static analysis. CFI confines execution in a statically built CFG. Furthermore, it ensures that return addresses are valid by using a protected shadow stack. Suppose that the execution sequences that are paths in the CFG, conforming to proper function call and return semantics, constitute the valid execution language E_v.

We now identify the essential control-flow events. Like CFI, we assume the presence of NWC. As recognized by Abadi et al., any dynamically computed control-flow transfer may feasibly target any basic block. Since they can generate invalid sequences regardless of previous control flow, they are independent anomaly generators (IAG). Returns from functions are dependent anomaly generators (DAG) because they can generate anomalies during an impossible path attack [33]. They are correlated with prior function calls, which are anomaly correlating (AC) events. Therefore, B_e contains all basic blocks that have such instructions. Notice that branch instructions, which have static target addresses are not anomaly generators because both target blocks are valid according to the static CFG.

The blocks in B_e are exactly those covered by CFI. Therefore, if E_v^{CFI} is the basic block sequences considered valid by CFI, then according to Corollary 2, $E_v^{CFI} = E_v$, making CFI the most precise statically constructed sequence based model. Any other system call approach based on static analysis [9, 31, 16, 13] considers the basic block sequences E_v^S as valid, where $E_v \subseteq E_v^S$. Therefore, *CFI subsumes all system call sequence based IDS built on static analysis.*

Dynamic analysis based approaches relying on execution language $E'_v \subseteq E_v$ that are more restrictive than statically constructed models. The system call sequence based models utilizing dynamic analysis [12, 10, 15] recognize basic block sequences $E_v^{S'}$ as valid where $E_v^{S'} \subseteq E_v^S$. When compared with CFI, we cannot say that $E_v^{S'} \subseteq E_v^{CFI}$, nor can we say that $E_v^{CFI} \subseteq E_v^{S'}$. Our formal framework therefore proves the intuition that neither of the approaches are more precise than the other. Each may detect attacks that the other does not. However, according to Corollary 1, a more precise control-flow model for dynamic analysis exists. Such an approach will be as precise as E_v', becoming fundamentally more precise than the system call based counterpart because $E_v' \subseteq E_v^{S'}$.

5   Incomplete Analysis and Hybrid Approaches

The precision of control-flow sequence models depends on the exposure of control-flow events in a program. To be as precise as possible, the essential basic blocks at least need to be identified and covered. This is generally straightforward for source code or for binaries with compiler generated hints. However, due to known undecidable problems [25] there is no static or dynamic binary analysis technique that guarantees complete coverage of code for arbitrary binaries. In such situations, an unchecked control-transfer instruction may be exploited by an attacker without being detected by a control-flow sequence based approach. On the other hand, system-call based methods achieve complete coverage of system calls by default because the system call interface can be completely mediated.

A trend toward combining the power of control flows with system calls is evident from PAID [23] with its recent improvements [24]. Intuitively, the advantage of a hybrid approach is that even if an attacker can escape the control-flow verification and execute injected code, a system-call based check should be able to detect invalid system call sequence. However, we show that *hybrid sequence approaches are not fundamentally more precise than control-flow sequence based approaches even in the case of incomplete binary analysis*. One point to note is that PAID considers system call arguments, but since our framework does not consider data, the theoretical results are applicable to sequence based hybrid approaches only.

5.1   The Effect of Incomplete Analysis

In order to help us analyze the effect of models resulting from incomplete analysis, we consider the models that would have resulted if the program could have been analyzed completely. Assume the original definitions of E_v, C_v, B_v and B_e to hold for the models found in the complete case. Let B_v' be the discovered set of basic blocks and E_v' be the valid execution language due generated due to incomplete analysis. Let the essential basic blocks for the incomplete case be B_e'.

The following theorem proves that if the events from the essential basic blocks in the discovered region (B_e') are exposed by a control-flow based scheme, then the IDS detects any attack that exploits a control-transfer instruction in the undiscovered region.

Theorem 4. *Any feasible execution sequence e that uses an anomaly generating (AG) control-flow event from a basic block in $b \in B_v - B_v'$ is not in E_v'.*

Proof. Without loss of generality, we can assume that e started in the known region of code, i.e. in the blocks B_v'. Since $b \notin B_v'$, prior to any control-flow event emanating from b there must be a control-flow event that transitions outside from B_v'. Such an event is of the form $c = (b_1, b_2)$ where $b_1 \in B_v'$ and $b_2 \notin B_v'$. This event c has to be an anomaly generating event (AG) because it turns a valid sequence invalid. Therefore,

$b_1 \in B'_e$ and accordingly is exposed. A simplified control-flow model will therefore detect it as an anomaly, resulting in $e \notin E'_v$. □

Hence, as long as the essential blocks in the discovered region of code are exposed and checked, there can be no undetected attacks that try to exploit unchecked transfers in the undiscovered code.

5.2 Hybrid Models

We can represent hybrid models consisting of both system call and control-flow information in our framework in order to analyze their precision. The alphabet of our hybrid language is $\Sigma_H = \Sigma_C \cup \Sigma_S$, containing both control-flow events and system calls. We can formally describe the derivation as a homomorphism h_h, which has the effects of h_s to add system call information from any basic block, and the effects of h_{ce} to keep a subsequence of exposed control-flow events from blocks in B_h. The homomorphism $h_h : \Sigma_C^* \rightarrow \Sigma_H^*$ is defined as following:

$$h_h((b_1, b_2)) = \begin{cases} (b_1, b_2)s, & b_1 \in B_h \text{ and } b_2 \text{ calls } s \in \Sigma_S \\ (b_1, b_2), & b_1 \in B_h \text{ and no syscall in } b_2 \\ s, & b_1 \notin B_h \text{ and } b_2 \text{ calls } s \in \Sigma_S \\ \epsilon, & \text{otherwise} \end{cases}$$

Using the above homomorphism, the valid sequence model for the hybrid language H_v can be found from the comprehensive control-flow langauge C_v, by $H_v = h_h(C_v)$. Compared to the pure control-flow and the system-call based models, hybrid models constrain both the control-flow and system call sequences. Therefore, the basic block sequences considered valid by the hybrid model are not less constrained than other two. Assume that the basic block sequences considered valid by a hybrid, a control-flow sequence and a system call sequence models are E_v^H, E_v^C and E_v^S respectively. The following corollary can be very easily derived from our framework.

Corollary 5. *If a hybrid model and a pure control-flow sequence model expose the control-flow events from the same set of basic blocks, then $E_v^H \subseteq E_v^C$ and $E_v^H \subseteq E_v^S$.*

The above shows the relative precision of the three approaches in the general case. However, we will show that in the case that the essential basic blocks are exposed, hybrid models and control-flow models become equal in precision.

It can be proved in a manner similar to Theorem 3 that $C_v = h_{cs}^{-1}(H_v) \cap C_f$ when the essential blocks are exposed, i.e. $B_h = B_e$. Therefore, basic block sequences considered valid by the hybrid model then becomes precise as the valid execution language, i.e. $E_v^H = E_v$. Therefore:

Corollary 6. *If all essential basic blocks B_e are exposed, then a hybrid model is equivalent in precision to a control-flow model, i.e. $E_v^H = E_v^C = E_v \subseteq E_v^S$.*

All that is required to make control-flow based approaches as precise as hybrid models is the coverage of essential basic blocks. We have also seen in the previous section that even for incomplete binary analysis, it is sufficient to cover essential basic blocks in the discovered region of code. Moreover, it is straightforward to identify essential basic blocks in the discovered region of code. Therefore, this shows that control-flow based approaches can be as precise as hybrid models in all cases; hybrid approaches do not have any fundamental advantage over control-flow models. Further research in creating more precise hybrid models may not be fruitful because eventually these systems will become precise enough to make the system call information in the models redundant.

6   Control-Flow Based IDS Using External Monitoring

Traditionally, system call based IDSes have used an external monitor. CFI uses efficient inlined monitoring to keep the overhead of monitoring at the fine-grained control-flow level low. Although control-flow based methods have been proven to be more precise than system calls, using an external monitor would provide a fair comparison of performance between the two paradigms. We provide evidence against the intuition that an external monitor shifting to this control-flow interface will incur significant overhead. We implement and evaluate a precise control-flow based approach built on static analysis and using external monitoring.

External monitoring has several advantages including easier development and debugging. It can also be easily deployed as a centralized security service. Moreover, it is a more generalized approach that does not rely on tricks to protect memory access to the inlined model or require hardware features such as NXD.

Our external monitor reduces the number of control-flow events that require exposure without losing model precision. We used a run-time program transformation to restrict the feasible executions of a program and hence reduce essential basic blocks. We begin by presenting the implementation details and then demonstrate the validity of the implementation by testing detection of multiple synthetic attacks and real attacks against a collection of test programs. Finally, our performance tests show a surprisingly low cost for external monitoring at the control-flow level.

6.1   Construction Via Static Binary Analysis and Rewriting

Our selection of control-flow instructions to model and monitor is similar to CFI. Our model contains a list of valid target addresses for each dynamically computed control-transfer instruction, and a PDA-like stack that stores calling context used to validate the targets of function returns. Like CFI, sequence information is not explicitly required; the stack checks the subsequences of calls and returns. We first construct the static CFG of a program. Then, for each control-transfer instruction that has a dynamically computed target, we use the CFG to identify valid target addresses.

Our system constructs models for dynamically-linked Linux ELF binaries on the x86 architecture. We use *DynInst* [19], a binary analysis and instrumentation library, as our low-level static analyzer. The one-time model construction procedure rewrites the binary program to expose control-flow operations to the external monitor. We use DynInst to replace monitored control-flow instructions with single-byte software breakpoints (the INT3 instruction) that can be securely intercepted by an external monitor.

That monitor limits the program's execution by the model every time the program is subsequently loaded for execution. Using the *ptrace* system call, the monitor intercepts the software breakpoints previously inserted by DynInst. For each interception, the target of a control transfer is extracted from the program's context or memory. This method of extracting control-flow information ensures that an attacker cannot pass fake information to the monitor. We implemented the control-flow model itself as a hash table. We key the table on value pairs—a source and destination address for control-flow events. The hash table is sparse with few collisions, providing O(1) average time complexity for lookups. After verification, as DynInst had overwritten the original control-flow instructions with breakpoints, the monitor emulates the execution of the clobbered control flow before returning execution control to the monitored process. During execution, our system also intercepts dynamic library loads and updates the model with valid target addresses for indirect jumps that use the GOT.

An external monitor requires context switches into and out of the monitor at every event. We reduce the number of events that the monitor checks by restricting feasible execution of a program (Corollary 4). We use a transformation similar to function inlining. By creating duplicate copies of functions and replacing function call and return instructions with static jump instructions, we remove the necessity of exposing these control transfers to the monitor. In order to reduce code space explosion, we apply a *hot code optimization* that first identifies function calls executed at a high rate at run-time and then performs this transformation. The monitor uses DynInst to alter the code of the monitored process during execution. We ensure that the memory region where the inlined copy resides is write-protected by invoking necessary kernel services.

6.2 Attack Detection

Our approach has the same precision as inlined CFI. We evaluated the attack detection ability of our system after first ensuring the static analyzer and our implementation introduced no false positives for our test programs on normal workloads. We conducted two types of experiments: detection of real attacks against standard Linux programs and detection of various arbitrary code execution attacks against a vulnerable synthetic program.

Our first test evaluated the ability of the external monitor in detecting actual attacks against Linux programs with published vulnerabilities and exploits (Table 1). We ensured that the exploits successfully worked on the vulnerable programs. We then constructed models for each program and used our system to monitor the execution of each program. As expected, the IDS successfully detected every attack before arbitrary code was executed.

Second, we tested the ability of the control-flow based model to detect a collection of injected code and existing code attacks against a synthetic program. The program contains a vulnerability that allows an attacker to write anywhere in data. We created synthetic exploits that modify various code pointers inside the applications' memory: return addresses on the stack, global offset table (GOT) entries used for locating shared library functions, and function pointers. We tested each control-flow modification with three different classes of targets: injected code, code in the middle of a function, and

Table 1. Detection capability of external control-flow IDS on real applications

Application	Vulnerability type	Exploit code URL	Detected
imapd 10.234	Stack buffer overflow	[3]	√
thttpd 2.21	Stack buffer overflow	[4]	√
indent 2.2.9	Heap overflow	[1]	√
GnuPG 1.0.5	Format string vulnerability	[2]	√

Table 2. Detection of synthetic tests for various kinds of arbitrary code execution

Attack Step	Injected	Existing (inside function)	Existing (function start)
Change return address	√	√	√
Modify GOT	√	√	√
Modify function pointer	√	√	×

the entry point of a libc function. Table 2 contains the results of our synthetic attack detection tests.

In all but one synthetic test, our IDS successfully detected the attacks when execution was about to be diverted before the code executed. For the failed test, our IDS missed the attack due to the imprecision introduced in the statically-recovered CFG of the binary code at indirect calls. The target address was a valid function entry point and was thus classified as a normal control-flow transfer by our model. This imprecision demonstrates a shortcoming of static binary analysis that may not be present in static source code analysis or in dynamic analysis.

6.3 Performance Impact of External Control-Flow Monitoring

We evaluated the performance overhead on several real-world applications by measuring the execution-time overhead on programs representing both I/O-bound and CPU-bound applications. Table 3 summarizes the results. All timing values represent an average over 5 executions. We first measured each application's average unmonitored runtime, shown in the results as "Base time". To determine the time cost of external monitoring of control flow, we then ran the programs with our external monitor. "Monitored time" indicates monitored program execution time. We additionally show the percentage increase in execution time and the percentage increase in program code size due to function body replication during the hot code optimization.

These results show that an external monitor can efficiently detect attacks at the fine-grained control-flow level. Our hot code optimization inlining functions called at high rates effectively balanced the need for fast execution verification with the need to use extra memory responsibly. For example, the I/O-bound applications such as httpd and cat incurred a low monitoring overhead and therefore no inlining of code was performed. On the other hand, inlining was crucial for the CPU-bound and function-call-bound program gzip for which the crippling performance loss of over 4,000% was brought down to only a 23.1% degradation in speed for an 11.3% increase in space. For comparison, the Dyck model [17] produced a 3% overhead for cat for which our system incurs a 1.2% overhead. The earlier model, however, had a 0% overhead for gzip, which has a main loop that repeatedly calls functions to compress or decompress data, making only a few system calls. The Dyck model hence can be efficient for this

Table 3. Performance results for various applications. Time values are in real-time units.

Application	Base time (sec)	Monitored time (sec)	Time overhead	Inlining space overhead
thttpd	20.40	21.23	4.0%	0.0%
SQLite	55.44	66.04	19.1%	8.8%
gzip	11.03	13.59	23.1%	11.3%
cat	10.06	10.18	1.2%	0.0%

program. Our model instead adds overhead due to the initial control-flow checks and the run-time program transformation needed to optimize away the function calls.

Our control-flow model requires considerably less memory than system call based models such as VPStatic [9] or PAID [23] because it is similar to a single-state PDA. In summary, our IDS ties the power of precise control-flow checks with the convenience of external system call monitoring while keeping performance comparable to previous system-call based approaches.

7 Conclusion

We presented a formal framework for understanding and comparing the attack detection capability of anomaly detection approaches that characterize normal program execution behavior by modeling and monitoring a set of program generated events. In our principal contribution, we showed that for any system call sequence based approach, there always exists a more precise control-flow based approach. In order to derive more efficient and simplified models, we provided the theory behind selecting essential control-flow events that require exposure. In addition, we proved that control-flow models are more precise even in the case of incomplete analysis, showing that hybrid approaches that include system calls provide only redundant detection. Finally, we used the ideas of reducing essential control-flow events in the program with appropriate transformations in order to make external monitoring at the control-flow level feasible. Our static analysis based approach provides better precision while having performance overhead comparable to previous system-call based approaches.

Acknowledgments

This material is based upon work supported by the National Science Foundation under Grant No. 0133629. Any opinions, findings, and conclusions or recommendations expressed in this material are those of the authors and do not necessarily reflect the views of the National Science Foundation. We would like to thank Paul Royal for his help in this research.

References

1. GNU Indent Local Heap Overflow Vulnerability,
   http://www.securityfocus.com/bid/9297/
2. GnuPG Format String Vulnerability,
   http://www.securityfocus.com/bid/2797/
3. imapd Buffer Overflow Vulnerability,
   http://www.securityfocus.com/bid/130/
4. thttpd defang Buffer Overflow Vulnerability,
   http://www.securityfocus.com/bid/8906/
5. Abadi, M., Budiu, M., Erlingsson, U., Ligatti, J.: Control-Flow Integrity: Principles, Implementations, and Applications. In: Proceedings of ACM Computer and Communications Security (CCS), Alexandria, Virginia, November 2005, ACM Press, New York (2005)
6. Abadi, M., Budiu, M., Erlingsson, U., Ligatti, J.: A theory of secure control flow. In: Lau, K.-K., Banach, R. (eds.) ICFEM 2005. LNCS, vol. 3785, Springer, Heidelberg (2005)

7. Bhatkar, S., Chaturvedi, A., Sekar, R.: Dataflow anomaly detection. In: IEEE Symposium on Security and Privacy, Oakland, California, May 2006, IEEE Computer Society Press, Los Alamitos (2006)
8. Chen, H., Wagner, D.: MOPS: An infrastructure for examining security properties of software. In: ACM Conference on Computer and Communications Security (CCS), Washington, DC, November 2002, ACM Press, New York (2002)
9. Feng, H., Giffin, J., Huang, Y., Jha, S., Lee, W., Miller, B.: Formalizing sensitivity in static analysis for intrusion detection. In: Proceedings of the IEEE Symposium on Security and Privacy, Oakland, California, May 2004, IEEE Computer Society Press, Los Alamitos (2004)
10. Feng, H., Kolesnikov, O., Fogla, P., Lee, W., Gong, W.: Anomaly detection using call stack information. In: Proceedings of the IEEE Symposium on Security and Privacy, Oakland, California, May 2003, IEEE Computer Society Press, Los Alamitos (2003)
11. Forrest, S., Hofmeyr, S.A., Somayaji, A., Longstaff, T.A.: A sense of self for unix processes. In: Proceedings of the IEEE Symposium on Security and Privacy, Oakland, California, May 1996, IEEE Computer Society Press, Los Alamitos (1996)
12. Gao, D., Reiter, M., Song, D.: Gray-box extraction of execution graphs for anomaly detection. In: Proceedings of the 11th ACM Conference on Computer and Communications Security (CCS), Washington, DC, October 2003, ACM Press, New York (2003)
13. Gao, D., Reiter, M.K., Song, D.: On gray-box program tracking for anomaly detection. In: USENIX Security Symposium, San Diego, California (August 2004)
14. Garvey, T., Lunt, T.: Model-based intrusion detection. In: Proceedings of the 14th National Computer Security Conf. (NCSC), Baltimore, Maryland (June 1991)
15. Ghosh, A., Schwartzbard, A., Schatz, M.: Learning program behavior profiles for intrusion detection. In: Proceedings of the 1st USENIX Workshop on Intrusion Detection and Network Monitoring, Santa Clara, California (April 1999)
16. Giffin, J., Jha, S., Miller, B.: Detecting manipulated remote call streams. In: Proceedings of the 11th USENIX Security Symposium, San Francisco, California, August 2002 (2002)
17. Giffin, J., Jha, S., Miller, B.: Efficient context-sensitive intrusion detection. In: Proceedings of the 11th Annual Network and Distributed Systems Security Symposium (NDSS), San Diego, California, February 2004 (2004)
18. Giffin, J.T., Jha, S., Miller, B.P.: Automated discovery of mimicry attacks. In: Zamboni, D., Kruegel, C. (eds.) RAID 2006. LNCS, vol. 4219, Springer, Heidelberg (2006)
19. Hollingsworth, J.K., Miller, B.P., Cargille, J.: Dynamic program instrumentation for scalable performance tools. In: Proceedings of the Scalable High Performance Computing Conference, Knoxville, Tennessee (May 1994)
20. Ko, C., Fink, G., Levitt, K.: Automated detection of vulnerabilities in privileged programs by execution monitoring. In: Proceedings of the 10th Annual Computer Security Applications Conference (ACSAC), Orlando, Florida (December 1994)
21. Kruegel, C., Kirda, E., Mutz, D., Robertson, W., Vigna, G.: Automating mimicry attacks using static binary analysis. In: Proceedings of the USENIX Security Symposium, Baltimore, Maryland (August 2005)
22. Kruegel, C., Mutz, D., Valeur, F., Vigna, G.: On the detection of anomalous system call arguments. In: Snekkenes, E., Gollmann, D. (eds.) ESORICS 2003. LNCS, vol. 2808, Springer, Heidelberg (2003)
23. Lam, L., Chiueh, T.: Automatic extraction of accurate application-specific sandboxing policy. In: Recent Advances in Intrusion Detection, Sophia Antipolis, France, September 2004 (2004)
24. Lam, L., Li, W., Chiueh, T.: Accurate and automated system call policy-based intrusion prevention. In: The International Conference on Dependable Systems and Networks (DSN), Philadelphia, PA, USA (June 2006)
25. Landi, W.: Undecidability of static analysis. ACM Letters on Programming Languages and Systems (LOPLAS) 1(4), 323–337 (1992)

26. Lee, W., Stolfo, S., Mok, K.: A data mining framework for building intrusion detection models. In: Proceedings of the IEEE Symposium on Security and Privacy, Oakland, California, May 1999, IEEE Computer Society Press, Los Alamitos (1999)
27. Sekar, R., Bendre, M., Bollineni, P., Dhurjati, D.: A fast automaton-based method for detecting anomalous program behaviors. In: Proceedings of the IEEE Symposium on Security and Privacy, Oakland, California, May 2001, IEEE Computer Society Press, Los Alamitos (2001)
28. Tan, K., Killourhy, K.S., Maxion, R.A.: Undermining an anomaly-based intrusion detection system using common exploits. In: Wespi, A., Vigna, G., Deri, L. (eds.) RAID 2002. LNCS, vol. 2516, Springer, Heidelberg (2002)
29. Vigna, G., Kruegel, C.: Handbook of Information Security. ch. Host-based Intrusion Detection Systems. Wiley, Chichester (December 2005)
30. Wagner, D.: Static Analysis and Computer Security: New Techniques for Software Assurance. Ph.D. dissertation, University of California at Berkeley (2000)
31. Wagner, D., Dean, D.: Intrusion detection via static analysis. In: Proceedings of the IEEE Symposium on Security and Privacy, Oakland, California, May 2001, IEEE Computer Society Press, Los Alamitos (2001)
32. Wagner, D., Soto, P.: Mimicry attacks on host based intrusion detection systems. In: Proceedings of the Ninth ACM Conference on Computer and Communications Security (CCS), Washington, DC, November 2002, ACM Press, New York (2002)
33. Xu, H., Du, W., Chapin, S.J.: Context sensitive anomaly monitoring of process control flow to detect mimicry attacks and impossible paths. In: Jonsson, E., Valdes, A., Almgren, M. (eds.) RAID 2004. LNCS, vol. 3224, Springer, Heidelberg (2004)
34. Zhang, T., Zhuang, X., Lee, W., Pande, S.: Anomalous path detection with hardware support. In: Proceedings of the International Conference on Compilers, Architectures and Synthesis of Embedded Systems (CASES), San Francisco, CA (July 2005)

Comparing Anomaly Detection Techniques for HTTP

Kenneth L. Ingham[1] and Hajime Inoue[2]

[1] University of New Mexico, Computer Science Department, Albuquerque, NM,
87131, USA
ingham@cs.unm.edu
[2] Carleton University School of Computer Science Ottawa, ON, K1S 5B6, Canada
hinoue@ccsl.carleton.ca

Abstract. Much data access occurs via HTTP, which is becoming a universal transport protocol. Because of this, it has become a common exploit target and several HTTP specific IDSs have been proposed as a response. However, each IDS is developed and tested independently, and direct comparisons are difficult. We describe a framework for testing IDS algorithms, and apply it to several proposed anomaly detection algorithms, testing using identical data and test environment. The results show serious limitations in all approaches, and we make predictions about requirements for successful anomaly detection approaches used to protect web servers.

Keywords: Anomaly detection, Intrusion detection, Comparison, HTTP, Hypertext transport protocol.

1 Introduction

The Hypertext Transfer Protocol (HTTP) [14] has become a universal transport protocol. For example, it is used for file sharing [19], payment processing [12], remote procedure calls [29], streaming media [1], and even protocols such as SSH [40]. Custom web applications and the rush toward Web Services [3] mean that in the future, we can expect heavier use of HTTP. Robertson et al. [32] claimed that many web applications are written by people with little expertise in security and that web-based vulnerabilities represent 25% of the total security flaws reported in the Common Vulnerabilities and Exposures list (CVE) [5] 1999 through 2005.

The importance of HTTP and the security problems have led many researchers to propose intrusion detection systems (IDSs) for use with HTTP. Unfortunately, the proposed IDSs suffer from one or more of the following problems:

- The proposed IDS is not fully described and the source code is not available.
- The test data is not available, preventing a direct comparison.
- The test data is not labeled, preventing replication.
- The test data is not representative of traffic seen today.

C. Kruegel, R. Lippmann, and A. Clark (Eds.): RAID 2007, LNCS 4637, pp. 42–62, 2007.

To address this problem, we describe a framework for comparing IDS algorithms, and we use this framework to compare several anomaly IDS algorithms under identical circumstances. This framework[1] and the attack data[2] are open source to encourage further experimentation. Under more rigorous testing, not all algorithms perform as well as the initial tests showed, and we discuss why some algorithms do better than others.

Three basic architectures of IDSs exist: signature detection, specification, and anomaly detection. We focus in this paper on anomaly detection. Signature detection systems cannot detect novel attacks, while specification systems require skills well beyond those commonly used when developing web applications. Additionally, whenever the protected program changes, the specification must be updated. Although we test only anomaly IDSs, the framework can be applied to signature and specification based algorithms as well.

The organization of the paper is as follows. The following section, Section 2, sets the stage by describing previous IDS testing, with a focus on systems designed for HTTP. We then briefly describe the test framework and test data in Section 3. The specific algorithms we tested are described in Section 3.3, followed by the test results in Section 4. Our discussion of the results follows in Section 5, while Section 6 concludes the paper with a summary of our results and a discussion of future work.

2   Prior Work

There are at least two reasons to testing IDSs: (1) to verify that an algorithm is effective and efficient at detecting attacks, and (2) to compare two or more algorithms to determine the better under various metrics.

Most IDS testing is little more than asking, "Does the IDS detect one or a few attacks?" Better are researchers who ask the question, "Which of the following attacks can the IDS detect?" Even this testing is often acknowledged as weak.

Good testing is repeatable; the data are available to other researchers facilitating direct comparisons of the results, the training data are representative of real systems, and the attack data accurately represent the diversity of attacks. A good test also compares two or more valid approaches (i.e., no straw man arguments). The results of a good test should provide guidance about which system or algorithm performs best under different circumstances. To this point, most IDSs for web servers have been weakly tested, and/or the tests are limited in their scope. In their review of IDS testing, Athanasiades et al. state that they do not believe this problem will ever be properly solved [2].

There are several explanations for the scarcity of good IDS testing. Identifying appropriate data is difficult—the data must be representative of realistic operating conditions. Data collected live from a network might be subject to

---

[1] The parser, framework and algorithm implementation code is available from the Comprehensive Perl Archive Network (CPAN) at
http://cpan.org/modules/by-authors/id/I/IN/INGHAM/
[2] The attack data is available at http://www.i-pi.com/HTTP-attacks-JoCN-2006/

privacy concerns. Synthetic data must be shown to represent real data on a target network accurately. In order to test an IDS, researchers need a collection of intrusions and vulnerable machines on which to test the intrusions. Because a library of intrusions represents a threat to vulnerable systems, researchers often use disconnected networks for testing to ensure that the attack does not escape into unprotected networks.

Setting up and maintaining a good, protected network is resource-intensive, both in the costs of the hardware, as well as in system administration support to set up and maintain a diversity of machines needed to ensure a good test environment. Exploits are specific to operating system and version, as well to to specific compilers, libraries, and other software. An intrusion is likely to fail if any part of the execution environment is different than expected. Because of this, a machine, or virtual machine, may be required for each new intrusion added to the attack corpus.

Finally, Debar noted that a set of criteria for evaluating an IDS does not exist [11]. Even if such criteria were available, the most careful comparisons, such as Warrender et al. [39], lack enough information to be repeatable.

2.1 Frameworks for Testing

A framework for testing is one way of reproducibility by providing a setup in which different IDSs can be tested under identical conditions. Three researchers or research groups have established such frameworks:

- The first published papers about an IDS testing framework and methodology were from Puketza et al. [30,31] at UC Davis. Unless they failed to publish further work, they built the framework and then tested only one IDS: NSM [17,18].
- Wan and Yang [37] developed a framework for testing sensors that used the Internet Engineering Task Force (IETF) Intrusion Detection Working Group (IDWG) Intrusion Detection Message Exchange Format (IDMEF) [6]. Their framework might be useful, but the paper describes only a preliminary version.
- IBM Zurich [11] set up a laboratory for testing IDSs. Their normal data came not only from recordings of user sessions, but also from the IBM test suites for the AIX operating system. While this test suite is not representative of actual user interactions, it exercises normal functionality of the product.

2.2 Data Sets for Testing HTTP IDSs

Using a good data set is critical for the test. The training and test data must be representative of the web server(s) to be protected, and the attacks used for testing need to illustrate the diversity of attacks existing today. Given the diversity between web sites, the ideal situation is to use data collected from the server to be protected. These data often have privacy issues associated with them, preventing other researchers from using it and thereby hindering repeatability. This tension has resulted in some researchers using open, less-representative data, while others use closed but more accurate data sets.

The DARPA/MIT Lincoln Laboratories IDS tests of 1998 and 1999 produced the most prominent data sets [15,24]. Many researchers in IDS research used these data because large data sets are scarce and the dataset provides an immediate comparison with the original Lincoln Labs test. Open datasets allow comparison of methods, but careful analysis of the relevant papers is required to combine and compare the results. Furthermore, differences in testing methodologies make direct comparison difficult.

However, this data set is not without its critics. McHugh [27,28] pointed out that the DARPA/MIT Lincoln Laboratories IDS test used generated data, but the MIT researchers never did any tests to show that the generated data was representative of real data. Additionally, they did no tests to verify that their attacks were representative of real attacks. The Lincoln Labs data set is also quite dated, as web behavior has evolved significantly over the years.

When testing IDSs for HTTP, researchers using the Lincoln Labs data sets have only four web attacks. When systems developed using these data are tested on a broader data set, their performance suffers; confirmation of this assertion appears in this paper. In spite of these limitations, Wang and Stolfo [38], Mahoney [25], and Mahoney and Chan [26] Vargiya and Chan [36] used one or both of these data sets for testing their IDSs, at least a portion of which were for protecting web servers. Estévez-Tapiador et al. [13] used these data as normal behavior, but they developed their own attack database to supplement the attacks in the Lincoln Labs data.

Recognizing the shortcomings of the Lincoln Labs data, other researchers have used test data that is more representative for the servers the IDS is protecting. However, these data are unavailable for others to use, eliminating direct comparisons. For example, Kruegel et al. [22,23] tested their system using extensive normal data sets from multiple sites (including Google).[3] For a portion of their 12 attacks, they used attacks against software that ran on one of their data source web servers. Wang and Stolfo [38] used data collected from their departmental web server as an additional source of data, but they did not filter attacks from the data and therefore used it only for testing the training. Tombini et al. [35] collected data from two production web servers, one academic, and one industrial, with a combined total of over five million HTTP requests from web server log files. Estévez-Tapiador et al. [13] used 1500 attack requests representing variants of 85 distinct attacks, the largest attack database reported to date.

Another important HTTP data issue is how much of the HTTP request the IDS used. While most attacks to date have been in the requested resource path, some attacks target other regions of the request. For example, Apache Sioux [8] exhausts Apache's memory by a repeated header line. Wang and Stolfo [38], in different experiments, modeled the packet payload, the first and last 100 bytes,

---

[3] The Google data was not even available to the researchers; they sent their programs to Google, who returned the results.

and also the first 1000 bytes of the connection. Kruegel and Vigna and Kruegel et al. [22,23] obtained their test data from web server log files, and only looked at CGI programs. Web server log files are a popular data source; Tombini et al. [35] and Robertson et al. [32] also used them. Unfortunately, log files contain only a small portion of most HTTP requests, and attacks not in the resource path are unlikely to appear in the log files.

3   Experimental Setup

To perform rigorous tests of HTTP IDS algorithms, the test circumstances and data must be identical. Testing requires data representative of what production web servers receive. Quality test data is difficult to obtain; organizations with the most interesting data typically consider it confidential. Therefore, we collected data for testing from four web sites. The attack data needs to be representative of the broad range of attacks existing today. Since, as we noted in Section 2.2, no public database of attacks exists, we compiled our own. Due to space limitations, full details of the experimental setup are described by Ingham [20].

3.1   Data

The normal data set is a collection of HTTP requests received by to the University of New Mexico Computer Science departmental web server (cs.unm.edu), as well as aya.org, explorenm.com, and i-pi.com. The training data was from one week, and the normal test data is from the following week. All attacks were filtered from the data using a combination of *snort* and manual inspection. All the data sets contain the *entire* HTTP request.[4] These include information not usually found in the log files. Having the HTTP header lines allows testing for attacks not contained in the requested resource path.

The attack database contains 63 attacks, some of which are variants of the same vulnerability—either a different exploit for the same vulnerability or the same exploit against a different operating system. We include the variants because some IDS algorithms will find some variants easier to detect than others. As one example, some of the Nimda variants are short, allowing detection by the length algorithm, while others are average length.

The attacks were collected from the following sources: Attacks against web servers under test (attacks in the wild); BugTraq and the SecurityFocus archives http://www.SecurityFocus.com/; the Open Source Vulnerability Database http://www.osvdb.org/; the Packetstorm archives http://Packetstorm.widexs.nl/; and Sourcebank http://archive.devx.com/sourcebank/. In many cases, the attack programs from these sources contained bugs, and we had to modify the program before it would produce malicious web requests. Note that we did not test to verify whether the attacks produced could actually compromise the targeted web application.

---

[4] These data were captured using a *snort* filter which reconstructs the application layer portion.

The attack database contains the following categories of attacks: buffer over-flow; input validation error (other than buffer overflow); signed interpretation of unsigned value; and URL decoding error. The attacks targeted different web servers: Active Perl ISAPI; AltaVista Search Engine; AnalogX SimpleServer; Apache with and without mod_php; CERN 3.0A; FrontPage Personal Web Server; Hughes Technologies Mini SQL; InetServ 3.0; Microsoft IIS; NCSA; Netscape FastTrack 2.01a; Nortel Contivity Extranet Switches; OmniHTTPd; and PlusMail. The target operating systems for the attacks include the follow-ing: AIX; Linux (many varieties); Mac OS X; Microsoft Windows; OpenBSD; SCO UnixWare; Solaris x86; Unix; VxWorks; and any x86 BSD variant.

3.2 The Algorithm Test Framework

A framework allows testing a collection of algorithms in the same environment, ensuring that each algorithm is working under identical conditions. By provid-ing a common interface, testing any IDS algorithm that uses this interface is straightforward, and the surrounding support code is reused. The framework for running the tests was designed to work with anomaly detection algorithms, but it is general enough to work with signature and specification systems—these sys-tems simply need no training before testing. As an example, it was easy to write an IDS algorithm object to use *snort* signatures for HTTP requests. Detailed descriptions of the test framework are available in [20].

Some algorithms require that the data be tokenized. For these algorithms, we implemented a parser that breaks the HTTP request into tokens based on the those specified in the HTTP standard, RFC 2616 [14]. The tokens are a combination of the token type (e.g., method) and optionally the value (e.g., GET). In practice, most of the values are necessary to properly distinguish attacks from normal requests. The result is a stream of tokens combined with the associated values.

Instead of using tokens, some algorithms use a string representation for the request. This (much simpler) representation is also available from the parser.

3.3 Algorithms

We consider algorithms from Kruegel and Vigna [22], who developed a linear combination of six measures (length, a character distribution measure, a Markov Model, presence/absence of parameters, order of parameters, and whether para-meter values were enumerated or random), and applied them to CGI parameters. For some of the six algorithms, we also consider them in isolation. We also im-plemented the character distribution metric described by Wang and Stolfo [38], and the DFA induction and n-grams described by Ingham et al. and Ingham [21,20].

These algorithms are either proposed by often cited papers in the IDS com-munity, similar to those algorithms but using different data or representations, or successful in related domains. In short, we tested algorithms claimed to be or likely to be successful in HTTP-based anomaly intrusion detection.

Request Length. Observing that buffer overflows and cross-site scripting attacks tend to be longer than normal CGI attribute values, one measure used by Kruegel and Vigna [22] was the mean μ and variance σ^2 of attribute lengths. These values were calculated from training data.

For testing, the system calculated the probability p that an attribute would have the observed length l by:

$$p = \frac{\sigma^2}{(l - \mu)^2}$$

Character Distributions. Buffer-overflow attacks often have a distinctive character distribution. Two research groups have compared the character distribution of test instances to the distribution in the training data. Wang and Stolfo [38] used a character distribution metric on similarly-sized packets. Kruegel and Vigna [22] used a character distribution as one of six tests.

Mahalanobis distance. Wang and Stolfo [38] measured the Mahalanobis distance, d, between two distributions. For efficiency reasons they used a measure they called the *simplified Mahalanobis distance*:

$$d(x, \overline{y}) = \sum_{i=0}^{n-1} \frac{|x_i - \overline{y}_i|}{\overline{\sigma}_i + \alpha} < \infty$$

n is 256 for the ASCII character set. The α term is a smoothing factor so that the distance does not become infinite when $\overline{\sigma}_i$ is 0. Wang and Stolfo did not specify how they calculate α; for the results reported in this paper, $\alpha = 0.001$. Wang and Stolfo set the distance threshold to 256 (one standard deviation). Using this value means that rare distributions are anomalous; consequently it reports false positives even when tested on the training data set.

Our implementation differs with Wang and Stolfo's slightly. They correlated packet length with character frequencies. Our data consists only of the data at the application layer; the raw packets containing the data were not stored. Therefore, we apply this method to the complete request. Note that while the different packet sizes may have a given character distribution, an attacker can easily control the packet size, allowing them to use packets of a size with a better match for the character distribution.

χ^2 *of idealized character distribution.* As one of six tests, Kruegel and Vigna [22] use a measure of relative character frequency. They produced a sorted list of character frequencies f_c containing the relative frequency of the character c. Their example is the string `passwd`, where the absolute frequency distribution is 2 for `s`, 1 for `a`, `d`, `p`, and `w`, and 0 for all other characters. The relative frequencies are then $f = (\frac{1}{3}, \frac{1}{6}, \frac{1}{6}, \frac{1}{6}, \frac{1}{6}, 0, ..., 0)$; note that f_6 through f_{256} are 0. Kruegel and Vigna noted that relative frequencies decrease slowly for non-attack requests, but have a much steeper decline for buffer overflows, and no decline for random data.

They called the character distribution induced from the training data the *idealized character distribution* ($\mathcal{ICD}$) and noted that $\sum_{i=1}^{256} \mathcal{ICD}(i) = 1.0$. As mentioned in the prior paragraph, the $\mathcal{ICD}$ is sorted so most common frequency is $\mathcal{ICD}(1)$ and the least common is $\mathcal{ICD}(256)$. $\mathcal{ICD}$ is calculated during training as the average over the character distributions of the requests in the training data.

For testing, they binned the $\mathcal{ICD}$ (the expected distribution, calculated through training) and the distribution of the test request (observed distribution) into six bins as follows:

Bin	1	2	3	4	5	6
i	1	2–4	5–7	8–12	13–16	17-256

where $i \in [1, 256]$. For example, bin 4 contains $\sum_{i=8}^{12} ICD(i)$. Once binned, they then use a χ^2 test to determine if the character distribution of CGI parameter values is similar to that of the training data:

$$\chi^2 = \sum_{i=1}^{6} \frac{(O_i - E_i)^2}{E_i}$$

where E_i is bin i for the $\mathcal{ICD}$, and O_i is bin i for the observed distribution. χ^2 is compared to values from a table and the corresponding probability is the return value.

CGI Parameter Measures. Kruegel and Vigna [22] used three different observations about CGI parameters. First, they noted that since CGI parameters are set programmatically, the normal order of the parameters is fixed. If a human generates the path, the order could be different, and they presumed this change indicated a potential attack. For similar reasons, they also noted CGI parameters are supplied even when they have no value. The result is a regularity in the number, name, and order of the parameters. Their system learned the parameters present for a given CGI program path. When testing an instance, the return value is 1 if the same parameters appeared in the training data as in the test instance, and 0 otherwise.

Similar to the presence and absence test, Kruegel and Vigna noted that some CGI parameter values are selected from a finite set (enumerated), and others are effectively random. In the training phase, they test to see whether the number of parameter values stays small compared to the number of examples. If it does, then the parameter values are enumerated and the algorithm performs no generalization. Otherwise, it accepts any value during testing.

DFA. We use a one-pass, $O(nm)$ DFA induction algorithm where n is the number of samples in the training data set and m is the average number of tokens per sample. The algorithm does not require negative examples. This algorithm is described in detail by Ingham et al. [21].

A DFA by itself is simply a language acceptor; however, we expect some variation in normal behavior not incorporated in the DFA induction algorithm.

When testing, the algorithm notes when it is unable to make a transition on a token. If a state exists which is a destination of that token, the DFA is adjusted to that state. If not, the algorithm uses the next token and tries again. The number of missed tokens is used to calculate the similarity s between the DFA model and an HTTP request:

$$s = \frac{\text{\# of tokens reached by valid transitions}}{\text{\# of tokens in the HTTP request}} \in [0,1]$$

The similarity measure reflects the proportion of the request requiring changes for the DFA to accept the request. Using proportionality instead of a raw miss count allows complex requests to have greater variability than simpler ones.

Markov Model. A Markov model is a nondeterministic finite automaton (NFA) with probabilities associated with the transitions. A Markov model differs from a DFA in that multiple transitions might exist for a given token, and a probability is associated with each transition. The probability of a given string of tokens can be calculated as the sum of the probabilities of each independent path through the NFA that can generate the string of tokens. The probability of a given path is the product of the probabilities of each of the transitions, and this probability is interpreted as the similarity measure for the testing. Similar to a DFA, a Markov Model represents the structure of the HTTP request through a directed graph.

For an anomaly detection system, the traditional approach is to build an NFA that exactly matches the training data. Through a series of state merging operations, it is compressed and hence it becomes more general (and, as a side effect, it becomes a DFA with probabilities). For more details about Markov model induction, see the work by Stolcke [34] and Stolcke and Omohundro [33]. Warrender et al. noted that building a generalized Markov model is $\mathcal{O}(n^2)$ [39].

Markov models have been shown to be an effective but time-consuming algorithm for system-call based intrusion detection [39]. Kruegel and Vigna [22] used a Markov model as a portion of the IDS for protecting web servers, but after noting that the probability of any given request string is small, they used their Markov model as a DFA, noting only whether or not the model was capable of generating the string in question.

Our Markov model implementation is a modification of the DFA algorithm described in Section 3.3. When learning the DFA, the number of times that a transition is taken is recorded, and the probability of taking a given transition is the fraction of the sum of all of the transitions that the taken transition represents. This approach is not exactly the same as a more traditional Markov model, but the result is similar in size and effect to a Markov model after generalization.

Linear Combination. Combining IDSs is a logical step once more than one IDS is available. The system developed by Kruegel and Vigna [22] was limited to HTTP CGI requests, and consisted of a linear combination of the **length**, **character distribution**, **order**, and **presence or absence** of CGI parameter values. Additionally, it also included a test for which CGI parameter values were **enumerated or random**, and a **Markov model** to learn the structure of those values.

The threshold for normal for each algorithm was determined dynamically, chosen to be 10% above the highest value obtained in training. Calculating the threshold requires a second pass over the training data, testing it to find the maximum value for each measure. For testing, each algorithm was equally weighted and the system produced a binary normal/abnormal signal.

n-grams. An n-gram [9] is a substring generated by sliding a window of length n across a string of tokens. The result is a set of strings of length n. For example, given the string abcdef and $n = 3$, the resulting 3-grams are: abc, bcd, cde, and def. The similarity measure considers the presence or absence of the test n-grams in the set of n-grams learned from the training data:

$$s = \frac{\text{\# of } n\text{-grams from the request also in the training data}}{\text{\# of } n\text{-grams in the HTTP request}} \in [0, 1]$$

The n-gram algorithm can use either tokens or strings from the data source. Early testing showed poor results for strings, so we report results using tokens as the alphabet.

Targeted Generalization Heuristics. To improve the accuracy of the n-gram and DFA induction algorithms, we also applied several heuristics that increase the generalization. These check that certain data types have a valid (parsable) format. If so, they return a small, enumerated set of values dependent on the heuristic. The data types that are checked for valid form are host names, IP addresses, dates, various hash values (PHP session IDs, HTTP entity tags, etc), floating point numbers (HTTP q-values), and email addresses. Ingham and Ingham et al. provide a detailed description of these heuristics in [20,21].

4   Results

The traditional method for reporting IDS results is a receiver operating characteristic (ROC) curve that shows the tradeoff between identifying real attacks (true positives) and incorrectly flagging non-attack requests as an attack (false positives) [16]. True or false positives are represented in the ROC curves presented here as the fraction of the attack database or test data set properly or improperly identified. Each set of connected points represents a different data set used with the algorithm, and each point represents a different similarity threshold for distinguishing normal from abnormal. A perfect algorithm would have a point at $(0, 1)$ (the upper-left corner of the graph) indicating no false positives and 100% correct identification of attacks. In order to better see the most accurate range, the plots only show the X axis values in $[0, 0.1]$. The portion of the plot in the rest of the X axis represents a range where the false positives would be too high for production use; we visit this claim in Section 4.7. The axes in these plots indicate the actual fraction of true and false positives in the test.

To ease comparisons between algorithms, most of the ROC plots have the same scale; one required a different scale to present the data, and this fact is noted in the plot description.

McHugh noted several potential problems in presenting IDS test results with ROC curves [28]. His first objection is that some researchers presented curves with only one measured point and assumed continuity from (0,0), through their point, to (1,1). We present plots with 128 uniformly divided points in [0,1]. No assumption is made about (0,0) or (1,1). McHugh also pointed out that for the ROC curves to be comparable, the unit of analysis must be the same. For every test in this paper, this unit of analysis is always one HTTP request. The tests we performed used the data and framework described in Section 3.

4.1   Length

Accuracy is below 80% true positive at tolerable false positive rates (see Figure 1). This measure can detect some buffer overflows and cross-site scripting attacks, however, attacks such as the Apache chunked transfer error [4] and some variants of Nimda [10] are short enough to pass as normal; if they are too short, padding to increase the length is easy. Therefore, a minimum length will never stop an attack other than by a simplistic attacker. Because this algorithm accepts many strings that are not legal HTTP, an attacker has great freedom in the construction of her attack.

If this algorithm were to be applied to tokens, it would overgeneralize. Consider how many sentences with n words are valid English-language sentences. Therefore, this algorithm is unlikely to ever be useful in isolation. It might be applied as one of several algorithms, assuming non-attack requests have a tight enough upper bound on their length.

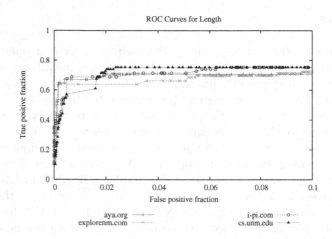

Fig. 1. Receiver Operating Characteristic curves showing the accuracy of the length algorithm

4.2   Character Distributions

Our Mahalanobis distance results (see Figure 2) differ from Wang and Stolfo's [38]. Note that the cs.unm.edu accuracy is lower than other sites, indicating that the measure's accuracy depends on the mix of HTTP requests. Wang and Stolfo reported true positive rates about 90% with a 20% false positive rate on the Lincoln Labs data. Trained and tested using their own departmental server, the false positive rate improved, ranging from 0.0084% to 1.3%. They found their system did not always detect variants of exploits used during training. A possible explanation is their dependence on packet size in their calculations. As we noted in Section 3.3, an attacker can easily manipulate packet size, so we question the usefulness of this correlation.

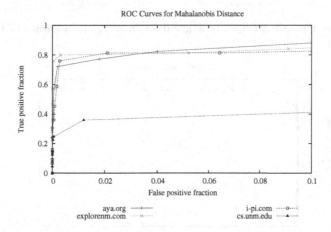

Fig. 2. Receiver Operating Characteristic curves showing the accuracy of the Mahalanobis distance algorithm

Figure 3 contains the χ^2 distance results. This algorithm performs poorly on all data sets, with a true positive rate at or below 40%.

The Mahalanobis distance and χ^2 distance algorithms generalize by allowing similar, instead of identical, character distributions. Unfortunately, this approach fails. The HTTP protocol is flexible enough that an attack can be padded to give a character distribution considered close enough to normal, especially with the myriad ways of encoding data allowed by the standards. To make the problem worse for these metrics, some attacks such as the Apache chunked transfer error [4] and some variants of Nimda [10] use a character distribution that might pass as normal without padding, and had the attacker needed to, she could have easily made minor changes to the attack (such as putting the proper host name or IP address in the `Host:` field) as needed to ensure a valid character distribution. The problem is that the set considered normal is so large that it includes many of the attacks in the attack database, regardless of if the attack is legal HTTP or not.

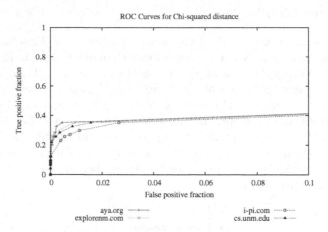

Fig. 3. Receiver Operating Characteristic curves showing the accuracy of the χ^2 distance algorithm

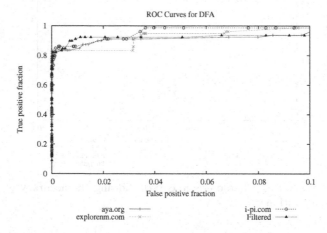

Fig. 4. Receiver Operating Characteristic curves showing the accuracy of the DFA algorithm

Wang and Stolfo [38] tested the Mahalanobis distance using the MIT Lincoln Labs data (Section 2.2). This data set contains only four HTTP attacks. In the years since the MIT data were collected, attack characteristics have changed; our more comprehensive attack data set illustrates the effect of this difference on this algorithm (Figure 2).

4.3   DFA

Figure 4 shows the DFA accuracy. The DFA can achieve better than 80% true positive rate at a false positive rate of less than 0.1%, which is better than all but the 6-grams. At slightly higher false positive rates, it achieves true positive rates of over 90%.

The DFA induced using tokens is a directed graph representing the structure of the HTTP request. Generalization occurs in the DFA generation described in [21]. It also occurs when one or more "missed tokens" are allowed. These generalizations are limited compared to that performed by the length and character distribution algorithms. The better true positive rate relative to all of the other algorithms shows that the model is even more accurate than that of the n-grams.

4.4   Markov Model

The Markov model result values are in $[0, 10^{-13}]$ with many values as small as 10^{-300}. These small values make it appear that the algorithm identifies everything (both normal traffic and attacks) as abnormal. To better understand these results, Figure 5 shows the data plot where the similarity value from the Markov model m has been transformed into a new similarity value s by $s = \frac{1}{|\log_e(m)|}$, and the plot scale has been changed so the data appears (making these plots not directly comparable to the rest of the ROC plots in this paper). This transformation means that the data cannot go through the point $(0,0)$, and all of the data appears on the plot. The log transformed Markov model provides 94% accuracy on cs.unm.edu data, but with an unacceptable false positive rate. The results on the other web sites show an even better true positive rate, but the false positive rate remains unacceptably high.

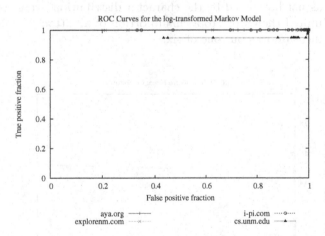

Fig. 5. Receiver Operating Characteristic curves showing the accuracy of the Markov model algorithm. Note that the scale on this plot does not match the scale of the other plots.

In a Markov model, normal requests might have a probability of 0 due to minor differences from the instances in the training data. If the model was induced from filtered data, attacks would also result in a probability of 0, and the model has a hard time distinguishing between these two cases. The Markov model's generalization is traditionally achieved by allowing probabilities within a given range. The diversity of normal requests means any given normal request is unlikely, and perpetual novelty of HTTP data leads to normal requests with a probability of 0. The combination of these two factors means that the Markov model is a poor model for HTTP requests. Our results applying a Markov model to the tokens of the complete HTTP request using tokens mirror those of Kruegel and Vigna applying it to CGI parameters [22]. They reported that the Markov model suffered because HTTP requests are so diverse that the probability of any given request is low. When working with complete requests, the problem is even worse, because the increased number of tokens increases the normal level of diversity, resulting in lower probabilities for any given HTTP request.

4.5   Linear Combination

The linear combination results are in Figure 6. The accuracy is best on the cs.unm.edu data, but the true positive rate is only around 60%. On the other web sites, it is less accurate. Kruegel and Vigna reported a true positive rate of 100% and false positive rates less than 0.000650. The disparity is explained by the attacks attempted—in contrast to their attack database which was constructed solely of attacks in CGI parameters, these attacks account for only 40% of the attacks in our database.

Most of the discrimination the linear combination came from the **order, presence or absence**, and **enumerated or random** tests which did not generalize. We found it was not hampered by the character distribution overgeneralization because they limited their work to a small portion of all attacks (CGI parameters) and this measure was but one of six.

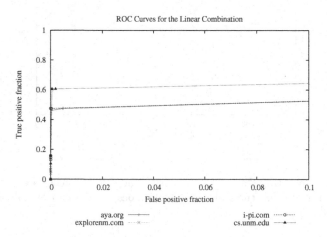

Fig. 6. Receiver Operating Characteristic curves showing the accuracy of the linear combination algorithm

The method of combining IDSs itself determines the generalization of the combined algorithm. If all models must agree that a request is normal, the least general usually determines a request is abnormal. Combining overgeneralizing detectors such as length and character distribution will usually indicate a normal request (including for many attacks), and therefore contribute little to the discrimination power of the combination; combining overgeneralizing detectors results in a system that overgeneralizes.

4.6 *n*-Grams

Results for 6-grams[5] are in Figure 7. The accuracy starts at around 85% true positive rate with a low false positive rate, making this algorithm comparable to the DFA for accuracy.

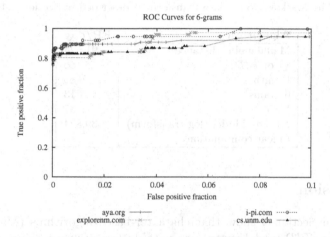

Fig. 7. Receiver Operating Characteristic curves showing the accuracy of the 6-gram algorithm

n-grams effectively model the structure, or grammar, of a request by encoding sequences of tokens as a directed graph in a manner similar to the DFA and Markov Model. *n*-grams minimize false positives by allowing a small number of mismatches, and it is better able to tell normal requests from nonsense.

4.7 False Positives

A human system administrator would have to inspect false positives to determine if they represent normal traffic or attacks. When comparing the algorithms, a useful metric is the load that the algorithm would place on this person. Table 1 shows the false positive rate per day, assuming a true positive rate of only 80% is required. This table presents data using the cs.unm.edu data sets and shows that only the 6-grams and the DFA have a false positive rate that might be acceptable for a web site like the UNM CS department.

Most previous research has reported false positives as the fraction of the non-attack test data misidentified, which is the value shown in the ROC plots presented in the earlier sections. This result can be misleading for web sites if a

---

[5] Preliminary tests showed $n = 6$ to be optimal.

human must evaluate the abnormal requests to determine if if they represent attacks. A 1% false positive rate on a lightly-visited web site may be tolerable; the same percentage on Amazon.com or Google.com would require a large full-time staff. A false positive rate of 0.01 corresponds to 917, 50, 8, and 43 false positives per day for cs.unm.edu, aya.org, i-pi.com, and explorenm.com respectively. In the 1999 DARPA/MIT Lincoln Laboratories IDS tests, they stated that above 10 false positives per day is a high rate [15].

Table 1. False positive rate per day for the algorithms, trained and tested using the cs.unm.edu data. Algorithms marked with ∞ did not achieve a threshold 80% true positive rate. The Markov Model data transform is described in Section 4.4.

Algorithm	FP/day
Mahalanobis distance	91,524
χ^2 of $\mathcal{ICD}$	∞
Length	∞
6-grams	13
DFA	37
Markov Model (log transform)	39,824
Linear combination	∞

5   Discussion

The results in Section 4 show that character-based algorithms (Mahalanobis distance, χ^2 of $\mathcal{ICD}$, and Length) are notably less accurate than two of the token-based algorithms (DFA, n-grams). Tokens represent a higher lexical unit, and are used by the system to represent meaning; attacks often represent nonsensical requests. With the need to "ship the product yesterday" and other deadlines, programmers often focus on making the system work under common circumstances and spend fewer resources on exceptional cases. Additionally, to consider all of the ways in which exceptional states may be represented requires thinking in ways many programmers were not trained. In our attack database, most, if not all, of the attacks are nonsensical. The ability to represent more of the meaning of a HTTP request improves the ability of an algorithm to discriminate between normal and abnormal. Presumably the normal requests do not represent nonsense. Applying these concepts to the algorithms we tested, the DFA and n-grams learn the higher-level structure of valid HTTP requests, and so therefore they can use this structure to better tell if a request is normal or not.

Both token based algorithms share a weakness in their similarity measures in that they cannot discern between a novel request with a few new tokens and an attack with a small number of tokens. This was responsible for some of the missed attacks. Another attack missed by the DFA can be traced to a user typo.

The pair of tokens // appeared in the training data, causing an edge from the node corresponding to the path separator / back to itself. Unfortunately, the beck attack [7] used a multitude of /s to cause an out-of-memory condition in an older version of Apache.

The idea of representing the meaning of the request allows us to make a prediction: Statistics such as character distribution applied to tokens rather than characters may be more accurate than when the same statistic is applied to the characters making up the request. However, the relationships between tokens is important to the semantics. Statistics on tokens are likely to be less accurate unless the measure can represent these relationships. In effect, by ignoring the relationships between tokens, measures such as the character distribution algorithms applied to tokens will continue to overgeneralize, and therefore be more prone to mimicry attacks. Consider as an example all English-language sentences with a specific distribution of words versus the sentences that are well-formed and not nonsense.

6   Conclusion

This paper evaluated and compared seven different different anomaly intrusion detection algorithms for HTTP under realistic conditions. This testing is more rigorous than any HTTP IDS testing reported to date. For this comparison we implemented an open-source IDS testing framework. In addition, we developed the most comprehensive open database of HTTP attacks designed for IDS testing.

Most previous IDS approaches for HTTP have represented the request as a character string. The work we report is one of the first to use tokens from parsing the request, and the first to use these tokens with DFA induction and n-grams. These algorithms detect more attacks than earlier approaches. One reason for this improved accuracy is that we use the complete HTTP request instead of just a portion—most previous IDSs ignore portions of the request and obviously cannot detect attacks in the ignored portions.

Our test results are explained by two factors. The first is the data representation of the HTTP request. We have shown that the token-based methods result in algorithms with a better ability to discriminate between sense and nonsense, and as a result, between legitimate requests and attacks. The second factor is generalization. We included several heuristics for generalization the algorithms using tokens. A detailed discussion of the effects of generalization is out of scope for this paper but is provided by Ingham in [20].

This research has shown that all the algorithms have an unacceptable false positive rate. We need additional algorithms and heuristics to improve performance. Furthermore, our work implies that new approaches should be token based, because they better represent HTTP requests than current algorithms. We hope that the IDS testing framework described in this paper encourages further research.

Acknowledgments

We thank the anonymous reviewers for their comments and suggestions. The first author was partially supported by National Science Foundation grant ANIR-9986555. The second author is supported by the Canadian Government through MITACS.

References

1. Apple Computer: Tunneling RTSP and RTP over HTTP (2006) (accessed September 13, 2006), http://developer.apple.com/ documentation/QuickTime/ QTSS/Concepts/chapter_2_section_14.html
2. Athanasiades, N., Abler, R., Levine, J., Owen, H., Riley, G.: Intrusion detection testing and benchmarking methodologies. In: IEEE-IWIA '03: Proceedings of the First IEEE International Workshop on Information Assurance (IWIA'03), Washington, DC, USA, page 63, IEEE Computer Society, Los Alamitos (2003)
3. Booth, D., Haas, H., McCabe, F., Newcomer, E., Champion, M., Ferris, C., Orchard, D.: Web services architecture. Technical Report W3C Working Group Note 11 February 2004, World Wide Web Consortium (W3C) (2004) (accessed 2007-04-05), online at http://www.w3.org/TR/ws-arch/
4. Cohen, C.F.: CERT advisory CA-2002-17 Apache web server chunk handling vulnerability (July 2002) (accessed July 24, 2002), http://www.cert.org/advisories/CA-2002-17.html
5. Corporation, M.: Common vulnerabilities and exposures (accessed June 16, 2006), http://cve.mitre.org/
6. Curry, D., Debar, H.: Intrusion detection message exchange format data model and extensible markup language (XML) document type definition (December 2002) (accessed January 1, 2003), http://www.ietf.org/internet-drafts/draft-ietf-idwg-idmef-xml-09.txt
7. cve.mitre.org: CVE-1999-0107 (July 1999) (accessed September 3, 2006), http://www.cve.mitre.org/cgi-bin/cvename.cgi?name=CVE-1999-0107
8. cve.mitre.org: CVE-1999-1199 (September 2004) (accessed October 30, 2005), http://www.cve.mitre.org/cgi-bin/cvename.cgi?name=CVE-1999-1199
9. Damashek, M.: Gauging similarity with n-grams: language-independent categorization of text. Science 267(5199), 843–848 (1995)
10. Danyliw, R., Dougherty, C., Householder, A., Ruefle, R.: CERT advisory CA-2001-26 Nimda worm (September 2001), http://www.cert.org/advisories/CA-2001-26.html
11. Debar, H., Dacier, M., Wespi, A., Lampart, S.: An experimentation workbench for intrusion detection systems. Technical Report RZ 6519, IBM Research Division, Zurich Research Laboratory, 8803 Rüuschlikon, Switzerland (September 1998)
12. Eastlake, D., Khare, R., Miller, J.: Selecting payment mechanisms over HTTP (2006) (accessed September 13, 2006), http://www.w3.org/TR/WD-jepi-uppflow-970106
13. Estévez-Tapiador, J.M., García-Teodoro, P., Díaz-Verdejo, J.E.: Measuring normality in http traffic for anomaly-based intrusion detection. Journal of Computer Networks 45(2), 175–193 (2004)
14. Fielding, R., Gettys, J., Mogul, J., Frystyk, H., Masinter, L., Leach, P., Berners-Lee, T.: Hypertext transfer protocol—HTTP/1.1. RFC 2616 (June 1999) (accessed October 2, 2002), ftp://ftp.isi.edu/in-notes/rfc2616.txt

15. Haines, J.W., Lippmann, R.P., Fried, D.J., Tran, E., Boswell, S., Zissman, M.A.: 1999 DARPA intrusion detection system evaluation: Design and procedures. Technical Report TR-1062, Lincoln Laboratory, Massachusetts Institute of Technology, Lexington, MA, USA (February 2001)
16. Hancock, J., Wintz, P.: Signal Detection Theory. McGraw-Hill, New York (1966)
17. Heberlein, L.: Network security monitor (NSM)—final report. Technical report, University of California at Davis Computer Security Lab, Lawrence Livermore National Laboratory project deliverable (1995), http://seclab.cs.ucdavis.edu/papers/NSM-final.pdf
18. Heberlein, L., Dias, G., Levitt, K., Mukherjee, B., Wood, J., Wolber, D.: A network security monitor. In: 1990 IEEE Computer Society Symposium on Research in Security and Privacy, Oakland, CA, USA, May 7–9, 1990, pp. 296–304. IEEE Computer Society Press, Los Alamitos, CA, USA (1990)
19. Hernández, L.O., Pegah, M.: WebDAV: what it is, what it does, why you need it. In: SIGUCCS '03: Proceedings of the 31st annual ACM SIGUCCS conference on User services, New York, NY, USA, pp. 249–254. ACM Press, New York (2003)
20. Ingham, K.L.: Anomaly Detection for HTTP Intrusion Detection: Algorithm Comparisons and the Effect of Generalization on Accuracy. PhD thesis, Department of Computer Science, University of New Mexico, Albuquerque, NM, 87131 (2007)
21. Ingham, K.L., Somayaji, A., Burge, J., Forrest, S.: Learning DFA representations of HTTP for protecting web applications. Computer Networks 51(5), 1239–1255 (2007)
22. Kruegel, C., Vigna, G.: Anomaly detection of web-based attacks. In: Proceedings of the 10th ACM conference on Computer and communications security, pp. 251–261. ACM Press, New York (2003)
23. Kruegel, C., Vigna, G., Robertson, W.: A multi-model approach to the detection of web-based attacks. Computer Networks 48(5), 717–738 (2005)
24. Lippmann, R., Haines, J., Fried, D., Korba, J., Das, K.: The 1999 DARPA off-line intrusion detection evaluation. Computer Networks 34(4), 579–595 (2000)
25. Mahoney, M.V.: Network traffic anomaly detection based on packet bytes. In: Proceedings of the 2003 ACM Symposium on Applied computing, pp. 346–350. ACM Press, New York (2003)
26. Mahoney, M.V., Chan, P.K.: Learning nonstationary models of normal network traffic for detecting novel attacks. In: Proceedings of the eighth ACM SIGKDD international conference on Knowledge discovery and data mining, pp. 376–385. ACM Press, New York (2002)
27. McHugh, J.: The 1998 Lincoln Laboratory IDS evaluation—a critique. In: Debar, H., Mé, L., Wu, S.F. (eds.) RAID 2000. LNCS, vol. 1907, pp. 145–161. Springer, Heidelberg (2000)
28. McHugh, J.: Testing intrusion detection systems: a critique of the 1998 and 1999 DARPA intrusion detection system evaluations as performed by Lincoln Laboratory. ACM Transactions on Information and Systems Security 3(4), 262–294 (2000)
29. Microsoft Corporation: Exchange server 2003 RPC over HTTP deployment scenarios (2006) (accessed Sept 13, 2006), http://www.microsoft.com/technet prodtechnol/exchange/2003/library/ex2k 3rpc.mspx
30. Puketza, N., Chung, M., Olsson, R., Mukherjee, B.: A software platform for testing intrusion detection systems. IEEE Software 14(5), 43–51 (1997)
31. Puketza, N.J., Zhang, K., Chung, M., Mukherjee, B., Olsson, R.A.: A methodology for testing intrusion detection systems. IEEE Transactions on Software Engineering 22(10), 719–729 (1996)

32. Robertson, W., Vigna, G., Kruegel, C., Kemmerer, R.A.: Using generalization and characterization techniques in the anomaly-based detection of web attacks. In: Network and Distributed System Security Symposium Conference Proceedings: 2006. Internet Society (2006) (accessed February 12, 2006), http://www.isoc.org/isoc/conferences/ndss/06/proceedings/html/2006/papers/anomaly_signatures.pdf

33. Stolcke, A., Omohundro, S.: Hidden Markov Model induction by bayesian model merging. In: Hanson, S.J., Cowan, J.D., Giles, C.L. (eds.) Advances in Neural Information Processing Systems, vol. 5, pp. 11–18. Morgan Kaufmann, San Mateo, CA (1993)

34. Stolcke, A., Omohundro, S.M.: Best-first model merging for hidden Markov model induction. Technical Report TR-94-003, International Computer Science Institute, 1947 Center Street, Suite 600, Berkeley, CA, 94704-1198 (1994)

35. Tombini, E., Debar, H., Mé, L., Ducassé, M.: A serial combination of anomaly and misuse IDSes applied to HTTP traffic. In: 20th Annual Computer Security Applications Conference (2004)

36. Vargiya, R., Chan, P.: Boundary detection in tokenizing network application payload for anomaly detection. In: Proceedings of the ICDM Workshop on Data Mining for Computer Security (DMSEC). Workshop held in conjunction with The Third IEEE International Conference on Data Mining, November 2003, pp. 50–59 (2003) (accessed April 5, 2006), available at http://www.cs.fit.edu/~pkc/dmsec03/dmsec03notes.pdf

37. Wan, T., Yang, X.D.: IntruDetector: a software platform for testing network intrusion detection algorithms. In: Seventeenth Annual Computer Security Applications Conference, New Orleans, LA, USA, December 10–14, 2001, IEEE Computer Society, Los Alamitos, CA, USA (2001)

38. Wang, K., Stolfo, S.J.: Anomalous payload-based network intrusion detection. In: Jonsson, E., Valdes, A., Almgren, M. (eds.) RAID 2004. LNCS, vol. 3224, pp. 203–222. Springer, Heidelberg (2004)

39. Warrender, C., Forrest, S., Pearlmutter, B.A.: Detecting intrusions using system calls: Alternative data models. In: IEEE Symposium on Security and Privacy, pp. 133–145. IEEE Computer Society Press, Los Alamitos (1999)

40. Wiers, D.: Tunneling SSH over HTTP(S) (2006) (accessed September 13, 2006), http://dag.wieers.com/howto/ssh-http-tunneling/

Swaddler: An Approach for the Anomaly-Based Detection of State Violations in Web Applications

Marco Cova, Davide Balzarotti, Viktoria Felmetsger, and Giovanni Vigna

Department of Computer Science,
University of California Santa Barbara
Santa Barbara, CA 93106-5110, USA
{marco,balzarot,rusvika,vigna}@cs.ucsb.edu

Abstract. In recent years, web applications have become tremendously popular, and nowadays they are routinely used in security-critical environments, such as medical, financial, and military systems. As the use of web applications for critical services has increased, the number and sophistication of attacks against these applications have grown as well. Most approaches to the detection of web-based attacks analyze the interaction of a web application with its clients and back-end servers. Even though these approaches can effectively detect and block a number of attacks, there are attacks that cannot be detected only by looking at the external behavior of a web application.

In this paper, we present Swaddler, a novel approach to the anomaly-based detection of attacks against web applications. Swaddler analyzes the internal state of a web application and learns the relationships between the application's critical execution points and the application's internal state. By doing this, Swaddler is able to identify attacks that attempt to bring an application in an inconsistent, anomalous state, such as violations of the intended workflow of a web application. We developed a prototype of our approach for the PHP language and we evaluated it with respect to several real-world applications.

Keywords: Web Attacks, Anomaly Detection, Dynamic Analysis, Code Instrumentation.

1 Introduction

Web applications are quickly becoming the most common way to access services and functionality. Even applications such as word processors and spreadsheets are becoming web-based because of the advantages in terms of ubiquitous accessibility and ease of maintenance.

However, as web applications become more sophisticated, so do the attacks that exploit them. Some of these attacks are evolutions of well-known attacks, such as buffer overflows or command injections. In addition, there are attacks that are specific to web applications, such as forceful browsing and parameter manipulation.

C. Kruegel, R. Lippmann, and A. Clark (Eds.): RAID 2007, LNCS 4637, pp. 63–86, 2007.
© Springer-Verlag Berlin Heidelberg 2007

Web applications are usually implemented as a number of server-side components, each of which can take a number of parameters from the user through both the request parameters (e.g., an attribute value) and the request header (e.g., a cookie). These components need to share and maintain state, so that the application can keep track of the actions of a user as he/she interacts with the application as a whole.

There are several attacks that exploit erroneous or inconsistent state management mechanisms in order to bypass authentication and authorization checks. Unfortunately, even though there are a number of tools and techniques to protect web applications from attacks, these approaches analyze the external behavior of an application, such as its request/response flow [2,33] or its interaction with back-end databases [22,32,13], and do not take into account the *internal state* of a web application in order to identify anomalous or malicious behavior.

In this paper, we present Swaddler, a novel approach to the detection of attacks against web applications. The approach is based on a detailed characterization of the internal state of a web application, by means of a number of anomaly models. More precisely, the internal state of the application is monitored during a learning phase. During this phase the approach derives the profiles that describe the normal values for the application's state variables in critical points of the application's components. Then, during the detection phase, the application's execution is monitored to identify anomalous states.

The approach has been implemented by instrumenting the PHP interpreter and has been validated against real-world applications. Our experiments show that by modeling the internal state of a web application one can detect attacks that cannot be identified by examining the external flow of requests and responses only. For example, attacks that violate the intended workflow of an application cannot be detected by examining requests and responses in isolation.

The contributions of our paper are the following:

- We introduce a novel approach that analyzes the internal state of a web application using anomaly detection techniques. To the best of our knowledge, there are no other approaches that are able to analyze a web application's state at the granularity that our approach supports.
- We show that anomaly detection based on both the value of single variables and the relationships among multiple variables is an effective way to detect complex attacks against web applications.
- We demonstrate that our technique is able to detect attacks that mainstream techniques based on request analysis are unable to detect, such as workflow violations.

The rest of this paper is structured as follows. In Section 2, we describe our threat model and the type of attacks that our approach detects using a sample application. Then, in Section 3, we present our approach to modeling the state of a web application to detect complex attacks. In Section 4, we describe the implementation of our tool, and, in Section 5, we present a number of experiments that we carried out to evaluate its effectiveness. Finally, Section 6 presents related work and Section 7 concludes.

2   Threat Model

Web applications are the target of many different types of attacks. In this section, we present two common classes of attacks: the ones that exploit errors in the input validation process and the ones that exploit flaws in the enforcement of an application's intended workflow.

2.1   Input Validation Attacks

Input validation attacks exploit the application's inability to properly filter the values of the parameters provided by the user, allowing an attacker to inject malicious data (e.g., a piece of JavaScript code) into a web application. In particular, the two most common attacks that belong to this category are SQL injection and cross-site scripting (XSS).

A web application is vulnerable to a SQL injection attack when the input provided by the user is used to compose a database query without being previously sanitized. A SQL injection attack can allow a malicious user to execute arbitrary queries on the database server. As a result, the attacker can steal sensitive information and/or modify the information stored in the database tables.

Consider, for example, a typical web application where the authentication module compares the user-provided credentials with the known accounts contained in the database. The username provided by the user is used to compose the query, without any checks on its contents:

```
"SELECT * FROM users WHERE name = '" + userName + "';"
```

Since the username is not sanitized, it can be crafted by the attacker so that arbitrary SQL code is injected into the query. For example, if the value of the user name is set to `';DROP TABLE users;`, the database would evaluate the `DROP` query just after the `SELECT` one.

In cross-site scripting attacks, an attacker is able to force a user's web browser to evaluate attacker-supplied code (typically JavaScript) in the context of a trusted web site. The goal of these attacks is to circumvent the browsers' *same-origin policy*, which prevents scripts or documents loaded from one site from getting or setting the properties of documents originating from other sites.

In a typical XSS attack, the attacker inserts the malicious code as part of a message that is stored by the web application (e.g., JavaScript code is added to a blog comment). When a normal user accesses the page that shows the message, the malicious code is evaluated by the user's browser under the assumption that it originates from the vulnerable application rather than from the attacker. Therefore, the malicious code has access to sensitive information associated with the trusted web site, such as login credentials stored in cookies.

SQL injection and XSS attacks are very common and very dangerous at the same time. However, there is a large number of static and dynamic techniques to detect this kind of input validation attacks [15,13,26,30,35,20,21]. For this reason, in this paper we concentrate on the less-known and often-overlooked attacks against the workflow of web applications.

```
include 'config.php';
session_start();
$username = $_GET['username'];
$password = $_GET['password'];
if($username == $admin_login
   && $password == $admin_pass) {
  $_SESSION['loggedin'] = 'yes';
  $_SESSION['username'] = $admin_login;
} else if(checkuser($username,$password)) {
  $_SESSION['loggedin'] = 'yes';
  $_SESSION['username'] = $username;
} else {
  diefooter("Login failed");
}
```
login.php

```
include 'config.php';
session_start();
if($loggedin != 'yes'
   || $username != $admin_login) {
  diefooter("Unauthorized access");
}
printusers();
```
admin/viewusers.php

Fig. 1. Authentication bypass vulnerability in the store application

2.2 Workflow Violation Attacks

Workflow violation attacks exploit logical errors in web applications in order to bypass the intended workflow of the application. The intended workflow of a web application represents a model of the expected user interactions with the application. Examples of workflow violation attacks include authentication and authorization bypass, parameter tampering, and code inclusion attacks.

To better illustrate this class of attacks, we present a small PHP application that contains a number of common workflow vulnerabilities. The application is a simple online store that sells different items to its users. New users can register and, once logged in, browse and buy the items available in the store. The application uses the standard PHP session mechanism [27] to store the session information and the shopping carts of the users. In addition, the store provides an administrative interface to manage the inventory and to review information about its users.

The first example of vulnerability contained in the store application is an authentication bypass vulnerability. The program uses two session variables, `loggedin` and `username`, to keep track of whether a user is currently logged in and if she has administrative privileges. A simplified version of the code of `login.php`, the application module that initializes these variables, is shown in Figure 1. Every time the user requests one of the administrative pages, the variables `loggedin` and `username` are checked, as shown in `viewusers.php` in Figure 1, to verify that the user is correctly authenticated as administrator.

Since the application utilizes the PHP session mechanism, the session variables are kept inside the superglobal _SESSION array. However, if the `register_globals` option of the PHP interpreter is enabled, an application can refer to a session variable by simply using the variable name, as if it was a normal global variable. Since our application uses this "shortcut" to access the session variables (unfortunately a common practice among inexperienced developers), an attacker can easily bypass the checks by providing the required variables as part of the GET request to one of the protected pages. In fact, when `register_globals` is enabled, the PHP interpreter automatically binds the parameters coming from the user's requests to

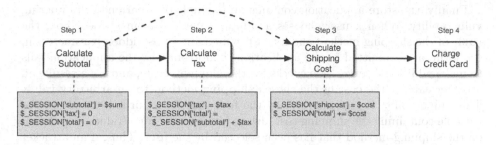

Fig. 2. Checkout workflow in the store application

global variables. Thus, if the variable `loggedin` is not present in the session (i.e, the user did not authenticate herself), it can be provided by an attacker using the request parameters, as shown in the following request:

`http://store.com/admin/viewusers.php?loggedin=yes&username=admin`

The `login.php` module is the only part of the application that sets the `loggedin` and `username` variables, and, as it can be seen from the code given in Figure 1, the variable `username` is set to the administrator's name only if a user provides the correct administrator's name and password. Thus, even if the attacker manages to bypass the authorization check in `viewusers.php`, she will not be able to set the `_SESSION['username']` to the correct value. Thus, the attack would force the application to move into an anomalous state (corresponding to the administrative code being executed with the `_SESSION['username']` not set to the expected *admin* value).

The store application is also vulnerable to a second workflow violation attack. In this case, the attack exploits the fact that the application computes the amount of money to be charged to the user's credit card in several different steps. During the checkout phase, the user navigates through several pages where she has to provide various pieces of information, including her state of residency (for tax calculation), shipping address, shipping method, and credit card number. For simplicity, suppose that the checkout process consists of four main steps as shown in Figure 2, where the first three steps calculate the purchase total based on the user-provided information and the final step proceeds with the order submission. Now, suppose that the application fails to enforce the policy that the *Step 3* page should be accessible only after *Step 2* has been completed. As a result of this flaw, an attacker can directly go from *Step 1* to *Step 3* by simply entering the correct URL associated with *Step 3*. In this case, the total amount charged to the attacker's credit card will be equal to the shipping cost only.

It is important to note that while this attack would be very difficult to detect analyzing the HTTP traffic, it clearly manifests itself as an anomaly in the web application state. In fact, under a normal operation, the total amount charged to the user is always equal to the sum of the purchased price, taxes and shipping cost. However, if the user is able to change the order of the steps in the checkout process, this relationship will not hold.

Finally, the store application contains an example of a parameter tampering vulnerability. When a user chooses a shipping method from a select box, the name of the shipping method and its cost, which are set as hidden parameters in the form, are submitted to the application. Unfortunately, the application fails to make additional server-side checks for the shipping costs, and, as a result, an attacker can set the cost of the chosen shipping method to an arbitrary value. This vulnerability is characterized by the fact that, in a normal execution, the variable containing the shipping cost always assumes the same values, depending on the shipping method that has been selected by the user. Thus, if an attacker tampers with the hidden parameter to change the shipping cost to an arbitrary value, the `_SESSION['shipcost']` variable will assume an anomalous value that can be easily detected analyzing the state of the application.

3   Approach

As shown in the previous section, not all web-based attacks rely on sending malicious input to web applications. Some of them exploit weaknesses in the intended workflow of the application, allowing the user to navigate through the different application's modules in a way that leads the application to an insecure state. In this case, the attacker performs a sequence of actions in which all the provided input values can be perfectly harmless, and the vulnerability is exploited through the particular order (or timing) of the various requests.

This type of attacks can be very difficult to detect "from the outside," that is, using sensors that only analyze HTTP requests and responses in isolation. Nevertheless, regardless of how the attack is performed, its final effect is to force the application to enter an insecure state. For this reason, we believe that a more effective approach to the detection of workflow attacks consists of monitoring, at runtime, the state of the web application "from the inside." This is true, of course, under the assumption that there is a strong relationship between insecure and anomalous states, i.e., any insecure state is also likely anomalous and vice versa.

Before describing our approach, which we call Swaddler, we need to introduce the concept of *web application state*. We define the state of a web application at a certain point in the execution as the information that survives a single client-server interaction: in other words, the information associated with the *user session*. Part of this information is kept on the server, while part of it can be sent back and forth between the user's browser and the server in the form of cookies, hidden form fields, and request parameters.

Given this definition of application state, it is possible to associate each instruction of the application with a model of the state in which that instruction is normally executed. For example, code contained in the admin directory of our sample application shares the fact that, when it is executed, the variable `_SESSION['username']` should always be equal to *admin*. Any runtime violation of this requirement represents the evidence that a low-privilege user was able to access an administrative functionality bypassing the constraints implemented by the application's developer.

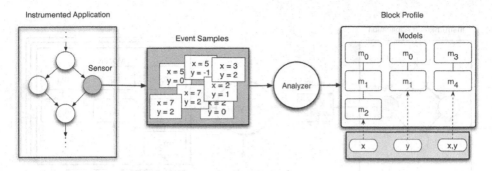

Fig. 3. Description of the training phase

Ideally, a complete set of these relationships among code execution points and state variables would be provided by the developers as part of the application's specification. However, since in reality this information is never explicitly provided, the models of the normal state for each program instruction have to be inferred from a set of attack-free execution traces. To perform this task, we propose to automatically instrument the web application with the code required to extract the runtime values of state variables. Depending on the language in which the application is developed, this instrumentation can be performed in several ways. For example, in our prototype implementation we decided to add the instrumentation as a module to the PHP interpreter. This solution allows our approach to be applied to a large set of web applications without the need to modify the source code of the applications.

Swaddler associates a model of the web application state with each instruction executed by the application. However, this solution can be optimized by limiting the instrumentation to the first instruction of each basic block. A *basic block* is a sequence of consecutive statements in which flow of control enters at the beginning and leaves at the end without halt or possibility of branching except at the end [1]. In fact, since the control-flow inside a basic block is a simple sequence of instructions without branches, the application state at the beginning of the basic block univocally determines the state of each instruction inside the block. Once the models that describe the normal state associated with each basic block have been properly extracted, they can be used to detect (and prevent) attacks that violate the normal application state.

Figure 3 and Figure 4 show the architecture of our anomaly detection system during the training and detection phases. Swaddler consists of two main components: the *sensor* and the *analyzer*. The sensor is represented by the instrumentation code, which collects the application's state data (i.e., the values of state variables) at the beginning of each basic block, and encapsulates them in an *event* that is sent to the analyzer. An event generated by the sensor defines a mapping between the variable names and their current values. For each basic block of the application, the analyzer maintains a *profile*, i.e., a set of statistical models used to characterize certain features of the state variables. These models can be used to capture various properties of single variables as well as

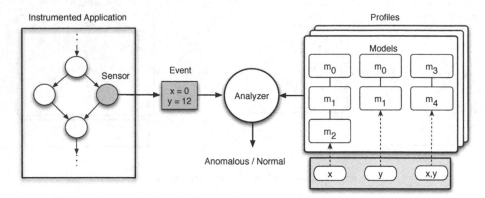

Fig. 4. Description of the detection phase

to describe complex relationships among multiple variables associated with a block. In training mode, profiles for application blocks are established using the events generated by the sensor, while in detection and prevention modes these profiles are used to identify anomalous application states. When an anomalous state is detected, the analyzer raises an alert message, and, optionally, it can immediately stop the execution of the application.

Since Swaddler is based on anomaly detection techniques, it can be vulnerable to mimicry attacks [34], in which an attacker crafts an exploit in a way that closely resembles normal activity (or normal state values). Therefore, in principle, one could find a way to perform an attack that brings a web application into an insecure state without triggering any alert. Nonetheless, the fine granularity at which our approach analyzes the application state makes this type of attacks much more difficult to perform.

Even though our approach is general and, in principle, can be applied to other languages and execution environments, in the following sections we will describe in detail the solution that we have developed for the PHP language.

4 Implementation

The implementation of our approach consists of two main components: the *sensor*, which is an extension of the PHP interpreter that probes the current state of an executing application, and the *analyzer*, which is an anomaly-based system that determines the normality of the application's state. In the current prototype, the sensor is implemented as a module of the open-source Zend Engine interpreter [36] and the analyzer is built on top of the libAnomaly framework [31].

4.1 Event Collection

The Zend Engine is the standard interpreter for the PHP language. It implements a virtual machine that is responsible for parsing programs written in PHP and compiling them into an intermediate format, which is then executed.

To probe an application's state and generate responses to detected attacks, our implementation extends the Zend Engine in two points of its processing cycle: after the standard compilation step is completed and before the standard execution step is initiated. Whenever the execution of a PHP script is requested (e.g., in response to a user's request to a web application), the Zend Engine parses the script's source code, checks for its correctness, and compiles it into a sequence of statements in an intermediate, architecture-independent language. The binary representation of each statement holds a reference to a handler function, which interprets the statement and changes the state of the virtual machine accordingly. During execution, the Zend Engine decodes in turn each statement and dispatches it to its handler function.

Our extension is invoked by the engine after it has produced the compiled version of a program. The extension performs a linear scan of the sequence of intermediate statements, identifies the corresponding basic blocks, and associates a unique ID with each of them. The first statement of each basic block is modified by overwriting its handler with a custom instrumentation handler. The effect of this modification is that, during the program's execution, our instrumentation code is invoked each time a basic block is entered.

The cost of this phase is linear in the number of intermediate statements, which is proportional to the size of the program. By default, the Zend Engine does not cache the intermediate statements for reuse during subsequent executions, and, therefore, the compilation and our instrumentation of the application's code is repeated for every access of the page. However, if one of the available caching mechanisms is added to the standard engine, our technique will be able to take advantage of the caching functionality, thus reducing the cost of the instrumentation.

After the compilation step, the Zend Engine starts executing the application's code. Our instrumentation handler is invoked every time the first statement of a basic block is executed. The instrumentation handler creates an event corresponding to the basic block being executed and makes the event available to the analyzer for inspection. The event contains the information collected about the current application state. Since in the current implementation of our approach we focus on the detection of workflow-based attacks, by default the events contain the values of the variables defined in the application's session, i.e., the content of the _SESSION array. In our experiments we found this information to be sufficient to detect most of the workflow attacks. However, the system can be configured to extract other parts of the application's state. For example, one could use the content of the _REQUEST array (a global array automatically populated by the interpreter with the values of the user's input to the application) to detect attacks that exploit insufficient validation of input parameters. In addition, further customizations of the sensor are possible if more information is known about an application. For example, if one knows that only some portions of the application's state can be used to attack the application, one could configure the sensor to only extract those parts of the state. Note that all the configurable settings of the sensor (e.g., the set of state variables to extract or the models to use) are set by using the standard .htaccess mechanism and, therefore, can be changed on-the-fly without the need to modify the sensor's code.

After delivering an event to the analyzer, the instrumentation handler behaves differently depending on the current execution mode. During training, it takes no further action. However, if the system is in detection or prevention mode, and it has determined that the state associated with the block about to be executed is anomalous, an alert is generated, the request is logged, and, in prevention mode, the execution is automatically blocked.

When the sensor has finished its processing (and the execution has not been abnormally terminated), it invokes the original handler of the statement, passing the control back to the Zend Engine. The execution of the statement, then, proceeds as in the normal, unmodified interpreter.

Our implementation, based on the modification of the web application's interpreter, has several strengths. First, the sensor has direct access to all of the interpreter's data structures, and, thus, it has an unambiguous view of the application's state. Other implementation strategies of our approach, e.g., those based on the analysis of request/response traces, would have to infer the application's state and, thus, in general, would provide a less precise input to the analyzer component. Second, the sensor has the capability of blocking attacks before they reach a vulnerable point in the application.

4.2   Anomaly Detection

Our implementation of the detection engine is based on a modified version of the libAnomaly framework [31]. The anomaly detection process uses a number of different models to identify anomalous states for each basic block of a web application. A model is a set of procedures used to evaluate a certain feature of a state variable associated with the block (e.g., the range of its possible values) or a certain feature that involves multiple state variables (e.g., the presence and absence of a subset of them). Each block has an associated *profile* that keeps the mapping between variables and models. Consider, for example, a block of code in a web application whose corresponding state can be described with two variables, username and password. Suppose that one wants to associate a certain number of different models with each of these variables in order to capture various properties, such as length and character distribution, that their values can take under normal execution. In this case there will be a profile, associated with the block, that contains a mapping between each variable and the corresponding models. Whenever an event is generated for that block, the profile is used to find the models to evaluate the features of the state variables.

In our implementation, the task of a model is to assign a probability value to a feature of a state variable or a set of state variables associated with the block that is about to be executed. This value reflects the probability of the occurrence of a given feature value with regards to an established model of "normality." The assumption is that feature values with a sufficiently low probability indicate a potential attack. The overall anomaly score of a block is derived from the probability values returned by the models that are associated with the block and its variables. The anomaly score value is calculated through the weighted sum shown in Equation 1. In this equation, w_m represents the weight associated with model m, while p_m is the probability value returned by model m.

$$AnomalyScore = \sum_{m \in Models} w_m * p_m \qquad (1)$$

A model can operate in one of two modes, training or detection. The training phase is required to determine the characteristics of normal events (that is, the profile of a block according to specific models) and to establish anomaly score thresholds to distinguish between regular and anomalous values of the state variables. This phase is divided into two steps. During the first step, the system creates a profile and trains the associated models for each block in the applications. During the second step, suitable thresholds are established. This is done by evaluating the states associated with the blocks using the profiles created during the previous step. For each block, the most anomalous score (i.e., the lowest probability) is stored in the block's profile and the threshold is set to a value that is a certain adjustable percentage lower than this minimum. The default setting for this percentage is 10%. By modifying this value, the user can adjust the sensitivity of the system and perform a trade-off between the number of false positives and the expected detection accuracy.

Once the profiles have been created—that is, the models have learned the characteristics of normal events and suitable thresholds have been derived—the system switches to detection mode. In this mode, anomaly scores are calculated and anomalous states are reported.

libAnomaly provides a number of built-in models that can be combined to model different features. By default, block profiles are configured to use all the available models with equal weights. However, to improve performance, if some application-specific knowledge is available, the user can configure profiles to only use a subset of the models, or fine-tune the way they are combined.

In Swaddler, we used a number of existing libAnomaly models to represent the normal values of single variables and we developed two additional models to capture relationships among multiple variables associated with a block. We describe the models we used in the next two sections.

4.3   Univariate Models

In the context of this paper, we will use the term *univariate models* to refer to the anomaly models that are used to capture various properties of single variables associated with a block. libAnomaly already contains a number of univariate models. These models can be used to characterize the normal length of a variable (*Attribute Length* model), the structure of its values (*Attribute Character Distribution* model), the set of all the possible values (*Token Finder* model), etc. In the following, we provide a brief description of some of the univariate models used by the current Swaddler implementation. A more in-depth description of these and other available models can be found in [25,20].

Token Finder. In our implementation, the purpose of the Token Finder model is to determine whether the values of a certain variable are drawn from a limited set of possible alternatives (i.e., they are elements of an enumeration). In web applications, certain variables often take one of few possible values. For example, in our shopping cart application, the variable _SESSION['shipcost'] can be set to one of three predefined values depending on which shipping method is chosen by the user. If a malicious user attempts to set her shipping cost to a value that is not part of the enumeration, the attack is detected. When no enumeration can be identified, it is assumed that the attribute values are random.

The classification of an argument as an enumeration or as a random value is based on the observation that the number of different occurrences of variable values is bound by some unknown threshold t in the case of an enumeration while it is unrestricted in the case of random values. During the training phase, when the number of different values for a given variable grows proportionally to the total number of its samples, the variable is characterized as random. If such an increase cannot be observed, the variable is modeled with an enumeration.

Once it has been determined that the values of a variable are tokens drawn from an enumeration, any value seen during the detection phase is expected to appear in the set of known values. When this happens, 1 is returned by the model (indicating normality), and 0 is returned otherwise (indicating an anomalous condition). If it has been determined that the variable values are random, the model always returns 1.

Attribute Length. The length of a variable value can be used to detect anomalous states, for example when typical values are either fixed-size tokens (as it is common for session identifiers) or short strings derived from human input. In these cases, the length of the parameter values does not vary significantly between executions of the same block. The situation may look different when malicious input is passed to the program. For example, XSS attacks that attempt to inject scripts in pages whose content is generated dynamically, often require to send an amount of data that can significantly exceed the length of legitimate parameters.

Thus, the goal of this model is to approximate the actual but unknown distribution of the length of values of a variable and detect instances that significantly deviate from the observed normal behavior. During the training phase, the value length distribution is approximated through the sample mean and variance. Then, during the detection phase, the abnormality of a given value for a variable is assessed by the "distance" of the given length from the mean value of the length distribution. The calculation of this distance is based on the Chebyshev inequality [3].

Attribute Character Distribution. The attribute character distribution model captures the concept of a "normal" or "regular" value of a variable by looking at its character distribution. The approach is based on the observation that values of variables in web applications are mostly human-readable and mostly are drawn from a small subset of the ASCII characters. In case of attacks that send binary data or repetitions of a single character, a completely different character distribution can be observed.

During the training phase, the idealized character distribution of a variable values (i.e., the distribution that is perfectly normal) is approximated based on the sorted relative character frequencies that were observed. During the detection phase, the probability that the character distribution of a string parameter fits the normal distribution established during the training phase is calculated using a statistical test (Pearson χ^2-test).

4.4 Multivariate Models

In the context of this paper, we will use the term *multivariate models* to refer to anomaly models that are used to capture relationships among multiple variables associated with a block. In particular, Swaddler adds two multivariate models to the libAnomaly framework: a *Variable Presence or Absence model*[1] and a *Likely Invariants* model.

Variable Presence or Absence. The purpose of the Variable Presence or Absence model is to identify which variables are expected to be always present when accessing a basic block in an application. For example, in our sample store application, the variables _SESSION['loggedin'] and _SESSION['username'] have to be always present when accessing one of the administrative pages. When a malicious user tries to directly access one of the protected pages, these variables will not be present and the attack will be detected.

During the training phase, the model keeps track of which variables are always set when accessing a particular block of code. Based on this information, each state variable associated with the block is given a weight, where variables that were always present are given a weight of 1 and variables that were sometimes absent are given a weight in the range from 0 to 1, depending on the number of times that the variable has been seen. The total score for a block is calculated as the sum of all variables scores divided by the number of variables in the block. This score is always between 0 and 1.

During the detection phase, the total score of the block is calculated based on the established weights. Therefore, the absence of a variable with a higher weight results in a lower score for the state associated with the block.

Likely Invariants. A program invariant is a property that holds for every execution of the program. If the property is not guaranteed to be always true in all the possible executions, it is called a *likely invariant*. To be able to automatically detect and extract state-related likely invariants, we integrated the Daikon engine [5,6] in the libAnomaly framework.

Daikon is a system for the dynamic detection of likely invariants, which was originally designed to infer invariants by observing the variable values computed over a certain number of program executions. Daikon is able to generate invariants that predicate both on a single variable value (e.g., $x == 5$) and on complex

---

[1] Even though based on similar idea, this model is different from the *Attribute Presence or Absence* model described in [20].

compositions of multiple variables (e.g., $x > abs(y)$, $y = 5 * x - 2$). Its ability to extract invariants predicating on multiple variables is one of the main reasons for including Daikon in our tool.

In training mode, Daikon observes the variable values at particular program points decided by the user. In order to integrate it in our system, we developed a new component that translates the events generated by our sensor into the Daikon trace format. Our component is also able to infer the correct data type of each variable, by analyzing the values that the variables assume at runtime. The output of this type inference process is required for the correct working of the Daikon system.

At the end of the training phase, the Daikon-based model calculates the set of likely invariants and computes the probability that each of them appears in a random data set. If this is lower than a certain threshold (i.e., if it is unlikely that the invariant has been generated by chance) the invariant is kept, otherwise it is discarded.

For example, in our store application, Daikon detects that the block of code that charges the user's credit card is associated with the following invariants on the state variables:

```
loggedin == 'yes'
total > price
```

This means that, when the basic block is executed, the `loggedin` variable is always set to *yes* (because the user must be logged in order to be able to buy items) and the `total` value charged to the user is always greater than the price of the purchased items (because of the taxes and shipping costs).

When the system switches to detection, all the invariants that apply to the same block are grouped together. The algorithm then automatically generates the C++ code of a function that receives as a parameter an event created by the sensor. The function performs three actions:

- it fetches the value of the variables predicated by the invariants (in our example, `loggedin`, `total`, and `price`);
- it verifies that the runtime type of each variable is correct (in our example, we expect `total` and `price` to be integers and `loggedin` to be a string);
- finally, it evaluates the invariants, which, in our example, are represented by the following snippet of C++ code:

```
if (strcmp(loggedin, "yes")!=0) return 0;
if (total <= price) return 0;
return 1;
```

The result of the function is a value (0 or 1) that represents whether the application state associated with the PHP block violates the likely invariants inferred during the training phase. This value is then combined with the ones provided by the other `libAnomaly` models to decide if the state is anomalous or normal as a whole.

Table 1. Applications used in the experiments. For each application, we report the number of files that compose the application as an indication of its size, and the known attacks against it, if any. Vulnerabilities are referenced by their Common Vulnerabilities and Exposures ID (CVE) or their Bugtraq ID (BID).

Application Name	PHP Files	Description	Known Vulnerabilities
BloggIt 1.01	24	Blog engine	CVE-2006-7014
PunBB 1.2.4	67	Discussion board system	BID 20786
Scarf 2006-09-20	18	Conference management system	CVE-2006-5909
SimpleCms	22	Content management system	BID 19386
WebCalendar 1.0.3	123	Calendar application	BID 23054

5 Evaluation

We evaluated our system on several real-world, publicly available PHP applications, which are summarized in Table 1. BloggIt is a blog application that allows users to manage a web log, publish new messages, and comment on other people's entries. PunBB is a discussion board system that supports the building of community forums. Scarf is a conference management application that supports the creation of different sessions, the submission of papers, and the creation of comments about a submitted paper. SimpleCms is a web application that allows a web site maintainer to write, organize, and publish online content for multiple users. WebCalendar is an online calendar and event management system. These applications are a representative sample of the different type of functionality and levels of complexity that can be found in commonly-used PHP applications.

The evaluation consisted of a number of tests in a live setting with each of the test applications. All the experiments were conducted on a 3.6GHz Pentium 4 with 2 GB of RAM running Linux 2.6.18. The server was running the Apache web server (version 2.2.4) and PHP version 5.2.1. Apache was configured to serve requests using threads through its `worker` module.

Attack-free data was generated by manually operating each web application and, at the same time, by running scripts simulating user activity. These scripts controlled a browser component (the KHTML component of the KDE library [16]) in order to exercise the test applications by systematically exploring their workflow.

In particular, for each application, we identified the set of available user profiles (e.g., administrator, guest user, and registered user) and their corresponding atomic operations (e.g., login, post a new message, and publish a new article), and then we combined these operations to model a typical user's behavior. For example, a common behavior of a blog application's administrator consists of visiting the home page of the blog, reading the comments added to recent posts, logging in, and, finally, publishing a new entry. The sequences of requests corresponding to each behavior were then replayed with a certain probability reflecting how often one expects to observe that behavior in the average application traffic.

In addition, we developed a number of libraries to increase the realism of the test traffic. In particular, one library was used to create random user identities to be used in registration forms. In this case, we leveraged a database of real names, addresses, zip codes, and cities. Another library was used to systematically explore a web site from an initial page in accordance with a selected user profile's behavior. For example, when simulating a blog's guest user, the library extracts from the current page the links to available blog posts, randomly chooses one, follows it, and, with a certain probability, leaves a new comment on the post's page by submitting the corresponding form.

We used this technique to generate three different datasets: the first was used for training the `libAnomaly` models, the second for choosing suitable thresholds, and the third one was the clean dataset used to estimate the false positive rate of our system.

Since our tests involved applications with known vulnerabilities (and known exploits), it was not sensible to collect real-world attack data by making our testbed publicly accessible. Therefore, attack data was generated by manually performing known or novel attacks against each application, while clean background traffic was directed to the application by using the user simulation scripts. We used the datasets produced this way to assess the detection capability of our system.

5.1 Detection Effectiveness

We evaluated the effectiveness of our approach by training our system on each of the test applications. For these experiments, we did not perform any fine-tuning of the models, equal weights were assigned to each model, and we used the default 10% threshold adjustment value. Then, we recorded the number of false positives generated when testing the application with attack-free data and the number of attacks correctly detected when testing the application with malicious traffic.

Table 2 summarizes the results of our experiments. The size of the training and clean sets is expressed as the number of requests contained in each dataset. Coverage represents the number of lines in each application that have been executed at least once during training. Note that in all cases the coverage was less than 100%. Unexplored paths usually correspond to code associated with the handling of error conditions or with alternative configuration settings, e.g., alternative database libraries or layout themes. The false positives column reports the total number of legitimate requests contained in the clean set that Swaddler incorrectly flagged as anomalous during the detection phase. The attack set size illustrates the number of different malicious requests contained in the attack dataset of each application. This reflects the number of different attacks we used to exploit the vulnerabilities present in the application. For example, an authentication bypass vulnerability can be exploited to get access to several restricted pages. In this case, the attack set contained requests to gain access to

Table 2. Detection effectiveness

Application	Training Set Size (# requests)	Coverage (%)	Clean Set Size (# requests)	False Positives	Attack Set Size (# requests)	Attacks Detected
BloggIt	9779	91	1586	0	15	15
PunBB	10200	67	1360	5	1	1
Scarf	9615	86	1000	1	10	10
SimpleCms	9333	95	1969	0	10	10
WebCalendar	19800	66	3300	1	1	1

each of these pages. Finally, the last column reports how many of these malicious requests were successfully identified by Swaddler.

In our experiments, all attacks were successfully detected by Swaddler. For each application, we describe the vulnerability exploited by the corresponding attacks and how our system detected the attacks.

BloggIt is vulnerable to two types of attacks. First, it contains a known authentication bypass vulnerability that allows unauthenticated users to access administrative functionality. More precisely, the application stores in the session variable `login` the value "ok" if the user has been successfully authenticated. Whenever a user requests a restricted page, the page's code correctly checks whether the user has logged in by inspecting the session variable, and, if not, redirects her to the login page. However, the page's code fails to stop the execution after issuing the redirection instruction to the user's browser, and continues executing the code that implements the restricted functionality. Our system easily detects this attack: for example, the Variable Presence or Absence model returns a high anomaly score if the restricted code is accessed when the session does not contain the `login` variable; similarly, the Likely Invariant and Token Finder models produce an alert if the `login` variable has a value other than "ok".

The second flaw in BloggIt is a novel file injection vulnerability that we discovered. The application allows users to upload files on the server. The uploaded files can then be accessed online and their content (e.g., a picture) be used in blog entries and comments. However, if the uploaded file's name terminates with the `php` extension and a user requests it, the application interprets the file's content as a PHP script and blindly executes it, thus allowing an attacker to execute arbitrary commands. Our system detects the attack since all models report high anomaly scores for the unknown blocks associated with the injected script.

PunBB is vulnerable to a known file injection attack that allows arbitrary code to be executed. In fact, PunBB utilizes a user-controlled variable to present the site in the language chosen by the user, by including appropriate language files. Unfortunately, the variable value is not sanitized and, therefore, it can be modified by an attacker to include malicious code. Also in this case, Swaddler detects the attack when the blocks corresponding to the injected code are executed.

Scarf is vulnerable to a known authentication bypass attack. One of its administrative pages does not check the user's status and allows any user to arbitrarily change site-wide configuration settings (e.g., user profiles information, web site configuration). The status of a user is stored in the application's session using three variables, namely, `privilege`, `user_id`, and `email`. The flaw can be exploited by users that do not have an account on the vulnerable web site or by registered users that lack administrative privileges. In the first case, during an attack the vulnerable page is accessed with an empty session, and thus all our models will report a highly anomalous score; in the second case, the session variables contain values that, for example, are not recognized by the Token Finder model and that do not satisfy the predicates learned by the Likely Invariant model.

SimpleCms is vulnerable to a known authentication bypass attack. It insecurely uses the `register_globals` mechanism in a way similar to the example application described in Section 2. An attacker can simply set the request parameter `loggedin` to 1 and have access to the administrative functionality of the application. Note that this allows the attacker to bypass the authorization check but does not modify the corresponding variable in the session. Therefore, during an attack, all our models report high anomalous scores.

Finally, WebCalendar is vulnerable to a file inclusion attack. In this case, the vulnerability cannot be exploited to execute arbitrary code, but it allows an attacker to modify the value of several state variables, and, by this, to gain unauthorized privileges. Swaddler detects the attack since several models, e.g., the Token Finder and Likely Invariant, flag as anomalous the modified variables.

In our experiments, Swaddler raised a few false positives. Our analysis indicates that, in all cases, the false alarms were caused by the execution of parts of the applications that were exercised by a limited number of requests during the training phase. For example, this is the case with pages that handle the submission of complex forms containing a large number of input parameters: during training, only a subset of all the possible combinations of the input parameters were tested, and, therefore, the models associated with the portions of the page that were least visited were not sufficiently trained.

5.2   Detection Overhead

Our system introduces runtime overhead in two points during the request-serving cycle. First, for each request, some time is spent to analyze and instrument the compiled code of the requested application's page. We refer to this overhead as "instrumentation overhead". Second, during execution, whenever a basic block is entered, the analyzer has to determine whether the current state is anomalous. We call the total time spent performing this operation "detection overhead".

A test was performed to quantify the overhead introduced by our system. For each application, we ran again the requests contained in the clean set used during the detection evaluation and we recorded the time required to perform instrumentation and detection.

Table 3. Detection overhead

Application	Avg. Instrumentation Overhead (msec)	Avg. Detection Overhead (msec)
BloggIt	5	8
PunBB	23	115
Scarf	3	13
SimpleCms	1	5
WebCalendar	15	75

Table 3 presents the results of this test. It shows the average overhead per user's request broken down in its instrumentation and detection components. A direct comparison of the average request-serving time on our modified PHP interpreter and the standard interpreter is presented in Figure 5.

There are two main factors influencing the performance of our tool: the number of state variables that need to be analyzed for each basic block and the number of basic blocks that are traversed when serving a page. To better assess how these factors influence the performance of our system, we measured the Swaddler overhead on a set of test programs. Each program defines a certain number of variables in its session and executes a well-defined number of basic blocks. The values of the defined session variables were chosen carefully in order to avoid artificial simplifications in the trained models (e.g., the values used were not random to avoid that, in detection mode, the Token Finder model would immediately return a normal value). Furthermore, the same number of session variables was defined in all basic blocks, so that the corresponding models had to be trained in all the basic blocks of the program.

We ran the test programs on the standard PHP interpreter and on a version of the interpreter extended with our tool (after performing the training phase) and recorded the difference in the running time in the two cases. Figure 6 shows how the overhead introduced by our system changes as a function of the number of executed basic blocks and the number of examined state variables.

The overhead grows linearly as the number of executed basic blocks increases. This was expected because there is both an instrumentation and a detection overhead associated with each basic block in the program. Similarly, the overhead increases roughly linearly with the number of state variables defined. This can be explained observing that, during detection, the current value of each state variable must be extracted from the execution context and must be checked with respect to the appropriate anomaly models.

In many cases, by tuning the two performance factors (number of executed blocks and number of modeled state variables), it is possible to limit the overhead caused by our instrumentation. First, sometimes it is possible to identify state variables whose value is unlikely to be affected by an attack. For example, an

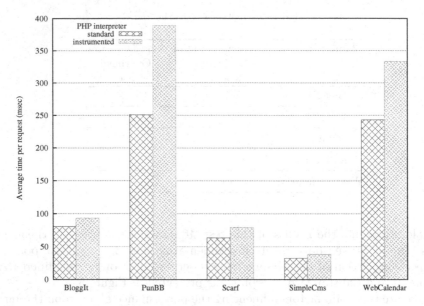

Fig. 5. Total overhead for each application

application might store in a state variable the background color preferred by the current user. In this case, it is reasonable that an attack will not manifest itself with anomalous modifications to that variable. Therefore, the variable can be excluded from the subset of the monitored application state without affecting the detection capability of our tool and reducing the detection overhead.

Second, sometimes the number of basic blocks executed by an application causes the overhead to be larger than it is desired. For example, an application might execute some blocks in a loop a large number of times. In this case, it is possible to configure our sensor so that, during a request, the instrumentation routine is invoked no more than a certain number of times for each block. If an attack manifests itself even if the analyzer monitors the execution of loops only up to a certain bound, this optimization will reduce the overhead without introducing false negatives.

The results of the performance tests both on real-world applications and on synthesized programs indicate that our approach introduces an acceptable overhead for most applications. These results are quite encouraging especially considering that performance was not a priority in the implementation of the current prototype of our tool.

6   Related Work

The work described in this paper is related to different previous research results in the intrusion detection field. First of all, there is a corpus of work on detecting

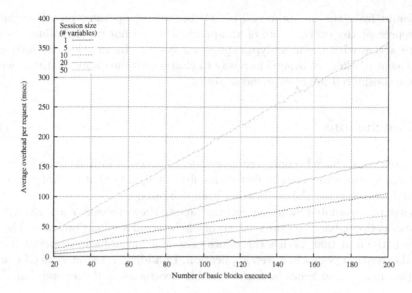

Fig. 6. Factors influencing the overhead

intrusions using anomaly detection techniques (see, for example, [4,17,11,23,14,9]), which we cannot discuss in detail here.

However, there are several proposed anomaly detection approaches that are more closely related to the solution proposed here. First of all, there is the previous work from our group on performing anomaly detection of web-based attacks by analyzing the requests and replies exchanged between clients and servers [20,21]. This previous work introduced the idea of using statistical models to characterize the normal values of the parameters of web requests. This work suggested that this technique could be applied to other event streams and resulted in the libAnomaly framework, which is used (and extended) in the research presented here. The main difference between the two approaches resides in the type of attacks that can be detected. More precisely, the analysis of requests and replies does not allow for the identification of attacks that subvert the intended, normal workflow of a web application.

Another set of results that this work is related to is in the contextualization of intrusion detection, that is, the use of detection models that take into account the different phases (or states) in which an application might be when an attack is executed. The contextualization has been initially introduced in intrusion detection systems that analyze sequences of system calls as a countermeasure against mimicry attacks [34]. For example, in [28,29] the detection of anomalous system call sequences is contextualized using the program counter value at the moment of the system call invocation. Extensions to this approach leveraged the call stack information to characterize different execution states [8,10,7,12].

The combination of contextualization techniques with the detection of anomalous system calls based on the analysis of their parameters was proposed in [24]. Even though this approach is also based on libAnomaly [19,18,25], our approach is different from the one proposed in [24] because it operates on the variables that represent the overall state of an application and not on the values used in its interaction with the underlying operating system. In addition, we introduce the concept of likely invariants as a way to characterize anomalous states, which was not considered in these previous works.

7   Conclusions

Web applications have become a common way to access information and services. These applications are vulnerable to a number of attacks that cannot always be detected by observing the application from the outside.

This paper presented Swaddler, an approach to the detection of attacks against web applications, based on the analysis of the internal application state. The approach is the first that models the values of session variables in association with critical execution points in a web application. In addition, we introduced a novel detection model that relies on multi-variable invariants to detect web-based attacks.

We developed a prototype of our system for the PHP language and we evaluated it against several real-world applications. The results show that by leveraging the internal, hidden state of a web application it is possible to detect attacks that violate its intended workflow, confirming our hypothesis that any insecure state usually corresponds to an anomalous state.

Future work will focus on two directions. First, we will extend our approach to consider other parts of the internal state of an application. Second, we will focus on optimizations that will reduce the overhead introduced by the instrumentation of the PHP interpreter.

Acknowledgments

This research was partially supported by the National Science Foundation, under grants CCR-0238492 and CCR-0524853.

References

1. Aho, A.V., Sethi, R., Ullman, J.: Compilers: Principles, Techniques, and Tools. Addison-Wesley Longman Publishing Co., Inc., Redwood City,CA, USA (1986)
2. Almgren, M., Debar, H., Dacier, M.: A Lightweight Tool for Detecting Web Server Attacks. In: Proceedings of the Network and Distributed System Security Symposium (NDSS), San Diego, CA (February 2000)
3. Billingsley, P.: Probability and Measure, 3rd edn. Wiley-Interscience, Chichester (April 1995)
4. Denning, D.: An Intrusion Detection Model. IEEE Transactions on Software Engineering 13(2), 222–232 (1987)

5. Ernst, M.D., Cockrell, J., Griswold, W.G., Notkin, D.: Dynamically discovering likely program invariants to support program evolution. IEEE Transactions on Software Engineering 27(2), 99–123 (2001) (A previous version appeared in ICSE '99, Proceedings of the 21st International Conference on Software Engineering, pp. 213–224, Los Angeles, CA, USA (May 19–21, 1999))
6. Ernst, M.D., Perkins, J.H., Guo, P.J., McCamant, S., Pacheco, C., Tschantz, M.S., Xiao, C.: The Daikon system for dynamic detection of likely invariants. Science of Computer Programming (2007)
7. Feng, H., Giffin, J., Huang, Y., Jha, S., Lee, W., Miller, B.: Formalizing Sensitivity in Static Analysis for Intrusion Detection. In: Proceedings of the IEEE Symposium on Security and Privacy, Oakland, CA, May 2004, IEEE Computer Society Press, Los Alamitos (2004)
8. Feng, H., Kolesnikov, O., Fogla, P., Lee, W., Gong, W.: Anomaly Detection Using Call Stack Information. In: Proceedings of the IEEE Symposium on Security and Privacy, May 2003, IEEE Computer Society Press, Los Alamitos (2003)
9. Forrest, S.: A Sense of Self for UNIX Processes. In: Proceedings of the IEEE Symposium on Security and Privacy, Oakland, CA, May 1996, pp. 120–128. IEEE Computer Society Press, Los Alamitos (1996)
10. Gao, D., Reiter, M., Song, D.: Gray-Box Extraction of Execution Graphs for Anomaly Detection. In: Proceedings of the 11th ACM Conference on Computer and Communication Security (CCS), Washington, DC, USA, October 2004, pp. 318–329. ACM Press, New York (2004)
11. Ghosh, A., Wanken, J., Charron, F.: Detecting Anomalous and Unknown Intrusions Against Programs. In: Proceedings of the Annual Computer Security Application Conference (ACSAC'98), Scottsdale, AZ, December 1998, pp. 259–267 (1998)
12. Giffin, J., Jha, S., Miller, B.: Efficient Context-Sensitive Intrusion Detection. In: Proceedings of 11th Network an Distributed System Security Symposium, San Diego, California (February 2004)
13. Halfond, W., Orso, A.: AMNESIA: Analysis and Monitoring for NEutralizing SQL-Injection Attacks. In: Proceedings of the International Conference on Automated Software Engineering (ASE'05), November 2005, pp. 174–183 (2005)
14. Javitz, H.S., Valdes, A.: The SRI IDES Statistical Anomaly Detector. In: Proceedings of the IEEE Symposium on Security and Privacy, May 1991, IEEE Computer Society Press, Los Alamitos (1991)
15. Jovanovic, N., Kruegel, C., Kirda, E.: Pixy: A Static Analysis Tool for Detecting Web Application Vulnerabilities. In: Proceedings of the IEEE Symposium on Security and Privacy, May 2006, IEEE Computer Society Press, Los Alamitos (2006)
16. KDE Project: KDE HTML widget, http://api.kde.org/3.5-api/kdelibs-apidocs/khtml/html/
17. Ko, C., Ruschitzka, M., Levitt, K.: Execution Monitoring of Security-Critical Programs in Distributed Systems: A Specification-based Approach. In: Proceedings of the 1997 IEEE Symposium on Security and Privacy, Oakland, CA, May 1997, pp. 175–187. IEEE Computer Society Press, Los Alamitos (1997)
18. Kruegel, C., Mutz, D., Robertson, W., Valeur, F.: Bayesian Event Classification for Intrusion Detection. In: Omondi, A.R., Sedukhin, S. (eds.) ACSAC 2003. LNCS, vol. 2823, Springer, Heidelberg (2003)
19. Kruegel, C., Mutz, D., Valeur, F., Vigna, G.: On the Detection of Anomalous System Call Arguments. In: Snekkenes, E., Gollmann, D. (eds.) ESORICS 2003. LNCS, vol. 2808, pp. 326–343. Springer, Heidelberg (2003)

20. Kruegel, C., Vigna, G.: Anomaly Detection of Web-based Attacks. In: Proceedings of the 10th ACM Conference on Computer and Communication Security (CCS '03), Washington, DC, October 2003, pp. 251–261. ACM Press, New York (2003)
21. Kruegel, C., Vigna, G., Robertson, W.: A Multi-model Approach to the Detection of Web-based Attacks. Computer Networks 48(5), 717–738 (2005)
22. Lee, S.Y., Low, W.L., Wong, P.Y.: Learning Fingerprints for a Database Intrusion Detection System. In: Gollmann, D., Karjoth, G., Waidner, M. (eds.) ESORICS 2002. LNCS, vol. 2502, Springer, Heidelberg (2002)
23. Lee, W., Stolfo, S., Mok, K.: Mining in a Data-flow Environment: Experience in Network Intrusion Detection. In: Proceedings of the 5th ACM SIGKDD International Conference on Knowledge Discovery & Data Mining (KDD '99), San Diego, CA, August 1999, ACM Press, New York (1999)
24. Mutz, D.: Context-sensitive Multi-model Anomaly Detection. PhD thesis, UCSB (June 2006)
25. Mutz, D., Valeur, F., Kruegel, C., Vigna, G.: Anomalous System Call Detection. ACM Transactions on Information and System Security 9(1), 61–93 (2006)
26. Nguyen-Tuong, A., Guarnieri, S., Greene, D., Evans, D.: Automatically Hardening Web Applications Using Precise Tainting. In: Proceedings of the 20th International Information Security Conference (SEC'05), May 2005, pp. 372–382 (2005)
27. PHP: Session Support in PHP, http://php.net/manual/en/ref.session.php/
28. Sekar, R., Bendre, M., Bollineni, P., Dhurjati, D.: A Fast Automaton-Based Method for Detecting Anomalous Program Behaviors. In: Proceedings of the IEEE Symposium on Security and Privacy, Oakland, CA, May 2001, IEEE Computer Society Press, Los Alamitos (2001)
29. Sekar, R., Venkatakrishnan, V., Basu, S., S, B., DuVarney, D.: Model-carrying code: A practical approach for safe execution of untrusted applications. In: Proceedings of the ACM Symposium on Operating Systems Principles, ACM Press, New York (2003)
30. Su, Z., Wassermann, G.: The Essence of Command Injection Attacks in Web Applications. In: Proceedings of the 33rd Annual Symposium on Principles of Programming Languages (POPL'06), pp. 372–382 (2006)
31. The Computer Security Group at UCSB: libAnomaly Project Homepage, http://www.cs.ucsb.edu/~seclab/projects/libanomaly
32. Valeur, F., Mutz, D., Vigna, G.: A Learning-Based Approach to the Detection of SQL Attacks. In: Julisch, K., Krügel, C. (eds.) DIMVA 2005. LNCS, vol. 3548, Springer, Heidelberg (2005)
33. Vigna, G., Robertson, W., Kher, V., Kemmerer, R.: A Stateful Intrusion Detection System for World-Wide Web Servers. In: Omondi, A.R., Sedukhin, S. (eds.) ACSAC 2003. LNCS, vol. 2823, pp. 34–43. Springer, Heidelberg (2003)
34. Wagner, D., Soto, P.: Mimicry Attacks on Host-Based Intrusion Detection Systems. In: Proceedings of the 9th ACM Conference on Computer and Communications Security, Washington DC, USA, November 2002, pp. 255–264. ACM Press, New York (2002)
35. Xie, Y., Aiken, A.: Static Detection of Security Vulnerabilities in Scripting Languages. In: Proceedings of the 15th USENIX Security Symposium (USENIX'06) (August 2006)
36. Zend: Zend Engine, http://www.zend.com/products/zend_engine

Emulation-Based Detection of Non-self-contained Polymorphic Shellcode

Michalis Polychronakis[1], Kostas G. Anagnostakis[2], and Evangelos P. Markatos[1]

[1] Institute of Computer Science, Foundation for Research & Technology – Hellas
{mikepo,markatos}@ics.forth.gr
[2] Institute for Infocomm Research, Singapore
kostas@i2r.a-star.edu.sg

Abstract. Network-level emulation has recently been proposed as a method for the accurate detection of previously unknown polymorphic code injection attacks. In this paper, we extend network-level emulation along two lines. First, we present an improved execution behavior heuristic that enables the detection of a certain class of non-self-contained polymorphic shellcodes that are currently missed by existing emulation-based approaches. Second, we present two generic algorithmic optimizations that improve the runtime performance of the detector. We have implemented a prototype of the proposed technique and evaluated it using off-the-shelf non-self-contained polymorphic shellcode engines and benign data. The detector achieves a modest processing throughput, which however is enough for decent runtime performance on actual deployments, while it has not produced any false positives. Finally, we report attack activity statistics from a seven-month deployment of our prototype in a production network, which demonstrate the effectiveness and practicality of our approach.

1 Introduction

Along with the phenomenal growth of the Internet, the number of attacks against Internet-connected systems continues to grow at alarming rates. From "one hostile action a week" 15 years ago [7], Internet hosts today confront millions of intrusion attempts every day [34]. Besides the constantly increasing number of security incidents, we are also witnessing a steady increase in attack sophistication. During the last few years, there has been a decline in the number of massive easy-to-spot global epidemics, and a shift towards more targeted and evasive attacks.

For example, attackers have been increasingly using techniques like polymorphism and metamorphism [28] to evade network-level detectors. Using polymorphism, the code in the attack vector —which is usually referred to as *shellcode*— is mutated so that each instance of the same attack acquires a unique byte pattern, thereby making fingerprinting of the whole breed very difficult. In its most naive form, the shellcode is encrypted using a simple algorithm, such as XOR-ing blocks of the original shellcode —which is also known as the *payload*— with a random key, and is prepended with a decryption routine that on runtime unveils and executes the encrypted payload.

Nowadays, the large and diverse number of polymorphic shellcode engines [13, 9, 33, 23, 20, 4, 27, 11, 1], along with their increased sophistication, makes imperative the

C. Kruegel, R. Lippmann, and A. Clark (Eds.): RAID 2007, LNCS 4637, pp. 87–106, 2007.
© Springer-Verlag Berlin Heidelberg 2007

need for effective and robust detection mechanisms. Along with the several research efforts towards this goal, we have recently proposed network-level emulation [22], a passive network monitoring approach for the detection of previously unknown polymorphic shellcode, which is based on the actual execution of network data on a CPU emulator. The principle behind network-level emulation is that the machine code interpretation of arbitrary data results to random code, which, when it is attempted to run on an actual CPU, usually crashes soon, e.g., due to the execution of an illegal instruction. In contrast, if some network request actually contains a polymorphic shellcode, then the shellcode runs normally, exhibiting a certain detectable behavior.

Network-level emulation does not rely on any exploit or vulnerability specific signatures, which allows the detection of previously unknown attacks. Instead, network-level emulation uses a generic heuristic that matches the runtime behavior of polymorphic shellcode. At the same time, the actual execution of the attack code on a CPU emulator makes the detector robust to evasion techniques such as highly obfuscated or self-modifying code. Furthermore, each input is inspected autonomously, which makes the approach effective against targeted attacks.

In this paper, we extend network-level emulation with an improved behavioral heuristic that allows the detection of a new class of polymorphic shellcodes, which are currently missed by the existing approach. The existing network-level emulation technique can detect only self-contained shellcode, which does not make any assumptions about the state of the vulnerable process. In this work, we enable the detection of a certain class of *non-self-contained* polymorphic shellcodes, which take advantage of a certain register that happens to hold the base address of the injected shellcode upon hijacking the instruction pointer. We also present two generic algorithmic optimizations that improve the runtime performance of the detector, and can be applied to network-level emulation irrespectively of the behavioral heuristic used. Finally, we report attack statistics from a real-world deployment of our prototype implementation, which we believe demonstrate the effectiveness and practicality of network-level emulation.

2   Related Work

The constant increase in the amount and sophistication of remote binary code injection attacks, and the consequent increase in the deployment and accuracy of defenses, have led to a coevolution of attack detection methods and evasion techniques.

Early approaches to network-level detection of zero-day worms relied on the identification of common byte sequences that are prevalent among multiple worm instances for the automated generation of NIDS signatures [14, 24]. Such approaches are effective only for fast spreading worms that do not use any form of payload obfuscation. As more tools for shellcode encryption and polymorphism became publicly available [13, 9, 33, 23, 20, 4, 27, 11, 1], subsequent automated signature generation approaches [18, 16] focused on the detection of polymorphic worms by identifying multiple common invariants among different worm instances. However, the first-level classifier on which such methods rely can result to evasion attacks [19].

An inherent limitation of the above approaches is that they are effective only after several instances of the same worm have reached the detector, which makes them

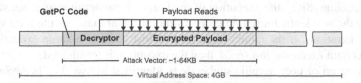

Fig. 1. A typical execution of a polymorphic shellcode using network-level emulation

ineffective against targeted attacks. Content-based anomaly detection can also identify worms that employ a certain degree of polymorphism by alerting on traffic with anomalous content distributions [30, 31], although it is prone to blending attacks [12].

In face of extensive polymorphism, slow propagating worms, and targeted attacks, several research efforts turned to static binary code analysis on network traffic for identifying the presence of polymorphic shellcode. Initial approaches focused on the identification of the sled component that often precedes the shellcode [29, 2]. Recent works aim to detect the polymorphic shellcode itself using various approaches, such as the identification of structural similarities among different worm instances [15], control and data flow analysis [8, 32], or neural networks [21].

Static analysis, however, cannot effectively handle code that employs advanced obfuscation methods, such as indirect jumps and self-modifications, so carefully crafted polymorphic shellcode can evade detection methods based on static analysis. Dynamic code analysis using network-level emulation [22] is not hindered by such obfuscations, and thus can detect even extensively obfuscated shellcodes but is currently able to detect only self-contained polymorphic shellcode. Zhang et al. [35] propose to combine network-level emulation with static and data flow analysis for improving runtime detection performance. However, the proposed method requires the presence of a decryption loop in the shellcode, and thus will miss any polymorphic shellcodes that use unrolled loops or linear code, such as those presented in Sec. 3.

2.1 Network-Level Emulation Overview

We briefly describe some aspects of the network-level emulation detection technique. The interested reader is referred to our previous work [22] for a thorough description of the approach and its implementation details.

The detector inspects the client-initiated data of each network flow, which may contain malicious requests towards vulnerable services. Any server-initiated data, such as the content served by a web server, are ignored. For TCP packets, the application-level stream is reconstructed using TCP stream reassembly. In case of large client-initiated streams, e.g., due to file uploads, only the first 64KB of the stream are inspected. Each input is mapped to a random memory location in the virtual address space of the emulator, as shown in Fig. 1. Since the exact location of the shellcode in the input stream is not known in advance, the emulator repeats the execution multiple times, starting from each and every position of the stream. We refer to complete executions from different positions of the input stream as *execution chains*. Before the beginning of a new execution, the state of the CPU is randomized, while any accidental memory modifications in the addresses where the attack vector has been mapped to are rolled back after the end of each execution. Since the execution of random code sometimes may not stop soon, e.g., due to the accidental formation of loop structures that may execute for a very large number of iterations, if the number of executed instructions in some execution chain reaches a certain *execution threshold*, then the execution is terminated.

The execution of polymorphic shellcode is identified by two key behavioral characteristics: the execution of some form of GetPC code, and the occurrence of several read operations from the memory addresses of the input stream itself, as illustrated in Fig 1. The GetPC code is used to find the absolute address of the injected code, which is mandatory for subsequently decrypting the encrypted payload, and involves the execution of some instruction from the `call` or `fstenv` instruction groups.

3   Non-self-contained Polymorphic Shellcode

The execution behavior of the most widely used type of polymorphic shellcode involves some indispensable operations, which enable network-level emulation to accurately identify it. Some kind of GetPC code is necessary for finding the absolute memory address of the injected code, and, during the decryption process, the memory locations where the encrypted payload resides will necessarily be read. However, recent advances in shellcode development have demonstrated that in certain cases, it is possible to construct a polymorphic shellcode which i) does not rely on any form of GetPC code, and ii) does not read its own memory addresses during the decryption process. A shellcode that uses either or both of these features will thus evade current network-level emulation approaches [22, 35]. In the following, we describe examples of both cases.

3.1   Absence of GetPC Code

The primary operation of polymorphic shellcode is to find the absolute memory address of its own decryptor code. This is mandatory for subsequently referencing the encrypted payload, since memory accesses in the IA-32 architecture can be made only by specifying an absolute memory address in a source or destination operand (except instructions like `pop`, `call`, or `fstenv`, which implicitly read or modify the stack). Although the IA-64 architecture supports an addressing mode whereby an operand can refer to a memory address relatively to the instruction pointer, such a functionality is not available in the IA-32 architecture.

The most common way of finding the absolute address of the injected shellcode is through the use of some form of GetPC code [22]. However, there exist certain exploitation cases in which none of the available GetPC codes can be used, due to restrictions in the byte values that can be used in the attack vector. For example, some vulnerabilities can be exploited only if the attack vector is composed of characters that fall into the ASCII range (or sometimes in even more limited groups such as printable-only characters), in order to avoid being modified by conversion functions like `toupper` or `isprint`. Since the opcodes of both `call` and `fstenv` have bytes that fall into these ranges, they cannot take part in the shellcode. In such cases, a possible workaround is to retrieve the address of the injected code through a register that during exploitation happens to point at the beginning of the buffer where the shellcode resides. If such a register exists, then the decoder can use it to calculate the address of the encrypted body.

```
 0   60000000  6A20          push 0x20             ; ecx points here
 1   60000002  6B3C240B      imul edi,[esp],0xb    ; edi = 0x160
 2   60000006  60            pusha                 ; push all registers
 3   60000007  030C24        add ecx,[esp]         ; ecx = 0x60000160
 4   6000000a  6A11          push 0x11
 5   6000000c  030C24        add ecx,[esp]         ; ecx = 0x60000171
 6   6000000f  6A04          push 0x4              ; encrypted block size
 7   60000011  6826191413    push 0x13141926
 8   60000016  5F            pop edi               ; edi = 0x13141926
 9   60000017  0139          add [ecx],edi         ; [60000171] = "ABCD"
10   60000019  030C24        add ecx,[esp]         ; ecx = 0x60000175
11   6000001c  6817313F1E    push 0x1e3f3117
12   60000021  5F            pop edi               ; edi = 0x1E3F3117
13   60000022  0139          add [ecx],edi         ; [60000175] = "EFGH"
14   60000024  030C24        add ecx,[esp]         ; ecx = 0x60000179
     . . .
```

Fig. 2. Execution trace of a shellcode produced by the "Avoid UTF8/tolower" encoder. When the first instruction is executed, ecx happens to point to address 0x60000000.

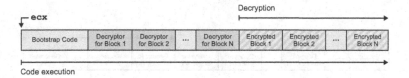

Fig. 3. Schematic representation of the decryption process for "Avoid UTF8/tolower" shellcode

Skape has recently published an alphanumeric shellcode engine that uses this technique [27]. Fig. 2 shows the execution trace of a shellcode generated using the implementation of the engine contained in Metasploit Framework v3.0 [1]. In this example, the register that is assumed to hold the base address of the shellcode is ecx. The shellcode has been mapped to address 0x60000000, which corresponds to the beginning of the vulnerable buffer. When the control flow of the vulnerable process is diverted to the shellcode, the ecx register already happens to hold the value 0x60000000. Instructions 0–5 calculate the starting address of the encrypted payload (0x60000171) based on its length and the absolute address contained in ecx.

The decryption process begins with instruction 7. An interesting characteristic of the decryptor is that it does not use any loop structure. Instead, separate transformation blocks comprising four instructions each (7–10, 11–14, ...) handle the decryption of different 4-byte blocks of the encrypted payload, as illustrated in Fig. 3. This results to a completely sequential flow of control for the whole decryption process. At the same time, however, the total size of the shellcode increases significantly, since for each four bytes of encrypted payload, an 11-byte transformation instruction block is needed.

3.2 Absence of Self-references

Another common characteristic of polymorphic shellcodes is that they carry the encrypted payload within the same attack vector, right after the decryptor code, as shown in Fig. 1. During execution, the decryptor necessarily makes several memory reads from the addresses of the encrypted payload in order to decrypt it. These self-references can be used as a strong indication of the execution of polymorphic shellcode [22]. However,

```
0    bfff0000  54              push esp              ; esp points here
1    bfff0001  58              pop eax               ; eax = BFFF0000
2    bfff0002  2D6C2D2D2D      sub eax,0x2d2d2d6c    ; eax = 92D1D294
3    bfff0007  2D7A555858      sub eax,0x5858557a    ; eax = 3A797D1A
4    bfff000c  2D7A7A7A7A      sub eax,0x7a7a7a7a    ; eax = BFFF02A0
5    bfff0011  50              push eax
6    bfff0012  5C              pop esp               ; esp = BFFF02A0
7    bfff0013  252D252123      and eax,0x2321252d    ; eax = 20012020
8    bfff0018  2542424244      and eax,0x44424242    ; eax = 00000000
9    bfff001d  2D2D2D2D2D      sub eax,0x2d2d2d2d    ; eax = D2D2D2D3
10   bfff0022  2D2D252D25      sub eax,0x252d252d    ; eax = ADA5ADA6
11   bfff0027  2D61675E65      sub eax,0x655e6761    ; eax = 48474645
12   bfff002c  50              push eax              ; [BFFF029C] = "EFGH"
13   bfff002d  2D2D2D2D2D      sub eax,0x2d2d2d2d    ; eax = 1B1A1918
14   bfff0032  2D5E5E5E5E      sub eax,0x5e5e5e5e    ; eax = BCBBBABA
15   bfff0037  2D79787878      sub eax,0x78787879    ; eax = 44434241
16   bfff003c  50              push eax              ; [BFFF0298] = "ABCD"
     . . .
```

Fig. 4. Execution trace of a shellcode produced by the "Encode" engine. The shellcode is assumed to be placed on the stack, and esp initially points to the first instruction.

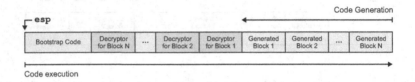

Fig. 5. Schematic representation of the decryption process for the "Encode" engine

it is possible to construct a shellcode that, although it carries an encrypted payload, will not result to any memory reads from its own memory addresses.

Figure 4 shows the execution trace of a shellcode produced by an adapted version of the "Encode" shellcode engine [26], developed by Skape according to a previous description of Riley Eller [11]. In this case, the vulnerable buffer is assumed to be located on the stack, so esp happens to point to the beginning of the shellcode. Instructions 0–6 are used to set esp to point far ahead of the decryptor code (in higher memory addresses). Then, after zeroing eax (instructions 7–8), the decryption process begins, again using separate decryption blocks (9–12, 13–16, ...) for each four bytes of the encrypted payload. However, in this case, each decryption block consists only of arithmetic instructions with a register and an immediate operand, and ends with a push instruction. Each group of arithmetic instructions calculates the final value of the corresponding payload block, which is then pushed on the stack. In essence, the data of the encrypted payload are integrated into the immediate values of the arithmetic instructions, so no actual encrypted data exist in the initial attack vector.

Due to the nature of the stack, the decrypted payload is produced backwards, starting with its last four bytes. When the final decrypted block is pushed on the stack, the flow of control of the decryptor will "meet" the newly built payload, and the execution will continue normally, as depicted in Fig. 5. Notice that during the whole execution of the shellcode, only two memory reads are performed by the two pop instructions, but not from any of the addresses of the injected code.

4   Non-self-contained Polymorphic Shellcode Detection

4.1   Approach

Achieving the effective detection of a certain class of polymorphic shellcodes using network-level emulation requires the fulfillment of two basic requirements. First, the detector should be able to accurately reproduce the execution of the shellcode in exactly the same way as if it would run within the context of the vulnerable process. Second, it should be possible to identify a certain execution behavior pattern that can be used as a strict heuristic for the effective differentiation between the execution of polymorphic shellcode and random code. In this section, we discuss these two dimensions regarding the detection of non-self-contained shellcode.

Enabling Non-self-contained Shellcode Execution. As discussed in the previous section, some shellcodes rely on a register that happens to contain the base address of the injected code, instead of using some form of GetPC code. Such shellcodes cannot be executed properly by the existing network-level emulation approach, since before each execution, all general purpose registers are set to random values. Thus, the register that is assumed to hold the base address will not have been set to the correct value, and the decryption process will fail. Therefore, our first aim is to create the necessary conditions that will allow the shellcode to execute correctly. In essence, this requires to set the register that is used by the shellcode for finding its base address to the proper value.

The emulator maps each new input stream to an arbitrary memory location in its virtual memory. Thus, it can know in advance the absolute address of the hypothetical buffer where the shellcode has been mapped, and as a corollary, the address of the starting position of each new execution chain. For a given position in the buffer that corresponds to the beginning of a non-self-contained shellcode, if the base register has been initialized to point to the address of that position, then the shellcode will execute correctly. Since we always know the base address of each execution chain, we can always set the base register to the proper value.

The problem is that it is not possible to know in advance which one of the eight general purpose registers will be used by the shellcode for getting a reference to its base address. For instance, it might be ecx or esp, as it was the case in the two examples of the previous section, or in fact any other register, depending on the exploit. To address this issue, we initialize all eight general purpose registers to hold the absolute address of the first instruction of each execution chain. Except the dependence on the base register, all other operations of the shellcode will not be affected from such a setting, since the rest of the code is self-contained. For instance, going back to the execution trace of Fig. 2, when the emulator begins executing the code starting with the instruction at address 0x60000000, all registers will have been set to 0x60000000. Thus, the calculations for setting ecx to point to the encrypted payload will proceed correctly, and the 9th instruction will indeed decrypt the first four bytes of the payload at address 0x60000171. Note that the stack grows downwards, towards lower memory addresses, in the opposite direction of code execution, so setting esp to point to the beginning of the shellcode does not affect its correct execution, e.g. due to push instructions that write on the stack.

Behavioral Heuristic. Having achieved the correct execution of non-self-contained shellcode on the network-level emulator, the next step is to identify a strict behavioral pattern that will be used as a heuristic for the accurate discrimination between malicious and benign network data. Such a heuristic should rely to as few assumptions about the structure of the shellcode as possible, in order to be resilient to evasion attacks, while at the same time should be specific enough so as to minimize the risk of false positives.

Considering the execution behavior of the shellcodes presented in the previous section, we can make the following observations. First, the absence of any form of GetPC code precludes the reliance on the presence of specific instructions as an indication of non-self contained shellcode execution, as was the case with the `call` or `fstenv` groups of instructions, which are a crucial part of the GetPC code. Indeed, all operations of both shellcodes could have been implemented in many different ways, using various combinations of instructions and operands, especially when considering exploits in which the use of a broader range of byte values is allowed in the attack vector. Second, we observe that the presence of reads from the memory locations of the input buffer during the decryption process is not mandatory, as demonstrated in Sec. 3.2, so this also cannot be used as an indication of non-self-contained shellcode execution.

However, it is still possible to identify some indispensable behavioral characteristics that are inherent to all such non-self-contained polymorphic shellcodes. An essential characteristic of polymorphic shellcodes in general is that during execution, they eventually unveil their initially concealed payload, and this can only be done by writing the decrypted payload to some memory area. Therefore, the execution of a polymorphic shellcode will unavoidably result to several memory writes to *different* memory locations. We refer to such write operations to different memory locations as *"unique writes."* Additionally, after the end of the decryption process, the flow of control will inevitably be transferred from the decryptor code to the newly revealed code. This means that the instruction pointer will move *at least once* from addresses of the input buffer that have not been altered before (the code of the decryptor), to addresses that have already been written during the same execution (the code of the decrypted payload). For the sake of brevity, we refer to instructions that correspond to code at any memory address that has been written during the same execution chain as *"wx-instructions."*

It is important to note that the decrypted payload may not be written in the same buffer where the attack vector resides [20]. Furthermore, one could construct a shellcode in which the unique writes due to the decryption process will be made to non-adjacent locations. Finally, wx-instructions may be interleaved with non-wx-instructions, e.g., due to self-modifications before the actual decryption, so the instruction pointer may switch several times between unmodified and modified memory locations.

Based on the above observations, we derive the following detection heuristic: *if at the end of an execution chain the emulator has performed W unique writes and has executed X wx-instructions, then the execution chain corresponds to a non-self-contained polymorphic shellcode.* The intuition behind this heuristic is that during the execution of random code, although there will probably be a lot of random write operations to arbitrary memory addresses, we speculate that the probability of the control flow to reach such a modified memory address during the same execution will be low. In the following, we elaborate on the details behind this heuristic.

Unique memory writes. The number of unique writes (W) in the heuristic serves just as a hint for the fact that at least a couple of memory locations have been modified during the same execution chain—a prerequisite for the existence of any wx-instructions. The parameter W cannot be considered as a qualitatively strong detection heuristic because the execution of random code sometimes exhibits a large number of accidental memory writes. The emulator does not have a view of the vulnerable process' memory layout, and thus cannot know which memory addresses are valid and writable, so it blindly accepts all write operations to any location, and keeps track of the written values in its own virtual memory. The decryption process of a polymorphic shellcode will too result to tens or even hundreds of memory writes. This makes the number of unique writes *per se* a weak indication for the execution of polymorphic shellcode, since random code sometimes results to a comparable number of writes.

Although this does not allow us to derive a threshold value for W that would be reached only during the execution of polymorphic shellcode, we can derive a lower bound for W, given that any regularly sized encrypted payload will require quite a few memory writes in order to be decrypted. Considering that the decryption of a 32-byte payload —a rather conservatively small size for a meaningful payload, as discussed in Sec. 5.2— would require at least 8 memory writes (using instructions with 4-byte operands), we set $W = 8$. This serves as a "negative" heuristic for deciding quickly the absence of shellcode, which effectively filters out a lot of execution chains with very few memory writes that cannot correspond to any functional polymorphic shellcode.

Execution of decrypted instructions. Although the number of unique writes alone cannot provide a strong positive indication for shellcode detection, we expected that the number of wx-instructions in random code would be very low, which would allow for deriving a definite detection threshold that would never be reached by random code. A prerequisite for the execution of code from a recently modified memory address is that the instruction pointer should first be changed to point to that memory address. Intuitively, the odds for this to happen in random code are quite low, given that most of the modified locations will be dispersed across the whole virtual address space of the emulator, due to the random nature of memory writes. Even if the control flow ever lands on such a memory address, most probably it will contain just a few valid instructions. In contrast, self-decrypting shellcode will result to the execution of tens or even hundreds of wx-instructions, due to the execution of the decrypted payload.

We conducted some preliminary experiments using real network traces and randomly generated data in order to explore the behavior of random code in terms of wx-instructions. The percentage of instruction chains with more than 8 unique writes and at least one wx-instruction was in the order of 0.01% for artificial binary data, while it was negligible for artificial ASCII data and real network traces. However, there were some rare cases of streams in which some execution chain contained as much as 60 wx-instructions. As we discuss in Sec. 5.2, the execution of the decrypted payload may involve less than 60 wx-instructions, so the range in which an accurate detection threshold value for X could exist is somehow blurred. Although one could consider the percentage of these outlying streams as marginal, and thus the false positive ratio as acceptable, it is still possible to derive a stricter detection heuristic that will allow for improved resilience to false positives.

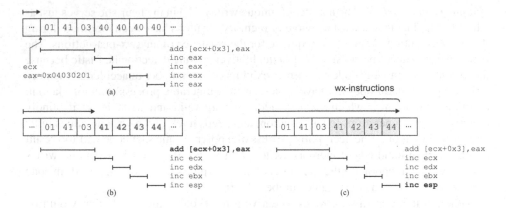

Fig. 6. An example of accidental occurrence of wx-instructions in random code

Second-stage execution. The existence of some execution chains with a large number of wx-instructions in random code is directly related to the initialization of the general purpose registers before each new execution. Setting all registers to point to the address of the first instruction of the execution chain facilitates the accidental modification of the input stream itself, e.g., in memory addresses farther (in higher memory addresses) from the starting position of the execution chain. An example of this effect is presented in Fig. 6. Initially (Fig. 6a), when the flow of control reaches the instruction starting with byte 01, ecx happens to point to the same instruction, and eax holds the value 0x04030201. The effective address calculation in add [ecx+0x3], eax (Fig. 6b) involves ecx, and its execution results to a 4-byte memory write within the buffer, right after the add instruction. This simple self-modification causes the execution of four wx-instructions (Fig. 6c). Note that after the execution of these four wx-instructions, the flow of control will continue normally with the subsequent instructions in the buffer, so the same effect may occur multiple times.

In order to mitigate this effect, we introduce the concept of *second-stage execution.* For a given position in the input stream, if the execution chain that starts from this position results to more than 8 unique writes and has at least 14 wx-instructions,[1] then it is ignored, and the execution from this position is repeated eight times with eight different register initializations. Each time, only one of the eight general purpose registers is set to point to the starting location. The remaining seven registers are set to random values.

The rationale is that a non-self-contained shellcode that uses some register for finding its base address will run correctly both in the initial execution, when all registers point to the starting position, as well as in one of the eight subsequent second-stage executions—the one in which the particular base register being used by the decryptor will have been properly initialized. At the same time, if some random code enters second-stage execution, the chances for the accidental occurrence of a large number of wx-instructions in any of the eight new execution chains are significantly lower, since now only one of the eight registers happens to point within the input buffer.

---

[1] As discussed in Sec. 5.2, a functional payload results to at least 14 wx-instructions.

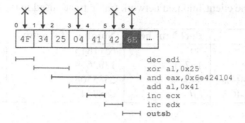

Fig. 7. Example of an illegal instruction path

Although second-stage execution incurs an eight times increase in the emulation overhead, its is only triggered for a negligible fraction of execution chains, so it does not incur any noticeable runtime performance degradation. At the same time, it results to a much lower worst-case number of accidental wx-instructions in benign streams, as shown in Sec. 5.1, which allows for deriving a clear-cut threshold for X.

4.2 Performance Optimizations

Skipping Illegal Paths. The main reason that network-level emulation is practically feasible and achieves a decent processing throughput is because, in the most common case, the execution of benign streams usually terminates early, after the execution of only a few instructions. Indeed, arbitrary data will result to random code that usually contains illegal opcodes or privileged instructions, which cannot take part in the execution of a functional shellcode. Although there exist only a handful of illegal opcodes in the IA-32 architecture, there exist 25 privileged instructions with one-byte opcodes, and several others with multi-byte opcodes. In the rest of this section, we use the term illegal instruction to refer to both privileged and actually illegal instructions.

A major cause of overhead in network-level emulation is that for each input stream, the emulator starts a new execution from each and every position in the stream. However, since the occurrence of illegal instructions is common in random code, there may be some instruction chains which all end to the same illegal instruction. After the execution of the first of these chains terminates (due to the illegal instruction), then any subsequent execution chains that share the same final instruction path with the first one will definitely end up to the same illegal instruction, if i) the path does not contain any control transfer instructions, ii) none of the instructions in the path was the result of a self-modification, and iii) the path does not contain any instruction with a memory destination operand. The last requirement is necessary in order to avoid potential self-modifications on the path that may alter its control flow. Thus, whenever the flow of control reaches any of the instructions in the path, the execution can stop immediately.

Consider for example the execution chain that starts at position 0 in the example of Fig. 7. Upon its termination, the emulator backtracks the instruction path and marks each instruction until any of the above requirements is violated, or the beginning of the input stream is reached. If any subsequent execution chain reaches a marked instruction, then the execution ceases immediately. Furthermore, the execution chains that would begin from positions 1, 3, 5, and 6, can now be skipped altogether.

Table 1. Details of the client-initiated network traffic traces used in the experimental evaluation

Name	Port Number	Number of streams	Total size
HTTP	80	6511815	5.6 GB
NetBIOS	137–139	1392679	1.5 GB
Microsoft-ds	445	2585308	3.8 GB
FORTH-ICS	*all*	668754	821 MB

Kernel Memory Accesses. The network-level detector does not have any information about the vulnerable process targeted by a particular attack. As already discussed, the emulator assumes that all accesses to any memory address are valid. In reality, only a small subset of these memory accesses would have succeeded, since the hypothetical vulnerable process would have mapped only a small subset of pages from the whole 4GB virtual memory space. Thus, memory writes outside the input buffer or the stack proceed normally and the emulator tracks the written values, while memory reads from previously unknown locations are executed without returning any meaningful data, since their contents are not available to the network-level detector. The execution cannot stop on such unknown memory references, since otherwise an attacker could hinder detection by interspersing instructions that read arbitrary data from memory locations known in advance to belong to the address space of the vulnerable process [22].

The network-level emulation approach assumes that the whole 4GB of virtual memory may be accessible by the shellcode. However, user-level processes cannot access the address space of the OS kernel. In Linux, the kernel address space begins at address 0xC0000000 and takes up the whole upper 1GB of the 4GB space. In Windows, the upper half of the 4GB space is allocated for kernel use. A functional shellcode would never try to access a memory address in the kernel address space, so any instructions in random code that accidentally try to access some kernel memory location can be considered illegal. For simplicity, the emulator assumes as legal all memory accesses up to 0xBFFFFFFF, i.e., excludes only the common kernel space of both OSes, since it cannot know in advance which OS is being targeted.

5   Experimental Evaluation

5.1   Deriving a Robust Detection Threshold

The detection algorithm is based on a strict behavioral pattern that matches some execution characteristics of non-self-contained polymorphic shellcode. In order to be effective and practically applicable, a heuristic based on such a behavioral pattern should not falsely identify benign data as polymorphic shellcode. In this section, we explore the resilience of the detector to false positives using a large and diverse attack-free dataset.

We accumulated full payload packet traces of frequently attacked ports captured at FORTH-ICS and the University of Crete across several different periods. We also captured a two hour long trace of all the TCP traffic of the access link that connects FORTH-ICS to the Internet. Since we are interested in client-initiated traffic, which contains requests to network services, we keep only the packets that correspond to the

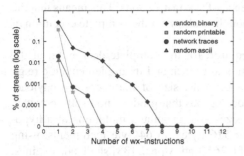 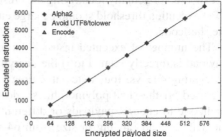

Fig. 8. Number of wx-instructions found in benign streams

Fig. 9. Number of instructions required for complete decryption

client-side stream of each TCP flow. For large flows, which for example may correspond to file uploads, we keep the packets of the first 64KB of the stream. Trace details are summarized in Table 1. Note that the initial size of the FORTH-ICS trace, before extracting the client-initiated only traffic, was 106GB. We also generated a large amount of artificial traces using three different kinds of uniformly distributed random content: binary data, ASCII-only data, and printable-only characters. For each type, we generated four million streams, totaling more than 160GB of data.

We tested our prototype implementation of the detection heuristic with second-stage execution enabled using the above dataset, and measured the maximum number of accidental wx-instructions among all execution chains of each stream. The execution threshold of the emulator was set to 65536 instructions. Figure 8 presents the results for the different types of random data, as well as for the real network streams (the category "network traces" refers collectively to all network traces listed in Table 1). We see that random binary data exhibit the largest number of wx-instructions, followed by printable data and real network traffic. From the four million random binary streams, 0.8072% contain an execution chain with one wx-instruction, while in the worst case, 0.00014% of the streams resulted to seven wx-instructions. In all cases, no streams were found to contain an execution chain with more than seven wx-instructions.

Based on the above results, we can derive a lower bound for the number of wx-instructions (parameter X of the detection heuristic) that should be found in an execution chain for flagging the corresponding code as malicious. Setting $X=8$ allows for no false positives in the above dataset. However, larger values are preferable since they are expected to provide even more improved resilience to false positives.

5.2 Non-self-contained Shellcode Detection

CPU execution threshold. As discussed in Sec. 4.1, the execution of non-self-contained shellcode will exhibit several wx-instructions, due to the execution of the decrypted payload. However, a crucial observation is that most of these wx-instructions will occur *after* the end of the decryption process, except perhaps any self-modifications during the bootstrap phase of the decryptor [22,33]. Thus, the emulator should execute the shellcode for long enough in order for the decryption to complete, and then for the decrypted payload to execute, for actually identifying the presence of wx-instructions. This means that the CPU execution threshold should be large enough to allow for the complete execution of the shellcode.

The number of executed instructions required for the complete decryption of the payload is directly related to i) the decryption approach and its implementation (e.g., decrypting one vs. four bytes at a time), and ii) the size of the encrypted payload. We used off-the-shelf polymorphic shellcode engines that produce non-self-contained shellcode to encrypt payloads of different sizes. We generated mutations of a hypothetical payload ranging in size from 64 to 576 bytes, in 64-byte increments, using the Avoid UTF8/tolower [1, 27], Encoder [11, 26], and Alpha2 [33] shellcode engines. The size of the largest IA-32 payload contained in the Metasploit Framework v3.0, windows/adduser/reverse_http, is 553 bytes, so we chose a slightly larger value of 576 bytes as a worst case scenario.

Figure 9 shows the number of executed instructions for the complete decryption of the payload, for different payload sizes. As expected, the number of instructions increases linearly with the payload size, since all engines spend an equal amount of instructions per encrypted byte during decryption. Alpha2 executes considerably more instructions compared to the other two engines, and in the worst case, for a 576-byte payload, takes 6374 instructions to complete. Thus, we should choose an execution threshold significantly larger than the 2048 instructions that is suggested in the existing network-level emulation approach [22].

Setting a threshold value for X. A final dimension that we need to explore is the minimum number of wx-instructions (X) that should be expected during shellcode execution. As we have already mentioned, this number is directly related to the size of the encrypted payload: the smaller the size of the concealed code, the fewer the number of wx-instructions that will be executed. As shown in the previous section, the threshold value for X should be set to at least 8, in order to avoid potential false positives. Thus, if the execution of the decrypted payload would result to a comparable number of wx-instructions, then we would not be able to derive a robust detection threshold.

Fortunately, typical payloads found in remote exploits usually consist of much more than eight instructions. In order to verify the ability of our prototype implementation to execute the decrypted payload upon the end of the decryption process, we tested it with the IA-32 payloads available in Metasploit. Note that although the network-level emulator cannot correctly execute system calls or follow memory accesses to addresses of the vulnerable process, whenever such instructions are encountered, the execution continues normally (e.g., in case of an int 80 instruction, the code continues as if the system call had returned). In the worst case, the linux/x86/exec family of payloads, which have the smallest size of 36 bytes, result to the execution of 14 instructions. All other payloads execute a larger number of instructions. Thus, based on the number of executed instructions of the smallest payload, we set $X=14$. This is a rather conservative value, given that in practice the vast majority of remote exploits in the wild are targeting Windows hosts, so in the common case the number of wx-instructions of the decrypted payload will be much higher.

Payloads targeting Linux hosts usually have a very small size due to the direct invocation of system calls through the int 80 instruction. In contrast, payloads for Windows hosts usually involve a much higher number of instructions. Windows shellcode usually does not involve the direct use of system calls (although this is sometimes possible [5]), since their mapping often changes across different OS versions, and some crucial operations, e.g., the creation of a socket, are not readily offered through system calls. Instead, Windows shellcode usually relies on system API calls that offer a wide range of advanced functionality (e.g., the ability to download a file from a remote host through HTTP using just one call). This, however, requires to first locate the necessary library functions, which involves finding the base address of kernel32.dll, then resolving symbol addresses, and so on. All these operations result to the execution of a considerable number of instructions.

In any case, even a conservative value for $X=14$, which effectively detects both Linux and Windows shellcode, is larger enough than the seven accidental wx-instructions that were found in benign data, and thus allows for a strong heuristic with even more improved resilience to false positives.

5.3 Processing Throughput

In this section, we evaluate the raw processing throughput of the proposed detection algorithm. We have implemented the new detection heuristic on our existing prototype network-level detector [22], which is based on a custom IA-32 CPU emulator that uses interpretive emulation. We measured the user time required for processing the network traces presented in Table 1, and computed the processing throughput for different values of the CPU execution threshold. The detector was running on a PC equipped with a 2.53GHz Pentium 4 processor and 1GB RAM, running Debian Linux (kernel v2.6.18). Figure 10 presents the results for the four different network traces.

As expected, the processing throughput decreases as the CPU execution threshold increases, since more cycles are spent on streams with very long execution chains or seemingly endless loops. We measured that in the worst case, for port 445 traffic, 3.2% of the streams reach the CPU execution threshold due to some loop when using a threshold higher than 8192. This percentage remains almost the same even when using a threshold as high as 131072 instructions, which means that these loops would require a prohibitively large number of iterations until completion.

Overall, the runtime performance has been slightly improved compared to our previous network-level emulation prototype. Although the algorithmic optimizations presented in Sec. 4.2 offer considerable runtime performance improvements, any gain is compensated by the more heavy utilization of the virtual memory subsystem and the need to frequently undo accidental self-modifications in the input stream.

Port 80 traffic exhibits the worst performance among all traces, with an almost constant throughput that drops from 12 to 10 Mbit/s. The throughput is not affected by the CPU execution threshold because i) the zero-delimited chunk optimization[2] is not effective because HTTP traffic rarely contains any null bytes, and ii) the execution chains

---

[2] Given that in the vast majority of exploits the attack vector cannot contain a null byte, the detector skips any zero-byte delimited regions smaller than 50 bytes, since they are too small to contain a functional polymorphic shellcode [22].

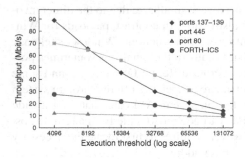 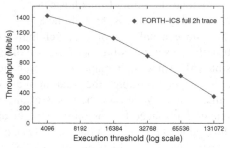

Fig. 10. Raw processing throughput for different execution thresholds

Fig. 11. Raw processing throughput for the complete 2-hour trace

of port 80 traffic have a negligible amount of endless loops, so a higher CPU execution threshold does not result to the execution of more instructions due to extra loop iterations. However, ASCII data usually result to very long and dense execution chains with many one or two byte instructions, which consume a lot of CPU cycles.

We should stress that our home-grown CPU emulator is highly unoptimized, and the use of interpretive emulation results to orders of magnitude slowdown compared to native execution. It is expected that an optimized CPU emulator like QEMU [6] would boost performance, and we plan in our future work to proceed with such a change.

Nevertheless, the low processing throughput of the current implementation does not prevent it from being practically usable. In the contrary, since the vast majority of the traffic is server-initiated, the detector inspects only a small subset of the total traffic of the monitored link. For example, web requests are usually considerably smaller than the served content. Note that all client-initiated streams are inspected, in both directions. Furthermore, even in case of large client-initiated flows, e.g., due to file uploads, the detector inspects only the first 64KB of the client stream, so again the vast amount of the traffic will not be inspected. Indeed, as shown in Fig. 11, when processing the complete 106GB long trace captured at FORTH-ICS, the processing throughput is orders of magnitude higher. Thus, the detector can easily sustain the traffic rate of the monitored link, which for this 2-hour long trace was on average around 120 Mbit/s.

6   Real-World Deployment

In this section, we present some attack activity results from a real-world deployment of our prototype detector implementation. The detector is installed on a passive monitoring sensor that inspects the traffic of the access link that connects part of an educational network with hundreds of hosts to the Internet. The detector has been continuously operational since 7 November 2006, except a two-day downtime on January.

As of 14 June 2007, the detector has captured 21795 attacks targeting nine different ports. An overall view of the attack activity during these seven months is presented in Fig. 12. The upper part of the figure shows the attack activity according to the targeted port. From the 21795 attacks, 14956 (68.62%) were launched from 5747 external IP addresses (red dots), while the rest 6839 (31.38%) originated from 269 infected hosts in

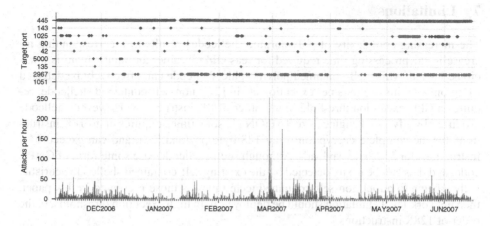

Fig. 12. Overall attack activity from a real-world deployment of our prototype detector

the monitored network (gray dots). Almost one third of the internal attacks came from a single IP address, using the same exploit against port 445. The bottom part of the figure shows the number of attacks per hour of day. There are occasions with hundreds of attacks in one hour, mostly due to bursts from a single source that horizontally attacks all active hosts in local neighboring subnets. The vast majority of the attacks (88%) target port 445. Interestingly, however, there also exist attacks to less commonly attacked ports like 1025, 1051, and 5000. We should note that for all captured attacks the emulator was able to successfully decrypt the payload, while so far has zero false positives.

For each identified attack, our prototype detector generates i) an alert file with generic attack information and the execution trace of the shellcode, ii) a raw dump of the re-assembled TCP stream, iii) a full payload trace of all attack traffic (both directions) in libpcap format,[3] and iv) the raw contents of the modified addresses in the virtual memory of the emulator, i.e., the decrypted shellcode.

Although we have not thoroughly analyzed all captured attacks, we can get a rough estimate on the diversity of the different exploitation tools, worms, or bots that launched these attacks, based on a simple analysis of the decrypted payloads of the captured poly-morphic shellcodes. Computing the MD5 hash of the decrypted payload for all above attacks resulted to 1021 unique payloads. However, grouping further these 1021 pay-loads according to their size, resulted to 64 different payload size groups. By manu-ally inspecting some of the shellcodes with same or similar lengths, but different MD5 hashes, we observed that in most cases the actual payload code was the same, but the seeding URL or IP address from where the "download and execute" shellcode would retrieve the actual malware was different. Our results are in accordance with previous studies [17] and clearly show that polymorphic shellcodes are extensively used in the wild, although in most cases they employ naive encryption methods, mostly for con-cealing restricted payload bytes.

---

[3] Anonymized full payload traces of some attacks are available from
http://lobster.ics.forth.gr/traces/

7   Limitations

The increasing complexity of polymorphic shellcodes results to a corresponding increase in the processing time required for reasoning weather an input stream is malicious. Indeed, while self-contained polymorphic shellcode can effectively be detected using only 2K instructions per execution chain [22], non-self-contained shellcode, requires a CPU execution threshold in the order of 8K instructions. However, shellcode produced by advanced engines like TAPiON [4] sometimes requires up to 16K instructions for the complete decryption of an 128-byte payload [22], and can exceed 64K instructions for 512-byte payloads. Although such shellcodes use some form of GetPC code, and thus can be easily detected by the existing self-contained shellcode heuristic, if they begin to adopt non-self-contained techniques as those presented in this paper, then network-level emulation should be deployed with high execution thresholds, in the order of 128K instructions.

Fortunately, even in case we have to spend so many cycles per inspected input, network-level emulation is still practical, although with a reduced throughput, as we showed in Sec. 5.3. However, in the extreme case, an attacker could construct a decryptor that could spend millions of instructions, maybe even before the actual decryption process has begun at all, just for reaching the execution threshold before revealing any signs of polymorphic behavior [22]. Such "endless" loops are a well-known problem in the area of dynamic code analysis, and we are not aware of any effective solution so far. Fortunately, the percentage of benign streams that reach the execution threshold is under 3.2%, as discussed in Sec. 5.3, so if attackers start to employ such evasion techniques, network-level emulation can still be useful as a first-stage anomaly detector for application-aware NIDS like shadow honeypots [3], by considering as suspicious all streams that reach the execution threshold.

Finally, here we have considered only the class of non-self-contained shellcode that takes advantage of some register to get a reference to the absolute address of the injected code in order to decrypt. However, it could be possible to construct a shellcode that during decryption uses some data or code from memory locations with a priori known contents, which should remain constant across all vulnerable systems. Since the network-level detector lacks any host-level information, it would not be able to execute such shellcode properly. In general, however, the use of hard-coded addresses is avoided because it results in more fragile code [25], especially since address space randomization has become prevalent in popular OSes, and significantly complicates the implementation of polymorphic shellcode engines. In our future work, we plan to explore ways to augment the network-level detector with host-level context [10] for enabling the detection of a broader class of non-self-contained shellcodes.

8   Conclusion

In this paper, we have presented a novel approach for the detection of a certain class of non-self-contained polymorphic shellcodes using dynamic code analysis of network-level data. We have extended previous work on network-level emulation to correctly handle the execution and identify the behavior of polymorphic shellcodes that do not use any form of GetPC code, but instead rely on some register that happens during exploitation to contain the base address of the injected code. This demonstrates that in certain cases where some certain host-level state is used by the shellcode, detection at the network level is still possible.

Such advanced analysis comes at the cost of spending more CPU cycles per input, which reduces the runtime throughput of the detector, but still allows it to achieve a decent performance on real-world deployments. However, certain evasion methods are still possible, and the problem of effectively tackling them at the network-level remains open. Nevertheless, we believe that the ability to accurately detect previously unknown polymorphic shellcodes with virtually zero false positives, and the simplicity of its deployment, make network-level emulation an effective and practical defense method.

References

1. Metasploit project (2006), http://www.metasploit.com/
2. Akritidis, P., Markatos, E.P., Polychronakis, M., Anagnostakis, K.: STRIDE: Polymorphic sled detection through instruction sequence analysis. In: Proceedings of the 20th IFIP International Information Security Conference (IFIP/SEC) (June 2005)
3. Anagnostakis, K., Sidiroglou, S., Akritidis, P., Xinidis, K., Markatos, E., Keromytis, A.D.: Detecting targeted attacks using shadow honeypots. In: Proceedings of the 14th USENIX Security Symposium, August 2005, pp. 129–144 (2005)
4. Bania, P.: TAPiON (2005), http://pb.specialised.info/all/tapion/
5. Bania, P.: Windows Syscall Shellcode (2005),
   http://www.securityfocus.com/infocus/1844
6. Bellard, F.: QEMU, a fast and portable dynamic translator. In: Proceedings of the USENIX Annual Technical Conference, FREENIX Track, pp. 41–46 (2005)
7. Bellovin, S.M.: There be dragons. In: Proceedings of the Third USENIX UNIX Security Symposium, pp. 1–16 (1992)
8. Chinchani, R., Berg, E.V.D.: A fast static analysis approach to detect exploit code inside network flows. In: Valdes, A., Zamboni, D. (eds.) RAID 2005. LNCS, vol. 3858, Springer, Heidelberg (2006)
9. Detristan, T., Ulenspiegel, T., Malcom, Y., Underduk, M.: Polymorphic shellcode engine using spectrum analysis. Phrack 11(61) (August 2003)
10. Dreger, H., Kreibich, C., Paxson, V., Sommer, R.: Enhancing the accuracy of network-based intrusion detection with host-based context. In: Julisch, K., Krügel, C. (eds.) DIMVA 2005. LNCS, vol. 3548, Springer, Heidelberg (2005)
11. Eller, R.: Bypassing MSB Data Filters for Buffer Overflow Exploits on Intel Platforms,
    http://community.core-sdi.com/~juliano/bypass-msb.txt
12. Fogla, P., Sharif, M., Perdisci, R., Kolesnikov, O., Lee, W.: Polymorphic blending attacks. In: Proceedings of the 15th USENIX Security Symposium (2006)
13. K2: ADMmutate (2001), http://www.ktwo.ca/ADMmutate-0.8.4.tar.gz
14. Kim, H.-A., Karp, B.: Autograph: Toward automated, distributed worm signature detection. In: Proceedings of the 13th USENIX Security Symposium, pp. 271–286 (2004)
15. Kruegel, C., Kirda, E., Mutz, D., Robertson, W., Vigna, G.: Polymorphic worm detection using structural information of executables. In: Valdes, A., Zamboni, D. (eds.) RAID 2005. LNCS, vol. 3858, Springer, Heidelberg (2006)

16. Li, Z., Sanghi, M., Chen, Y., Kao, M.-Y., Chavez, B.: Hamsa: Fast signature generation for zero-day polymorphic worms with provable attack resilience. In: Proceedings of the 2006 IEEE Symposium on Security and Privacy, pp. 32–47. IEEE Computer Society Press, Los Alamitos (2006)
17. Ma, J., Dunagan, J., Wang, H.J., Savage, S., Voelker, G.M.: Finding diversity in remote code injection exploits. In: Proceedings of the 6th ACM SIGCOMM on Internet measurement (IMC), pp. 53–64. ACM Press, New York (2006)
18. Newsome, J., Karp, B., Song, D.: Polygraph: Automatically generating signatures for polymorphic worms. In: Proceedings of the IEEE Security & Privacy Symposium, May 2005, pp. 226–241. IEEE Computer Society Press, Los Alamitos (2005)
19. Newsome, J., Karp, B., Song, D.: Paragraph: Thwarting signature learning by training maliciously. In: Zamboni, D., Kruegel, C. (eds.) RAID 2006. LNCS, vol. 4219, Springer, Heidelberg (2006)
20. Obscou: Building IA32 'unicode-proof' shellcodes. Phrack 11(61) (August 2003)
21. Payer, U., Teufl, P., Lamberger, M.: Hybrid engine for polymorphic shellcode detection. In: Julisch, K., Krügel, C. (eds.) DIMVA 2005. LNCS, vol. 3548, pp. 19–31. Springer, Heidelberg (2005)
22. Polychronakis, M., Markatos, E.P., Anagnostakis, K.G.: Network-level polymorphic shellcode detection using emulation. In: Büschkes, R., Laskov, P. (eds.) DIMVA 2006. LNCS, vol. 4064, pp. 54–73. Springer, Heidelberg (2006)
23. Rix: Writing IA32 alphanumeric shellcodes. Phrack 11(57) (August 2001)
24. Singh, S., Estan, C., Varghese, G., Savage, S.: Automated worm fingerprinting. In: Proc. of the 6th Symposium on Operating Systems Design & Implementation (OSDI) (December 2004)
25. sk: History and Advances in Windows Shellcode. Phrack 11(62) (July 2004)
26. Skape: Shellcode text encoding utility for 7bit shellcode,
    http://www.hick.org/code/skape/nologin/encode/encode.c
27. Skape: Implementing a Custom x86 Encoder. Uninformed 5 (September 2006)
28. Ször, P., Ferrie, P.: Hunting for metamorphic. In: Proceedings of the Virus Bulletin Conference, September 2001, pp. 123–144 (2001)
29. Toth, T., Kruegel, C.: Accurate Buffer Overflow Detection via Abstract Payload Execution. In: Wespi, A., Vigna, G., Deri, L. (eds.) RAID 2002. LNCS, vol. 2516, Springer, Heidelberg (2002)
30. Wang, K., Cretu, G., Stolfo, S.J.: Anomalous Payload-based Worm Detection and Signature Generation. In: Valdes, A., Zamboni, D. (eds.) RAID 2005. LNCS, vol. 3858, Springer, Heidelberg (2006)
31. Wang, K., Parekh, J.J., Stolfo, S.J.: Anagram: A Content Anomaly Detector Resistant to Mimicry Attack. In: Zamboni, D., Kruegel, C. (eds.) RAID 2006. LNCS, vol. 4219, Springer, Heidelberg (2006)
32. Wang, X., Pan, C.-C., Liu, P., Zhu, S.: Sigfree: A signature-free buffer overflow attack blocker. In: Proceedings of the USENIX Security Symposium (August 2006)
33. Wever, B.-J.: Alpha 2 (2004),
    http://www.edup.tudelft.nl/~bjwever/src/alpha2.c
34. Yegneswaran, V., Barford, P., Ullrich, J.: Internet intrusions: global characteristics and prevalence. In: Proceedings of the 2003 ACM SIGMETRICS international conference on Measurement and modeling of computer systems, pp. 138–147. ACM Press, New York (2003)
35. Zhang, Q., Reeves, D.S., Ning, P., Lyer, S.P.: Analyzing network traffic to detect self-decrypting exploit code. In: Proceedings of the ACM Symposium on Information, Computer and Communications Security (ASIACCS), ACM Press, New York (2007)

The NIDS Cluster: Scalable, Stateful Network Intrusion Detection on Commodity Hardware

Matthias Vallentin[3], Robin Sommer[2,1], Jason Lee[2], Craig Leres[2],
Vern Paxson[1,2], and Brian Tierney[2]

[1] International Computer Science Institute
[2] Lawrence Berkeley National Laboratory
[3] TU München

Abstract. In this work we present a *NIDS cluster* as a scalable solution for realizing high-performance, stateful network intrusion detection on commodity hardware. The design addresses three challenges: *(i)* distributing traffic evenly across an extensible set of analysis nodes in a fashion that minimizes the communication required for coordination, *(ii)* adapting the NIDS's operation to support coordinating its *low-level* analysis rather than just aggregating alerts; and *(iii)* validating that the cluster produces sound results. Prototypes of our NIDS cluster now operate at the Lawrence Berkeley National Laboratory and the University of California at Berkeley. In both environments the clusters greatly enhance the power of the network security monitoring.

1 Introduction

The performance required to implement effective network security monitoring poses major challenges for the underlying hardware. Many network intrusion detection systems (NIDSs), both open-source and commercial, are based on inexpensive commodity hardware. However, today the processing required to analyze even a single well-loaded Gbps traffic stream at any significant depth is beyond the reach of single workstations, and the technology trends threaten to widen this gap in the future, not narrow it [10].

Faced with this performance gap, we must abide either *(i)* curtailing our analysis, *(ii)* turning to expensive, custom hardware, or *(iii)* employing some form of *load-balancing* to split the analysis across multiple commodity systems. In this work we pursue the third of these, because of the appeal of retaining the great flexibility and cost benefits of using commercial PC hardware. With this approach a "frontend" divides the traffic stream among the analysis nodes, each of which gets a share of the total network traffic to analyze in depth.

Conceptually, such a setup is easy to extend with increasing traffic volumes by simply deploying more boxes. However, the key challenge with such a system is how to *correlate* the analysis performed by each node, as otherwise attacks that span more than what one system sees will go undetected.

Unfortunately, this is where things get tricky. While all major NIDS provide support for multi-system configurations, typically individual instances (often

C. Kruegel, R. Lippmann, and A. Clark (Eds.): RAID 2007, LNCS 4637, pp. 107–126, 2007.

termed *sensors*) connect to a central manager that correlates their results. The information exchanged tends to be very high-level: often just alerts that already present the *conclusion* of a sensor's analysis. Many inter-connection attacks, however, require much finer-grained correlation. As a simple example, to reliably detect a scan we need to track connection attempts across the full traffic stream. Hence, instead of correlating results, what we really need is to correlate the underlying *analysis*.

In this work, we build such a system. We term it the *NIDS cluster*: a set of commodity PCs that collaboratively analyze a traffic stream without sacrificing accuracy of the detection. Individual cluster nodes run instances of a NIDS and transparently exchange low-level analysis state to compose a global picture of the network activity. As a whole, the cluster transparently performs the same analysis a single instance of the NIDS would if it could cope by itself with the full network load.

When designing our system we faced three challenges: *(i)* distributing traffic across the nodes in a fashion that minimizes the communication required for correlation, yet avoids overloading any particular node; *(ii)* adapting the NIDS's operation to support coordinating its lower-level; and *(iii)* validating that the cluster produces sound results. We will discuss each of these in depth.

The original motivation for our work arose from the operational network monitoring setup at the Lawrence Berkeley National Laboratory (LBNL), which connects thousands of users/hosts to the Internet via a 10 Gbps access link. The lab's primary monitoring is done using Bro [9], an open-source NIDS running on commodity hardware. Since no single instance of the system can analyze LBNL's traffic in sufficient depth, over time the setup evolved into a configuration that uses a number of separate, uncoordinated Bro instances running on an inhomogeneous set of PCs (and even this setup still cannot analyze all traffic). Each instance performs a dedicated task (e.g., one analyzes only HTTP traffic) in isolation, and each system individually reports its results to the Lab's analysts. Thus, we desired to remedy the lack of coordinated analysis without sacrificing the very major benefits of using commodity, general-purpose hardware.

Thus, when designing the NIDS cluster we naturally targeted Bro as the underlying analysis engine for the backend nodes. In addition to fitting with the operational environment, Bro had the significant benefit that it already provides mechanisms for coordinating lower-level analysis (rather than only high-level results such as alerts) by means of its *independent state* framework [17]. Due to our choice of Bro, in the subsequent discussion we sometimes have to delve into particulars of the system. We note, however, that generally our approach applies well to other systems that support general low-level messaging functionality.

We now operate a prototype of our NIDS cluster at LBNL in parallel with the sites' operational monitoring, which it will eventually replace. Another prototype installation monitors the access link of the University of California at Berkeley (UCB), and an earlier prototype ran at *IEEE Supercomputing 2006*, the premier international conference on high performance computing, networking and storage. There, two separate clusters monitored the conference's primary 1 Gbps backbone network as well as portions of the 100 Gbps *High Speed Bandwidth Challenge* network.

We structure the remainder of this paper as follows. In § 2 we present the primary design objectives of the NIDS cluster. In § 3 we discuss the design and implementation of schemes for evenly distributing load across the cluster nodes, and in § 4 the design and implementation of the backend nodes. In § 5 we perform a trace-based evaluation to gauge the performance and accuracy of the cluster, followed in § 6 by a discussion of live performance as observed in our current cluster installations at LBNL and UCB. § 7 discusses related work, with conclusions in § 8.

2 Design Objectives and Resulting Architecture

With the NIDS cluster we aim to realize in-depth, yet inexpensive, network monitoring in high-performance environments. To do so in a manner suitable for *operational* security monitoring, the design must satisfy a number of objectives:

Transparency. The system should convey to the operator the impression of interacting only with a single NIDS, producing results as a single NIDS would *if* it could cope with the total load.

Scalability. Since network traffic volumes grow with time, we want to be able to easily add more nodes to the cluster to accommodate an increased load. Ideally, the cluster's performance scales *linearly*, i.e., the amount of additional resources necessary is a linear function of the increase in network load.

Commodity hardware. In general, we want to leverage the enormous flexibility and economies-of-scale that operation on commodity hardware can bring over use of custom hardware (e.g., ASICs or FPGAs). However, for monitoring very high-speed links, we may need to resort to specialized hardware for the *frontends*, as these need to process packets at full line-rate.

Ease of Use. The operator should interact with the system using a single host as the primary interface, both for accessing aggregated analysis results and for tuning the system's configuration.

Ease of Maintenance. Replacing failed components should be a straight-forward operation that does not impair the analysis of other components unaffected by the defect. If the hardware setup allows, hot-spares should be able to automatically take over.

Driven by these design objectives, we architect the NIDS cluster in terms of four main components (see Figure 1): *frontend nodes* distribute the traffic to a set of *backend nodes*. The backends run the NIDS instances that perform the traffic analysis and exchange state via *communication proxies*. Finally, a central *manager node* provides the cluster's centralized user interface.

There is typically one frontend per monitored link. Each frontend forwards each packet it receives to exactly one backend node in charge of the packet. Frontend nodes operate at line-speed and are therefore the most performance-critical components of the cluster. In the next section we discuss their operation and different options for implementing them.

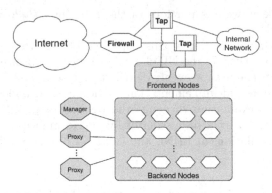

Fig. 1. Cluster architecture

Backend nodes are commodity PCs with two NICs: one for receiving traffic from the frontend, and one for communication with the manager and the communication proxies. Each backend node analyzes its share of the traffic using an instance of the NIDS, forwards results to the rest of the cluster as necessary, and receives information from other backends required for global analysis of activity. All backend nodes are using the same NIDS configuration and thus perform the same analysis on their traffic slices.

The communication proxies are a technical tool to avoid direct communication among all backend nodes, which does not scale well due to requiring fully meshed communication channels. Often a single proxy node suffices. It connects to each backend, forwarding information it receives from any of them to the others.

The manager node provides the operator-interface to the cluster. It aggregates and potentially filters the results of the backend nodes to provide the user with a coherent view of the overall analysis. The manager also facilitates easy management of the cluster, such as performing configuration updates and starting/stopping of nodes.

While conceptually proxies and managers are separate entities, we can combine them on a single host or co-resident with a backend system if their individual workloads permit (as is the case for some of our current installations).

3   Distributing Load

We begin with the question of how to divide the network traffic across the cluster's backend nodes. We first discuss and evaluate different distribution schemes, and then present options to implement them in the frontend nodes, as well as implications for coping with failure.

3.1   Distribution Schemes

The most straight-forward approach by which the frontend can achieve an even distribution of the incoming traffic would be a packet-based, round-robin scheme:

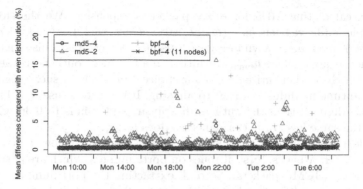

Fig. 2. Hash simulation

each node will see the same number of packets, arriving at the same rate. However, all major NIDSs keep significant *per-flow state*, e.g., to facilitate reassembling TCP byte streams, and thus a packet-based scheme would entail major communication overhead.

Flow-based schemes (all packets belonging to the same flow go to the same backend node) hold more promise as they result in load-balancing at the same granularity as used by the lower layers of backend analysis. Such schemes avoid inter-node communication for any analysis which is limited to the scope of a single flow—by far the largest share in most NIDSs. For example, traditional Snort-style signature matching requires no communication if we employ flow-based distribution. In addition, recent research suggests that the resource usage of a NIDS scales primarily with the number of flows [2], and thus a flow-based distribution scheme should impose a similar processing load on all backend nodes. We assess this claim in § 5.

To keep the frontend nodes as simple as possible, we focus on stateless distribution schemes. A simple approach is hashing a *flow identifier* derived from each packet's header into the set $\{0, \ldots, n-1\}$, with n being the number of backend nodes. For TCP and UDP traffic, for example, the identifier might be the 4-tuple (*addr1, port1, addr2, port2*). We could then use MD5 to generate a hash from such tuples: $h_{md5_4}(addr1, port1, addr2, port2) := MD5(addr1 + port1 + addr2 + port2) \mod n$. By using addition, this hash is commutative with respect to a flow's source and destination, so we map all packets of a flow in both directions to the same backend.

Figure 2 shows the result of applying several such hashes (for $n = 10$) to a day's worth of TCP traffic at UCB (231 million connections). Let N_i be the number of flows that began during each 5-minute interval i. An ideal distribution scheme across n backends assigns $M_i := N_i/n$ flows to each backend. For each interval, the plot shows the mean differences between a hash-generated distribution and M_i, as a percentage of M_i. As we would expect, we see that the h_{md5_4} hash (black circles) performs very well: the standard deviation σ of its variation from the ideal M_i is just 0.35%.

However, calculating MD5 for every packet is expensive. We therefore explore a simpler additive hash, $h_{bpf_4}(addr1, port1, addr2, port2) = (addr1 + port1 + addr2 + port2)$ mod n.[1], shown in Figure 2 using green crosses. This scheme has $\sigma = 1.31$, not as good as for h_{md5_4}, resulting in a few more outliers. However, it turns out that the outliers arise due to our choice of $n = 10$: for such an additive hash, a non-prime modulus can lead to aliasing. If we instead use $n = 11$ (blue crosses in the figure), then the outliers disappear, and σ falls to 0.36, yielding essentially the same level of performance as does h_{md5_4}.

Yet, while hashing on the 4-tuple yields a nice distribution of flows across backends, it also has drawbacks. First, it relies on port numbers, which are not always well-defined (e.g., ICMP packets). Second, extracting the port numbers can be somewhat complicated for fast hardware (per § 3.2) since their location within a packet is not necessarily fixed (due to IP options or nested IPv6 headers). Third, and most importantly, 4-tuple hashing cannot cope with IP fragments, as not all fragments contain the ports. Thus, a frontend would need to reassemble fragments, which requires maintaining state.

Accordingly, we also examine a third type of hash based *only* on addresses: $h_{md5_2}(addr1, addr2) = md5(addr1 + addr2)$ mod n. While this hash is easy to implement, we expect it to lack the evenness of the 4-tuple hashes, since all traffic between the same two hosts will map to the same hash. The question is whether in a large network the diversity of source and destination addresses already suffices to still yield similar loads on the backend nodes. We show the results in the figure using red triangles, finding that while h_{md5_2} has $\sigma = 1.55$, the unevenness is fairly mild. (We omit similar results for an analogous h_{bpf_2} hash to keep the plot legible.)

In addition, there are in fact some significant benefits to using 2-tuple hashing rather than 4-tuple: hashing just by addresses decreases communication overhead for per-host-pair forms of analysis. For example, a single cluster node can detect port scans without any inter-node correlation. In our cluster installations we therefore choose to rely on a 2-tuple hash despite its slightly lower performance. Accordingly, we also use it for our evaluation in § 5.

Finally, we note that in practice the load of a NIDS is quite difficult to predict even if we know exactly what traffic it processes [4]. Thus, even with a completely even distribution scheme the actual *processing* load on the backends differs. We return to this point in § 5.

3.2   Frontend Implementation

We can consider implementing the frontend using either specialized hardware, or purely in software. Regarding specialized hardware, we experimented with the P10 appliance from Force10 Networks, which features two 10 Gbps ports and the ability to draw upon an FPGA to inspect traffic across the ports at line rate. We programmed the FPGA to calculate hashes and in real-time rewrite the destination MAC address of each packet to be that of the corresponding backend

---

[1] We call this hash h_{bpf_4} because it can be implemented as a BPF filter [2].

node. We report on our experiences in § 6 below.[2] Alternatively, we find in our testing that software frontends, while slower, can provide sufficient performance for up to 2 Gbps. The most successful approach we have experimented with is based on Click [7] which, running entirely within a Linux kernel, can similarly rewrite the destination addresses.

3.3 Recovery from Failure

One of the design objectives for the NIDS cluster is *Ease of Maintenance*: if a component fails, it should be simple to replace it, ideally in an automated fashion and without interrupting unaffected components. For the front end, this is difficult without employing fully redundant hardware. However, for the other components, we can do so as follows.

If a backend node fails, the immediate effect is that its slice of the network traffic becomes unmonitored. All other components, however, continue to work unaffected. To prepare for backend failures, we can run additional nodes as hot spares. During normal operation, hot spares are configured the same as the other backends, but do not receive any traffic. Once the cluster detects the failure of a backend (e.g., via a heartbeat mechanism), a hot spare can assume the MAC address of the failed node and continue the node's monitoring. While the hot spare will not have the internal state of the failing node, it automatically receives a copy of all globally-shared state from its proxy when it connects to the cluster.

If a communication proxy fails, the backends connected to it will no longer be able to correlate their analysis with other nodes. However they continue analyzing their traffic slices locally, including further accumulation of local state. A hot-spare proxy then take over by connecting to all affected backends, which then automatically resume propagating their state updates via the new connections. However, the system will be in a state of partial inconsistency due to the state updates lost during the fail-over period.

If the manager fails, the cluster loses its reporting and logging facilities, but the backends and proxies continue their monitoring unaffected. If they also log locally, there is no loss of analysis results, even though they are no longer aggregated centrally during the manager outage. Once detected, a new manager can quickly takeover: like a proxy, it only needs to connect to the backends and they will automatically begin forwarding their results to the new manager.

4 Distributing Analysis

We now turn to devising the cluster's backend analysis. As noted above, we base our implementation on the Bro NIDS. Bro's flexibility makes it well-suited

---

[2] We have also developed an FPGA-based NIDS frontend that we term a "Shunt" that we can adapt to this purpose [22], but we do not yet have it at a stage to evaluate in this context.

to the task. In contrast to most other NIDSs, Bro is fundamentally neither anomaly-based nor signature-based. Instead, it is partitioned into a *protocol analysis component* ("event engine") and a *policy script component*. The former feeds the latter by generating a stream of *events* that reflect different types of activity detected using protocol analysis. For example, when the analyzer sees the establishment of a TCP connection, it generates a `connection_established` event; when it sees an HTTP request, it generates `http_request`, and for the corresponding reply, `http_reply`.

Bro's event engine is *policy-neutral*: it does not consider any particular events as reflecting trouble. It simply makes the events available to the policy script interpreter. The interpreter then executes scripts written in Bro's custom scripting language in order to define the response to the stream of events. Because the language includes rich data types, persistent state, and access to timers and external programs, the response can incorporate a great deal of context in addition to the event itself. The script's reaction to a particular event can range from updating arbitrary state (for example, tracking types of activity by address or address pair, or grouping related connections into higher-level "sessions") to generating alerts.

Almost all of Bro's event engine processing executes on a per-flow fashion, and thus does not require correlation of state across flows.[3] Therefore, we can restrict exchange of analysis state between backend nodes to script-level logic.

At the script-level, Bro provides extensive support for remote communication by means of its *independent state* framework [17]. The framework provides two communication primitives: *remote event subscription* and *synchronized variables*. With the former, one Bro instance can subscribe to any events from the event stream of remote peers; it will then transparently receive these events at its script-layer just as does the event source itself. With the latter, Bro instances can share *any* script-level data structure with a set of peers. Any change performed by one peer is transparently propagated to the others, creating a globally shared data structure. For our cluster, we use event subscription for the communication between the manager node and the backends, and synchronized variables for correlating analysis between backends.

To install Bro on the NIDS cluster, we need to set up three different types of Bro instances: *(i)* backends to analyze each slice of traffic; *(ii)* proxies to propagate state information across the backends; and *(iii)* a central manager to collect and aggregate the results of the backends.

Managers and proxies are straight-forward to construct. The manager is a Bro instance that connects to each backend and subscribes to the events corresponding to their analysis output: *alarm* events, generated upon detecting malicious activity, and *log* events, generated whenever the backend logs information to

---

[3] There is one exception: Bro's stepping stone detector [23] correlates flows *inside* the event engine. However, this analysis could just as well be done at the script layer, and so for our evaluation we have decided to ignore supporting its functionality.

a local file.[4] When the manager receives a remote *alarm* event, it processes it according to its local alarm configuration (e.g., determining which merit paging the operator), just as if the alarm had been locally generated. This approach allows the operator to easily centralize (and dynamically change) the alarm policy for the entire cluster. When the manager receives a *log* event, it writes the content into a corresponding local file; thus, the manager's log files reflect the aggregation of all of the backends' log files in real-time.

Different from the manager, the proxies operate in a fully policy-neutral fashion. Each proxy connects to a subset of the backend nodes, as well as to all other proxies. Proxies subscribe to the stream of state operations from all of their peers. Once they receive an operation from a peer, they forward it to all of the others. The receivers then apply the operation locally (or propagate the operation further in the case of multiple proxies).

Setting up the backend Bro instances consists of two step: *(i)* choosing an analysis configuration suitable for the environment, and *(ii)* adapting the processing to correlate state across the cluster. The first step does not differ from setting up a traditional, single Bro instance, and we therefore do not discuss it in more detail. With regard to correlating state, per our observation above, Bro performs its inter-connection analysis (almost) exclusively at the script-level, and thus we focus on identifying script-level variables that require synchronization across the backends. To do so, we examined each of Bro's standard scripts to determine which variables require synchronization between peers. By providing this synchronization, each peer obtains the *full* decision context while processing only a subset of the entire traffic.

Our analysis of the scripts revealed that many of them in fact perform only intra-connection analysis, and hence do not require any modification. In particular, most of the scripts analyzing the content of application-layer protocols do not correlate information across connection boundaries. (For example, while Bro's primary SMTP script maintains a table of all active SMTP sessions, the analysis of each individual one does not require access to the state of any other SMTP session.)

Some scripts, however, do require information from multiple connections. A prominent example is the scan detector, which counts connection attempts per source address. If these reach a certain threshold, the system raises an alarm. In the cluster setup, the scan detector now must count across backends; we therefore synchronize the corresponding tables of counters (which simply entails annotating the corresponding script variables with the attribute &synchronized). Other examples of scripts needing synchronization are the worm detector (which maintains a global list of infected hosts) and the SMTP relay detector (which identifies open SMTP relays by associating incoming with outgoing mails). Overall, we needed to synchronize 29 script-level variables spanning 19 different types of analysis.

---

[4] Bro differs from many other NIDS in that it keeps extensive logs of all network traffic, independent of whether activity is deemed malicious or not. These logs include one-line summaries of each flow, and transcripts of application-layer protocol dialogs for a wide range of protocols—invaluable for forensic analyses.

When adapting the scripts in this fashion, we sometimes leveraged the specific traffic distribution schemes implemented by our frontends (see § 3.1). Since the 2-tuple scheme we used directs all traffic between the same two hosts to a single backend, we do not need to synchronize state that only associates connections between the same two endpoints (for example, detection of port scans). However, since this optimization depends on the frontend distribution scheme, we structured our script modifications so that the user can selectively apply them based on *a priori* knowledge of how traffic will be distributed.

In general, there are trade-offs between the overhead that synchronization requires and the benefits one gains from it. For example, FTP data connections are *usually* instantiated between the same endpoints (addresses) as the corresponding FTP control connections. When that holds, a purely address-based distribution scheme obviates the need for inter-node communication. However, in principle FTP can involve a third address in such transfers, and thus not synchronizing knowledge between nodes can potentially lead to misclassifications. In our current configuration we still choose to *not* propagate such information in favor of avoiding the communication overhead. (Note that some, but not all, of the attack uses of such third-party FTP already manifest in the control session, and thus can be detected without synchronization.)

To adapt the backend analysis to the cooperative cluster setting, ideally it would suffice to simply go through all of Bro's analysis scripts and synchronize all variables used to correlate state across flows. However, in practice we encountered subtleties when doing so which merit discussion.

So far, we have assumed that synchronizing a variable works in a fully transparent and reliable fashion: at all times all peers agree on the variable's value; each operation is immediately reflected in all instances. However, in practice real-time requirements impede this model, as it would require global locking across mutually-exclusive data structures. The Bro system therefore relies on *loose synchronization* [17], which propagates state changes in a best-effort fashion without any kind of locking. Doing so can lead to race conditions, and therefore changes the semantics of the script processing.

While we cannot avoid such race conditions, we can mitigate their impact. We devised several strategies to do so, addressing the common situations we encountered. One example arises from the specific way in which some scripts use nested tables. The scan detector, for example, uses a table of source addresses mapping into sets of destination addresses to count how many unique victims a scanner has so far contacted. When a new source begins to scan, there is initially no entry for it in the outer table. However, the first connection attempts the source makes are often noticed by multiple backends at almost the same time, and thus each of them then assigns a freshly instantiated set of destination addresses to the corresponding source address. Because of loose synchronization, it is unpredictable what sort of picture these fresh creations plus additions will eventually result in at each peer. We addressed this problem by introducing *mergeable* sets into the scripting language: if new content is assigned to a mergeable set, the distributed result is the *union* of old and new content, rather than the new content replacing the old.

A number of other such examples arose; see [18] for a detailed discussion. (We note that all of our changes, including the mergeable sets, will be part of the next Bro release.)

Finally, we equipped the manager node with a set of tools to ease maintenance. Rather basically, a set of shell scripts provide means to control and monitor the cluster operation on all nodes (e.g., start and stop the cluster), based on a central configuration file that specifies which systems are backends, proxies, and manager. More interesting is on-the-fly reconfiguration, such as installing a modified alert policy, which such scripts also support via the *independent state* framework. Similarly, the operator can inspect the state of all nodes during runtime, e.g., to examine the contents of script-level variables on all of the backends. The scripts for doing so run a temporary Bro instance on the manager node that connects to all the cluster nodes, either sending out a configuration update or querying for internal state.

5 Evaluation

We evaluate the performance of our cluster setup as follows. We first first introduce our evaluation methodology. We then use it to assess the analysis accuracy of the cluster in comparison with running a single system. To understand how the cluster design scales, we next measure backend CPU load as we vary the number of nodes. Finally, we look at the overhead due to inter-node communication.

5.1 Methodology

For the bulk of our evaluation, we operate the system offline on previously captured traces. In contrast to running on live traffic (including traffic replayed into a testbed), this approach ensures reproducible results with multiple runs. When running multiple times on the same trace with different configurations, we can attribute any changes in performance directly to the configuration change.

However, the cluster's distributed processing introduces a few complications. First, as each backend node sees a different slice of traffic, we need one trace per backend node. Thus, we first capture a full trace and then split it up into slices using the h_{bpf_2} hash scheme discussed in § 3.1. We then copy one slice to every backend node and run each NIDS instance offline on its subset of the trace. The second difficulty arises due to inter-node communication: the NIDS, running offline, can process a trace more quickly than in real-time—since the nodes consume packets as fast as possible, even if in actuality the packets would not yet have arrived—leading to desynchronization between the backend nodes. To address this problem, the Bro system provides a *pseudo-realtime* mode [17]: if enabled, the trace analysis deliberately inserts delays into its processing that echo the inter-packet gaps observed when capturing the trace. That is, the analysis of the trace proceeds with the same speed as it would when running live, thereby synchronizing it with real-time, and hence with inter-node communication.

We conducted our evaluation in the LBNL environment, using the same cluster hardware that our live prototype runs (§ 6). The cluster consists of 10 backend nodes and one node for manager and proxy. All systems are 3.6 GHz dual-CPU Intel Pentium D with 2 GB RAM. We use a single Bro instance as both manager and proxy, and configured the backends to reflect the full operational Bro setup used at LBNL (the complete range of analysis that to date has been spread across a number of uncoordinated nodes). In addition, we enabled Bro's general capability to detect and analyze applications running on non-standard ports [3], which is infeasible for LBNL's current operational setup because it requires in-depth analysis of *all* packets.

We captured a 2+ hour, full-packet trace around noon on March 1st, 2007, comprising 97 GB, 134 M packets, and 1.5 M source/destination pairs. The average throughput corresponds to 113 Mbps, with a per-second peak of 261 Mb. 88% of the packets were TCP, 9.7% UDP, and 2.3% ICMP. The most prevalent TCP protocols were HTTPS (18.6% of the packets), followed by HTTP (12.0%), and SSH (10.3%). 40.8% of the TCP traffic was not classifiable by well-known ports, with a large share quite likely due to Grid protocols.

5.2   Accuracy

Ideally, a NIDS cluster produces the same output as a single NIDS would. Therefore, we first compared our cluster's output (as aggregated by the manager node) with the results of a single Bro instance running offline on the full trace. We examined both the *alarms* and the activity *logs* generated (per § 4).

Of the 2661 alarms reported by the single Bro, all were also raised by the cluster, i.e., the new setup does not miss any intrusion attempts. Upon closer inspection, we however found two differences. First, of the 252 address scans reported by the single Bro, two scanners were flagged significantly later by the cluster. The first scanner performed a quick but extremely short scan, contacting 39 different destinations within 1 sec but then no further contact for an interval exceeding the scan detector's time-out. While a single Bro can notice such a scan easily, the latency of the communication between the backends delays the cluster in doing so. The second initially missed scanner performed 5 small bursts of connection attempts: roughly 10 attempts each time, set 10 sec apart. This was only detected when the backends later generated summaries of their shared state (rather than upon propagation of the shared state, due to the activity-triggered nature of the current scan detection algorithm). In both cases, the final alarm generated by the backend agrees with the summary produced by the single Bro.

The second difference arose because the details of context accompanying an alarm can differ. Timestamps vary slightly (on the order of 0.1 sec) and, for example, the scan detector can report a different number of connections attempts in its initial alarm, with both effects due to communication delays and semantics slightly differing due to the distributed setup. Apart from these minor differences, we find that the cluster produces alarms closely matching those of a single Bro processing the same input.

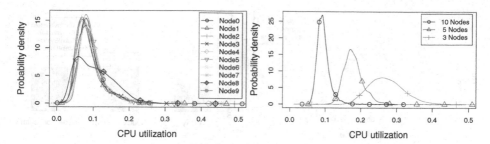

Fig. 3. Probability densities of backends' CPU load (left), and probability densities for varying numbers of backends (right)

Next, we compared the activity logs. The main discrepancies we encountered were differences in timing, e.g., the begin and duration logged for connections differed slightly. This is expected due to the pseudo-realtime mode, which can only approximately reproduce the exact timing of the trace. (Timing would similarly differ in a live setting.) Except for such timing issues, we found only one other major type of difference between the logs, which was also an artifact of our test-bed setup: when the Bros on the backends terminate, they generate a final spike of log activity. However, as Bro tears down the communication to the manager immediately at that point, the corresponding log events are not reliably forwarded anymore. Thus, the manager is missing some of the activity at the end of the processed trace. In a live setting, this problem does not occur because the nodes run continuously.

Overall, we conclude that the cluster yields very similar results as a single NIDS—well within the variation we see operationally for a single NIDS due to differences in timing and minor configuration variations—and therefore achieves an acceptable degree of transparency.

5.3 Performance

We now assess the performance of the NIDS cluster in terms of CPU load and communication overhead. We first examine how well our frontend balances the processing load across the backends. We then perform a series of measurements with different numbers of backends to assess the scalability of the approach. Finally, we take a look at the overhead introduced by the communication.

Load-balancing. In §3.1 we found that overall the h_{bpf_2} hashing scheme yields a good distribution in terms of the number of flows assigned to each node. However, even assignment does not automatically imply even *processing* loads on all backends, as different types of connections require different degrees of analysis (see [4]). To examine the backend CPU load, we again run the cluster on the captured trace, using the same configuration as described above. For each backend, we logged the amount of user CPU time consumed per second by the NIDS's analysis. Figure 3(left) shows the distribution of these per-second load samples for each backend. We see that nine of the ten backends (all except

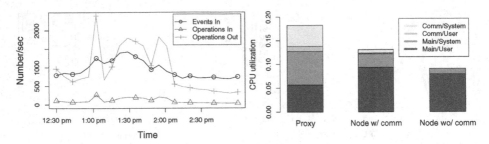

Fig. 4. State exchanged by manager/proxy (left), and CPU load of manager/proxy & one node (right)

node 8) show very similar distributions, indicating quite similar CPU loads. Across these nine backends, the *largest* mean CPU utilization was 10.0%, and the largest standard deviation $\sigma = 4.8\%$, reflecting that both the loads and the load fluctuations leave ample headroom for increases in traffic.

However, backend node 8 shows a notably different density shape (mean 10.7%, $\sigma = 5.7\%$). We examined the slice of the trace processed by node 8 and found that the slice contains a *single* TCP connection which makes up 86% of the trace's total bytes (33 GB of 38 GB!). Just by being assigned this one connection, node 8 receives a significantly larger share of the overall traffic (other nodes on average received 6.5 GB). Note, though, that pretty much any flow-based traffic distribution scheme will wind up introducing this disparity, since it manifests at even the finest flow-based granularity. However, even so node 8's CPU load 8 stayed well within a manageable range (below 30% for 99.5% of the time).

We conclude that overall our traffic distribution imposes quite similar processing loads across the nodes, and that the 10-node setup has sufficient headroom to easily cope with the occasional traffic spikes induced, even when performing the full range of operational analysis *plus* dynamic protocol detection.

Scaling. We next examine how the backend load scales with the number of analysis nodes. Figure 3(right) plots the CPU utilization for setups with 3, 5, and 10 backends. For each run, we first averaged the one-second CPU samples (see above) across all nodes, and then plotted the probability density of these mean CPU loads. In the plot we see that the load indeed scales nearly linearly with the number of nodes: the mean load for 3 nodes is 27.4%, for 5 nodes it is 18.0%, and for 10 nodes it is 9.4%, with the corresponding values of σ being 5.5%, 3.0%, and 2.0%.

Overhead. Compared to running a single Bro instance, the cluster setup introduces overhead in terms of communication. We now examine the volume of state exchanged between the cluster nodes and the additional amount of processing it requires. All measurements reported in this section use 10 backend nodes.

We first look at the amount of state exchanged between the cluster nodes. For the combined manager/proxy node, Figure 4(left) shows the number of incoming and outgoing state operations as well as the number incoming events (this node does not generate its own events). As *alarm* events are relatively rare, almost all of the incoming events are *log* events reflecting summaries of transport-level and application-level activity.

On average, one log event consumes 200 bytes when transmitted wire in its binary form. Incoming state operations correspond to updates to synchronized variables; each of these triggers 9 outgoing operations due to the proxy broadcasting the update to the other backends.[5] On average, one state operation consumes about 140 bytes.

Examining the state operations in more detail reveals that by far the largest fraction (97%) are triggered by the scan detector, unsurprising because scan detection is naturally quite expensive in terms of communication (to first order, *each* connection might be part of a scan and thus needs to be propagated).

To understand the processing burden that propagating events and operations imposes on the cluster nodes, Figure 4(right) shows the average CPU load over the course of our trace for *(i)* the manager/proxy, and *(ii)* an arbitrary backend node with and without any communication. For the proxy, we see that a significant amount of the processing time (11.5%) is system time. Apart from logging to disk, this time primarily reflects communication input/output: over the course of the trace, the proxy sends in total 101/918 MB in/out.

The mean CPU time consumed by the proxy is rather low in our evaluation (6.3%). However, as the proxy cannot do a real broadcast but has to individually send each operation to every receiver, its CPU usage increases with the number of backends. Depending on the traffic, this could in principle cause the proxy to become a bottleneck, especially during traffic spikes that suddenly generate a large number of events/operations. Yet, due to the flexibility of our cluster architecture, we can easily divide the load between multiple proxies. In our current installation (see §6), we in fact run two proxies, and also separate the manager so that logging and operations broadcasting can be performed on different hosts.

Looking at the exemplary node in Figure 4(right), we see that enabling communication increases its mean total CPU usage by 42.9% (though still to below 15% in absolute terms). In fact, 23% of the increase occurs in a child process that Bro uses to manage inter-Bro communication; thus, on a dual CPU machine this portion does not decrease the processing capacity of the main process. Overall, the overhead for a node's communication is non-negligible but also is not dominant. Furthermore, due to the proxy architecture the amount of communication that a node performs is independent of the number of backend nodes, providing good scaling properties.

6   Installations

We have installed operational NIDS clusters at LBNL and UC Berkeley, which here we discuss in turn.

---

[5] Due to Bro's communication framework using TCP, this is not a network-layer broadcast.

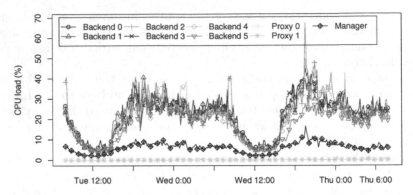

Fig. 5. CPU load on UC Berkeley cluster

The Bro cluster at LBNL consists of one frontend (classifier) node, one node each for the manager and communication proxy, and ten backend nodes. Each is a 3.6 GHz dual-CPU Intel Pentium D with two GB of memory and two GigE network interface ports, one for packet capture and one for communication. Optical splitters provide copies of each direction of wide area traffic. Since LBNL's current aggregate utilization is less than 10 Gbps, we merge these into a single 10 Gbps stream, fed into a Force10 P10 appliance. The P10 classifies the packets according to a variant of the h_{bpf_2} hash (which uses xor rather than addition) and injects them into a 10 Gbps uplink port on a Force10 S50 switch. The switch distributes the packets to GigE-connected analysis nodes according to their rewritten MAC addresses.

We run the manager and communication proxy each on a dedicated node. The manager collects log files from all backends, archiving them for forensic analysis, and responding to real-time alarms. In typical operation, backend nodes consume less then 2% CPU for packet analysis and less than 1% CPU for communication, the manager consumes around 5% CPU, and the proxy node consumes around 2% CPU. We have seen bursts of traffic consume up to 40% CPU on the backends, 25% CPU on the proxy, and 15% CPU on the manager for short periods of time. The backends report very little packet loss (less than .0001%). On average we monitor 32K pkts/sec and 28 MB/sec of traffic on this cluster.

The Bro cluster at UC Berkeley monitors the campus's two 1 GigE upstream links, which are mirrored via SPAN ports from two separate routers. There are two frontend nodes running Click to distribute the traffic (Dell PowerEdge 850; Intel Pentium D 920 dual-core; Linux 2.6), one for each SPAN port; and currently six backend nodes (Sun Fire X2100; AMD Opteron 180 dual-core; FreeBSD 6.1). An HP ProCurve 3500 switch connects frontends and backends.

The traffic volume seen at UCB is huge, 3–5 TB per day. As our six backends do not suffice to analyze the total traffic in full, until we can add more nodes we limit the analysis to half of the traffic volume by enabling only one of the frontends. We use two proxy instances to balance the communication load. The proxies, as well as the manager, run in addition with the traffic analysis on one of the backends each. For the manager, it appears that its disk I/O decreases the analysis capacity of the backend process running on the same host (we see occasional packet drops at similar loads that the other backends have no trouble with). Figure 6 shows the processing load of the different processes over a time period of two days. The specifics of the UC Berkeley network posed some challenges. First, Bro's scan detector imposed significant load on the cluster due to the large number of connections in this environment (about 2500/sec on average). On the one hand, these generate large numbers of propagated state operations. On the other hand, counting connection attempts for all sources requires a great deal of memory. The latter highlights a drawback of our approach to clustering: while we split the CPU load across the multiple nodes, each backend keeps a complete copy of all (synchronized) state. To counter both effects, we added two new options to Bro's scan detector: the first limits the synchronization of scanner state to sources for which one of the backends has at least seen 5 (default) different destinations locally. The second option stops synchronizing scanner state for sources once they have scanned at least 500 (default) destinations. With this tuning, the scan detector performs well on the cluster.

We encountered a similar problem with Bro's IRC analyzer, which tracks a significant amount of state for each IRC user encountered. Being a campus network, the share of IRC traffic is relatively large, and therefore these data structures grow quickly. Since they are synchronized, each backend keeps its own copy of the full set. For now we have disabled parts of the IRC analysis in favor of having the memory available for other types of analysis.

More generally, these problems highlight how existing ways of structuring analyses are not always well-suited for a distributed setup. With the cluster platform now in place, we plan to investigate analysis algorithms specifically designed for multi-node processing. For example, a distributed, probabilistic scan detector has the potential to significantly reduce communication and memory requirements.

7 Related Work

To our knowledge, the approach we have framed in this work—employing a cluster of commodity systems to perform load-balanced intrusion detection that coordinates lower-level analysis across nodes—is a novel development. That said, the more general notion of applying clusters to construct scalable network services has seen significant exploration in prior work. Fox et. al. mention several advantages clusters provide, including *incremental scalability*, *high availability*, and the *cost-effectiveness* of commodity PCs [5]. The performance of network intrusion detection has been extensively studied in the past [12,15,16,14]. All studies conclude that it is imperative to cope with the induced load that growing network traffic imposes. Schaelicke and Freeland argue that system-level optimizations such as *interrupt coalescing* and *rule-set pruning* as well as architectural techniques can significantly improve performance and reduce packet loss [14]. While previous work primarily focuses on the design of a NIDS cluster processing frontend [16,8], we look in addition at the challenges that intra-NIDS communication raises.

Numerous different NIDSs are available today. The focus and range of application vary for each system. To our knowledge, only a few systems feature a tunable and flexible communication sub-system that we can leverage to build a NIDS cluster. Snort [13] is the most widespread open-source NIDS. Snort runs on commodity hardware, utilizing *libpcap* to enable platform independent packet capturing. The detection engine is misuse-based. Around a core of numerous signatures, various plugins enhance its functionality. Despite the lack of a communication sub-system, Kruegel et. al. built a flow-based load-balancer on top of Snort [8]. Their approach maintains connection tables to forward packets belonging to the same flow to the corresponding sensor, but does not extend to inter-sensor communication. The *State Transition Analysis Technique (STAT)* tool suite [19] is a set of distributed intrusion detection tools based on misuse-detection. STAT models intrusions as sequences of attack scenarios reflected by state transition diagrams, and supports inclusion of network-based, host-based, and application-based sensors. The *MetaSTAT Infrastructure* [21] provides the communication sub-system and control infrastructure to enable distributed coordination of STAT-based applications. STAT-based tools fan out into $\{U, N, Net, Win, Web, Alert\} STAT$, each designed for a different application domain. In particular, *NetSTAT* [20] is the network-based component responsible for network communication. If it is impossible for the system to detect an attack completely, the NetSTAT propagates the partially configured scenario containing state information to other probes. EMERALD [11] is a distributed hybrid intrusion detection framework designed for large-scale enterprise network operation; it is not openly available. The architecture of EMERALD uses a layered approach to support hierarchical organization of monitors. Each monitor can subscribe to events and propagate correlated results. Prelude [1] is a distributed NIDS that relies on the IDMEF [6] standard to exchange events. In its framework, sensors are connected to managers, which process and correlate alerts. In a distributed setup, multiple managers can also act as relay managers that report to a central manager. However, none of the existing approaches provided a sufficiently flexible means to share arbitrary policy-neutral state, unlike the approach we pursue with our NIDS cluster.

8   Conclusion

In this work we set out to build a *NIDS cluster* as a scalable solution to realizing high-performance, stateful network intrusion detection on commodity hardware. The cluster consists of a frontend that distributes traffic evenly across an extensible set of backend nodes. Each backend examines its slice of the traffic in-depth and correlates its analysis with the rest of the cluster. Different from traditional multi-system NIDS setups, our cluster exchanges *low-level* state information across all the backends and thereby transparently creates the impression of interacting with a single NIDS.

In the process of developing the NIDS cluster, we examined different traffic distribution schemes for the frontend and experimented with both hardware and software implementations. We adapted the open-source Bro NIDS to run on the backends, and conducted a trace-based evaluation of the cluster to ensure that the cluster achieves *transparency* (output matches that of a stand-alone system) and good performance with respect to scalability and communication overhead.

A prototype of the cluster runs at the Lawrence Berkeley National Laboratory in parallel with the site's operational security monitoring, which it will eventually replace. Another prototype monitors the access links of UC Berkeley. With the cluster infrastructure now in place, we plan to further investigate the development of analysis algorithms specifically tailored for a distributed setting, allowing us to decrease communication overhead. Even without this, the NIDS cluster already increases the computational power of network security analysis far beyond what is currently feasible in these environments.

Acknowledgments

We would like to thank Mark Dedlow for testing and improving the cluster configuration, Christian Kreibich for valuable feedback, Livio Ricciulli and Force10 for implementing our hashing scheme on their P10 appliance, and Nicholas Weaver for his help with setting up the UCB cluster. Parts of this work were produced under the auspices of the Institute for Information Infrastructure Protection (I3P) research program. The I3P is managed by Dartmouth College, and supported under Award number 2003-TK-TX-0003 from the U.S. Department of Homeland Security, Science and Technology Directorate. Points of view in this document are those of the author(s) and do not necessarily represent the official position of the U.S. Department of Homeland Security, the Science and Technology Directorate, the I3P, or Dartmouth College. This work was also supported by NSF Awards STI-0334088, ITR/ANI-0205519, and CNS-0627320. Any opinions, findings, and conclusions or recommendations expressed in this material are those of the authors or originators and do not necessarily reflect the views of the National Science Foundation.

References

1. Blanc, M., Oudot, L., Glaume, V.: Global Intrusion Detection: Prelude Hybrid IDS. Technical report (2003)
2. Dreger, H.: Operational Network Intrusion Detection: Resource-Analysis Tradeoffs. PhD thesis, TU München (2007)
3. Dreger, H., Feldmann, A., Mai, M., Paxson, V., Sommer, R.: Dynamic Application-Layer Protocol Analysis for Network Intrusion Detection. In: Proc. USENIX Security Symposium (2006)
4. Dreger, H., Feldmann, A., Paxson, V., Sommer, R.: Operational Experiences with High-Volume Network Intrusion Detection. In: Proc. ACM Conference on Computer and Communications Security, ACM Press, New York (2004)

5. Fox, A., Gribble, S.D., Chawathe, Y., Brewer, E.A., Gauthier, P.: Cluster-Based Scalable Network Services. In: Proc. Symposium on Operating Systems Principles (1997)
6. Intrusion Detection Message Exchange Format, http://www.ietf.org/html.charters/idwg-charter.html
7. Kohler, E., Morris, R., Chen, B., Jannotti, J., Kaashoek, F.: The Click Modular Router. ACM Transactions on Computer Systems 18(3) (August 2000)
8. Kruegel, C., Valeur, F., Vigna, G., Kemmerer, R.A.: Stateful Intrusion Detection for High-Speed Networks. In: Proc. IEEE Symposium on Research on Security and Privacy, IEEE Computer Society Press, Los Alamitos (2002)
9. Paxson, V.: Bro: A System for Detecting Network Intruders in Real-Time. Computer Networks 31(23–24), 2435–2463 (1999)
10. Paxson, V., Asanovic, K., Dharmapurikar, S., Lockwood, J., Pang, R., Sommer, R., Weaver, N.: Rethinking Hardware Support for Network Analysis and Intrusion Prevention. In: Proc. USENIX Hot Security (2006)
11. Porras, P.A., Neumann, P.G.: EMERALD: Event Monitoring Enabling Responses to Anomalous Live Disturbances. In: Proc. National Information Systems Security Conference (1997)
12. Puketza, N.J., Zhang, K., Chung, M., Mukherjee, B., Olsson, R.A.: A Methodology for Testing Intrusion Detection Systems. IEEE Transactions on Software Engineering 22(10), 719–729 (1996)
13. Roesch, M.: Snort: Lightweight Intrusion Detection for Networks. In: Proc. Systems Administration Conference (1999)
14. Schaelicke, L., Freeland, C.: Characterizing Sources and Remedies for Packet Loss in Network Intrusion Detection. In: Proc. IEEE Symposium on Workload Characterization, IEEE Computer Society Press, Los Alamitos (2005)
15. Schaelicke, L., Slabach, T., Moore, B., Freeland, C.: Characterizing the Performance of Network Intrusion Detection Sensors. In: Proc. Symposium on Recent Advances in Intrusion Detection (2003)
16. Schaelicke, L., Wheeler, K., Freeland, C.: SPANIDS: A Scalable Network Intrusion Detection Loadbalancer. In: Proc. Computing Frontiers Conference (2005)
17. Sommer, R., Paxson, V.: Exploiting Independent State For Network Intrusion Detection. In: Proc. Computer Security Applications Conference (2005)
18. Vallentin, M.: Transparent Load-Balancing for Network Intrusion Detection Systems. Bachelor's Thesis, TU München (2006)
19. Vigna, G., Eckmann, S.T., Kemmerer, R.A.: The STAT Tool Suite. In: Proc. DARPA Information Survivability Conference and Exposition (2000)
20. Vigna, G., Kemmerer, R.A.: NetSTAT: A Network-based Intrusion Detection System. Journal of Computer Security 7(1), 37–71 (1999)
21. Vigna, G., Kemmerer, R.A., Blix, P.: Designing a Web of Highly-Configurable Intrusion Detection Sensors. In: Proc. Symposium on Recent Advances in Intrusion Detection (2001)
22. Weaver, N., Paxson, V., Gonzalez, J.M.: The Shunt: An FPGA-Based Accelerator for Network Intrusion Prevention. In: Proc. ACM Symposium on Field Programmable Gate Arrays, February 2007, ACM Press, New York (2007)
23. Zhang, Y., Paxson, V.: Detecting Stepping Stones. In: Proc. USENIX Security Symposium (2000)

Cost-Sensitive Intrusion Responses
for Mobile Ad Hoc Networks

Shiau-Huey Wang, Chinyang Henry Tseng, Karl Levitt, and Matthew Bishop

Computer Security Laboratory, University of California, Davis, CA, 95616 USA
{angelaw,ctseng,knlevitt,bishop}@ucdavis.edu

Abstract. This paper addresses how to perform cost-sensitive responses to routing attacks on Mobile Ad Hoc Networks (MANET). There have been numerous research efforts on securing MANET protocols using cryptography or intrusion detection techniques. However, few writings have addressed MANET intrusion response. Most research on automated response for wired networks focuses on how to select the best response action to improve the security posture and availability of the system in a cost effective manner. We borrow this cost sensitive concept and develop a cost model for MANET. Two indices, Topology Dependency Index (TDI) and Attack Damage Index (ADI), are developed to reflect the response cost and attack damage, respectively. TDI measures the positional relationship between nodes and the attacker, and ADI represents the routing damage caused by the attacker. Response cost, routing damage brought by the isolation response, can be calculated from TDI. Comparing TDI with ADI helps the response agents ("RA") to perform Adaptive Isolation while maintaining good network throughput. The simulation results show that launching adaptive isolations according to the comparison of TDI and ADI gives better network throughput than direct isolation. Therefore, the main contribution of our solution is to keep network connectivity when launching isolation responses and to do so such that good quality of network routing services is maintained.

Keywords: MANET, Response Agent (RA), Topology Dependency Index (TDI), Attack Damage Index (ADI), adaptive isolation, attack damage, response cost.

1 Introduction

In traditional wireless networks, which have a fixed infrastructure, all mobile devices use wireless radio to communicate with a base station connecting to a wired network. However, a base station does not exist under some circumstances where a wired infrastructure is not available or not effective, such as on battlefields, or in disaster areas. These needs are served by Mobile Ad Hoc Networks (MANET). MANET [1, 2,3] is a set of nodes that can communicate with each other without a static base station. These mobile nodes act as both routers and hosts, exchanging routing control messages with each other to establish routing topologies. Routing protocols in

C. Kruegel, R. Lippmann, and A. Clark (Eds.): RAID 2007, LNCS 4637, pp. 127–145, 2007.
© Springer-Verlag Berlin Heidelberg 2007

MANET enable mobile nodes to maintain reliable routing tables in order to adapt to the dynamic environment.

MANETs are vulnerable to attacks because of open radio media, no central authority point, and decentralized cooperation. Many Intrusion Detection Systems (IDS) have been proposed for different MANET routing protocols [4, 5, 6, 7, 8, 9,10]. In summary, the current trend of MANET IDS is to deploy a distributed IDS with cooperative decision algorithms. Each mobile host has an IDS deployed, which is running a local detection engine that analyzes local data thereby detecting intrusions. A cooperative detection mechanism depends on all nodes participating cooperatively in the intrusion detection process. Although many IDS have been developed for MANET, there is limited work concentrating on response systems specifically in MANET except isolating uncooperative nodes according to nodes' reputation observed from their behaviors [26,27,28,29]. Our target is designing an automated response system, which is compatible with distributed, network-based Intrusion Detection Systems for proactive protocols in MANET.

In this paper, we develop a cost sensitive response model, which considers the node criticality and attack damage. First, we discuss the vulnerability, our attack model, and the corresponding responses for MANET. Subsequently, our solution model focuses on the response of isolating the attacker. The main contribution of our solution is the ability to keep network connectivity when launching isolation responses. We develop two indices, Topology Dependency Index (TDI) and Attack Damage Index (ADI), to reflect response cost, attack damage, and relative topology change. TDI is used to measure the routing dependency of the attackers' neighboring nodes on the attacker, and ADI is used to represent the routing damage caused by the attacker. By using TDI, we can evaluate the response cost, which means, in other words, how much damage the isolation response caused to the routing service. Comparing TDI with ADI helps the response agents (RAs) to determine when and how to appropriately isolate the attacker with low response cost. When RA detects a routing attack, if TDI is zero or ADI is larger than 2* TDI, RA would determine to isolate the attacker temporarily, which is called "Adaptive Isolation." The simulation results show that adaptive isolation is better than complete isolation, temporary isolation, and information recovery without isolation.

The remainder of this paper is organized as follows. Related works are discussed in Section 2. Section 3 discusses the background, and introduces our attack model together with the corresponding responses of MANET. Section 4 outlines the problem statement and the solution characteristics. Section 5 presents our proposed solution and evaluation of the solution occurs in section 6. We summarize our conclusions and anticipated future work in Section 7.

2 Related Works

There have been numerous research efforts on securing MANET protocols using cryptography to prevent attackers from participating into the protocol [13, 14, 15] or using an intrusion detection technique to further improve the security of MANET [4, 5, 6, 10, 13]. Until now, research has been focused on detection. We can find few writings on automated response in a MANET environment.

Conversely, automated response has been studied for wired networks. Most research focuses on how to select the best response action to ensure that the response action will improve the security posture and availability of the system. Notification and manual response techniques are used by traditional response systems. However, these two categories are not proactive in countering an intrusion and leave a period of vulnerability between the point when the intrusion has been detected and the point when the first response is taken. Therefore, automatically responding to an attack as soon as possible is critical to an intrusion detection system.

The first step of automatically responding to intrusions is to use decision tables. In order to solve inflexibility of static decision tables, such as false positives and negative side effects caused by a response, more complicated response systems using expert systems are also developed in CSM [22] and EMERALD [23] and Toth [24]. These papers contribute the idea that confidence metrics and severity metrics of detected attacks are included in the response process. Confidence metrics show the confidence of an intrusion detection system when detecting some attacks. The more confidence, the lower false positives should be. Severity metrics rate all potential negative impacts a response might cause for legitimate users. Therefore, response with higher severity metrics is launched only when the confidence metrics of attacks is relatively on the same level.

Balepin [16] uses a cost model to reason about automated response. It is designed to work with a specification based intrusion detection system and the responses are at the host level instead of at the network level. The cost model enables the design of the optimal response strategy even in the presence of uncertainty. Tyluki [17] employs an approach based on Control Theory to identify network oriented automated response for countering denial-of-service attacks. A study by Toth [18] proposes a promising model for automating intrusion response. They construct dependency trees that model configuration of the network and give an outline of a cost model for estimating the effect of a response. These approaches, designed for wired networks or hosts, usually assume fixed configuration and the topology cannot be directly applicable to MANET.

Tseng [4, 5] has developed an IDS for MANET proactive protocol, Optimized Link State Routing (OLSR), using a specification based approach by specifying four constraints of normal behaviors of participating nodes. If a node does not operate within these constraints, it will potentially be vulnerable to an attack. This IDS work inspires a general model of automated response system (ARS) for MANET [11, 12]. In these works, each mobile node is deployed with an IDS agent together with an ARS agent and 1-hop neighbors then monitor each other. After observing anomalies, IDS will pass alarms to ARS for advanced processing. The response system is developed with consideration for the unique characteristics of MANET, mobility and dynamic topology. It starts with responding to attacks on MANET routing and three major stages in this automated response model are exchanging messages for alarm processing and alarm validation, cost-sensitive response selection, and damage recovery. An efficient message exchange framework among distributed response agents has been addressed [12]. Our work borrows the cost sensitive response concept and proposes a new solution to address challenges in MANET.

3 Mobile Ad Hoc Networks and Vulnerability

3.1 Mobile Ad Hoc Network (MANET)

In traditional wireless networks with a fixed infrastructure, all mobile devices use wireless radio to communicate with a base station, which then connects to a wired network. However, a base station does not exist under some circumstances, or a wired infrastructure is not available or ineffective, for example in battlefields or disaster areas. Therefore, Mobile Ad Hoc Networks (MANET) are needed. MANET consists of mobile nodes sharing wireless channels to communicate with each other without a pre-established infrastructure. In MANET, mobile nodes act as both routers and hosts, exchanging routing control messages with each other to establish routing. Routing protocols for MANET generally fall into one of the two categories: proactive or reactive protocols.

Proactive routing maintains routes to all destinations at all times, regardless of whether they are needed or not. In contrast, reactive or on-demand routing protocols initiate routes only when there is data to send. Ad Hoc On-Demand Distance Vector (AODV) and Optimized Link State Routing Protocol (OLSR) are representative examples of reactive and proactive protocols, respectively. AODV only provides partial topology information to nodes which participate in an active route. For example, in AODV, every node on an active route only knows its own next hops towards the source and destination of the route. Therefore, in our opinion, a proactive protocol is easier to be designed and protected by security systems because it provides complete topology information to every node all the time, and such that intrusion detection and response systems have more sufficient routing information for attack analysis and detecting malicious behaviors. As a result, we use OLSR, a proactive routing protocol, as our design target in this paper.

3.2 Vulnerability of MANET

Wireless links are particularly vulnerable to eavesdropping, replay, spoofing, and other attacks. Especially in MANET, there is no fixed infrastructure and each node acts as both a router and a host. Therefore, all the network activities rely on cooperation of all nodes. If some node behaves uncooperatively and maliciously, for example, dropping or modifying packets, services provided by MANET will fail. Several studies have been done analyzing the vulnerabilities of MANET protocols [5, 6, 7, 19, 20]. We summarize the vulnerabilities and classify these threats in MANET. The classifications are presented below.

Insiders VS. Outsiders. MANET vulnerability can be categorized into outsider and insider attacks. Outsider attacks can be detected by traffic pattern analysis, which does not require breaking the cryptography system; or can be eavesdropping, which can be prevented with authentication [21, 22]. If the attacker gains the privilege to participate in the network, either by physically catching and compromising a good node or by bypassing the authentication, then it becomes an insider. In the MANET intrusion detection systems (IDSs) we have surveyed, most of these IDSs focus on detecting insider attacks. Since our Automated Response System (ARS) is designed for cooperating with these IDSs, we narrow down the threat scope to insider attacks only.

Routing Services VS. Packet Delivery Services. Threats can also be categorized into attacks to routing services and attacks to packet delivery services. Attacks to routing services can be achieved by disrupting the integrity or authenticity of routing control packets. For example, the malicious node can modify routing packets to prevent correct routing construction or prevent a correct existing path from being used by other nodes, or construct a virtual route. Conversely, packet delivery services disruption can be achieved by modifying or dropping data packets delivered from the source node. Compared with routing control messages, attacks to data packets have less impact since they only influence the communication between the sender and the receiver. While in routing service attacks, the attack damages will propagate and the correctness of routing tables at each node that receives infected routing packets is destroyed. In table 1, we list possible attacks on routing services by modifying different fields of routing packets to achieve different goals.

Table 1. Possible modified fields of routing control packets and its influences

Modified Field	Influences
IP	address spoofing
Sequence #	routing packet freshness
Hop Count	shortest path calculation
TTL	flooding
Neighbor List	Routing table

In addition to the attack categories discussed above, there are other attack types mainly concerning confidentiality. One is location privacy and the other is traffic pattern analysis. These two attacks are particularly sensitive to the military environment. Nodes need to hide their location and keep their tasks secret from their enemy.

3.3 Attack Model

In this subsection, we present the attack model on which our response system is based and, in section 5 will discuss what responses should be taken against different types of attacks. Because of the IDS [4,5] our work bases on, our attack model simply focuses on *insider attacks* to *routing services* as discussed in section 3.2. In the attack model, we further categorize attacks into authenticity, integrity, and availability, which are discussed below.

Authenticity. Attackers can spoof others' IP addresses to send either correct or incorrect routing messages. However, if a node impersonates others to send correct routing messages, it causes no harm to routing services. Therefore, the attack model only includes the case of *spoofing others to send incorrect routing information*. We assume that TESLA authentication [22] is used to protect the authenticity of routing packets, therefore IDSs will detect the impersonation instead of reporting the victim being spoofed as the attacker.

Integrity. In this category of attacks, there is no spoofing issue belonging to the category of authenticity. In other words, in the category of attacks against integrity, IDSs have detected exactly who the attacker is. There are two major ways to disrupt the integrity of routing packets. One is *Fabrication*, which generates a non-existed routing packet, carrying incorrect routing information. The other is *Modification*, which modifies the contents of an existing routing packet. However, the damage results of integrity disruption by utilizing both ways are the same – incorrect routing information to damage the correctness of routing tables.

Availability. There are two major ways to disrupt the availability of routing. Attackers can either drop packets to refuse to cooperatively provide routing services, or jam the network channel with a large amount of traffic.

Table 2. This table summarizes our attack model along with its correspondingly preliminary responses, which are discussed in 3.4 subsequently. The table includes three categories of attacks: attacks against authenticity by spoofing IP addresses, attacks against integrity by modifying contents of packets or even fabricates a non-existed packet, and finally attacks against availability by dropping packets or flooding packets to jam the channel.

	Attack Method	Example Attack	Responses
Authenticity	Spoofing	Impersonation	Send correct information
Integrity	Fabrication	Bogus route error	Send correct information & Isolation
	Modification	add or delete routes	
Availability	Jamming	Paralyze the channel	Relocation
	Dropping	Denial of service	Isolation

3.4 Possible Responses

There are three fundamental responses: information recovery, isolation, and relocation.

Information Recovery. This response involves sending correct routing messages and recovering the corrupted routing tables at each node in real time. This response should be taken when attacks against integrity and authenticity were detected. Dropping attacks may not require this response because packets still propagate to the entire network by the nature of flooding. In this response, ARS will ask the node who has the correct information to re-broadcast the correct routing packets and do so such that wrong routing information at each node is overwritten. It has no additional message overhead in proactive routing protocols because it can be performed by periodical routing control messages. For example, in OLSR, correct routing information can be broadcast and flooded by Hello and Topology Control (TC) messages.

Isolation. Once a malicious node is detected, the most intuitive response is to isolate the node to prevent any advanced attacks. In isolation response, the neighbors of the malicious node will totally ignore the malicious node by neither forwarding packets through it nor accepting any packets from it. Furthermore, isolation response can be performed to a different degree. We introduce two new terms for isolation: complete isolation and temporary isolation.

Complete Isolation. *Complete Isolation* means *EVERY* response agent surrounding the attacker will totally ignore the packets sent from the attacker. This type of isolation simply treats the attacker as a non-existent node and stops communicating with it. Gradually, the attacker will disappear from routing tables of all nodes in the network because no one will receive his routing control messages.

Temporary Isolation. This is a complete isolation that has in addition the **time-wise** concept. Permanent isolation means completely isolating the attacker forever. While in **temporary** isolation, once the attacker is isolated completely, it might be released and participate in the routing again. If the attack pattern is observed, the response system can determine permanent or temporary isolation against the attacker. For example, if the attack rate is high with a constant frequency, permanent isolation is considered, and vice versa.

Relocation. A relocation response is taken when the attacker is so critical in topology that it cannot be directly isolated. For example, in figure 1, node 6 and 7 are the only two nodes to bridge two sub-networks, A and B. Therefore, isolating node 6 will cause network partition. Therefore, another node, for example, node 11, can be relocated as close to node 6 and then isolate node 6 later. In this way, the network connectivity is maintained. Global positioning system (GPS) can assist the response systems in locating a certain area close to the attacker and within which one of nodes can be selected to be relocated.

3.5 Fundamental Responses for Attack Model

These fundamental responses can apply to the attacks of our attack model as listed in table 2.

Authenticity. As mentioned in 3.3, this category only includes the case of *spoofing others to send incorrect routing information.* In this case, the Intrusion Detection System (IDS) can only detect the corrupted routing messages without knowing who actually sent them since the attacker spoofs the IP. As a result, in the category of attacks against authenticity, the only response is to *correct corrupted routing information for information recovery.*

Availability. Attacks against availability include dropping and jamming. When jamming attacks happen, the victims affected by the attacker need to either switch the radio frequency or move out of the attacker's transmission range to avoid being jammed, which is a type of *relocation.* This might be a "group" relocation, which means every node moves together in the same direction and with the same speed.

Such that they can be away from the attacker as well as keep connectivity with each other. Regarding dropping attacks, isolation is the only response, especially when the dropping rate is high and constant.

Integrity. In this category of attacks, IDSs have detected exactly who the attacker is and what the corrupted contents are. So the response should be *isolating the attacker* to prevent the routing information from being corrupted by the attacker.

4 Problem Statement and Solution Characteristics

4.1 Problem Statement

In wired networks, router topology depends on manual configuration. The administrator manually chooses the gateway and determines the routing hierarchy. Since the routers are deployed by humans, the router distribution tends to be normal and the topology is fixed and expected. Unlike normal and pre-established router distribution in wired networks, topology of MANETs is more dynamic in terms of random node distribution and topology change caused by node mobility. Therefore, when performing a response, the attacker's criticality in the topology should be evaluated in deciding a proper response. Intuitively, *isolating* the malicious node is the most fundamental response. However, although a response can stop attacks, it may also partially or completely bring down services and cause denial of service to legitimate users. For example, in figure 1, isolating node 6 or node 7 will partition a network into sub-networks A and B, which may bring more routing damages than the attack itself. Therefore, a proper response is expected to alleviate the damage and to sustain services as well. In order to avoid causing more damage after responding, a comparison between *attack damage* and *response cost* needs to be performed. In this context, **cost** is defined as the **negative** impacts to the routing. In this paper, we propose a solution for performing this comparison.

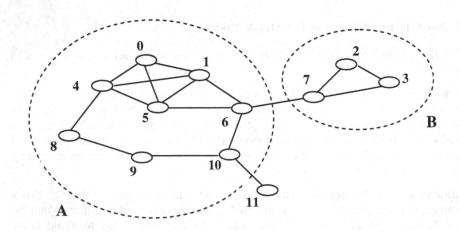

Fig. 1. Example Topology

4.2 Solution Characteristics

Distributed architecture. In wired networks, both IDSs and ARSs can be deployed on gateways, switches, or a particular centralized node. However, MANET has neither static topology nor a central point. Because of the decentralized nature of MANETs, the architecture of most IDSs developed for MANETs [2, 3, 4, 5, 6] is fully distributed rather than using a central monitoring point. In order to cooperate with these main-trend IDSs of MANETs, distributed architecture should be adopted for developing ARSs.

Automated. As we introduced in section 3, the attack model of our response system focuses on attacks against routing. Routing is the main service provided by MANETs. Therefore, it is critical to recover the routing faults in real time. If the attack is not stopped promptly, the attack damage will propagate to the entire network and the unattended attacker may launch recurring attacks. Consequently, the performance of delivering packets will be seriously degraded and so much so that the quality of routing service is deteriorated. In order to circumvent the degradation of the network and achieve real-time response, an automated response system is required.

5 Solution

As discussed previously, simply isolating the attacker might cause more damage than the attack itself. In order to avoid this problem, we need to develop some matrix to determine when and how to isolate the attacker. For MANET routing, network topology is the most fundamental element used to determine the response cost. In the early stage of designing this cost model, we focused on developing indices to reflect the *attack damage* and the *node criticality* in the routing topology. In this section, we introduce the *Topology Dependency Index (TDI)* and the *Attack Damage Index (ADI)*, which are used to represent node criticality and attack damage, respectively.

5.1 Topology Dependency Index (TDI)

We propose a new term, "Topology Dependency Index" (TDI), and develop an algorithm to calculate this index. TDI is then used to represent the routing dependency of some particular node upon the attacker. For example, *TDI(N, A)* can tell us how much *N's* routing service will be disrupted if the attacker *A* is isolated. Therefore, TDI can represent **Response Cost, which is** the negative impact caused by a response.

Definition of TDI. Each of Attacker's 1-hop neighbors (response agents) will calculate their TDIs of the Attacker. TDI can represent how much of their routing depends upon the attacker. TDI is defined as follow:

$$TDI(\ N,\ Attacker\ ) = |\ A\ |$$

Where N and the Attacker are neighbors and,
A = set of nodes that N cannot reach without taking the Attacker as the next hop.

Two cases for TDI value:

TDI(N, Attacker) = 0. It means the Attacker is not a critical node to N in topology since N's reach ability to all other nodes is not influenced by the Attacker at all. In this case, the Attacker can be isolated from N's point of view.

TDI(N, Attacker) > 0. It means N's reach ability to some nodes is influenced by the Attacker. Therefore, if the Attacker is isolated from the network, N cannot reach some set of nodes. In other words, N must take the Attacker as the next hop in order to reach some set of nodes. In this case, ARS residing on N may not consider isolating the Attacker as the response. Otherwise, some links will be broken and might bring more routing damage than the attack itself.

Algorithm of Calculating TDI(N, Attacker):

Step 1:
> *N will count the number C1 of its routing table entries*

Step 2:
> *After taking the Attacker away from all its routing control messages, N recalculates its routing table and gets C2 of new routing table entries*

Step 3:
> *TDI(N, Attacker) =| C1–C2 |*

5.2 Attack Damage Index

Attack Damage Index (ADI) is used to indicate the damage caused by an attack. When a node detects an attack, it will calculate the damage in terms of the number of nodes were affected by this attack. Each response agent will calculate how many routes from itself to other nodes changes after attacks. Here is the scenario of how we define the *route change: before attacks happen, node A takes node B as the next hop to reach node C. However, after attacks, node A takes another node D, instead of node B, to reach node C.* This is a basic example of how we define the route change, which is used to determine the attack damage.

Definition of ADI. Each of Attacker's 1-hop neighbors (response agents) will calculate their ADIs caused by the Attacker. This can represent how many routes from each of the response agents to other nodes are changed after the attack.

$$ADI(\ N, Attacker\ ) = |\ B\ |$$

Where N and the Attacker are neighbors and,
B = set of nodes whose routes from N to them change after attacks.

Algorithm of Calculating ADI(N, Attacker):

Step 1:
> *N calculates the corrupted routing table T1 using the incorrect routing information.*

Step 2:
> *N calculates the correct routing table T2 by using correct routing information.*

Step 3:

> *Compare all entries of T1 with those of T2. If any of T1's entry is missing or has a different next hop or has a different hop count, then increase **Count** by 1.*

Step 4:

> *Return **Count**, which represents ADI.*

5.3 Discussion on TDI and ADI

Both of the complexity of TDI and ADI algorithms are in O (number of nodes of the entire network), which is the same as the complexity of calculating routing tables of the protocol. Since protocol performance has proven to be good, the overhead of calculating TDI and ADI is good.

When ADI is calculated by a Response Agent (RA), RA needs to check which route from it to some other particular node changes. By checking if any route from it to other nodes changes or not, RA compares the correct routing table with the corrupted routing table. If any entry misses, or either the next hop or hop count changes, it will be a route which is affected by the attack. There are some intuitive objections arguing that it cannot detect all affected routes. However, our explanations are given.

First argument. In a routing table, given that both the next hop and the hop count of some routing entry does not change, is it possible that some point-to-point links on the route still change?

Clarification. No. According to the routing algorithm, if a new route whose next hop and hop count towards some particular node equal to those of the current route, it will keep the current route. Therefore, if both the next hop and the hop count do not change, it means the entry is not influenced by the attack.

Second argument. Only the neighboring nodes of the attacker calculate ADIs. Can these ADIs represent or reflect the overall damage of the entire network?

Clarification. Yes. Usually, the attacker manipulated the routing information to make it more attractive to other nodes such that it will be chosen as their next hop towards other destinations. Given this attack purpose, any wrong route involving the attacker must contain at least one of the attacker's neighbors. Therefore, ADIs calculated by the attacker's neighbors can proportionally reflect the overall attack damage of the entire network.

5.4 Adaptive Isolation

A discussion comparing TDI and ADI begins by noting that both TDI and ADI use "node" as their unit. Therefore, it is easy for an RA to compare them with each other and perform isolation properly. There are three basic cases when comparing TDI with ADI:

ADI > TDI: represents the case where attack damage caused by the attack itself is more severe than the damage caused by isolating the attacker. Therefore, isolating the attacker is the proper selection for response.

ADI < TDI: represents the case where isolating the node will cause more routing damage than the attack itself. Obviously, directly isolating the attacker is not a good response. It is better if another node can be relocated to replace the attacker's position in the topology and then isolation response can be performed against the attacker.

ADI ~ TDI: represents the case where attack damage and response cost is similar. The cost of a disconnected node is larger than that of a forged neighbor because the node loses the two-way connection to a disconnected node and only the one-way connection to a forged neighbor. So the node should isolate the attack while ADI > 2 * TDI.

Therefore, we isolate the attacker according to the comparison of TDI and ADI, and we call this technique "adaptive isolation." If TDI is zero, the attacker will be isolated since isolating the attacker will cause no attack damage. If TDI > 0, the node isolate the attacker only when ADI > 2 * TDI. Since the topology is dynamic, the isolation will last one minute, and new ADI and TDI will be calculated again.

6 Evaluation

6.1 Case Study

Two scenarios, based on the topology in figure 2, are described and discussed below.

Scenario 1: Node 8 is the attacker lying near node 2 and node 3 are his neighbors.
Detection: node 4 and node 9 detected this falsified routing information.
TDI and ADI calculation: $TDI_4(8) = 0$, $ADI_4(8) = 2$;
$\qquad\qquad\qquad\qquad\quad TDI_9(8) = 0$, $ADI_9(8) = 2$.
In this scenario, both node 4 and node 9 can simply isolate the attacker. That their TDI equals to 0 means isolating the attacker does not influence their reach ability to other nodes in the network. On the other hand, their ADI are greater than 0 as well as greater than their TDI. Therefore, it is easy to determine *Isolation* as the response because ADI is greater than TDI, which means attack damage is more severe than *response cost*.

Scenario 2: Node 10 is the attacker lying near node 0 is his neighbor.
Detection: node 6, node 9 and node 11 detected this falsified routing information.
TDI and ADI calculation: $TDI_6(10) = 1$, $ADI_6(10) = 0$;
$\qquad\qquad\qquad\qquad\quad TDI_9(10) = 1$, $ADI_9(10) = 1$;
$\qquad\qquad\qquad\qquad\quad TDI_{11}(10) = 10$, $ADI_{11}(10) = 2$.
In this scenario, node 11 definitely does not want to isolate node 10 because of much higher TDI than ADI, which indicates it will cause more routing damage than attack itself. For node 6, TDI is greater than zero and ADI is zero so node 6 does not isolate node 10. Regarding node 9, its TDI equals to its ADI so ADI is not large enough to trigger the isolation. Therefore, in this scenario, node 6, 8 and 9 only perform attack recovery, and they do not isolate the attacker because the cost of isolation is larger than attack damage.

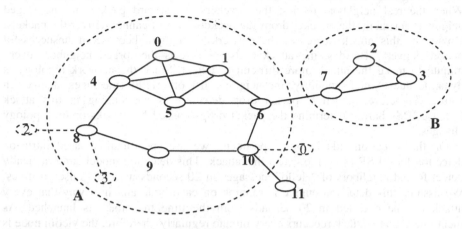

Fig. 2. Example Topology with Attacks

6.2 Experiment

We implemented our experiments on OLSR routing protocol [1] using GloMoSim as the simulation tool. GloMoSim is a clean and scalable simulation tool designed for MANET and it supports 802.11 and the Ground Reflection (Two-Ray) Model. This radio model has both a direct path and a ground reflected propagation path between the transmitter and the receiver. The radio range is about 250 meters calculated with the following parameters [25]— antenna height: 150cm, transmission power: 5dBm, antenna gain: 0, sensitivity: 91 dBm, and receiving threshold: 81 dBm. Nodes are randomly placed in the equally divided cells in the field. The total simulation time is 600 seconds and the bandwidth is 2 Mbps.

In the experiments all mobile nodes follow the *Random Waypoint* Mobility Model. Furthermore, we designed a random traffic generation model and implemented it in our experiment, which focuses on end-to-end traffic. Because nodes are placed in the equally divided cells, most of the nodes are connected and able to communicate with each other. In this model, each node randomly chooses a destination from the set of all other nodes and sends a 1024K-byte UDP packet to the selected destination every other second. If a destination receives a UDP packet, it is a successful transmission and vice versa. Therefore, the successful delivery rate is **number of received UDP packets of destinations / number of sent packets from sources** in the whole network. Moreover, this delivery rate is the measurement representing **network throughput** in the experiment. The reason for designing this traffic model is that we want to experiment with the network traffic sent from each node since MANET is a fully distributed network, where each node is treated equally.

While evaluating our solution, we simplified our attack model to consider **integrity** only because we are mainly interested in the impacts of launching different ways of isolations under different combinations of TDI and ADI. In the experiment, the attacker selects some number of non-neighboring nodes (3 nodes by default) as the victims, and adds them into its neighbor list with its new "Hello" message. Next, the attacker's real neighbors who receive the forged "Hello" message are attracted by the forged neighbors and add the incorrect routing information into their routing table. When the real neighbors request the attackers to forward packets to the forged neighbors for them, the attacker drops the packets since it cannot deliver the packets. Obviously, this attack decreases the network throughput because of unsuccessful packet delivery. Besides, the attacker also re-selects the forged neighbors every minute to make the attack more difficult to detect. Since the network topology is dynamic due to node mobility, the neighbor list of "Hello" messages changes in nature. Therefore, statistical packet drop detection is challenging in this attack because IDSs hardly determine the packet drops caused by attacks or by topology changes.

On the detection side in our experiment, we use specification based intrusion detection for OLSR [4] [5] to detect this attack. This detection model can practically detect forged neighbors of "Hello" messages in 20 seconds with low false positives. We assume this detection engine is running on each node and in a way that every attack can be detected in 20 seconds from the time the attack is launched. As mentioned, a new attack reoccurs every minute regularly, therefore, the victim node is under attack in the first 20 seconds and is recovered in the remaining 40 seconds.

The purposes of our experiments are to observe the difference between attacks with prompt responses and attacks without responses. Furthermore, we are also interested in knowing the effects of performing isolation with and without considering TDI and ADI. For these purposes, we develop 6 testing modes, which are described as follows:

Mode 0: Normal traffic generated by our traffic model without any attack.

Mode 1: Normal traffic. The attack is running without detection.

Mode 2: Normal traffic with attack running. The attack is detected in 20 seconds and the corrupted routing information will be recovered by sending correct information. However, in this mode, the attacker is not isolated.

Modes 3, 4, and 5 have the attack, information recovery as well as different degrees of isolation responses. The scenarios of the traffic pattern, attack pattern and information recovery are exactly the same in these three modes. The only difference among them is the way isolations are performed.

Mode 3: Normal traffic with attack running. The attack is detected in 20 seconds and the corrupted routing information will be recovered sending correct information. Meanwhile, the attacker is isolated completely, which means every neighboring node of the attacker refuses to communicate with the attacker from this point on.

Mode 4: Once the attacker is identified, it will be isolated for one minute, which is temporary isolation.

Mode 5: In mode 5, we want to test the effectiveness of adaptive isolation, which is our proposed solution. If ADI is larger than 2* TDI or TDI is 0, the attacker is isolated for one minute.

6.3 Experiment Results

We run these 6 test modes according to three kinds of matrices: attack degree, mobility, and scalability.

Attack degree. We tested 1 to 7 forged neighbors in a 10-node network with no mobility. When the number of forged neighbors is 5, the attack damage significantly increases since half of the nodes are forged as the attacker's neighbors. If the number is 7, almost every node becomes the forged neighbor. From figure 3, as the attack damage increases (number of forged nodes increases), our proposed solution: adaptive isolation running in mode 5 works better than other recovery methods of other modes.

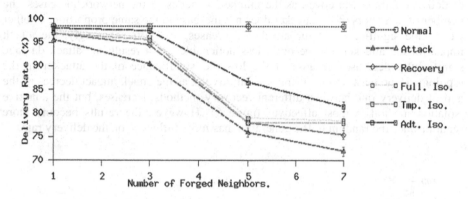

Fig. 3. Delivery Rate in different Attack Degrees

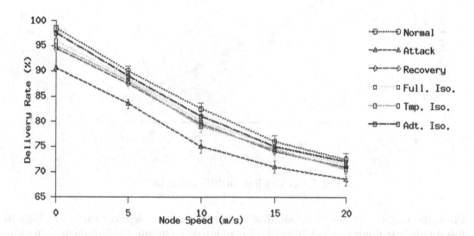

Fig. 4. Delivery Rate in different mobility

Mobility. Here we run the six test modes with differing degrees of node speed. With no mobility, attack damage is obvious, and clearly, the adaptive isolation works better than any other mode except mode 0 (no attack). As the node speed increases, the delivery rate significantly decreases due to unstable connectivity between nodes. Furthermore, the attack damage also decreases because the mobility itself already brought broken links while updating new routing topologies. So, the performance difference between different modes with different response methods becomes less noticeable. However, from figure 4, mode 5 with adaptive isolation still works the best and has the highest network throughput. In addition, although node pause time is also a factor of node mobility, it does not show much impact on the delivery rate. Therefore, we do not discuss it in this context.

Scalability. As the number of nodes increases, the delivery rate decreases because each packet transmission involves more hops and as a result, it has higher possibility of delivery failure. Moreover, as the number of nodes of the network increases, the number of neighbors of the attacker does not increase in the same proportion. In other words, the significance of the attacker decreases, and correspondingly, the attack impact of the attacker also becomes less noticeable. As a result, the attack damage significantly decreases because of the lowered significance of the attacker in the topology as the network size increases. Intuitively, as the attack impact decreases, the gap of delivery rate between different recovery methods decreases, but the adaptive isolation method is most effective (figure 5). However, the results become more random since the random traffic generation has more influence on the delivery rate.

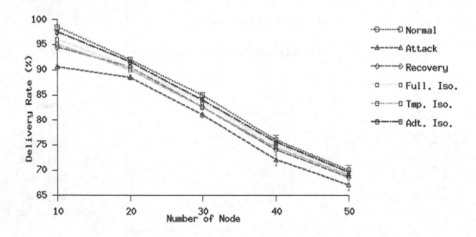

Fig. 5. Delivery Rate in different scalability

From the results, we can conclude that the ranking of the delivery rate from high to low in six test modes is: (1) Normal, (2) Adaptive Isolation, (3) Complete Isolation, (4) Temporary Isolation, (5) Information recovery only without isolation, (6) Attack without Detection and Responses. Therefore, isolating the attacker helps to improve the network throughput compared with performing information recovery only. Furthermore, isolating the attacker adaptively by referencing the comparison between TDI and ADI also increases the network throughput. Therefore, consideration of the comparison of attack damage and response cost indeed increases the quality of routing services after taking responses has been proven.

7 Conclusion and Anticipated Future Work

We developed Topology Dependency Index (TDI) to represent the response cost and Attack Damage Index (ADI) to measure the routing damage brought by the attack. Comparing TDI with ADI helps the Response Agents (RAs) to perform the adaptive isolation. From the simulation results, the importance of prompt responses, information recovery, and isolation is shown. Launching instant responses can increase the network throughput of the attacked network. Furthermore, performing adaptive isolation smartly by comparing TDI and ADI improves the network throughput even more than regular complete isolation.

In addition to attack damage (ADI) and response cost (TDI), some other factors can be considered, such as attack pattern, node reputation, and alarm confidence. **Attack pattern** means attack frequency in this context. For example, if a malicious node drops or modifies 80% of the packets, the response will tend to be isolation and route through another node. Furthermore, if the attacking rate is high and constant, permanent isolation is preferred. If attacks happen sporadically, temporary isolation might be chosen. Besides attack pattern, node reputation and blacklist approach [26,27] can be used to detect and react to packet drop attacks. **Node reputation** and **alarm confidence** are also good references for deciding responses, which will be integrated into our solution model. The better reputation of the reporting node and the worse reputation of the reported node, the higher confidence of this alarm and severe responses can be taken. For instance, an ID agent A with bad reputation raises an alarm against a suspicious node N with good reputation. The Response agent should be more conservative when launching a response because it might be a false alarm. These topics will be covered in our future work.

References

1. Clausen, T.T., Jacquet, P.: Optimized link state routing protocol (OLSR). IETF RFC3626
2. Perkins, C., Belding-Royer, E., Das, S.: Ad hoc on-demand distance vector (AODV) routing. IETF RFC 3561
3. Ogier, R., Templin, F., Lewis, M.: Topology Dissemination Based on Reverse-Path Forwarding (TBRPF). IETF RFC3684
4. Tseng, C.H., Wang, S.-H., Ko, C., Levitt, K.: DEMEM: Distributed Evidence-Driven Message Exchange Intrusion Detection Model For MANET. In: Zamboni, D., Kruegel, C. (eds.) RAID 2006. LNCS, vol. 4219, Springer, Heidelberg (2006)
5. Tseng, C.H., Song, T., Balasubramanyam, P., Ko, C., Levitt, K.: A Specification-based Intrusion Detection Model for OLSR. In: Valdes, A., Zamboni, D. (eds.) RAID 2005. LNCS, vol. 3858, Springer, Heidelberg (2006)
6. Tseng, C., Balasubramanyam, P., Ko, C., Limprasittiporn, R., Rowe, J., Levitt, K.: A Specification-Based Intrusion Detection System For AODV. In: Proceedings of the ACM Workshop on Security in Ad Hoc and Sensor Networks (SASN'03) (October 2003)
7. Ning, P., Sun, K.: How to Misuse AODV: A Case Study of Insider Attacks against Mobile Adhoc Routing Protocols. In: Proceedings of the 4th Annual IEEE Information Assurance Workshop, West Point, June 2003, pp. 60–67. IEEE Computer Society Press, Los Alamitos (2003)

8. Buchegger, S., Le Boudec, J.-Y.: Performance Analysis of the CONFIDANT Protocol (Cooperation Of Nodes: Fairness In Dynamic Ad-hoc NeTworks). In: Proceedings of the 3rd ACM international symposium on Mobile ad hoc networking & computing, Lausanne, Switzerland, June 2002, ACM Press, New York (2002)
9. Zhang, Y., Lee, W.: Intrusion Detection in Wireless Ad-Hoc Networks. In: Proceedings of The Sixth International Conference on Mobile Computing and Networking (MobiCom 2000), Boston, MA (August 2000)
10. Huang, Y.-a., Lee, W.: A cooperative intrusion detection system for ad hoc networks. In: Proceedings of the 1st ACM workshop on Security of ad hoc and sensor networks, October 2003, ACM Press, New York (2003)
11. Wang, S.-H., Tseng, C.H., Ko, C., Gertz, M., Levitt, K.: A general automatic response model for MANET. In: Proceeding of First IEEE International Workshop on Next Generation Wireless Networks, December 2005, IEEE Computer Society Press, Los Alamitos (2005)
12. Tseng, C.H., Wang, S.-H., Levitt, K.: DRETA: Distributed Routing Evidence Tracing and Authentication intrusion detection Model for MANET. In: ASIACCS 2007 (2007)
13. Yi, S., Naldurg, P., Kravets, R.: Security-aware routing protocol for wireless ad hoc networks. In: Proceeding of ACM MobiHoc 2001 (October 2001)
14. Zhou, L., Haas, Z.J.: Securing ad hoc networks. IEEE Network 13(6), 24–30 (1999)
15. Sanzgiri, K., Dahill, B., Levine, B.N., Shields, C., Belding-Royer, E.M.: A secure routing protocol for ad hoc networks. In: Proceeding of the Tenth IEEE International Conference on Network Protocols, IEEE Computer Society Press, Los Alamitos (2002)
16. Balepin, I., Maltsev, S., Rowe, J., Levitt, K.: Using Specification-Based Intrusion Detection for Automated Response. In: Vigna, G., Krügel, C., Jonsson, E. (eds.) RAID 2003. LNCS, vol. 2820, Springer, Heidelberg (2003)
17. Tylutki, M., Levitt, K.N.: Mitigating Distributed Denial of Service Attacks Using a Proportional-Integral-Derivative Controller. In: Vigna, G., Krügel, C., Jonsson, E. (eds.) RAID 2003. LNCS, vol. 2820, Springer, Heidelberg (2003)
18. Toth, T., Kruegel, C.: Evaluating the impact of automated intrusion response mechanisms. In: 18th Annual Computer Security Applications Conference, Las Vegas, Nevada (December 9-13, 2002)
19. Prasant, M., Srikanth, K. (eds.): Ad Hoc Networks: Technologies and Protocols (2004)
20. Hu, Y.-C., Perrig, A., Johnson, D.B.: A Secure On-Demand Routing Protocol for Ad Hoc Networks. In: The 8th ACM International Conference on Mobile Computing and Networking, September 2002, ACM Press, New York (2002)
21. Canetti, P.R., Tygar, D., Song, D.: The TESLA broadcast authentication protocol. Cryptobytes (RSA Laboratories, Summer/Fall 2002) 5(2), 2–13 (2002)
22. White, G., Fisch, E., Pooch, U.: Cooperating security managers: A peer-based intrusion detection system. IEEE Network 10, 20–23 (1996)
23. Porras, P., Neumann, P.: EMERALD: event monitoring enabling responses to anomalous live disturbances. In: Proceedings of the 1997 National Information Systems Security Conference (1997)
24. Toth, T., Kruegel, C.: Evaluating the impact of automated intrusion response mechanisms. In: 18th Annual Computer Security Applications Conference, Las Vegas, Nevada (December 9-13, 2002)
25. Nuevo, J.: A Comprehensible GloMoSim Tutorial (March 2004)
26. He, Q., Wu, D., Khosla, P.: SORI: A Secure and Objective Reputation-based Incentive Scheme for Ad-hoc Networks (2004)

27. Buchegger, S., Le Boudec, J.-Y.: Performance Analysis of the CONFIDANT Protocol (Cooperation Of Nodes - Fairness In Dynamic Ad-hoc NeTworks. In: Proceedings of MobiHoc 2002, Lausanne (June 2002)
28. Buchegger, S., Le Boudee, J.-Y.: Self-Policing Mobile Ad Hoc Networks by Reputation Systems. IEEE Communications Magazine 43(7), 101–107 (2005)
29. Lindsay, S.Y., Wei, Y., Zhu, H., Liu, K.J.R.: Information Theoretic Framework of Trust Modeling and Evaluation for Ad Hoc Networks. IEEE Journal on Selected Areas in Communications 24(2), 305–317 (2006)

ELICIT: A System for Detecting Insiders Who Violate Need-to-Know

Marcus A. Maloof[1] and Gregory D. Stephens[2]

[1] Department of Computer Science,
Georgetown University, Washington, DC 20057, USA
maloof@cs.georgetown.edu
[2] Center for Integrated Intelligence Systems,
The MITRE Corporation, McLean, VA 22102, USA
gstephens@mitre.org

Abstract. Malicious insiders do great harm and avoid detection by using their legitimate privileges to steal information that is often outside the scope of their duties. Based on information from public cases, consultation with domain experts, and analysis of a massive collection of information-use events and contextual information, we developed an approach for detecting insiders who operate outside the scope of their duties and thus violate *need-to-know*. Based on the approach, we built and evaluated ELICIT, a system designed to help analysts investigate insider threats. Empirical results suggest that, for a specified decision threshold of .5, ELICIT achieves a detection rate of .84 and a false-positive rate of .015, flagging per day only 23 users of 1,548 for further scrutiny. It achieved an area under an ROC curve of .92.

Keywords: misuse, insider threat, anomaly detection.

1 Introduction

Recently, the FBI arrested analyst Leandro Aragoncillo after he allegedly "conducted extensive keyword searches relating to the Philippines" and "printed or downloaded 101 classified documents", also relating to the Philippines [1]. Although Aragoncillo was an intelligence analyst, information about the Philippines was "outside the scope of his assignments" [1].

We are interested in detecting this type of malicious insider, but the problem of detecting *insiders* is much more complex and multi-faceted. For instance, malicious insiders are often disgruntled [2], so better working environments could lead to a reduced threat. Better processes for screening employees could also reduce the threat. On corporate intranets, one may be able to deploy methods traditionally used against external intruders to counter an insider who is, say, attempting to gain unauthorized access to a server. In contrast, we are interested in detecting malicious insiders who operate within their privileges, but who engage in activity that is outside the scope of their legitimate assignments and thus violate *need-to-know*.

C. Kruegel, R. Lippmann, and A. Clark (Eds.): RAID 2007, LNCS 4637, pp. 146–166, 2007.

In this paper, we describe our efforts to develop and evaluate methods of detecting insiders who violate need-to-know. Based on analysis, research, and consultation with domain experts, we designed an approach that consists of four main steps. First, *decoders* process network traffic from protocols associated with the use of information into higher-level *information-use* events. Second, a suite of detectors, supplanted with contextual information about users, groups, and organizations, examines these events and issues alerts. Third, a Bayesian network uses these alerts as evidence and computes threat scores. Fourth, an interface presents events, alerts, and threat scores of users to security analysts. Based on this approach, we implemented a system named ELICIT, which stands for "Exploit Latent Information to Counter Insider Threats."

To support ELICIT's development and evaluation, we derived a data set from 284 days of network traffic collected from an operational corporate intranet. Over a period of 13 months, we processed 16 terabytes of raw packets into more than 91 million information-use events for more than 3, 900 users. We then examined these events to characterize the searching, browsing, downloading, and printing activity of individuals, groups of individuals, and the organization as a whole. We built 76 detectors and a Bayesian network that, together, produce an overall threat score for each user in the organization.

To evaluate our approach and ELICIT, a red team developed scenarios based on information from real, publicly-available cases. They translated the scenarios to the target environment and executed them during normal network operation. A trusted agent[1] used scripts to insert events of the scenarios into our collection of events. We then ran ELICIT, as would an analyst, in an effort to identify the users corresponding to the scenarios.

Over a period of two months, using a specified decision threshold of .5, ELICIT detected the insiders on 16 of the 19 days they were acting maliciously, corresponding to a detection rate of .84. During this same period, ELICIT scored an average of 1, 548 users per day, with an average of only 23 users scoring high enough to warrant further scrutiny, meaning that ELICIT's average false-positive rate is .015. By varying the decision threshold, we produced an ROC curve, the area under which was .92.

2   Problem Statement

There are many detection tasks important for securing systems, their software, and their information, such as detecting intruders [3,4], and anomalous command [5] and system-call [6] sequences. We focus on the task of detecting misuse, defined as legitimate users abusing their privileges.

Detecting misuse is a complex, multi-faceted problem, and malicious insiders, or simply *insiders*, may engage in a variety of activities. Insiders could use knowledge of their organization's intranet and behave in a manner similar to an intruder. Such activities could include scanning ports, executing buffer overflows,

---

[1] Herein, all uses of the term *trusted agent* refer to the person serving as the intermediary between the red team and the research team.

and cracking password files, and one can detect these activities with methods of intrusion detection. Insiders could also masquerade as another user by compromising his or her account. However, in our work, we are interested in detecting malicious insiders who do not engage in these activities.

In a computing system, access-control mechanisms yield a set of illegal and legal actions for each user. Such actions include viewing certain documents, and so, there will be documents that a user can and cannot view. Unfortunately, for large, dynamic organizations, it is difficult to design and maintain effective access control. Consequently, given the set of legal actions for a user, there is a set of such actions that is suspect, especially given contextual information about the user. In our work, we are interested in detecting insiders who browse, search, download, and print documents and files to which they have access, but that are inappropriate or uncharacteristic for them based on contextual information, such as their identity, past activity, and organizational context.

Our conception of detecting insiders is quite different than detecting external intruders. One rarely, if ever, has the contextual information for such intruders that one has for insiders. Our aim is to leverage this context for detection. It is also different than detecting internal intruders, since insiders who violate need-to-know do not need to break rules to achieve their goals. All detection systems must analyze events at correct levels of abstraction, and the insiders of interest to us usually gather and exfiltrate documents. Consequently, rather than detecting malicious activity based on connections, packets, or system-call sequences, we chose to detect insiders based on *information-use events*, which we describe further in the next section.

3   Data Collection

We derived the data set for our study from an operational corporate intranet. In the following subsections, we describe how we processed network traffic into *information-use events*, collected contextual information about users and the information they accessed, and developed scenarios for the purpose of evaluation.

3.1   Transforming Network Traffic into Information-Use Events

To collect network events, we placed passive sensors between clients and servers within a large corporate intranet for 284 days.[2] The sensors collected packets from network protocols correlated with the legitimate use of information, a critical aspect of our work. In total, we captured approximately 16 terabytes of data,

---

[2] We experienced three outages. Two months into the period, an administrative error resulted in an outage for two days. Three months later, an unanticipated network reconfiguration caused a near-complete loss of data for five days. Four months into collection, we discovered and corrected an error in the software that captured packets. Subsequent analysis indicating that the flawed version failed to capture about 9% of the packets, with the majority of the loss occurring during traffic bursts. Nonetheless, data from this period was helpful for analysis and development. Crucially, the red team did not execute the scenarios until after we resolved these problems.

Table 1. Information Stored for Events

Field	Actions							
	List	Delete	Read	Write	Move	Print	Query	Send
Protocol	X	X	X	X	X	X	X	X
File Name/Path	X	X	X	X	X	X	X	X
Start/Stop Time	X	X	X	X	X	X	X	X
Client/Server IP	X	X	X	X	X	X	X	X
User Name	X	X	X	X	X	X	X	X
Bytes			X	X				
Original File Name					X			
Printer						X		
Pages						X		
Search Phrase							X	
E-mail Headers								X

corresponding to 27 billion packets. In the collection, 61% of packets were from the SMB protocol, 35% were from HTTP, 3%, from SMTP, and 1%, from FTP.

We developed a series of *protocol decoders* to transform the packets into information-use events. These decoders also tracked authenticated users across sessions and captured clues about their identity, which aided in subsequent attribution. Off-line, the trusted agent used Ethereal [7] to filter and dissect packets, and then applied our decoders to produce information-use events. Over a period of 13 months, the decoders processed more than 3.7 billion packets, producing more than 91 million events, which we stored in a relational database.

Referring to Table 1, each event consisted of an action and variable number of fields. Decoders extracted eight actions. In our collection, 35.8% of the actions were lists of files or directories, 42.1% were reads, 12.9% were writes, 4.6% were deletes, 2.9% were sends of e-mail, 1.1% were search-engine queries, 0.4% were prints of documents, and 0.3% were moves of files or directories. The decoders also extracted fields such as the start and end time of the action, the protocol involved, and other pertinent information. Table 2 contains an example of a print event in which user p0314508p printed a document named Liz's form fax.doc to the printer \\spool2\335-HP. Values for all other fields are null.

With the exception of send, we selected these actions and fields based on analysis of past insider cases and hypotheses about which would be useful for detecting violations of need-to-know. Then, during decoder development, we implemented routines to capture information from e-mail because we realized that it would be useful for constructing social networks.

We did not collect data directly on clients, so our approach is network-based, rather than host-based. In the environment we monitored, it would have been impractical—though desirable—to instrument every machine with the software necessary to collect events. We also did not collect packets inbound from or outbound to the Internet due to concerns about privacy. If our approach were used in an organization where such technical and privacy issues could be resolved, ELICIT's design is flexible enough to accommodate these new sources of information.

Table 2. Example of the Relevant Fields of a Print Event

Field	Value
Action	print
Protocol	smb
File Name	Liz's form fax.doc
Start Time	2005-02-03 10:32:16.993
Stop Time	2005-02-03 10:32:17.003
Client IP	ddd.ddd.ddd.13
Server IP	ddd.ddd.ddd.239
User Name	p0314508p
Bytes	2672
Printer	\\spool2\335-HP
Pages	1

3.2   Collection of Contextual Information

In addition to events, we developed sensors that periodically collected contextual information about the users and the information they accessed and manipulated. This included information from an employee directory, such as name, office location, job description, seniority, and projects. We also copied the contents of files in users' public directories on a shared file system, and we extracted information from the directory structure itself, the branches of which often corresponded to users, projects, and the organization's business units. We stored this information in a database, and Table 3 shows an example.

With this contextual information, we were able to build simple social networks with e-mail traffic, use a person's job description in the analysis of his or her search-engine queries, and determine if someone printed to a printer close to his or her office. It also let us compare a user's behavior to that of peers, such as those with the same job description and those working on the same floor, in the same department, and on joint projects.

These comparisons illustrate a critical aspect of our work. We are not simply examining network events between client and server IP addresses. We are monitoring how users access and manipulate information, and we are coupling this activity with contextual information about the users and the information itself.

3.3   Data Anonymization

To protect the privacy of the users, the trusted agent removed, anonymized, or abstracted any identifying information before releasing it to us, the research team. The trusted agent removed hire dates and phone numbers, replaced names and user IDs with pseudonyms, and abstracted office numbers to their floor.

An important concern is whether the process of anonymization introduced artifacts that may have affected detection. For this study, phone numbers and hire dates were not important for detection, so their removal was not problematic. Name and user ID are not relevant for detection, but are critical as labels

Table 3. Example of Contextual Information for User p0314508p

Field	Value
User Name	p0314508p
E-mail Address	p0314508p
User ID	p0314508p
Home Directory	s:\p0314508p\public
Department	Accounts Payable
Division	Purchasing
Office Location	7th Floor
Job Title	General Accounting Specialist
Job Category	General Accounting
Job Level	3
Project 1	Accounts Payable
Project 2	Travel Accounting

connecting events and detector outputs. However, pseudonyms serve this purpose equally well.

Abstracting office location to its floor did make it difficult or impossible to conduct certain analyses, which may have negatively affected detection. For example, we could not identify relationships between people who shared offices or who worked in adjacent offices. Since ours is a research effort, we had to accept that there was certain information we simply could not use or collect. Nonetheless, even without this information, our results are promising.

3.4 Event Attribution

To use an individual's context, such as their job description or social network, we had to attribute each event to a user. Unfortunately, not all sessions, and thus not all events, had information about the user who produced them. For example, unprotected Windows file shares and web sites requiring no authentication generated events without identifying information. In the database, such events have null values for their user IDs.

Our collection contained three types of events: unattributed events, indirectly-attributed events, and events directly attributed to a user because of an observed successful authentication. For example, most SMB sessions begin with an authentication, and we can then attribute subsequent events of the session to the authenticated user. Indirectly attributed events are those with some type of user context, such as the sender's address in an e-mail. Of the more than 91 million events, 14.7% were directly attributed, 2.3% were indirectly attributed, and 83% were initially unattributed.

With network engineers familiar with the network environment, we devised two off-line methods to label unattributed events. Both used events occurring before and after an unattributed event. The first was a nearest-neighbor method that attributes an unattributed event to the user of the closest attributed event, as measured by time. The second method uses a kernel function to give more weight to the attributed events closer to the unattributed event. To reflect the uncertainty of attribution sources (e.g., due to configuration or human errors), network engineers determined measures of confidence for each, assigning print events a weight of .999, send events a weight of .99, and FTP events a weight of .9. Directly attributed events had a weight of 1 and unattributed events had a weight of 0.

An *attribution event* e_i is then a 3-tuple $\langle u_i, w_i, t_i \rangle$, where u_i is the ID of the attributed user, w_i is the weight, and t_i is the time of occurrence. For a given client IP address, there is a sequence of attribution events with and without attribution. Let S be a sequence of n events ordered by t_i, and let $S^{(u)}$ be the sequence of events from S attributed to user u:

$$S^{(u)} = \{ \langle u_i, w_i, t_i \rangle : \langle u_i, w_i, t_i \rangle \in S \wedge u_i = u \} .$$

If e_i is an unattributed event (i.e., $u_i = \emptyset$) occurring in the middle of sequence S (i.e., $i = n/2$), then we attribute e_i to the user in the sequence whose actions have the maximum weight. That is, given the kernel function

$$K(e_i, e_j) = w_j e^{-\gamma(t_i - t_j)^2} ,$$

where γ determines the width of the kernel,

$$u_i = \operatorname*{argmax}_{u \in S} \left(\sum_{e_j \in S^{(u)}} K(e_i, e_j) \right) .$$

For each unattributed event in a sequence, we applied both methods. With the kernel method, we set $\gamma = 5 \times 10^{-5}$ and used overlapping sequences of events that were 16 hours in length. If the weight calculated for an unattributed event was less than 1×10^{-5}, then the event remained unattributed. If both methods returned the same user ID, then we set the ID of the unattributed event to the inferred ID. If the methods did not agree, then the event remained unattributed.

To evaluate this procedure, we compared performance to our two network engineers. We randomly selected 100 unattributed events and applied our attribution procedure. We provided the same events to both experts, who independently attributed the events. They then resolved any differences to produce a single set of attributed events. Our procedure agreed with the experts on 99 of the 100 events. The disagreement involved an ambiguous event from a multi-user machine that belonged either to the end of one user's session or the beginning of another's.

Applying this procedure to all of the events, we were able to infer attribution for 65% of the previously unattributed events. About 28.6% of the events in the collection remained unattributable, but 82% of these originated from 25 hosts running automated processes. Those remaining were ambiguous events from clients with multiple, concurrent users.

3.5   The Need for Meta-Events

Early on, we noticed that users initiating certain simple actions produced an inordinate number of information-use events. Executing a find command on a

Table 4. Scenarios and Their Descriptions

Scenario	Description
s1	Employee who gathers technical information about aviation and aeronautics, topics that are outside the scope of the employee's duties.
s2	System administrator who obtains financial information, such as internal reports, disclosure statements, labor rates, and the like.
s3	Disgruntled employee who is to leave the company and gathers a large amount of widely varying documents containing sensitive, proprietary information.
s4	Employee who collects a large volume of information about *knowledge management*, which is unrelated to the employee's duties.
s5	Employee who gathers software relating to aviation from a proprietary, internal repository.

large, shared file system is one example. We also found that software automatically updating files on clients or servers often accounted for most of a user's "browsing" activity (e.g., software updating a public calendar from a personal calendar). While the information-use events of these sequences are interesting themselves, we did not want the number of events in a sequence to skew certain types of analyses.

As a result, we grouped certain sequences of directory and file events into *meta-events*. We segmented a user's events when there was a change in protocol, a change in the server's IP address, or when the separation between two events was greater than ten seconds. Over each segment, we computed the number of events in the segment, the rate at which the events occurred, and the percentage of list events in the segment. If a segment was longer than 20 events and the frequency of events was greater than two per second, then we labeled the segment as a meta-event. If the percentage of list events within the segment was greater than 90%, then we further labeled the segment as being the result of a find command. In the database, we used a unique identifier to label events of a meta-event. An additional field indicated whether the meta-event was the result of a list or find command. Although we determined these thresholds empirically, we found that this heuristic method worked well for our events.

3.6 Scenario Development and Execution

The data set described so far consists of activity for 3,983 users. It has proven invaluable for analysis and the development of detectors. However, it contains no known malicious activity, which limits our ability to evaluate our approach.

In response, a red team constructed fifteen scenarios inspired by public cases that involved the gathering of illicit information by individuals such as Aldrich Ames, Ryan Anderson, and Brian Regan. Domain experts reviewed the scenarios and adapted them to the network we monitored. Once approved, the red team

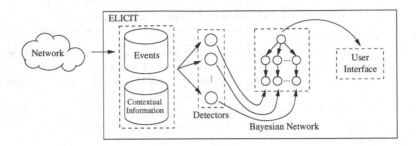

Fig. 1. ELICIT's architecture

executed the five scenarios listed in Table 4 during normal network operation. Three of the five scenarios were executed by two different members of the red team (i.e., S2, S3, and S4) in an effort to assess the role that individual personality might play in scenario execution and detection. This resulted in a total of eight scenario executions. (We did not execute the remaining scenarios because members of the red team were assigned to other projects; we plan to use the scenarios in future work.)

The red team used their legitimate accounts to execute scenarios during normal network operation, which let the trusted agent process the "benign" and scenario data together. Using the red team's detailed logs of their activity and demarcation events sent via e-mail, the trusted agent isolated and then removed the scenario events from the benign collection of information-use events. This let the trusted agent insert and remove individual scenarios at will.

The members of the red team were knowledgeable about insider activity and investigations. They were given the scenario and its translation, and instructed to achieve an objective (i.e., steal information) in a manner consistent with the scenario and its insider. These instructions identified specific topics, documents, and systems (e.g., financial), but their actions were not tightly scripted. Members were not told how to achieve their objective or the time over which an attack must occur. To make inserting and removing the scenario events possible, they were told not to intermix benign and malicious activity between demarcation events. While not all insider attacks follow this profile, many do because insiders often take advantage of windows of opportunity.

The research team and the red team worked in isolation with the trusted agent mediating interactions. The teams did not share domain experts, and the research team had no insight into the development, execution, collection, and insertion of scenarios and their events until *after the completion* of ELICIT's development and evaluation. Although the teams worked in isolation, in retrospect, they independently profiled some of the same insiders, such as Regan, Ames, and Hanssen. However, the red team also profiled insiders that the research team did not, such as Ryan Anderson and Ana Montes. The research team did not know how the red team would translate the scenarios (e.g., that aviation would be a topic of interest).

4   The ELICIT System

ELICIT is a research prototype designed to help analysts investigate malicious insiders. As shown in Fig. 1, it consists of four main components: a database of events and contextual information, a set of detectors, a Bayesian network, and a user interface.

As described previously, we processed packet data from the network and stored the resulting events in a relational database system. Based on our analysis of these events, consultation with experts, and public information about past cases, we designed and built detectors that, over specified periods of time, examine events in the database and return a set of alerts. A Bayesian inference network uses the alerts as evidence and computes, for each user, an overall threat score. Finally, ELICIT presents the users and their scores to an analyst through the user interface.

4.1   Detectors for Anomalous Activity

To date, we have developed 76 detectors that examine events for volumetric anomalies, suspicious behavior, and evasive behavior. We define each detector along three dimensions: the activity's type, its characteristics, and its context. The type of activity can be browsing, searching, downloading, and printing. Each detector examines characteristics of the activity, such as when the activity occurred, where it occurred, and how (or to what extent) it occurred. Finally, each detector evaluates activity in context with past activity, with the activity of organizational or professional peers, or with the activity of the peers in some social network.

Each detector works by taking as arguments a time period and a set of parameters, by examining each person's activity during the time period and relevant contextual information, and by issuing an alert, provided that the user's activity meets the detector's criteria for reporting. Some detectors use only the user's events that occurred during the specified period of time, while others analyze events of other types, of other users, or from other periods of time. Some detectors alert when users engage in specific activities, such as conducting searches using inappropriate terms. Others alert when some aspect of user activity is excessive or anomalous, which means that some measure of that activity falls into a rejection region.

We based each detector on a hypothesis about the activities in which malicious insiders might engage. We formed and supported each hypothesis with analysis of the events in our data collection, with advice from domain experts, with information from public cases, or with some combination thereof. As one might expect, we could not always support a hypothesis because one or more of the other sources refuted it. For example, if we found evidence of suspicious activity, but an expert advised that it was not indicative of malicious insiders, then a detector for that activity would be of little use, at least for the environment we monitored. It is important to note that detectors suitable for one environment may not be suitable for another.

Since we had no traces of real insider attacks and no models of insider behavior for the network we monitored, we consulted with three domain experts. For several years, they have performed technical analysis of active insider cases involving the theft or misuse of information. They were familiar with the network we monitored and its users. They advised us on the activities in which insiders might engage and helped determine the parameters of detectors.

To implement detectors, we used a variety of methods, including hand-coded rules, and parametric and nonparametric density estimation. We also exploited social networks. To set their parameters, we described and presented to our experts the observed activity in both textual and graphical form using events from the database and histograms of the activity of individual users and groups of users (e.g., with the same job title). The experts came to a consensus about what they considered excessive or anomalous, and we used this information to set the parameters and thresholds of the detectors. We make no claims that these are optimal settings, but based on observation and expert feedback, they seem to be reasonable estimates. Unfortunately, due to space restrictions, we cannot describe all 76 detectors, so we describe a representative few.

Sensitive Search Terms. Insiders use search engines to find, evaluate, and collect information. Most organizations can define a set of sensitive terms that appear in documents, but that would be inappropriate for use as query terms. The term *proprietary* is an example. With the help of domain experts, we constructed a list of thirteen such search terms, and if someone's query contains one of the terms on this list, then the detector issues an alert.

Printing to a Non-Local Printer. It is important to note that in the organizations of interest to us, printing a document is often the only way of removing information. Computers are on networks isolated from the Internet and have their USB ports and external storage systems disabled. Evidence from publicly-available documents suggests that insiders collect and print documents on topics outside the scope of their duties. Presumably, the insider's co-workers would recognize if the topic of a printed document were inappropriate. Consequently, to avoid suspicion, an insider may print inappropriate documents to a distant or non-local printer.

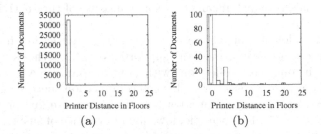

Fig. 2. Number of documents printed plotted against the distance of the printer from the user's office. (a) The fully scaled graph. (b) A version scaled to emphasize the bars right of the mode.

In the environment we monitored, an overwhelming majority of users printed to their local printer, as shown in Fig. 2. The graphs show the number of documents printed plotted against the distance to the printer when the user prints from his or her office. The distance is the number of floors from an individual's office to the printer.

As shown in Fig. 2a, over a six-week period, users printed 34,279 documents, with 32,475 of these documents sent to printers on the same floor as their office. In Fig. 2b, which contains a scaled version to emphasize the bars to the right of the mode, notice the small spike at a distance of four. Five users, all from the same department, were responsible for 22 of these 25 print jobs. We are unsure why these users would print from their offices to a printer four floors above. They may have been printing to a printer in a lab.

Writing a detector for non-local prints was quite easy. In the database, we stored each user's office location, each printer's location, and for each document printed, the user who issued the print command, the location where the user issued the print command, and the printer to which the user sent the document. The detector alerts if the user prints from his or her office to a printer on a different floor.

Anomalous Browsing Activity. To take into account a user's past activity, we implemented a number of detectors that alert when anomalous events occur. These include the size of a document printed, the number of documents downloaded, the number of search queries issued, and the like. One such detector alerts when a user browses an anomalous number of documents in a 15-minute period.

In the environment we monitored, in 15-minute periods, people often browsed few documents and rarely browsed many documents. Using a χ^2 test of goodness of fit, we determined that the number of documents browsed in 15-minute periods follows a folded-normal distribution [8].

For a given time period and user, the detector calculates the maximum number of browses for the user during a 15-minute interval within the time period. The detector then retrieves the number of browses during each 15-minute period going back a certain number of days from the start of the time period. It then estimates the parameters of a folded-normal distribution [8], the mean, the standard deviation, and the number of nonzero 15-minute intervals. Then, using the density function, it computes the probability that the user would conduct the maximum number of browses observed in the time period. If the probability is below a threshold, which we determined with the help of domain experts, then the detector alerts. We also implemented a version that uses a kernel-density estimator [9].

Retrieving Documents Outside of One's Social Network. Insiders often steal information to which they have access, but that is outside the scope of their duties, and thus, is not closely associated with them—closely associated in terms of topic and the information's owners and originators at individual and organizational levels. If the organization discovers that its information has been compromised, then this disassociation makes it more difficult to determine the leak's source.

For each individual of the organization, we automatically built a social network based on the people in their department, whom they e-mailed, and with whom they worked on projects. With nodes corresponding to people, we used unweighted directed arcs to represent these associations. We then examined the extent to which individuals retrieved documents from the public directories of people inside and outside their social network.

Over a period of five months, we tallied the number of documents that each user retrieved during each 15-minute interval. We then expressed this count as the percentage of documents retrieved from others who were outside the user's social network. Subject-matter experts selected as a threshold the percentage that they considered excessive. We built a detector that, when invoked, constructs a social network for each user and counts the number of documents retrieved from outside this network. If the count surpasses the threshold, then the detector alerts.

4.2   Bayesian Network for Ranking

For a given user, ELICIT's 76 detectors may alert in any combination. Presently, if a detector alerts, it simply reports true, so there are 2^{76} possible combinations of alerts. It is unlikely that any analyst would be able to understand such a set of alerts for all but the smallest of organizations or groups of users.

We wanted ELICIT to rank each user of the organization using a *threat score*. Naturally, each user's score would be based on the alerts that his or her activity produced. The simplest method would be to use as a score the total number of alerts, but alerts are not equally predictive of insider behavior, and benign users may engage in many of the same activities as does an insider. We considered asking experts to weight the alerts based on their correlation to malicious behavior, but this brought up the issue of how to combine weights, especially when detectors do not alert and there is an absence of evidence. There also may be other "external" events that cause benign users to change their behavior. For example, a task force created in response to a crisis may produce anomalous activity, such as searching, browsing, and printing during odd hours.

To cope with these challenges, with the help of domain experts, we designed and constructed a Bayesian inference network [10]. Our early designs, while accurate, were too complex, especially when we considered the task of eliciting probabilities from analysts. We settled on a three-level, tree-structured network (see Fig. 1) consisting of Boolean random variables.

The first level consists of one node for the random variable *MaliciousInsider*. The second and third levels correspond to the activities in which a malicious insider will or will not engage (e.g., using inappropriate search terms) and the detectors of those activities that will or will not alert, respectively. There are 76 nodes in both the second and third levels. The nodes of the second level represent the probability that a user will or will not engage in some activity given that he is and is not a malicious insider. The nodes of the third level represent the probability that a detector will or will not detect such activity given that it does and does not occur on the network.

For nodes of the top two levels, we elicited probabilities from three domain experts, mentioned previously. We conducted several sessions and elicited the conditional probabilities for all of the activities given that the insider was and was not malicious.

For the nodes of the bottom, detector level, we determined the conditional probabilities using either theoretical arguments or empirical methods. For these nodes, we set the probability of detection given that the activity occurs to 1. (Strictly speaking, these probabilities are not 1, and we discuss this issue further in Sect. 6.) To determine the probabilities of false alarm for the detectors, we first assumed the events in our collection are normal. For detectors based on, say, parametric estimators, we set the false-alarm rate based on the threshold that the detector uses to report anomalous events.

For example, a detector that alerts when a user prints an anomalously large number of documents uses an estimator based on a folded-normal distribution [8]. Our experts indicated that they would consider suspicious any number of jobs occurring with a probability of less than .015. Since the number of print jobs for a given user follows a folded-normal distribution and the events in our database are normal, the detector's false-alarm rate is also .015. For other detectors, we determined their false-alarm rate empirically, by calculation or by applying them and counting the number of alarms. For example, consider detectors that alert when activity occurs outside of normal working hours. Since we assumed that the events in our collection are normal, the false-alarm rate for such detectors is the proportion of events that occur outside of normal working hours.

When ELICIT invokes the detectors for a given user, for the detectors that alert, it sets to true the value of the nodes of the third level corresponding to those detectors. It then propagates this instantiated evidence throughout the network, thereby calculating a probability distribution for the node *MaliciousInsider*. We use $P(MaliciousInsider)$ as the user's threat score, and if it is above a specified decision threshold (e.g., .5), then ELICIT issues an alert for that user. We store all of this information in the database.

5 Evaluation

When we were ready to evaluate ELICIT, the trusted agent selected a scenario at random, inserted it into the database of events, and told us the month into which it was inserted. We ran ELICIT over the entire month and notified the trusted agent, who scored ELICIT's performance and removed the scenario's events from the database. The trusted agent then reported to the research team ELICIT's rank and threat score for each day the scenario's insider was active.

We evaluated ELICIT on eight scenario executions, and in Table 5, we present results for six of these executions. The table contains the member of the red team who executed the scenario, the day of activity, the number of preceding days

Table 5. ELICIT's Performance on Six Scenario Executions

Scenario	Executor	Active Day	Preceding Days of Inactivity	Sessions	Score	Rank	Detect
s1	RT4	1	–	1	.994	1	√
		2	1	1	.999	1	√
		3	2	1	.999	1	√
		4	3	1	.994	1	√
s2	RT1	1	–	3	.999	1	√
s2	RT4	1	–	1	.033	341	
		2	1	2	.999	1	√
		3	3	1	.999	1	√
s3	RT2	1	–	1	.999	1	√
		2	1	1	.999	1	√
		3	1	1	.999	1	√
		4	1	1	.984	2	√
s4	RT2	1	–	2	.999	2	√
		2	3	1	.999	1	√
		3	1	1	.992	2	√
		4	1	3	.999	1	√
		5	2	1	.587	20	√
s5	RT2	1	–	3	.071	149	
		2	1	5	.037	238	

of inactivity, the number of sessions per day, and the insider's threat score and relative ranking. Using a decision threshold of .5, we counted as a detection any insider scoring above this threshold. We present results for only six executions because when we analyzed the scenarios after completing ELICIT's evaluation, we noticed that for two of the executions (s3 and s4), an unintentional error in the settings of a user's web proxy routed the scenario's traffic around our sensors. We removed these two executions from further consideration.

As one can see, ELICIT detected insiders on 16 of the 19 days they were active. Notice that RT1 executed scenario s2 in one day, whereas RT4 executed it on three days spanning one week. With the exception of s5 and RT4's execution of s2, ELICIT detected the insiders on their first day of activity. ELICIT performed poorly on scenario s5, and we discuss the reason for this in the next section.

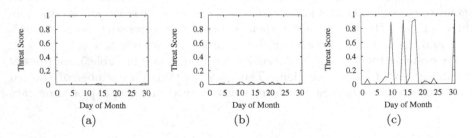

Fig. 3. Threat scores for three users for March

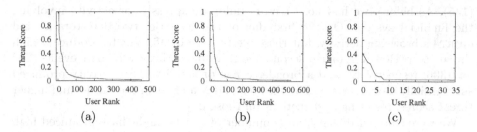

Fig. 4. Threat scores for all users for three days. (a) 462 users for 3/4/05, a Friday. (b) 523 users for 3/7/05, a Monday. (c) 36 users for 3/27/05, a Sunday.

6 Analysis and Discussion

After completing our evaluation of ELICIT, the red team provided information about the scenarios and their events, which we analyzed along with the threat scores for individual users and for all users. In Fig. 3, we present the threat scores for three users for the month of March. The scores of most users were similar to those pictured in Figs. 3a and 3b, which indicate little or no malicious activity. However, less typical are the scores in Fig. 3c, which spike above .9 on five different days. In an operational environment, ELICIT would flag and analysts would further investigate individuals with such scores.

In Fig. 4, we show the threat scores for all users on three different days. The scores in Figs. 4a and 4b are from work days, and those in Fig. 4c are from a Sunday (when there are fewer users). These plots are typical and illustrate how ELICIT scores users on different days and how few users obtain relatively high scores. During work days, ELICIT scored an average of 1,548 users, with 552 users scoring above 0. Of these, 23 users scored above .5.

Using .5 as the decision threshold, we estimated ELICIT's false-positive rate. Although our collection contains activity for 3,938 distinct users, during March and June, when the red team executed the scenarios, there were 1,548 active users on average. For these same months, not including the insiders, an average of 23 users scored above .5. Consequently, ELICIT's average false-positive rate is .015. Since ELICIT detected insiders on 16 of the 19 days they were active, its detection rate is .84. We constructed an ROC curve by varying the decision threshold and then approximated the area under the curve using the trapezoid rule, which yielded an area of .92.

We have conducted a thorough analysis of the scenarios and their events, but here, we can present only the key insights. We first examined why ELICIT failed to detect scenario S5, which required the member of the red team to retrieve proprietary software from an internal repository. Although our sensors captured the activity, we had not developed detectors to monitor that specific server. Put simply, our detectors were focused on documents rather than on software. We will address this issue in future work.

ELICIT did not detect the first day of activity of RT4's execution of S2. It consisted of the browsing of a specific financial system and relatively few events

(135). As before, we had no detectors tailored expressly for activity involving the financial system. On the first day of the scenario, two detectors alerted on RT4's browsing activity, but these alerts were insufficient to produce a high threat score. However, on the second and third days, there were more events (202 and 306, respectively) and a broader range of activity. This activity produced substantially more alerts—22 on the second day and 20 on the third—and higher threat scores, resulting in detections on those days.

We were concerned that a large number of events might have produced high threat scores. Indeed, of the scenarios we detected, all were in the 75th percentile in terms of the total number of *daily* events (i.e., accounting for both benign and anomalous activity). However, when we examined the correlation between the number of events and the threat scores for all users scoring above the decision threshold in the months of March and June, the coefficients were .026 and −.023, respectively. Consequently, we concluded that ELICIT's detections were not due to the number of events in the scenario executions.

We were also concerned that a red-team member's decision to run all of his or her sessions in a single day (versus one session per day) might have affected the daily threat scores. To investigate, for the days involving multiple sessions, we inserted each session individually and ran ELICIT. ELICIT did not detect the first session of the second day of RT4's execution of S2, and it did not detect the first session of the first day of RT1's execution of S2. On the other hand, evaluating ELICIT on the individual sessions did not result in any new detections. Ultimately, we concluded that a person's decision to execute multiple sessions in a single day did not significantly affect performance.

As for ELICIT's successes, our analysis suggests that based on the scenarios and their executions, the right detectors were alerting on the right activities. Scenarios S1, S2, and S4 involved employees who gathered information unrelated to their duties. Detectors for anomalous volumes of searching and browsing alerted, as did detectors indicating that there were queries atypical for the user.

As for ELICIT's false positives, we found no single consistent pattern of alerts that resulted in false alarms. However, individuals in non-technical administrative roles, representing 10% of the user population, accounted for 39% of all false alarms. Our analysis suggests that administrative staff engaged in many of the activities that ELICIT should detect: large amounts of activity and a breadth of activity spanning organizational boundaries.

Regarding the red-team member's incorrect proxy settings, in practice, insiders could attempt to route traffic around sensors. However, this requires specific, technical knowledge of sensor placement and traffic routing. The insider may obtain little feedback about the success of these countermeasures, and attempting such changes could increase the chance of being detected. In the organizations of interest to us, such changes could be a serious violation regardless of intent. Nonetheless, this illustrates the importance of complementary host-based approaches, which could make such attacks more difficult to launch.

Our results are significantly better than the current state of practice, which involves matching ad hoc patterns, auditing randomly-selected individuals, and auditing based solely on the volume of user activity. When interpreting our results, it is important to keep in mind that this task is quite different than detecting intrusions, which focuses on rule breaking.

False positives are always a concern, but the number of entities (i.e., users) that ELICIT processes per day is orders of magnitude smaller than the number of entities (e.g., connections) that intrusion-detection systems process in much shorter periods of time. Once ELICIT reports a detection, a user's historical activity and contextual information play a critical role in subsequent analysis. Such information is largely absent when investigating potential external intrusions. Indeed, ELICIT's interface provides enough information and context about individuals that analysts were able to quickly absolve false positives.

When interpreting the number of false positives, one must also take into account the cost of false negatives, which is substantially higher than that of other detection tasks. At stake is national security. We have not conducted a formal cost analysis. However, anecdotal evidence suggests that, because of the damage these insiders cause, organizations interested in detecting violations of need-to-know are willing to tolerate false positives at much higher rates than with other applications.

Two other important distinctions of this task are the rate of attack and the time over which attacks occur. Rather than occurring in milliseconds (in the case of worms), attacks by insiders who violate need-to-know occur over days, months, and even decades, in the case of Robert Hanssen. Publicly-available information suggests that insider activity occurs in bursts, like other types of attacks, but insider activity is spread over days and months. Consequently, analysts may have to investigate, say, ten false-positives per day, rather than thousands per hour.

As mentioned previously, the probabilities of detection are, strictly speaking, not 1. For example, we did have three days when our network sensors were down, there is a small percentage of events that we could not attribute to users, and there may have been packets that the sensors did not capture. These events certainly affect a detector's probability of detection in some way, but it is unclear whether there is a practical procedure for taking into account all of these factors and then estimating the probabilities. We suspect that most changes would be small and that many would uniformly change the probabilities of detection. This will affect the absolute probabilities, but not the relative probabilities, and we are most interested in a user's rank.

Eliciting probabilities from domain experts proved challenging. They had little difficulty specifying numeric thresholds and conditional probabilities for rules. However, for the detectors based on statistical methods, it was difficult to communicate how the detectors worked in a non-technical manner. Graphical aids and phrasing questions using percentages rather than probabilities helped, but even though all of the experts agreed on the importance of modeling individual activity, we still had trouble eliciting probabilistic cutoffs and conditional probabilities based on these cutoffs. Ultimately, it was easier for us to present and for experts to specify a number rather than a probability or a percentage.

We have attempted to convey that detecting malicious insiders is challenging and different than detecting intruders. One key difference is the availability of contextual information for insiders, information that one rarely has for intruders. With the help of such information, organizations must understand how its users access and manipulate information. To accomplish this, we must attribute actions to users, rather than to IP addresses, which in turn, raises important issues of privacy, especially for researchers.

Complicating matters is the lack of public data sets and information regarding insider behavior and activity. One solution is to engineer data sets. There have been attempts to do so for intrusion detection, mostly notably the MIT Lincoln Labs data set [11], but no similar data set exists for insider threat. Engineered data sets are not without problems, such as guaranteeing that the malicious activity is in correct proportion to the benign activity and that the benign activity is truly representative of the target environment [12]. Our collection of scenarios and information-use events is an attempt to address these concerns for insiders who violate need-to-know.

7 Related Work

We provide only a brief review of related work, but see Chapter 25 of Bishop [13] for a more complete survey. Denning [14] referred to specific instances of such activity as *leakage* and *inference* by legitimate users: Leakage involves a legitimate user leaking or exfiltrating information. Inference is inferring information based on queries to a database or a search engine.

One early attempt to address the problem of misuse was IDES [15], which used statistical profiles of user behavior to detect masqueraders by observing departures from established patterns. (It also applied rules to identify specific intrusions.) Another is UNICORN [16], which examined audit records for misuse by forming profiles using counts over multiple time scales and by applying rules to transform profiles into anomalies, into likely misuse events, and then into alarms. In contrast, ELICIT is geared more toward the misuse of user-level privilege and has a broader notion of context, such as social networks and job descriptions.

Several studies have examined methods of detecting masqueraders from command sequences [5,17,18]. The main points of departure between this work and ours are, we are monitoring network traffic; we are interested in legitimate users acting as themselves, but in a manner that is uncharacteristic and inappropriate; finally, to improve detection, we bring to bear contextual information about users and the information they access.

The research most similar to ours is that of Maybury et al. [19]. Workshop participants built a database of 11 million events collected over a period of 3 months from 18 hosts of a 31-node intranet with 75 users. There is overlap with our work, but they examined different sources of information, approaches, and insider profiles.

8   Concluding Remarks

In this paper, we described the construction and evaluation of ELICIT, a system designed to help analysts investigate insider threats. We are interested in malicious insiders who operate within their privileges, but outside the scope of their duties. This is quite different from intrusion detection. We stressed the importance of contextual information and of tracking how individuals access and manipulate information. One rarely has this information for detecting intruders, but it is critical for detecting insiders.

References

1. United States v. Leandro Aragoncillo and Michael Ray Aquino: Criminal complaint. District of New Jersey (September 9, 2005)
2. Keeney, M., et al.: Insider threat study: Computer system sabotage in critical infrastructure sector. Technical report, US Secret Service and CERT Program, Software Engineering Institute, Carnegie Mellon University, Pittsburgh, PA (May 2005)
3. Lee, W., Stolfo, S.J.: A framework for constructing features and models for intrusion detection systems. ACM Transactions on Information and System Security 3(4), 227–261 (2000)
4. Porras, P.A., Neumann, P.G.: EMERALD: Event monitoring enabling responses to anomalous live disturbances. In: Proceedings of the 20th NIST-NCSC National Information Systems Security Conference, pp. 353–365. National Institute of Standards and Technology, Gaithersburg, MD (1997)
5. Lane, T., Brodley, C.E.: Temporal sequence learning and data reduction for anomaly detection. ACM Transactions on Information and System Security 2(3), 295–331 (1999)
6. Hofmeyr, S.A., Forrest, S., Somayaji, A.: Intrusion detection using sequences of system calls. Journal of Computer Security 6(3), 151–180 (1988)
7. Ethereal, Inc.: Ethereal. Software (2007), http://www.ethereal.com
8. Leone, F.C., Nelson, L.S., Nottingham, R.B.: The Folded Normal Distribution. Technometrics 3(4), 543–550 (1961)
9. Silverman, B.W.: Density estimation for statistics and data analysis. Chapman & Hall/CRC, Boca Raton, FL (1998)
10. Jensen, F.V.: Bayesian networks and decision graphs. Statistics for Engineering and Information Science. Springer, New York, NY (2001)
11. Lippmann, R., et al.: The 1999 DARPA off-line intrusion detection evaluation. Computer Networks 34, 579–595 (2000)
12. McHugh, J.: Testing intrusion detection systems. ACM Transactions on Information and System Security 3(4), 262–294 (2000)
13. Bishop, M.: Computer security. Addison-Wesley, Boston, MA (2003)
14. Denning, D.E.: An intrusion-detection model. IEEE Transactions on Software Engineering SE-13(2), 222–232 (1987)
15. Lunt, T., et al.: IDES: A progress report. In: Proceedings of the Sixth Annual Computer Security Applications Conference. Applied Computer Security Associates, pp. 273–285. Silver Spring, MD (1990)

16. Christoph, G.G., et al.: UNICORN: Misuse detection for UNICOS^{TM}. In: Supercomputing '95, p. 56. IEEE Press, Los Alamitos, CA (1995)
17. Schonlau, M., et al.: Computer intrusion: Detecting masquerades. Statistical Science 16(1), 58–74 (2001)
18. Maxion, R.A.: Masquerade detection using enriched command lines. In: Proceedings of the International Conference on Dependable Systems and Networks, pp. 5–14. IEEE Press, Los Alamitos, CA (2003)
19. Maybury, M., et al.: Analysis and detection of malicious insiders. In: Proceedings of the 2005 International Conference on Intelligence Analysis, The MITRE Corporation, McLean, VA (2005)

On the Use of Different Statistical Tests for Alert Correlation – Short Paper

Federico Maggi and Stefano Zanero

Politecnico di Milano, Dip. Elettronica e Informazione
via Ponzio 34/5, 20133 Milano Italy
{fmaggi,zanero}@elet.polimi.it

Abstract. In this paper we analyze the use of different types of statistical tests for the correlation of anomaly detection alerts. We show that the Granger Causality Test, one of the few proposals that can be extended to the anomaly detection domain, strongly depends on good choices of a parameter which proves to be both sensitive and difficult to estimate. We propose a different approach based on a set of simpler statistical tests, and we prove that our criteria work well on a simplified correlation task, without requiring complex configuration parameters.

1 Introduction

One of the most challenging tasks in intrusion detection is to create a unified vision of the events, fusing together alerts from heterogeneous monitoring devices. This *alert fusion* process can be defined as the *correlation* of *aggregated* streams of alerts. *Aggregation* is the grouping of alerts that both are close in time and have similar features; it fuses together different "views" of the same event. Alert *correlation* has to do with the recognition of logically linked alerts. "Correlation" does not necessarily imply "statistical correlation", but statistical correlation based methods are sometimes used to reveal these relationships.

Alert fusion is more complex when taking into account *anomaly detection* systems, because no information on the type or classification of the observed attack is available to the fusion algorithms. Most of the algorithms proposed in the current literature on correlation make use of such information, and are therefore inapplicable to purely anomaly based intrusion detection systems.

In this work, we explore the use of *statistical causality tests*, which have been proposed for the correlation of IDS alerts, and which could be applied to anomaly based IDS as well. We focus on the use of *Granger Causality Test* (GCT), and show that its performance strongly depends on a good choice of a parameter which proves to be sensitive and difficult to estimate. We redefine the causality problem in terms of a simpler statistical test, and experimentally validate it.

2 Problem Statement and State of the Art

The desired output of an *alert fusion* process is a compact, high-level view of what is happening on a (usually large and complex) network. In this work we use

C. Kruegel, R. Lippmann, and A. Clark (Eds.): RAID 2007, LNCS 4637, pp. 167–177, 2007.
© Springer-Verlag Berlin Heidelberg 2007

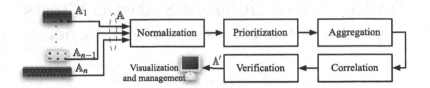

Fig. 1. A diagram illustrating alert fusion terminology as used in this work

a slightly modified version of the terminology proposed in [17]. Alerts streams are collected from different IDS sources, normalized and aggregated; alert correlation is the very final step of the process. In [17] the term "fusion" is used for the phase we name "aggregation", whereas we use the former to denote the whole process. Fig. 1 summarizes the terminology.

In [9] we propose a fuzzy time-based *aggregation* technique, showing that it yields good performance in terms of false positive reduction. Here, we focus on the more challenging *correlation* phase. Effective and generic correlation algorithms are difficult to design, especially if the objective is the reconstruction of complex attack scenarios.

A technique for alert correlation based on state-transition graphs is shown in [3]. The use of finite state automata enables for complex scenario descriptions, but it requires known scenarios signatures. It is also unsuitable for pure anomaly detectors which cannot differentiate among different types of events. Similar approaches, with similar strengths and shortcomings but different formalisms, have been tried with the specification of pre- and post-conditions of the attacks [15], sometimes along with time-distance criteria [12]. It is possible to mine scenario rules directly from data, either in a supervised [2] or unsupervised [5] fashion. Both approaches use alert classifications as part of their rules.

None of these techniques would work for anomaly detection systems, as they rely on alert names or classification to work. The best examples of algorithms that do not require such features are based on time-series analysis and modeling. For instance, [19] is based on the construction of time-series by counting the number of alerts occurring into sampling intervals; the exploitation of trend and periodicity removal algorithms allows to filter out predictable components, leaving *real* alerts only as the output. More than a correlation approach, this is a false-positive and noise-suppression approach, though.

The correlation approach investigated in [14] and based on the GCT also does not require prior knowledge, and it drew our attention as one of the few viable proposal for anomaly detection alert correlation in earlier literature. We will describe and analyze this approach in detail in Section 4.

3   Problems in Evaluating Alert Correlation Systems

Evaluation techniques for alert fusion systems are still limited to a few proposals, and practically and theoretically challenging to develop [9]. Additionally, the common problem of the lack of reliable sources of data for benchmarking impacts heavily also on the evaluation of correlation systems. Ideally, we need both host and network datasets, fully labeled, with complex attack scenarios described in detail. These data should be freely available to the scientific community. These requirements rule out real-world dumps.

The only datasets of this kind effectively available are the ones by DARPA (IDEVAL datasets). Of course, since this data set was created to evaluate IDS sensors and not to assess correlation tools, it does not include sensor alerts. The alerts have to be generated by running various sensors on the data. The 1999 dataset [7], which we used for this work, has many known shortcomings. Firstly, it is evidently and hopelessly outdated. Moreover, a number of flaws have been detected and criticized in the network traces [10, 11]. More recently, we analyzed the host-based system call traces, and showed [8, 21] that they are ridden with problems as well.

For this work these basic flaws are not extremely dangerous, since the propagation of attack effects (from network to hosts) is not affected by any of the known flaws of IDEVAL, and in fact we observed it to be quite realistically present. What could be a problem is the fact that intrusion scenarios are too simple and extremely straightforward. Additionally, many attacks are not detectable in both network and host data (thus making the whole point of correlation disappear). Nowadays, networks and attackers are more sophisticated and attack scenarios are much more complex than in 1999, operating at various layers of the network and application stack.

The work we analyze closely in the following [14] uses both the DEFCON 9 CTF dumps and the DARPA Cyber Panel *Correlation Technology Validation* (CTV) [4] datasets for the evaluation of an alert correlation prototype. The former dataset is not labeled and does not contain any background traffic, so in fact (as the authors themselves recognize) it cannot be used for a proper evaluation, but just for qualitative analysis. On the contrary, the DARPA CTV effort, carried out in 2002, created a complex testbed network, along with background traffic and a set of attack scenarios. The alerts produced by various sensors during these attacks were collected and given as an input to the evaluated correlation tools. Unfortunately, this dataset is not available for further experimentation.

For all the previous reasons, in our testing we will use the IDEVAL dataset with the following simplification: we will just try to correlate the stream of alerts coming from a single *host-based IDS* (HIDS) sensor with the corresponding alerts from a single *network-based IDS* (NIDS), which is monitoring the whole network. To this end, we ran two anomaly-based IDS prototypes (both described in [8, 20, 21]) on the whole IDEVAL testing dataset. We ran the NIDS prototype on `tcpdump` data and collected 128 alerts for attacks against the host `pascal.eyrie.af.mil` [6]. The NIDS also generated 1009 alerts related to other hosts. Using the HIDS prototype we generated 1070 alerts from the dumps of the host `pascal.eyrie.af.mil`. With respect to these alerts, the NIDS was capable of detecting almost 66% of the attacks with less than 0.03% of false positives; the HIDS performs even better with a detection rate of 98% and 1.7% of false positives.

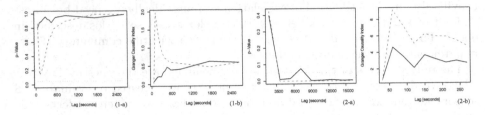

Fig. 2. p-value (-a) and GCI (-b) vs. p with $w = w_1 = 60s$ (1-) and $w = w_2 = 1800s$ (2-) "$NetP(k) \rightsquigarrow HostP(k)$" (dashed line), "$HostP(k) \rightsquigarrow NetP(k)$" (solid line)

In the following, we use this shorthand notation: Net is the substream of all the alerts generated by the NIDS. $HostP$ is the substream of all the alerts generated by the HIDS installed on `pascal.eyrie.af.mil`, while $NetP$ regards all the alerts (with `pascal` as a target) generated by the NIDS; finally, $NetO = Net \backslash NetP$ indicates all the alerts (with all but `pascal` as a target) generated by the NIDS.

4   The Granger Causality Test

In [14] Qin and Lee propose an interesting algorithm for alert correlation which seems suitable also for anomaly-based alerts. Alerts with the same feature set are grouped into collections of time-sorted items belonging to the same "type" (following the concept of type of [19]). Subsequently, frequency time series are built, using a fixed size sliding-window: the result is a time-series for each collection of alerts. The prototype then exploits the GCT [16], a statistical hypothesis test capable of discovering causality relationships between two time series when they are originated by linear, stationary processes. The GCT gives a stochastic measure, called *Granger Causality Index* (GCI), of how much of the history of one time series (the supposed cause) is needed to "explain" the evolution of the other one (the supposed consequence, or target). The GCT is based on the estimation of two models: the first is an *Auto Regressive* model (AR), in which future samples of the target are modeled as influenced only by past samples of the target itself; the second is an *Auto Regressive Moving Average eXogenous* (ARMAX) model, which also takes into account the supposed cause time series as an exogenous component. A statistical F-test built upon the model estimation errors selects the best-fitting model: if the ARMAX fits better, the cause effectively influences the target.

In [14] the unsupervised identification of "causally related" events is performed by repeating the above procedure for each couple of time-series. The advantage of the approach is that it does not require prior knowledge (even if it may use attack probability values, if available, for an optional prioritization phase). However, in a previous work [9] we showed that the GCT fails however in recognizing "meaningful" relationships between IDEVAL attacks.

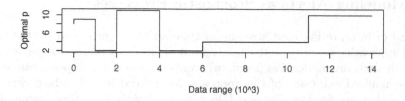

Fig. 3. The optimal time lag $\hat{p}$ given by the AIC criterion strongly varies over time

We tested the sensitivity of the GCT to the choice of two parameters: the sampling time, w, and the time lag p (that is, the order of the AR). In our simple experiment, the expected result is that $NetP \rightsquigarrow HostP$, and that $HostP \not\rightsquigarrow NetP$ (the $\rightsquigarrow$ indicates "causality" while $\not\rightsquigarrow$ is its negation). In [14] the sampling time was arbitrarily set to $w = 60s$, while the choice of p is not documented. However, our experiments show that the choice of these parameters can strongly influence the results of the test. In Fig. 2 (1-a/b) we plotted the p-value and the GCI of the test for different values of p ($w = 60s$). In particular, the dashed line corresponds to the test $NetP(k) \rightsquigarrow HostP(k)$, and the solid line to the test $HostP(k) \rightsquigarrow NetP(k)$. We recall that if the p-value is lower than the significance level, the null hypothesis is refused. Notice how different choices of p can lead to inconclusive or even opposite results. For instance, with $\alpha = 0.20$ and with $2 \leq p \leq 3$, the result is that $NetP(k) \rightsquigarrow HostP(k)$ and that $HostP(k) \not\rightsquigarrow NetP(k)$. As we detailed in [9] (Fig. 2 (2-a/b)), other values of p lead to awkward result that both $HostP(k) \rightsquigarrow NetP(k)$ and $NetP(k) \rightsquigarrow HostP(k)$.

A possible explanation is that the GCT is significant only if both the linear regression models are optimal, in order to calculate the correct residuals. If we use the *Akaike Information Criterion* (AIC) [1] to estimate the optimal time lag $\hat{p}$ over different windows of data, we find out that $\hat{p}$ wildly varies over time, as it is shown in Fig. 3. The fact that there is no stable optimal choice of p, combined with the fact that the test result significantly depends on it, makes us doubt that the Granger causality test is a viable option for general alert correlation. The choice of w seems equally important and even more difficult to perform, except by guessing.

Of course, our testing is not conclusive: the IDEVAL alert sets may simply not be adequate for showing causal relationships. Another, albeit more unlikely, explanation, is that the Granger causality test may not be suitable for anomaly detection alerts: in fact, in [14] it has been tested on misuse detection alerts. But in fact there are also theoretical reasons to doubt that the application of the Granger test can lead to stable, good results. First, the test is asymptotic w.r.t. p meaning that the results reliability decreases as p increases because of the loss of degrees of freedom. Second, it is based on the strong assumption of *linearity* in the auto-regressive model fitting step, which strongly depends on the observed phenomenon. In the same way, the stationarity assumption of the model does not always hold.

5 Modeling Alerts as Stochastic Processes

Instead of interpreting alert streams as time series (as proposed by the GCT-based approach), we propose to change point of view by using a stochastic model in which alerts are modeled as (random) events in time. This proposal can be seen as a formalized extension of the approach introduced in [17], which correlates alerts if they are fired by different IDS within a "negligible" time frame, where "negligible" is defined with a crisp, fixed threshold.

For simplicity, once again we describe our technique in the simple case of a single HIDS and a single NIDS which monitors the whole network. The concepts, however, can be easily generalized to take into account more than two alert streams, by evaluating them couple by couple. For each alert, we have three essential information: a timestamp, a "target" host (fixed, in the case of the HIDS, to the host itself), and the generating sensor (in our case, a binary value).

We reuse the scenario and data we already presented in Section 4 above. With a self-explaining notation, we also define the following random variables: T_{NetP} are the arrival times of network alerts in $NetP$ (T_{NetO}, T_{HostP} are similarly defined); ε_{NetP} (ε_{NetO}) are the delays (caused by transmission, processing and different granularity in detection) between a specific network-based alert regarding `pascal` (not `pascal`) and the corresponding host-based one. The actual values of each $T_{(.)}$ is nothing but the set of timestamps extracted from the corresponding alert stream. We reasonably assume that ε_{NetP} and T_{NetP} are stochastically independent (the same is assumed for ε_{NetO} and T_{NetO}).

In an *ideal* correlation framework with two equally perfect IDS with a 100% DR and 0% FPR, if two alert streams are correlated (i.e., they represent independent detections of the same attack occurrences by different IDSes [17]), they also are "close" in time. $NetP$ and $HostP$ should evidently be an example of such a couple of streams. Obviously, in the real world, some alerts will be missing (because of false negatives, or simply because some of the attacks are detectable only by a specific type of detector), and the distances between related alerts will therefore have some higher variability. In order to account for this, we can "cut off" alerts that are too far away from a corresponding alert in the other time series, presuming them to be singletons. In our case, knowing that single attacks did not last more than $400s$ in the original dataset, we tentatively set a cutoff threshold at this point.

Under the given working assumptions and the proposed stochastic model, we can formalize the correlation problem as a set of two statistical hypothesis tests:

$$H_0 : T_{HostP} \neq T_{NetP} + \varepsilon_{NetP} \; vs. \; H_1 : T_{HostP} = T_{NetP} + \varepsilon_{NetP} \quad (1)$$
$$H_0 : T_{HostP} \neq T_{NetO} + \varepsilon_{NetO} \; vs. \; H_1 : T_{HostP} = T_{NetO} + \varepsilon_{NetO} \quad (2)$$

Let $\{t_{i,k}\}$ be the observed timestamps of $T_i \; \forall i \in \{HostP, NetP, NetO\}$, the meaning of the first test is straightforward: within a random amount of time, ε_{NetP}, the occurring of a host alert, $t_{HostP,k}$, is preceded by a network alert, $t_{NetP,k}$. If this does not happen for a statistically significant amount of events, the test result is that alert stream T_{NetP} is *uncorrelated* to T_{HostP}; in this case,

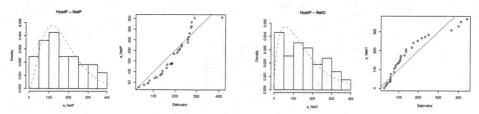

Fig. 4. Histograms vs. est. density (red dashes) and Q-Q plots, for both $\hat{f}_O$ and $\hat{f}_P$

we have *enough statistical evidence* for refusing H_1 and accepting the null one. Symmetrically, refusing the null hypothesis of the second test means that the $NetO$ alert stream (regarding to all hosts but `pascal`) is correlated to the alert stream regarding `pascal`.

Note that, the above two tests are strongly related to each other: in an ideal correlation framework, it cannot happen that both "$NetP$ is correlated to $HostP$" and "$NetO$ is correlated to $HostP$": this would imply that the network activity regarding to all hosts but `pascal` (which raises $NetO$) has to do with the host activity of `pascal` (which raises $HostP$) with the same order of magnitude of $NetP$, that is an intuitively contradictory conclusion. Therefore, the second test acts as a sort of "robustness" criterion.

From our alerts, we can compute a sample of ε_{NetP} by simply picking, for each value in $NetP$, the value in $HostP$ which is closest, but greater (applying a threshold as defined above). We can do the same for ε_{NetO}, using the alerts in $NetO$ and $HostP$.

The next step involves the *choice of the distributions* of the random variables we defined above. Typical distributions used for modeling random occurrences of timed events fall into the family of exponential *Probability Density Functions* (PDF)s [13]. In particular, we decided to fit them with Gamma PDFs, because our experiments show that such a distribution is a good choice for both the ε_{NetP} and ε_{NetO}.

The estimation of the PDF of ε_{NetP}, $f_P := f_{\varepsilon_{NetP}}$, and ε_{NetO}, $f_O := f_{\varepsilon_{NetO}}$, is performed using the well known *Maximum Likelihood* (ML) technique [18] as implemented in the `GNU R` software package: the results are summarized in Fig. 4. f_P and f_O are approximated by Gamma[3.0606, 0.0178] and Gamma [1.6301, 0.0105], respectively (standard errors on parameters are 0.7080, 0.0045 for f_P and 0.1288, 0.009 for f_O). From now on, the estimator of a given density f will be indicated as $\hat{f}$.

Fig. 4 shows histograms vs. estimated density (red, dashed line) and quantile-quantile plots (Q-Q plots), for both $\hat{f}_O$ and $\hat{f}_P$. We recall that Q-Q plots are an intuitive graphical "tool" for comparing data distributions by plotting the quantile of the first distribution against the quantile of the other one.

Considering that the samples sizes of $\varepsilon_{(.)}$ are around 40, Q-Q plots empirically confirms our intuition: in fact, $\hat{f}_O$ and $\hat{f}_P$ are both able to explain real data well, within inevitable but negligible estimation errors. Even if $\hat{f}_P$ and $\hat{f}_O$ are both Gamma-shaped, it must be noticed that they significantly differ in their

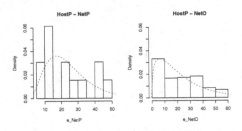

Fig. 5. Histograms vs. est. density (red dashes) for both $\hat{f}_O$ and $\hat{f}_P$ (IDEVAL 1998)

parametrization; this is a very important result since it allows to set up a proper criterion to decide whether or not ε_{NetP} and ε_{NetO} are generated by the same phenomenon.

Given the above estimators, a more precise and robust hypotheses test can be now designed. The Test 1 and 2 can be mapped into two-sided *Kolmogorov-Smirnov* (KS) tests [13], achieving the same result in terms of decisions:

$$H_0 : \varepsilon_{NetP} \sim f_P \text{ vs. } H_1 : \varepsilon_{NetP} \nsim f_P \tag{3}$$

$$H_0 : \varepsilon_{NetO} \sim f_O \text{ vs. } H_1 : \varepsilon_{NetO} \nsim f_O \tag{4}$$

where the symbol $\sim$ means "has the same distribution of". Since we do not know the real PDFs, estimators are used in their stead. We recall that the KS-test is a *non-parametric* test to compare a sample (or a PDF) against a PDF (or a sample) to check how much they differs from each other (or how much they fit). Such tests can be performed, for instance, with `ks.test()` (a GNU R native procedure): resulting p-values on IDEVAL 1999 are 0.83 and 0.03, respectively.

Noticeably, there is a significant statistical evidence to accept the null hypothesis of Test 3. It seems that the ML estimation is capable of correctly fitting a Gamma PDF for f_P (given ε_{NetP} samples), which double-checks our intuition about the distribution. The same does not hold for f_O: in fact, it cannot be correctly estimated, with a Gamma PDF, from ε_{NetO}. The low p-value for Test 4 confirms that the distribution of ε_{NetO} delays is completely different than the one of ε_{NetP}. Therefore, our criterion doest not only recognize noisy delay-based relationships among alerts stream *if they exists*; it is also capable of detecting if such a correlation does not hold.

We also tested our technique on alerts generated by our NIDS/HIDS running on IDEVAL 1998 (limiting our analysis to the first four days of the first week), in order to cross-validate the above results. We prepared and processed the data with the same procedures we described above for the 1999 dataset. Starting from almost the same proportion of host/net alerts against either `pascal` or other hosts, the ML-estimation has computed the two Gamma densities shown in Fig. 5: f_P and f_O are approximated by Gamma$(3.5127, 0.1478)$ and Gamma$(1.3747, 0.0618)$, respectively (standard errors on estimated parameters are 1.3173, 0.0596 for f_P and 0.1265, 0.0068 for f_O). These parameter are very similar to the ones we estimated for the IDEVAL 1999 dataset. Furthermore, with p-values of 0.51 and 0.09, the two KS tests confirm the same statistical discrepancies we observed on the 1999 dataset.

The above numerical results show that, by interpreting alert streams as random processes, there are several (stochastic) dissimilarities between net-to-host delays belonging to the same net-host attack session, and net-to-host delays belonging to different sessions. Exploiting these dissimilarities, we may find out the correlation among streams in an unsupervised manner, without the need to predefine any parameter.

6   Conclusions

In this paper we analyzed the use of of different types of statistical tests for the correlation of anomaly detection alerts, a problem which has little or no solutions available today. One of the few correlation proposals that can be applied to anomaly detection is the use of a *Granger Causality Test* (GCT). After discussing a possible testing methodology, we observed that the IDEVAL datasets traditionally used for evaluation have various shortcomings, that we partially addressed by using the data for a simpler scenario of correlation, investigating only the link between a stream of host-based alerts for a specific host, and the corresponding stream of alerts from a network based detector.

We examined the usage of a GCT as proposed in earlier works, showing that it relies on the choice of non-obvious configuration parameters which significantly affect the final result. We also showed that one of these parameters (the order of the models) is absolutely critical, but cannot be uniquely estimated for a given system. Instead of the GCT, we proposed a simpler statistical model of alert generation, describing alert streams and timestamps as stochastic variables, and showed that statistical tests can be used to create a reasonable criterion for distinguishing correlated and non correlated streams. We proved that our criteria work well on the simplified correlation task we used for testing, without requiring complex configuration parameters.

This is an exploratory work, and further investigations of this approach on real, longer sequences of data, as well as further refinements of the tests and the criteria we proposed, are surely needed. Another possible extension of this work is the investigation of how these criteria can be used to correlate anomaly and misuse-based alerts together, in order to bridge the gap between the existing paradigms of intrusion detection.

Acknowledgments

We need to thank prof. Ilenia Epifani and prof. Giuseppe Serazzi for their helpful comments, as well as the anonymous reviewers.

References

1. Akaike, H.: A new look at the statistical model identification. Automatic Control, IEEE Transactions on 19(6), 716–723 (1974)
2. Dain, O., Cunningham, R.: Fusing heterogeneous alert streams into scenarios. In: Proc. of the ACM Workshop on Data Mining for Security Applications, November 2001, pp. 1–13. ACM Press, New York (2001)
3. Eckmann, S., Vigna, G., Kemmerer, R.: STATL: An attack language for state-based intrusion detection. In: Proceedings of the ACM Workshop on Intrusion Detection, Atene, November 2000, ACM Press, New York (2000)
4. Haines, J., Ryder, D.K., Tinnel, L., Taylor, S.: Validation of sensor alert correlators. IEEE Security and Privacy 01(1), 46–56 (2003)
5. Julisch, K., Dacier, M.: Mining intrusion detection alarms for actionable knowledge. In: Proc. of the 8th ACM SIGKDD Int'l Conf. on Knowledge Discovery and Data Mining, New York, NY, USA, pp. 366–375. ACM Press, New York (2002)
6. Lippmann, R., Haines, J.W., Fried, D.J., Korba, J., Das, K.: The 1999 darpa off-line intrusion detection evaluation. Comput. Networks 34(4), 579–595 (2000)
7. Lippmann, R., Haines, J.W., Fried, D.J., Korba, J., Das, K.: Analysis and results of the 1999 DARPA off-line intrusion detection evaluation. In: Debar, H., Mé, L., Wu, S.F. (eds.) RAID 2000. LNCS, vol. 1907, Springer, Heidelberg (2000)
8. Maggi, F., Matteucci, M., Zanero, S.: Detecting intrusions through system call sequence and argument analysis (submitted for publication, 2006)
9. Maggi, F., Matteucci, M., Zanero, S.: Reducing false positives in anomaly detectors through fuzzy alert aggregation (submitted for publication, 2006)
10. Mahoney, M.V., Chan, P.K.: An analysis of the 1999 DARPA / Lincoln laboratory evaluation data for network anomaly detection. In: Vigna, G., Krügel, C., Jonsson, E. (eds.) RAID 2003. LNCS, vol. 2820, pp. 220–237. Springer, Heidelberg (2003)
11. McHugh, J.: Testing intrusion detection systems: a critique of the 1998 and 1999 DARPA intrusion detection system evaluations as performed by lincoln laboratory. ACM Trans. on Information and System Security 3(4), 262–294 (2000)
12. Ning, P., Cui, Y., Reeves, D.S., Xu, D.: Techniques and tools for analyzing intrusion alerts. ACM Trans. Inf. Syst. Secur. 7(2), 274–318 (2004)
13. Pestman, W.R.: Mathematical Statistics: An Introduction. Walter de Gruyter, Berlin (1998)
14. Qin, X., Lee, W.: Statistical causality analysis of INFOSEC alert data. In: Vigna, G., Krügel, C., Jonsson, E. (eds.) RAID 2003. LNCS, vol. 2820, pp. 73–93. Springer, Heidelberg (2003)
15. Templeton, S.J., Levitt, K.: A requires/provides model for computer attacks. In: NSPW '00: Proceedings of the 2000 workshop on New security paradigms, New York, NY, USA, pp. 31–38. ACM Press, New York (2000)
16. Thurman, W.N., Fisher, M.E.: Chickens, eggs, and causality, or which came first? American Journal of Agricultural Economics (1998)
17. Valeur, F., Vigna, G., Kruegel, C., Kemmerer, R.A.: A comprehensive approach to intrusion detection alert correlation. IEEE Trans. Dependable Secur. Comput. 1(3), 146–169 (2004)
18. Venables, W., Ripley, B.: Modern Applied Statistics with S. Springer, Heidelberg (2002)
19. Viinikka, J., Debar, H., Mé, L., Séguier, R.: Time series modeling for IDS alert management. In: Proc. of the 2006 ACM Symp. on Information, computer and communications security, New York, NY, USA, pp. 102–113. ACM Press, New York (2006)

20. Zanero, S.: Analyzing TCP traffic patterns using self organizing maps. In: Roli, F., Vitulano, S. (eds.) ICIAP 2005. LNCS, vol. 3617, pp. 83–90. Springer, Heidelberg (2005)
21. Zanero, S.: Unsupervised Learning Algorithms for Intrusion Detection. PhD thesis, Politecnico di Milano T.U., Milano, Italy (May 2006)

Automated Classification and Analysis of Internet Malware

Michael Bailey[1], Jon Oberheide[1], Jon Andersen[1], Z. Morley Mao[1],
Farnam Jahanian[1,2], and Jose Nazario[2]

[1] Electrical Engineering and Computer Science Department
University of Michigan
{mibailey,jonojono,janderse,zmao,farnam}@umich.edu
[2] Arbor Networks
{farnam,jose}@arbor.net

Abstract. Numerous attacks, such as worms, phishing, and botnets, threaten the availability of the Internet, the integrity of its hosts, and the privacy of its users. A core element of defense against these attacks is anti-virus (AV) software—a service that detects, removes, and characterizes these threats. The ability of these products to successfully characterize these threats has far-reaching effects—from facilitating sharing across organizations, to detecting the emergence of new threats, and assessing risk in quarantine and cleanup. In this paper, we examine the ability of existing host-based anti-virus products to provide semantically meaningful information about the malicious software and tools (or malware) used by attackers. Using a large, recent collection of malware that spans a variety of attack vectors (e.g., spyware, worms, spam), we show that different AV products characterize malware in ways that are inconsistent across AV products, incomplete across malware, and that fail to be concise in their semantics. To address these limitations, we propose a new classification technique that describes malware behavior in terms of system state changes (e.g., files written, processes created) rather than in sequences or patterns of system calls. To address the sheer volume of malware and diversity of its behavior, we provide a method for automatically categorizing these profiles of malware into groups that reflect similar classes of behaviors and demonstrate how behavior-based clustering provides a more direct and effective way of classifying and analyzing Internet malware.

1 Introduction

Many of the most visible and serious problems facing the Internet today depend on a vast ecosystem of malicious software and tools. Spam, phishing, denial of service attacks, botnets, and worms largely depend on some form of malicious code, commonly referred to as *malware*. Malware is often used to infect the computers of unsuspecting victims by exploiting software vulnerabilities or tricking users into running malicious code. Understanding this process and how attackers

C. Kruegel, R. Lippmann, and A. Clark (Eds.): RAID 2007, LNCS 4637, pp. 178–197, 2007.
© Springer-Verlag Berlin Heidelberg 2007

use the backdoors, key loggers, password stealers, and other malware functions is becoming an increasingly difficult and important problem.

Unfortunately, the complexity of modern malware is making this problem more difficult. For example, Agobot [3], has been observed to have more than 580 variants since its initial release in 2002. Modern Agobot variants have the ability to perform DoS attacks, steal bank passwords and account details, propagate over the network using a diverse set of remote exploits, use polymorphism to evade detection and disassembly, and even patch vulnerabilities and remove competing malware from an infected system [3]. Making the problem even more challenging is the increase in the number and diversity of Internet malware. A recent Microsoft survey found more than 43,000 new variants of backdoor trojans and bots during the first half of 2006 [20]. Automated and robust approaches to understanding malware are required to successfully stem the tide.

Previous efforts to automatically classify and analyze malware (e.g., AV, IDS) focused primarily on content-based signatures. Unfortunately, content-based signatures are inherently susceptible to inaccuracies due to polymorphic and metamorphic techniques. In addition, the signatures used by these systems often focus on a specific exploit behavior—an approach increasingly complicated by the emergence of multi-vector attacks. As a result, IDS and AV products characterize malware in ways that are inconsistent across products, incomplete across malware, and that fail to be concise in their semantics. This creates an environment in which defenders are limited in their ability to share intelligence across organizations, to detect the emergence of new threats, and to assess risk in quarantine and cleanup of infections.

To address the limitations of existing automated classification and analysis tools, we have developed and evaluated a dynamic analysis approach, based on the execution of malware in virtualized environments and the causal tracing of the operating system objects created due to malware's execution. The reduced collection of these user-visible system state changes (e.g., files written, processes created) is used to create a fingerprint of the malware's behavior. These fingerprints are more invariant and directly useful than abstract code sequences representing programmatic behavior and can be directly used in assessing the potential damage incurred, enabling detection and classification of new threats, and assisting in the risk assessment of these threats in mitigation and clean up. To address the sheer volume of malware and the diversity of its behavior, we provide a method for automatically categorizing these malware profiles into groups that reflect similar classes of behaviors. These methods are thoroughly evaluated in the context of a malware dataset that is large, recent, and diverse in the set of attack vectors it represents (e.g., spam, worms, bots, spyware).

This paper is organized as follows: Section 2 describes the shortcomings of existing AV software and enumerates requirements for effective malware classification. We present our behavior-based fingerprint extraction and fingerprint clustering algorithm in Section 3. Our detailed evaluation is shown in Section 4. We present existing work in Section 5, offer limitations and future directions in Section 6, and conclude in Section 7.

2   Anti-Virus Clustering of Malware

Host-based AV systems detect and remove malicious threats from end systems. As a normal part of this process, these AV programs provide a description for the malware they detected. The ability of these products to successfully characterize these threats has far-reaching effects—from facilitating sharing across organizations, to detecting the emergence of new threats, and assessing risk in quarantine and cleanup. However, for this information to be effective, the descriptions provided by these systems must be meaningful. In this section, we evaluate the ability of host-based AV to provide meaningful intelligence on Internet malware.

2.1   Understanding Anti-Virus Malware Labeling

In order to accurately characterize the ability of AV to provide meaningful labels for malware, we first need to acquire representative datasets. In this paper, we use three datasets from two sources, as shown in Table 1. One dataset, *legacy*, is taken from a network security community malware collection and consists of randomly sampled binaries from those posted to the community's FTP server in 2004. In addition, we use a large, recent six-month collection of malware and a six-week subset of that collection at the beginning of the dataset collection period. The *small* and *large* datasets are a part of the Arbor Malware Library (AML). Created by Arbor Networks, Inc. [1], the AML consists of binaries collected by a variety of techniques including Web page crawling [28], spam traps [26], and honeypot-based vulnerability emulation [2]. **Since each of these methods collects binaries that are installed on the target system without the user's permission, the binaries collected are highly likely to be malicious.** Almost 3,700 unique binaries were collected over a six-month period in late 2006 and early 2007.

Table 1. The datasets used in this paper: A large collection of legacy binaries from 2004, a small six-week collection from 2006, and a large six-month collection of malware from 2006/2007. The number of unique labels provided by five AV systems is listed for each dataset.

Dataset Name	Date Collected	Number of Unique MD5s	Number of Unique Labels				
			McAfee	F-Prot	ClamAV	Trend	Symantec
legacy	01 Jan 2004 - 31 Dec 2004	3,637	116	1216	590	416	57
small	03 Sep 2006 - 22 Oct 2006	893	112	379	253	246	90
large	03 Sep 2006 - 18 Mar 2007	3,698	310	1,544	1,102	2,035	50

After collecting the binaries, we analyzed them using the AV scanners shown in Table 2. Each of the scanners was the most recent available from each vendor at the time of the analysis. The virus definitions and engines were updated uniformly on November 20th, 2006, and then again on March 31st, 2007. Note that the first update occured more than a year after the *legacy* collection ended and one month after the end of the *small* set collection. The second update was 13 days after the end of the *large* set collection.

Table 2. Anti-virus software, vendors, versions, and signature files used in this paper. The *small* and *legacy* datasets were evaluated with a version of these systems in November of 2006 and both *small* and *large* were evaluated again with a version of these systems in March of 2007.

Label	Software	Vendor	Version	Signature File
McAfee	Virus Scan	McAfee, Inc.	v4900	20 Nov 2006
			v5100	31 Mar 2007
F-Prot	F-Prot Anti-virus	FRISK Software	4.6.6	20 Nov 2006
		International	6.0.6.3	31 Mar 2007
ClamAV	Clam Anti-virus	Tomasz Kojm and	0.88.6	20 Nov 2006
		the ClamAV Team	0.90.1	31 Mar 2007
Trend	PC-cillin Internet	Trend Micro, Inc.	8.000-1001	20 Nov 2006
	Security 2007		8.32.1003	31 Mar 2007
Symantec	Norton Anti-virus	Symantec	14.0.0.89	20 Nov 2006
	2007	Corporation	14.0.3.3	31 Mar 2007

AV systems rarely use the exact same labels for a threat, and users of these systems have come to expect simple naming differences (e.g., W32Lovsan.worm.a versus Lovsan versus WORM_MSBLAST.A) across vendors. It has always been assumed, however, that there existed a simple mapping from one system's name space to another, and recently investigators have begun creating projects to unify these name spaces [4]. Unfortunately, the task appears daunting. Consider, for example, the number of unique labels created by various systems. The result in Table 1 is striking—there is a substantial difference in the number of unique labels created by each AV system. While one might expect small differences, it is clear that AV vendors disagree not only on what to label a piece of malware, but also on how many unique labels exist for malware in general.

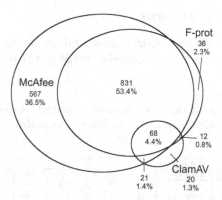

Fig. 1. A Venn diagram of malware labeled as SDBot variants by three AV products in the *legacy* dataset. The classification of SDBot is ambiguous.

One simple explanation for these differences in the number of labels is that some of these AV systems provide a finer level of detail into the threat landscape than the others. For example, the greater number of unique labels in Table 1 for F-Prot may be the result of F-Prot's ability to more effectively differentiate small variations in a family of malware. To investigate this conjecture, we examined the labels of the *legacy* dataset produced by the AV systems and, using a collection of simple heuristics for the labels, we created a pool of malware classified by F-Prot, McAfee, and ClamAV as SDBot [19]. We then examined the percentage of time each of the three AV systems classified these malware samples as part of the same family. The result of this analysis can be seen in Figure 1. Each AV classifies a number of samples as SDBot, yet the intersection of these different SDBot families is not clean, since there are many samples that are classified as SDBot by one AV and as something else by the others. It is clear that these differences go beyond simple differences in labeling—anti-virus products assign distinct semantics to differing pieces of malware.

2.2   Properties of a Labeling System

Our previous analysis has provided a great deal of evidence indicating that labeling across AV systems does not operate in a way that is useful to researchers, operators, and end users. Before we evaluate these systems any further, it is important to precisely define the properties an ideal labeling system should have. We have identified three key design goals for such a labeling system:

– **Consistency.** Identical items must and similar items should be assigned the same label.
– **Completeness.** A label should be generated for as many items as possible.
– **Conciseness.** The labels should be sufficient in number to reflect the unique properties of interest, while avoiding superfluous labels.

2.3   Limitations of Anti-Virus

Having identified consistency, completeness, and conciseness as the design goals of a labeling system, we are now prepared to investigate the ability of AV systems to meet these goals.

Table 3. The percentage of time two binaries classified as the same by one AV are classified the same by other AV systems. Malware is inconsistently classified across AV vendors.

	legacy					small				
	McAfee	F-Prot	ClamAV	Trend	Symantec	McAfee	F-Prot	ClamAV	Trend	Symantec
McAfee	100	13	27	39	59	100	25	54	38	17
F-Prot	50	100	96	41	61	45	100	57	35	18
ClamAV	62	57	100	34	68	39	23	100	32	13
Trend	67	18	25	100	55	45	23	52	100	16
Symantec	27	7	13	14	100	42	25	46	33	100

Consistency. To investigate consistency, we grouped malware into categories based on the labels provided by AV vendors. For each pair of distinct malware labeled as the same by a particular system, we compared the percentage of time the same pair was classified by other AV systems as the same. For example, two binaries in our *legacy* dataset with different MD5 checksums were labeled as

Table 4. The percentage of malware samples detected across datasets and AV vendors. AV does not provide a complete categorization of the datasets.

Dataset Name	AV Updated	Percentage of Malware Samples Detected				
		McAfee	F-Prot	ClamAV	Trend	Symantec
legacy	20 Nov 2006	100	99.8	94.8	93.73	97.4
small	20 Nov 2006	48.7	61.0	38.4	54.0	76.9
small	31 Mar 2007	67.4	68.0	55.5	86.8	52.4
large	31 Mar 2007	54.6	76.4	60.1	80.0	51.5

W32-Blaster-worm-a by McAfee. These two binaries were labeled consistently by F-Prot (both as msblast), and Trend (both as msblast), but inconsistently by Symantec (one blaster and one not detected) and ClamAV (one blaster, one dcom.exploit). We then selected each system in turn and used its classification as the base. For example, Table 3 shows that malware classified by McAfee as the same was only classified as the same by F-Prot 13% of the time. However, malware classified by F-Prot as the same was only classified as the same by McAfee 50% of the time. Not only do AV systems place malware into different categories, these categories don't hold the same meaning across systems.

Completeness. As discussed earlier, the design goal for completeness is to provide a label for each and every item to be classified. For each of the datasets and AV systems, we examined the percentage of time the AV systems detected a given piece of malware (and hence provided a label). A small percentage of malware samples are still undetected a year after the collection of the *legacy* datasets (Table 4). The results for more recent samples are even more profound, with almost half the samples undetected in the *small* dataset and one quarter in the *large* dataset. The one quarter undetected for the *large* set is likely an overestimate of the ability of the AV, as many of the binaries labeled at that point were many months old (e.g., compare the improvement over time in the two labeling instances of *small*). Thus, AV systems do not provide a complete labeling system.

Table 5. The ways in which various AV products label and group malware. AV labeling schemes vary widely in how concisely they represent the malware they classify.

	legacy(3,637 binaries)		*small*(893 binaries)	
	Unique Labels	Clusters or Families	Unique Labels	Clusters or Families
McAfee	116	34	122	95
F-Prot	1216	37	379	62
ClamAV	590	41	253	65
Trend	416	46	246	72
Symantec	57	31	90	81

Conciseness. Conciseness refers to the ability of the labeling system to provide a label that reflects the important characteristics of the sample without superfluous semantics. In particular, we find that a label that carries either too much or too little meaning has minimal value. To investigate this property, we examined the number and types of labels and groups provided by the AV systems. Table 5 shows the number of unique labels provided by the AV systems as well as the number of unique families these labels belong to. In this analysis, the family is a generalized label heuristically extracted from the literal string, which contains the portion intended to be human-readable. For example, the literal labels returned by a AV system W32-Sdbot.AC and Sdbot.42, are both in the "sdbot" family. An interesting observation from this table is that these systems vary widely in how concisely they represent malware. Vendors such as Symantec appear to employ a general approach, reducing samples to a small handful of labels and families. On the other extreme, FProt appears to aggressively label new instances, providing thousands of unique labels for malware, but still maintaining a small number of groups or families to which these labels belong.

3   Behavior-Based Malware Clustering

As we described in the previous section, any meaningful labeling system must achieve consistency, completeness, and conciseness, and existing approaches, such as those used by anti-virus systems, fail to perform well on these metrics. To address these limitations, we propose an approach based on the actual execution of malware samples and observation of their persistent state changes. These state changes, when taken together, make a behavioral fingerprint, which can then be clustered with other fingerprints to define classes and subclasses of malware that exhibit similar state change behaviors. In this section, we discuss our definition and generation of these behavioral fingerprints and the techniques for clustering them.

3.1   Defining and Generating Malware Behaviors

Previous work in behavioral signatures has been based at the abstraction level of low-level system events, such as individual system calls. In our system, the intent is to capture what the malware actually does on the system. Such information is more invariant and directly useful to assess the potential damage incurred. Individual system calls may be at a level that is too low for abstracting semantically meaningful information: a higher abstraction level is needed to effectively describe the behavior of malware. *We define the behavior of malware in terms of non-transient state changes that the malware causes on the system.* State changes are a higher level abstraction than individual system calls, and they avoid many common obfuscation techniques that foil static analysis as well as low-level signatures, such as encrypted binaries and non-deterministic event ordering. In particular, we extract simple descriptions of state changes from the raw event logs obtained from malware execution. Spawned process names, modified registry keys, modified file names, and network connection attempts are extracted from the logs and the list of such state changes becomes a behavioral profile of a sample of malware.

Observing the malware behavior requires actually executing the binaries. We execute each binary individually inside a virtual machine [27] with Windows XP installed. The virtual machine is partially firewalled so that the external impact of any immediate attack behaviors (e.g., scanning, DDoS, and spam) is minimized during the limited execution period. The system events are captured and exported to an external server using the Backtracker system [12]. In addition to exporting system events, the Backtracker system provides a means of building causal dependency graphs of these events. The benefit of this approach is that we can validate that the changes we observe are a direct result of the malware, and not of some normal system operation.

3.2   Clustering of Malware

While the choice of abstraction and generation of behaviors provides useful information to users, operators, and security personnel, the sheer volume of malware makes manual analysis of each new malware intractable. Our malware source observed 3,700 samples in a six-month period—over 20 new pieces per day. Each generated fingerprint, in turn, can exhibit many thousands of individual state changes (e.g., infecting every .exe on a Windows host). For example, consider the tiny subset of malware in table 6. The 10 distinct pieces of malware generate from 10 to 66 different behaviors with a variety of different labels, including disjoint families, variants, and undetected malware. While some items obviously belong together in spite of their differences (e.g., C and D), even the composition of labels across AV systems can not provide a complete grouping of the malware. Obviously, for these new behavioral fingerprints to be effective, similar behaviors need to be grouped and appropriate meanings assigned.

Table 6. Ten unique malware samples. For each sample, the number of process, file, registry, and network behaviors observed and the classifications given by various AV vendors are listed.

Label	MD5	P/F/R/N	McAfee	Trend
A	71b99714cddd66181e54194c44ba59df	8/13/27/0	Not detected	W32/Backdoor.QWO
B	be5f889d12fe608e48be11e883379b7a	8/13/27/0	Not detected	W32/Backdoor.QWO
C	df1cda05aab2d366e626eb25b9cba229	1/1/6/1	W32/Mytob.gen@MM	W32/IRCBot-based!Maximus
D	5bf169aba400f20cbe1b237741eff090	1/1/6/2	W32/Mytob.gen@MM	Not detected
E	eef804714ab4f89ac847357f3174aa1d	1/2/8/3	PWS-Banker.gen.i	W32/Bancos.IQK
F	80f64d342fddcc980ae81d7f8456641e	2/11/28/1	IRC/Flood.gen.b	W32/Backdoor.AHJJ
G	12586ef09abc1520c1ba3e998baec457	1/4/3/1	W32/Pate.b	W32/Parite.B
H	ff0f3c170ea69ed266b8690e13daf1a6	1/2/8/1	Not detected	W32/Bancos.IJG
I	36f6008760bd8dc057ddb1cf99c0b4d7	3/22/29/3	IRC/Generic Flooder	IRC/Zapchast.AK@bd
J	c13f3448119220d006e93608c5ba3e58	5/32/28/1	Generic BackDoor.f	W32/VB-Backdoor!Maximus

Our approach to generating meaningful labels is achieved through clustering of the behavioral fingerprints. In the following subsections, we introduce this approach and the various issues associated with effective clustering, including how to compare fingerprints, combine them based on their similarity, and determine which are the most meaningful groups of behaviors.

Comparing Individual Malware Behaviors. While examining individual behavioral profiles provides useful information on particular malware samples, our goal is to classify malware and give them meaningful labels. Thus malware samples must be grouped. One way to group the profiles is to create a distance metric that measures the difference between any two profiles, and then use the

Table 7. A matrix of the NCD between each of the 10 malware samples in our example

	A	B	C	D	E	F	G	H	I	J
A	0.06	0.07	0.84	0.84	0.82	0.73	0.80	0.82	0.68	0.77
B	0.07	0.06	0.84	0.85	0.82	0.73	0.80	0.82	0.68	0.77
C	0.84	0.84	0.04	0.22	0.45	0.77	0.64	0.45	0.84	0.86
D	0.85	0.85	0.23	0.05	0.45	0.76	0.62	0.43	0.83	0.86
E	0.83	0.83	0.48	0.47	0.03	0.72	0.38	0.09	0.80	0.85
F	0.71	0.71	0.77	0.76	0.72	0.05	0.77	0.72	0.37	0.54
G	0.80	0.80	0.65	0.62	0.38	0.78	0.04	0.35	0.78	0.86
H	0.83	0.83	0.48	0.46	0.09	0.73	0.36	0.04	0.80	0.85
I	0.67	0.67	0.83	0.82	0.79	0.38	0.77	0.79	0.05	0.53
J	0.75	0.75	0.86	0.85	0.83	0.52	0.85	0.83	0.52	0.08

metric for clustering. Our initial naive approach to defining similarity was based on the concept of edit distance [7]. In this approach, each behavior is treated as an atomic unit and we measure the number of inserts of deletes of these atomic behaviors required to transform one behavioral fingerprint into another. The method is fairly intuitive and straightforward to implement (think the Unix command *diff* here); however, it suffers from two major drawbacks:

- **Overemphasizing size.** When the size of the number of behaviors is large, the edit distance is effectively equivalent to clustering based on the length of the feature set. This overemphasizes differences over similarities.
- **Behavioral polymorphism.** Many of the clusters we observed had few *exact* matches for behaviors. This is because the state changes made by malware may contain simple behavioral polymorphism (e.g., random file names).

To solve these shortcomings we turned to normalized compression distance (NCD). NCD is a way to provide approximation of information content, and it has been successfully applied in a number of areas [25,29]. NCD is defined as:

$$NCD(x, y) = \frac{C(x + y) - min(C(x), C(y))}{max(C(x), C(y))}$$

where "x + y" is the concatenation of x and y, and C(x) is the zlib-compressed length of x. Intuitively, NCD represents the overlap in information between two samples. As a result, behaviors that are similar, but not identical, are viewed as close (e.g., two registry entries with different values, random file names in the same locations). Normalization addresses the issue of differing information content. Table 7 shows the normalized compression distance matrix for the malware described in Table 6.

Constructing Relationships Between Malware. Once we know the information content shared between two sets of behavioral fingerprints, we can combine various pieces of malware based on their similarity. In our approach, we construct a tree structure based on the well-known hierarchical clustering algorithm [11]. In particular, we use pairwise single-linkage clustering, which defines the distance between two clusters as the minimum distance between any two members of the clusters. We output the hierarchical cluster results as a tree graph in graphviz's dot format [14]. Figure 2 shows the generated tree for the malware in Table 6.

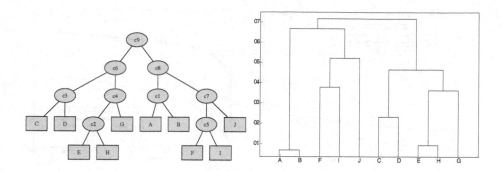

Fig. 2. On the left, a tree consisting of the malware from Table 6 has been clustered via a hierarchical clustering algorithm whose distance function is normalized compression distance. On the right, a dendrogram illustrating the distance between various subtrees.

Extracting Meaningful Groups. While the tree-based output of the hierarchical clustering algorithm does show the relationships between the information content of behavioral fingerprints, it does not focus attention on areas of the tree in which the similarities (or lack thereof) indicate an important group of malware. Therefore, we need a mechanism to extract meaningful groups from the tree. A naive approach to this problem would be to set a single threshold of the differences between two nodes in the tree. However, this can be problematic as a single uniform distance does not accurately represent the distance between various subtrees. For example, consider the dendrogram in Figure 2. The height of many U-shaped lines connecting objects in a hierarchical tree illustrates the distance between the two objects being connected. As the figure shows, the difference between the information content of subtrees can be substantial. Therefore, we require an automated means of discovering where the most important changes occur.

Table 8. The clusters generated via our technique for the malware listed in Table 6

Cluster	Elements	Overlap	Example
c1	C, D	67.86%	scans 25
c2	A, B	97.96%	installs a cygwin rootkit
c3	E, G, H	56.60%	disables AV
c4	F, I, J	53.59%	IRC

To address this limitation, we adopt an "inconsistency" measure that is used to compute the difference in magnitude between distances of clusters so that the tree can be cut into distinct clusters. Clusters are constructed from the tree by first calculating the inconsistency coefficient of each cluster, and then thresholding based on the coefficient. The inconsistency coefficient characterizes each link in a cluster tree by comparing its length with the average length of other links at the same level of the hierarchy. The higher the value of this coefficient, the less similar are the objects connected by the link. The inconsistency coefficient calculation has one parameter, which is the depth below the level of the current

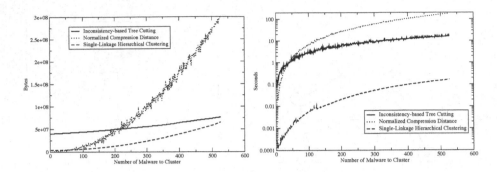

Fig. 3. The memory and runtime required for performing clustering based on the number of malware clustered (for a variety of different sized malware behaviors)

link to consider in the calculation. All the links at the current level in the hierarchy, as well as links down to the given depth below the current level, are used in the inconsistency calculation.

In Table 8 we see the result of the application of this approach to the example malware in Table 6. The 10 unique pieces of malware generate four unique clusters. Each cluster shows the elements in that cluster, the average number of unique behaviors in common between the clusters, and an example of a high-level behavior in common between each binary in the cluster. For example, cluster one consists of C and D and represents two unique behaviors of mytob, a mass mailing scanning worm. Five of the behaviors observed for C and D are identical (e.g., scans port 25), but several others exhibit some behavioral polymorphism (e.g., different run on reboot registry entries). The other three clusters exhibit similar expected results, with cluster two representing the cygwin backdoors, cluster three the bancos variants, and cluster four a class of IRC backdoors.

4   Evaluation

To demonstrate the effectiveness of behavioral clustering, we evaluate our technique on the *large* and *small* datasets discussed in section 2. We begin by demonstrating the runtime performance and the effects of various parameters on the system. We then show the quality or goodness of the clusters generated by our system by comparing existing AV groups (e.g., those labeled as SDBot) to our clusters. Next we discuss our clusters in the context of our completeness, conciseness, and consistency criteria presented earlier. Finally, we illustrate the utility of the clusters by answering relevant questions about the malware samples.

4.1   Performance and Parameterization

We now examine the memory usage and execution time for the hierarchical clustering algorithm. To obtain these statistics, we take random sub-samples of length between 1 to 526 samples from the *small* dataset. For each sub-sample,

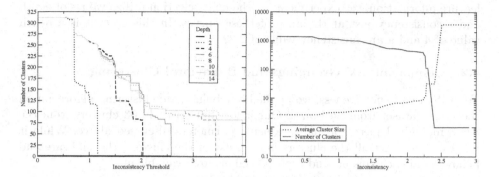

Fig. 4. On the left, the number of clusters generated for various values of the inconsistency parameter and depth. On the right, the trade-off between the number of clusters, the average cluster size, and the inconsistency value.

we analyze its run time and memory consumption by running ten trials for each. The experiments were performed on a Dell PowerEdge 4600 with two Intel Xeon MP CPUs (3.00GHz), 4 GB of DDR ECC RAM, 146G Cheetah Seagate drive with an Adaptec 3960D Ultra160 SCSI adapter, running Fedora Core Linux.

We first decompose the entire execution process into five logical steps: (1) trace collection, (2) state change extraction, (3) NCD distance matrix computation: an $O(N^2)$ operation, (4) clustering the distance matrix into a tree, (5) cutting the tree into clusters. We focus on the latter three operations specific to our algorithm for performance evaluation. Figure 3 shows the memory usage for those three steps. As expected, computing NCD requires the most memory with quadratic growth with an increasing number of malware for clustering. However, clustering 500 malware samples requires less than 300MB of memory. The memory usage for the other two components grows at a much slower rate. Examining the run-time in Figure 3 indicates that all three components can complete within hundreds of seconds for clustering several hundred malware samples.

Phases 1-4 of the system operate without any parameters. However, the tree-cutting algorithm of phase 5 has two parameters: the inconsistency measure and the depth value. Intuitively, larger inconsistency measures lead to fewer clusters and larger depth values for computing inconsistency result in more clusters. Figure 4 illustrates the effects of depth on the number of clusters produced for the *small* dataset for various inconsistency values. Values of between 4-6 for the depth (the 3rd and 4th colored lines) appear to bound the knee of the curve. In order to evaluate the effect of inconsistency, we fixed thedepth to 4 and evaluated the number of clusters versus the average size of the clusters for various inconsistency values in the *large* dataset. The results of this analysis, shown in Figure 4, show a smooth trade-off until an inconsistency value between 2.2 and 2.3, where the clusters quickly collapse into a single cluster. In order to generate clusters that are as concise as possible without, losing important feature information, the experiments in the next selection utilize values of depth and inconsistency just at the knee of these curves. In this case, it is a depth value of 4 and an inconsistency value of 2.22.

4.2   Comparing AV Groupings and Behavioral Clustering

To evaluate its effectiveness, we applied our behavioral clustering algorithm on the *large* dataset from Section 2. Our algorithm created 403 clusters from the 3,698 individual pieces of malware using parmeters discussed above. While it is infeasible to list all the clusters here, a list of the clusters, the malware and behaviors in each cluster, and their AV labels are available at
http://www.eecs.umich.edu/~mibailey/malware/.

As a first approximation of the quality of the clusters produced, we returned to our example in Section 2 and evaluated the clustering of various malware samples labeled as SDBot by the AV systems. Recall from our previous discussions that various AV systems take differing approaches to labeling malware—some adopt a general approach with malware falling into a few broad categories and others apply more specific, almost per sample, labels to each binary. We expect that a behavior-based approach would separate out these more general classes if their behavior differs, and aggregate across the more specific classes if behaviors are shared. Looking at these extremes in our sample, Symantec, who adopts a more general approach, has two binaries identified as back-door.sdbot. They were divided into separate clusters in our evaluation based on differing processes created, differing back-door ports, differing methods of process invocation or reboot, and the presence of AV avoidance in one of the samples. On the other extreme, FProt, which has a high propensity to label each malware sample individually, had 47 samples that were identified as belonging to the sdbot family. FProt provided 46 unique labels for these samples, nearly one unique label per sample. In our clustering, these 46 unique labels were collapsed into 15 unique clusters reflecting their overlap in behaviors. As we noted in Section 2, these grouping have differing semantics—both Symantec labels were also labled by FProt as SDBot, but obviously not all FProt labels were identified as SDBot by Symantec. Both of these extremes demonstrate the utility of our system in moving toward a labeling scheme that is more concise, complete, and consistent.

4.3   Measuring the Completeness, Conciseness and Consistency

We previously examined how the clusters resulting from the application of our algorithm to the *large* dataset compared to classification of AV systems. In this section, we examine more general characteristics of our clusters in an effort to demonstrate their quality. In particular, we demonstrate the completeness, conciseness, and consistency of the generated clusters. Our analysis of these properties, summarized in Table 9, are highlighted each in turn:

Completeness. To measure completeness, we examined the number of times we created a meaningful label for a binary and compared this to the detection rates of the various AV products. For AV software, "not detected" means no

Table 9. The completeness, conciseness, and consistency of the clusters created with our algorithm on the *large* dataset as compared to various AV vendors

AV	Completeness			Conciseness		Consistency
	Detected	Not Detected	% Detected	Unique Lables	Clusters or Families	Identical Behavior Labeled Identically
McAfee	2018	1680	54.6%	308	84	47.2%
F-Prot	2958	740	80.0%	1544	194	31.1%
ClamAV	2244	1454	60.7%	1102	119	34.9%
Trend	2960	738	80.0%	2034	137	44.2%
Symantec	1904	1794	51.5%	125	107	68.2%
Behavior	**3387**	**311**	**91.6%**	**403**	**403**	**100%**

signature matched, despite the up-to-date signature information. For behavioral clustering, "not detected" means that we identified no behavior. A unique aspect of this system is that our limiting factor is not whether we have seen a particular binary before, as in a signature system, but whether we are able to extract meaningful behavior. Any such behavior can be clustered in the context of any number of previously observed malware instances and differentiated, although this differentiation is clearly more valuable the more instances that are observed. In our experiments, roughly 311 binaries exhibited no behavior. The root cause of these errors, and a more complete discussion of the general limitations of dynamic path exploration, is available in the Limitations section. A striking observation from the table is that many AV software systems provide detection rates as low as 51%, compared to around 91% using behavioral clustering. It should be noted that these numbers are as much an indication of the mechanisms the vendors use to collect malware as the AV systems themselves, since signature systems can clearly only detect what they have seen before. While it would be unfair to judge the detection rates based on previously unseen malware, we hesitate to point out that our system for collection of these binaries is not unique. In fact, while individual AV system rates may vary, over 96 percent of the malware samples were detected by at least one of the AV systems. These samples are seen significantly more broadly than our single collection infrastructure and many AV systems fail to detect them.

Conciseness. Conciseness represented the ability of the labeling system to group similar items into groups that both reflected the important differences in samples, but were devoid of superfluous labels. As in Section 2, we evaluate conciseness by examining the characteristics of the grouping, or clusters, created by AV systems with those created by our system. We examine the number of unique labels generated by the AV systems and a heuristically-generated notion of families or groups of these labels extracted from the human readable strings. For example, the labels W32-Sdbot.AC and Sdbot.42, are both in the "sdbot" family. As we noted before, AV systems vary widely in how concisely they represent malware. Relative to other systems, our clusters strike a middle ground in conciseness, providing fewer labels than the total unique labels of AV systems, but more than the number of AV system families. This observation is consistent with the previous section— the AV system families exhibit multiple different behaviors, but these behaviors have much in common across individual labels.

Consistency. Consistency referred to the ability of a labeling system to identify similar or identical items in the same way. In the context of our behavioral system goals, this implies that identical behaviors are placed in the same clusters. In order to measure the consistency of the system, we examined the binaries that exhibited exactly identical behavior. In the *large* sample, roughly 2,200 binaries shared exactly identical behavior with another sample. When grouped, these 2,200 binaries created 267 groups in which each sample in the group had exactly the same behavior. We compared the percentage of time the clusters were identified as the same through our approach, as well as the various AV system. As expected, our system placed all of the identical behaviors in the same clusters. However, because consistency is a design goal of the system, the consistency value for our technique is more a measure of correctness than quality. What is interesting to note, however, is that AV systems obviously do not share this same goal. AV systems only labled *exactly identical behavior* with the same label roughly 31% to 68% percent of the time.

4.4   Application of Clustering and Behavior Signatures

In this subsection we look at several applications of this technique, in the context of the clusters, created by our algorithm from the *large* dataset.

Classifying Emerging Threats. Behavioral classification can be effective in characterizing emerging threats not yet known or not detected by AV signatures. For example, cluster c156 consists of three malware samples that exhibit malicious bot-related behavior, including IRC command and control activities. Each of the 75 behaviors observed in the cluster is shared with other samples of the group—96.92% on average, meaning the malware samples within the cluster have almost identical behavior. However, none of the AV vendors detect the samples in this cluster except for F-Prot, which only detects one of the samples. It is clear that our behavioral classification would assist in identifying these samples as emerging threats through their extensive malicious behavioral profile.

Resisting Binary Polymorphism. Similarly, behavioral classification can also assist in grouping an undetected outlier sample (due to polymorphism or some other deficiency in the AV signatures) together with a common family that it shares significant behaviors with. For example, cluster c80 consists of three samples that share identical behaviors with distinctive strings "bling.exe" and "m0rgan.org." The samples in this cluster are consistently labeled as a malicious bot across the AV vendors except Symantec, which fails to identify one of the samples. To maintain completeness, this outlier sample should be labeled similar to the other samples based on its behavioral profile.

Examining the Malware Behaviors. Clearly one of the values of any type of automated security system is not to simply provide detailed information on individual malware, but also to provide broad analysis on future directions of malware. Using the behavioral signatures created by our system, we extracted

Table 10. The top five behaviors observed by type

Network	Process	Files	Registry
connects to 80	execs cmd.exe	writes winhlp32.dat	uses wininet.dll
connects to 25	execs IEXPLORE.EXE	writes tasklist32.exe	uses PRNG
connects to 6667	execs regedit.exe	writes change.log	modifies registered applications
connects to 587	execs tasklist32.exe	writes mirc.ini	modifies proxy settings
scans port 80	execs svchost.exe	writes svchost.exe	modifies mounted drives

the most prevalent behaviors for each of the various categories of behaviors we monitor. The top five such behaviors in each category are shown in Table 10.

The network behavior seems to conform with agreed notions of how the tasks are being performed by most malware today. Two of the top five network behaviors involve the use of mail ports, presumably for spam. Port 6667 is a common IRC port and is often used for remote control of the malware. Two of the ports are HTTP ports used by systems to check for jailed environments, download code via the web, or tunnel command and control over what is often an unfiltered port. The process behaviors are interesting in that many process executables are named like common Windows utilities to avoid arousing suspicion (e.g., svchost.exe, tasklist32.exe). In addition, some malware uses IEXPLORE.EXE directly to launch popup ads and redirect users to potential phishing sites. This use of existing programs and libraries will make simple anomaly detection techniques more difficult. The file writes show common executable names and data files written to the filesystem by malware. For example, the winhlp32.dat file is a data file common to many Bancos trojans. Registry keys are also fairly interesting indications of behavior and the prevalence of wininet.dll keys shows heavy use of existing libraries for network support. The writing to PRNG keys indicates a heavy use of randomization, as the seed is updated every time a PRNG-related function is used. As expected, the malware does examine and modify the registered application on a machine, the TCP/IP proxy settings (in part to avoid AV), and it queries mounted drives.

5   Related Work

Our work is the first to apply automated clustering to understand malware behavior using resulting state changes on the host to identify various malware families. Related work in malware collection, analysis, and signature generation has primarily explored static and byte-level signatures [23,17] focusing on invariant content. Content-based signatures are insufficient to cope with emerging threats due to intentional evasion. Behavioral analysis has been proposed as a solution to deal with polymorphism and metamorphism, where malware changes its visible instruction sequence (typically the decryptor routine) as it spreads. Similar to our work, emulating malware to discover spyware behavior by using anti-spyware tools has been used in measurements studies [22].

There are several abstraction layers at which behavioral profiles can be created. Previous work has focused on lower layers, such as individual system calls [15,10],instruction-based code templates [6], the initial code run on malware infection (shellcode) [18], and network connection and session behavior [30]. Such behavior needs to be effectively elicited. In our work, we chose a higher abstraction layer for several reasons. In considering the actions of malware, it is not the individual system calls that define the significant actions that a piece of malware inflicts upon the infected host; rather, it is the resulting changes in state of the host. Also, although lower levels may allow signatures that differentiate malware, they do not provide semantic value in explaining behaviors exhibited by a malware variant or family. In our work, we define malware by what it actually does, and thereby build in more semantic meanings to the profiles and clusters generated.

Various aspects of high-level behavior could be included in the definition of a behavioral profile. Network behavior may be indicative of malware and has been used to detect malware infections. For example, Ellis et al. [9] extracted network-level features, such as similar data being sent from one machine to the next. In our work, we focus on individual host behavior, including network connection information but not the data transmitted over the network. Thus, we focus more on the malware behavior on individual host systems instead of the pattern across a network.

Recently, Kolter and Maloof [13] studied applying machine learning to classify malicious executables using n-grams of byte codes. Our use of hierarchical clustering based on normalized compression distance is a first step at examining how statistical techniques are useful in classifying malware, but the features used are the resulting state changes on the host to be more resistant to evasion and inaccuracies. Normalized information distance was proposed by Li et al. [16] as an optimal similarity metric to approximate all other effective similarity metrics. In previous work [29], NCD was applied to worm executables directly and to the network traffic generated by worms. Our work applies NCD at a different layer of abstraction. Rather than applying NCD to the literal malware executables, we apply NCD to the malware behavior.

6   Limitations and Future Work

Our system is not without limitations and shares common weaknesses associated with dynamic analysis. Since the malware samples were executed within VMware, samples that employ anti-VM evasion techniques may not exhibit their malicious behavior. To mitigate this limitation, the samples could be run on a real, non-virtualized system, which would be restored to a clean state after each simulation. Another limitation is the time period in which behaviors are collected from the malware execution. In our experiments, each binary was able to run for five minutes before the virtual machine was terminated. It is possible that certain behaviors were not observed within this period due to time-dependent or delayed activities. Previous research has been done to detect such time-dependent triggers [8]. A similar limitation is malware that depends on user input, such as responding to a popup message box, before exhibiting further malicious behavior, as mentioned in [22]. Finally, the capabilities and environment of our virtualized system stayed static throughout our experiments. However, varying the execution environment by using multiple operating system versions, including other memory resident programs such as anti-virus protection engines, and varying network connectivity and reachability may yield interesting behaviors not observed in our existing results. Recently, a generic approach to these and other problems associated with dynamic analysis has be suggested by Moser, et al. [21]. Their approach is based on exploring multiple execution paths through tracing and rewriting key input values in the system, which could yield additional behaviors unseen in our single execution path.

Our choice of a high level of abstraction may limit fine-grained visibility into each of the observed behaviors in our system. A path for future work could include low-level details of each state change to supplement the high-level behavior description. For example, the actual contents of disk writes and transmitted network packets could be included in a sample's behavioral profile. In addition, we plan to evaluate the integration of other high-level behavioral reports from existing systems, such as Norman [24] and CWSandbox [5], in the future. We will also investigate further clustering and machine-learning techniques that may better suit these other types of behavioral profiles. Finally, the causal graphs from Backtracker, which are used to identify the behaviors in our system, also include dependency information that is currently ignored. In future versions, this dependency information could be used to further differentiate behaviors.

7   Conclusion

In this paper, we demonstrated that existing host-based techniques (e.g., anti-virus) fail to provide useful labels to the malware they encounter. We showed that AV systems are *incomplete* in that they fail to detect or provide labels for between 20 to 49 percent of the malware samples. We noted that when these systems do provide labels, these labels are not *consistent*, both within a single naming convention as well as across multiple vendors and conventions. Finally, we demonstrated that these systems vary widely in their *conciseness*— from aggressive, nearly individual labels that ignore commonalities, to broad general groups that hide important details.

To address these important limitations, we proposed a novel approach to the problem of automated malware classification and analysis. Our dynamic approach executes the malware in a virtualized environment and creates a behavioral fingerprint of the malware's activity. This fingerprint is the set of all the state changes that are a causal result of the infection, including files modified, processes created, and network connections. In order to compare these fingerprints and combine them into meaningful groups of behaviors, we apply single-linkage hierarchical clustering of the fingerprints using normalized compress distance as a distance metric. We demonstrated the usefulness of this technique by applying it to the automated classification and analysis of 3,700 malware samples collected over the last six months. We compared the clusters generated to existing malware classification (i.e., AV systems) and showed the technique's completeness, conciseness, and consistency. Through these evaluations, we showed that this new technique provides a novel way of understanding the relationships between malware and is an important step forward in understanding and bridging existing malware classifications.

Acknowledgments

This work was supported in part by the Department of Homeland Security (DHS) under contract numbers NBCHC040146 and NBCHC060090, by the National Science Foundation (NSF) under contract number CNS 0627445 and by corporate gifts from Intel Corporation and Cisco Corporation. We would like to thank our shepherd, Jonathon Giffin, for providing valuable feedback on our submission as well as the anonymous reviewers for critical and useful comments.

References

1. Arbor malware library (AML) (2006), http://www.arbornetworks.com/
2. Baecher, P., Koetter, M., Holz, T., Dornseif, M., Freiling, F.: The nepenthes platform: An efficient approach to collect malware. In: Zamboni, D., Kruegel, C. (eds.) RAID 2006. LNCS, vol. 4219, Springer, Heidelberg (2006)
3. Barford, P., Yagneswaran, V.: An inside look at botnets. In: Series: Advances in Information Security, Springer, Heidelberg (2006)
4. Beck, D., Connolly, J.: The Common Malware Enumeration Initiative. In: Virus Bulletin Conference (October 2006)
5. Willems, C., Holz, T.: Cwsandbox (2007), http://www.cwsandbox.org/
6. Christodorescu, M., Jha, S., Seshia, S.A., Song, D., Bryant, R.E.: Semantics-aware malware detection. In: Proceedings of the 2005 IEEE Symposium on Security and Privacy (Oakland 2005), Oakland, CA, USA, May 2005, pp. 32–46. ACM Press, New York (2005)
7. Cormen, T.H., Leiserson, C.E., Rivest, R.L., Stein, C.: Introduction to Algorithms. MIT Press, Cambridge, MA (1990)
8. Crandall, J.R., Wassermann, G., de Oliveira, D.A.S., Su, Z., Wu, S.F., Chong, F.T.: Temporal Search: Detecting Hidden Malware Timebombs with Virtual Machines. In: Proceedings of ASPLOS, San Jose, CA, October 2006, ACM Press, New York (2006)
9. Ellis, D., Aiken, J., Attwood, K., Tenaglia, S.: A Behavioral Approach to Worm Detection. In: Proceedings of the ACM Workshop on Rapid Malcode (WORM04), October 2004, ACM Press, New York (2004)
10. Gao, D., Beck, D., Reiter, J.C.M.K., Song, D.X.: Behavioral distance measurement using hidden markov models. In: Zamboni, D., Kruegel, C. (eds.) RAID 2006. LNCS, vol. 4219, pp. 19–40. Springer, Heidelberg (2006)
11. Hastie, T., Tibshirani, R., Friedman, J.: The Elements of Statistical Learning: Data Mining, Inference, and Prediction. Springer, Heidelberg (2001)
12. King, S.T., Chen, P.M.: Backtracking intrusions. In: Proceedings of the 19th ACM Symposium on Operating Systems Principles (SOSP'03), Bolton Landing, NY, USA, October 2003, pp. 223–236. ACM Press, New York (2003)
13. Kolter, J.Z., Maloof, M.A.: Learning to Detect and Classify Malicious Executables in the Wild. Journal of Machine Learning Research (2007)

14. Koutsofios, E., North, S.C.: Drawing graphs with dot. Technical report, AT&T Bell Laboratories, Murray Hill, NJ (October 8, 1993)
15. Lee, T., Mody, J.J.: Behavioral classification. In: Proceedings of EICAR 2006 (April 2006)
16. Li, M., Chen, X., Li, X., Ma, B., Vitányi, P.: The similarity metric. In: SODA '03: Proceedings of the fourteenth annual ACM-SIAM symposium on Discrete algorithms, Philadelphia, PA, USA. Society for Industrial and Applied Mathematics, pp. 863–872 (2003)
17. Li, Z., Sanghi, M., Chen, Y., Kao, M., Chavez, B.: Hamsa: Fast Signature Generation for Zero-day Polymorphic Worms with Provable Attack Resilience. In: Proc. of IEEE Symposium on Security and Privacy, IEEE Computer Society Press, Los Alamitos (2006)
18. Ma, J., Dunagan, J., Wang, H., Savage, S., Voelker, G.: Finding Diversity in Remote Code Injection Exploits. In: Proceedings of the USENIX/ACM Internet Measurement Conference, October 2006, ACM Press, New York (2006)
19. McAfee: W32/Sdbot.worm (April 2003),
    http://vil.nai.com/vil/content/v_100454.htm
20. Microsoft: Microsoft security intelligence report: (January-June 2006) (October 2006), http://www.microsoft.com/technet/security/default.mspx
21. Moser, A., Kruegel, C., Kirda, E.: Exploring multiple execution paths for malware analysis. In: Proceedings of the IEEE Symposium on Security and Privacy (Oakland 2007), May 2007, IEEE Computer Society Press, Los Alamitos (2007)
22. Moshchuk, A., Bragin, T., Gribble, S.D., Levy, H.M.: A Crawler-based Study of Spyware in the Web. In: Proceedings of the Network and Distributed System Security Symposium (NDSS), San Diego, CA (2006)
23. Newsome, J., Karp, B., Song, D.: Polygraph: Automatically generating signatures for polymorphic worms. In: Proceedings 2005 IEEE Symposium on Security and Privacy, Oakland, CA, USA, May 8–11, 2005, IEEE Computer Society Press, Los Alamitos (2005)
24. Norman Solutions: Norman sandbox whitepaper (2003),
    http:// download.norman.no/whitepapers/whitepaper_Norman_SandBox.pdf
25. Nykter, M., Yli-Harja, O., Shmulevich, I.: Normalized compression distance for gene expression analysis. In: Workshop on Genomic Signal Processing and Statistics (GENSIPS) (May 2005)
26. Prince, M.B., Dahl, B.M., Holloway, L., Keller, A.M., Langheinrich, E.: Understanding how spammers steal your e-mail address: An analysis of the first six months of data from project honey pot. In: Second Conference on Email and Anti-Spam (CEAS 2005) (July 2005)
27. Walters, B.: VMware virtual platform. j-LINUX-J 63 (July 1999)
28. Wang, Y.-M., Beck, D., Jiang, X., Roussev, R., Verbowski, C., Chen, S., King, S.T.: Automated web patrol with strider honeymonkeys: Finding web sites that exploit browser vulnerabilities. In: Proceedings of the Network and Distributed System Security Symposium, NDSS 2006, San Diego, California, USA (2006)
29. Wehner, S.: Analyzing worms and network traffic using compression. Technical report, CWI, Amsterdam (2005)
30. Yegneswaran, V., Giffin, J.T., Barford, P., Jha, S.: An Architecture for Generating Semantics-Aware Signatures. In: Proceedings of the 14th USENIX Security Symposium, Baltimore, MD, USA, August 2005, pp. 97–112 (2005)

"Out-of-the-Box" Monitoring of VM-Based High-Interaction Honeypots

Xuxian Jiang and Xinyuan Wang

Department of Information and Software Engineering
George Mason University
Fairfax, VA 22030
{xjiang,xwangc}@ise.gmu.edu

Abstract. Honeypot has been an invaluable tool for the detection and analysis of network-based attacks by either human intruders or automated malware in the wild. The insights obtained by deploying honeypots, especially high-interaction ones, largely rely on the monitoring capability on the honeypots. In practice, based on the location of sensors, honeypots can be monitored either *internally* or *externally*. Being deployed inside the monitored honeypots, internal sensors are able to provide a semantic-rich view on various aspects of system dynamics (e.g., system calls). However, their very internal existence makes them visible, tangible, and even subvertible to attackers after break-ins. From another perspective, existing external honeypot sensors (e.g., network sniffers) could be made invisible to the monitored honeypot. However, they are not able to capture any internal system events such as system calls executed.

It is desirable to have a honeypot monitoring system that is invisible, tamper-resistant and yet is capable of recording and understanding the honeypot's system internal events such as system calls. In this paper, we present a virtualization-based system called *VMscope* which allows us to view the system internal events of virtual machine (VM)-based honeypots from outside the honeypots. Particularly, by observing and interpreting VM-internal system call events at the virtual machine monitor (VMM) layer, VMscope is able to provide the same deep inspection capability as that of traditional inside-the-honeypot monitoring tools (e.g., Sebek) while still obtaining similar tamper-resistance and invisibility as other external monitoring tools. We have built a proof-of-concept prototype by leveraging and extending one key virtualization technique called *binary transla-tion*. Our experiments with real-world honeypots show that VMscope is robust against advanced countermeasures that can defeat existing internally-deployed honeypot monitors, and it only incurs moderate run-time overhead.

1 Introduction

Malware that exploits network and system vulnerabilities has become an increasing threat to the information systems we are depending on daily: They not only actively take advantage of zero-day exploits [20,21,22] to compromise vulnerable machines, but also stealthily hide in infected machines and inflict contaminations over time [10,15], e.g., by deliberately avoiding fast propagation and using rootkits to protect themselves.

From the defender's perspective, security researchers have proposed and developed a variety of systems and tools to capture, analyze, and ultimately defend against these

C. Kruegel, R. Lippmann, and A. Clark (Eds.): RAID 2007, LNCS 4637, pp. 198–218, 2007.
© Springer-Verlag Berlin Heidelberg 2007

attacks. Among the most notable approaches, the honeypot [9] has been an invaluable and effective tool for researchers to observe and understand the exploits, methods and strategies used by attackers and malware. Particularly, high-interaction honeypots allow intruders to access a full-fledged operating system running unmodified vulnerable applications with few restrictions. By closely monitoring the entire process on how the honeypot is being probed, exploited, and misused, we can obtain unique insights on the (possibly zero-day) vulnerabilities [17,48,59] being exploited, the detailed intrusion steps used by the attacker, as well as the motivations behind the attack.

The effectiveness of using honeypots to obtain these insights heavily relies on the monitoring capability on the honeypots that are supposed to be compromised and controlled by the attacker or malware. Ideally, the monitoring should be 1) transparent to the honeypot; 2) tamper-resistant even after the attacker gains access and takes full control of the honeypot; and 3) capable of capturing and understanding honeypot system internal events such as system calls. Unfortunately, none of the existing honeypot monitoring approaches achieves all the above three goals at the same time. Note that based on the locations of sensors, existing honeypot monitoring approaches can be classified into two main categories: *internal* and *external*. The external monitoring remains invisible to the monitored honeypot but at the cost of losing the capability to capture the internal system events such as system calls executed. On the other hand, the internal monitoring deploys sensors inside the monitored honeypots and hence provides a semantic-rich view on various aspects of system dynamics. However, the sensors inside the honeypots could be detected, subverted and disabled by the attacker. For example, the de-facto high-interaction honeypot monitoring tool – Sebek [4] – could be completely disabled by NoSEBrEaK [35].

In this paper, we present a virtualization-based monitoring system called *VMscope* that gives us the same deep inspection capability as existing internal monitoring tools (e.g. Sebek) while being as transparent and tamper-resistant as existing external monitoring tools (e.g. a network sniffer). By deploying itself completely outside the VM-based honeypot (we call "out-of-the-box" monitoring in the rest of this paper), VMscope is tamper-resistant and transparent to the monitored system. Further, without requiring any modification to the monitored system, VMscope runs at the virtual machine monitor (VMM) layer and is capable of observing, recording, and understanding the parameters and semantics of various VM-internal system events including system calls. This gives us the same monitoring capability as existing internal sensors even though we do not have any sensors inside. As an example, once a *sys_read* system call of a VM is observed, VMscope will examine from outside the VM the corresponding system call parameters and understand which file is being opened for this read operation and what will be the return value or content after the system call is completed. Furthermore, these semantic-level information will be collected and stored outside the vulnerable honeypot system, which gives us better tamper-resistance than other conventional approaches.

More specifically, to enable "out-of-the-box" monitoring, VMscope leverages and extends one key software-based virtualization technique [1] called *binary translation* (implemented in VMware [16], VirtualBox[14], and QEMU [29]) to transparently observe,

---

[1] In this paper, we focus our discussion on software- based VMM implementations and leave the VMscope support for hardware-based virtualization as our future work.

interpret, and record interested VM events at runtime. Note there exists another comparable virtualization technique called *para-virtualization* (implemented in Xen [27] and User Mode Linux [34]), which, however, is undesirable for VMscope purposes. The reasons are: (1) Binary translation allows us to transparently support legacy OSes in VMs without any modification on the guest OSes while para-virtualization requires modification and recompiling of the guest OSes. Such a modification of the VM-based honeypot not only violates the transparency requirement but also introduces the risk of being detected and subverted; (2) Para-virtualization requires the access and modification of guest OS source code, which could significantly limit our choices of deploying commodity (commercial) OSes as honeypots. We point out that this design choice differentiates our approach from earlier Xen or UML-based system monitoring approaches [25,40,53]. In the meantime, being deployed completely "out-of-the-box", VMscope faces additional challenges, known as the "semantic gap" [31], when interpreting VM-internal events and state (Section 3).

To demonstrate the feasibility of "out-of-the-box" monitoring, we have implemented a proof-of-concept prototype based on an open-source binary translation-capable VMM prototype called QEMU [29]. Our experimental results with real-world honeypot deployment as well as the comparison with the de-facto honeypot monitoring tool (i.e., Sebek [4]) show that VMscope can achieve the same deep inspection capability as internal monitoring tools while, at the same time, being transparent and tamper-resistant against advanced attacks (e.g., NoSEBrEaK [35]).

The rest of the paper is organized as follows: Section 2 examines existing approaches in honeypot monitoring. Section 3 and 4 present the design and implementation of VMscope respectively. In Section 5, we show the experimental results with real-world honeypot incidents as well as the comparison between VMscope and Sebek. Section 6 reviews related works. Finally, we conclude in Section 7.

2   Traditional Honeypot Monitoring

Honeypot monitoring is one essential component in any honeypot deployment. Since VMscope is designed to monitor high-interaction VM-based honeypots, we briefly overview existing approaches that are used for high-interaction honeypot monitoring.

There exist two traditional ways to monitor honeypots: the network-based (i.e. external) approach and the host-based (i.e. internal) approach. The network-based approach uses traffic sniffers such as TCPDUMP [6] and Ethereal [2] to record every network packet sent to or received from the monitored honeypot; The host-based approach, on the other hand, uses specialized sensors deployed inside the honeypot to monitor and record interesting system events (e.g., specific system calls). Note that these two approaches are complementary and each one has its own unique strengths and weaknesses. The network-based approach is more transparent as the sniffers are deployed outside of the vulnerable honeypots. However, it is unable to observe honeypot internal events. Furthermore, its effectiveness is greatly minimized if the monitored network traffic is encrypted. In comparison, with internally deployed sensors, the host-based approach is able to observe the system events of the monitored honeypot. However, sensors deployed inside the honeypot could be detected and tampered with by the attacker.

Here we choose to use Sebek [4] – the de-facto honeypot monitoring tool that has been widely used in a variety of high-interaction honeypot systems [9,39] – to illustrate how honeypots are monitored in practice. In principle, Sebek works as follows:

- Firstly, Sebek installs itself as a loadable kernel module that will wrap or replace a number of sensitive system calls in the original OS kernel with its own implementations. For example, the latest Sebek development (version 3.2.0b) for Linux kernel 2.6 is interested in the following 11 system calls: *sys_open*, *sys_read*, *sys_readv*, *sys_pread64*, *sys_write*, *sys_writev*, *sys_pwrite64*, *sys_fork*, *sys_vfork*, *sys_clone*, *sys_socketcall*. To intercept these system calls, the corresponding system table entries will be overwritten by Sebek with its own system call handlers.
- Secondly, if the replacement is successful, the system call handlers provided by Sebek will intercept subsequent invocations of these replaced system calls and record their arguments as well as other context information (e.g., *UID* or *PID*). After that, Sebek's system call handlers will invoke the original system call service routines to complete the requested service.
- Finally, the collected information about the invoked system calls will be stealthily sent to a remote trusted Sebek server so that we can analyze the collected system call information in real-time or save the log for later investigation.

In order to reliably monitor potentially malicious activities happening inside the honeypot, internal sensors such as Sebek need to be stealthy and tamper-resistant. Unfortunately, any sensor inside the honeypot could be potentially detected, subverted, or evaded by sophisticated attackers after they gain complete control over the honeypot. For example, it has been successfully demonstrated [53] that, after the compromise of a Sebek-based honeypot, attackers can detect the existence of Sebek by identifying a variety of Sebek-introduced "anomalies": (1) the modification on the system call table by Sebek; (2) the inconsistency in the statistics (e.g., transmit-counters) of the Ethernet device on the system caused by Sebek; and (3) the existence of a hidden Sebek module in the honeypot. Furthermore, once identified, Sebek can be disabled or circumvented. For example, an attacker can choose to re-overwrite (e.g., unsebek [32]) those system call entries that are hooked by Sebek or use other alternative system calls (e.g., NoSE-BrEaK [35]) instead of those Sebek-hooked system calls (e.g., *sys_read*) to achieve the same goal. Further information about Sebek as well as possible attacks can be found in [4,35,53].

In summary, while existing host-based (i.e. internal) honeypot monitoring approaches are capable of observing and interpreting the honeypot's system internal events, they are fundamentally limited in achieving transparency and tamper-resistance due to the internal deployment of sensors inside the honeypot. Existing network-based (i.e. external) honeypot monitoring approaches are transparent, invisible and tamper-resistant, but they could not monitor honeypots' system internal events. In other words, currently available honeypot monitoring approaches would force the honeypot designer to either sacrifice the tamper-resistance for the deep inspection capability or sacrifice the deep inspection capability for the tamper-resistance of honeypot monitoring. In the rest of this paper, we show via VMscope that it is indeed possible to achieve transparency, tamper-resistance and deep inspection capability at the same time when monitoring honeypots.

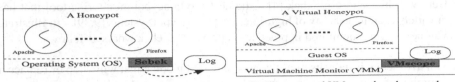

(a) The traditional Sebek-based approach   (b) The proposed VMscope-based approach

Fig. 1. A comparison between the traditional Sebek-based approach and the proposed VMscope-based approach in honeypot monitoring

3 VMscope

In this section, we present the VMscope design, which enables the deep inspection of VM-based high-interaction honeypots without deploying any sensors inside.

3.1 Placement of Event Logging

Figure 1 shows the main difference between VMscope and traditional (internal) honeypot monitoring tools (Sebek is chosen as the representative example). Unlike the traditional approach where the monitoring tools are deployed "inside the box", the placement of VMscope is unique in that it is deployed outside of the monitored VMs. Such "out-of-the-box" placement is desirable because it leverages the isolation property from virtual machines to strictly confine processes running inside the VM such that, even if they are compromised by attackers, it will be hard, if not impossible, to compromise the VMscope outside of the VM. In the meantime, since VMscope runs underneath the VM-based honeypots, it has access to all VM-internal system state and can intercept every network packet from/to the VM, indicating that it can still reliably monitor the system dynamics of a honeypot even after being compromised. In comparison, the effectiveness of existing tools including Sebek, which are deployed inside the monitored honeypots, becomes susceptible after the honeypot is compromised. The reason is that they could also be identified, circumvented, or compromised. The development of unsebek [32] as well as disclosed ptrace-related vulnerabilities [19] [2] clearly demonstrate this weakness.

The proposed VMscope approach also has another benefit in the way of collecting and saving honeypot logs. In order to protect the integrity and trustworthiness of collected honeypot logs, they can not be stored inside the vulnerable honeypot systems and typically should be securely transferred to a remote trusted location. The network-based transmission is *unavoidable* for traditional monitoring tools that are deployed "inside the box". Unfortunately, such transmission behavior can lead to certain side-effects (e.g., the transmit-counters of a particular NIC), some of which can be exploited by attackers to identify the very internal existence of these honeypot monitoring tools and cascadingly compromise them [53]. In comparison, VMscope directly stores the collected log data at the host domain, which is outside the monitored honeypot.

---

[2] In Section 5.1, we will describe a honeypot incident that exploits one ptrace vulnerability to completely compromise the honeypot.

3.2 Interception and Interpretation

The "out-of-the-box" deployment does significantly improve the tamper-resistance of VMscope. However, it also poses significant challenges on the interception and interpretation of interesting system call events that are currently happening inside monitored VMs. For instance, the external placement prevents VMscope from hooking system calls by directly overwriting certain entries in the VM's system call table.

The distinctions between two mainstream virtualization techniques (Section 1) are useful in understanding the well-known "semantic gap" challenge [31] when observing and interpreting the internal VM state/event at the VMM layer. Particularly, the modification on the guest OS source code by para-virtualization-based approaches naturally enables the interpretation of the VM state as the modified components are already a part of the guest OS kernel. However, the transparent support from binary translation-based approaches unintentionally creates a significantly larger gap in semantically understanding VM-internal state or events as the VMM is now completely running "out of the box".

Our approach leverages and extends the original binary translation technique to selectively rewrite other "interesting" instructions, in addition to those non-virtualizable instructions (e.g., *POPF*). More precisely, to intercept system call events of a VM, we are also interested in translating those system call instructions (e.g., *int $0x80* or *sysenter/sysexit*) that are being invoked by internal processes.

Moreover, the semantics implicitly associated with these system call instructions are used for their interpretation. Specifically, upon the interception of an interesting system call event, the corresponding interpretation code will be executed to understand and collect the associated context information to resolve the semantic gap. Note that, similar to the interception, the interpretation code is also running in the context of virtual machine monitor (VMM), *not* inside the guest VM. As such, VMscope instantiates a general methodology known as virtual machine introspection (VMI) [38], which allows to analyze software running in a VM by examining its system state from outside the VM. For example, upon the interception of a *sys_execve* event, we need to find out which new process is being launched. The answer lies in the arguments or the context of this system call. Specifically, for the *sys_execve* system call, the EBX register contains a memory address that points to the string of process file name; the ECX register has the memory address of an array of strings with all command line arguments (i.e., *argv[]*); and the EDX register contains the memory address of another array of strings with all environment settings (i.e., *envp[]*). Finally, we would like to point out that every above-mentioned memory address is a virtual address, which is specific to an internal process and would be different for different processes. As such, its interpretation requires the traversal of the page table of that particular process running inside the VM. We defer the technical discussion to Section 4.

3.3 Selection of System Events

It is important to select a right set of system events which could provide important "leads" to understand attackers' behavior. Since the main way for an attacker to inflict damages on a system is by making system calls, we choose system call events as the main source for honeypot logging. However, we do point out that VMscope is capable of capturing other system-wide events. For example, the context switch event is useful to identify the moment when a new process is being switched in for execution. Such event is valuable if additional monitoring events should be activated just for a particular process. In this paper, we only examine the application of collecting system call events for honeypot monitoring purposes. The exclusive focus on system call events is consistent with existing approaches [39,33] for honeypot log collection. Particularly, the fact that Sebek only replaces 11 system calls (Section 2) actually implies that VMscope may only need to intercept these 11 system calls.

However, we notice that a system call could be somehow substituted with other system calls to achieve the same goal. Consequently, the log with an incomplete set of system calls could not reveal a complete picture of attack behavior. Moreover, if these alternative system calls are not selected for interception, they can be leveraged by attackers to inflict their damages without being logged, hence significantly undermining the honeypot value. For example, the *sys_read* system call is commonly used to read a file's content and this event is mainly intercepted by Sebek to provide important information about attackers, including the keystrokes that are not possible to uncover by only analyzing encrypted network communication. A program or a malware can alternatively call *sys_mmap* or *sys_mmap2* to map the file into memory and directly use memory pointers to access the file content *without being logged*.

As another example, if a file is being opened (*sys_open*) and its content will be read (*sys_read*) and written (*sys_write*) to a network socket, a single system call, i.e., *sys_sendfile*, can be used to consolidate these two system calls *sys_read* and *sys_write* without undermining the functionality. In fact, a countermeasure tool called NoSE-BrEaK [35] has already been developed to effectively circumvent Sebek – the de-facto honeypot monitoring tool. More specifically, NoSEBrEaK could exploit and control a honeypot monitored by Sebek in such a way that any commands issued through NoSE-BrEaK will not be captured by Sebek. Considering these possible attacks, VMscope is designed to capture all system call events. We will present the comparison between VMscope and Sebek more thoroughly in Section 5.

Finally, we point out that VMscope captures all system call events during the lifetime of a monitored honeypot, starting from the first moment when it is booted to the last moment it is shut down. This is different from most of existing approaches that need a working normal system before activating the log collection. As such, there exists a window of vulnerability within which system call events will not be monitored and attackers could potentially exploit this vulnerability window to invoke certain backdoor services without being noticed. As an example, the loadable kernel module of Sebek is not able to capture those system call events executed during the system bootstrap phrase. We point out that some stealthy rootkits such as Suckit [56] is able to manipulate the system bootstrap process to start some backdoor services before launching logging processes. This interesting capability of VMscope can be uniquely used to detect any anomaly during the system's bootstrap process.

4   Implementation

We have implemented a proof-of-concept system based on an open-source emulation-based VM implementation called QEMU [29]. The two main reasons why we choose

QEMU are: (1) It implements a basic approach of performing dynamic binary translation, which is leveraged and extended by VMscope to observe and interpret interesting
system call events from outside the VM; (2) Upon the observation of VM system events,
we need to embed our own interpretation logic to extract related context information.
The open-source nature of QEMU provides great convenience and flexibility in making
our implementation possible.

4.1 Interception

To better understand how the interception of VMscope works, we need to first understand the dynamic binary translation technique of QEMU [29]. We briefly summarize
it as follows: (1) Firstly, QEMU splits each target CPU instruction into fewer simpler
instructions called *micro operations*, each of which is implemented by a small piece of
native C code and compiled by GCC to an object file; (2) The generated object file is
then used by a compile time tool called *dyngen*[29] to generate a dynamic code generator. The dynamic code generator will be invoked at runtime to dynamically translate
target instruction sequences into executable host code in the form of basic blocks.

To speed up the process of translating a sequence of target code, QEMU keeps translating the target code sequence until it encounters an *jmp* instruction (including other
variants such as *je/jne/jcxz/ljmp* instructions) or an instruction that will essentially modify the target CPU state in a way that cannot be deduced at translation time [29]. One
such example is the instruction – *repz stos %ax,%es:(%di)*, which will modify the zero
flag (ZF) in the target CPU state. Another example is the system call instruction in
Linux – *int $0x80*, which will trigger the transition from the user mode to the kernel
mode and directly modify the target CPU state. Another interesting trick of QEMU is
to take advantage of the native compiler to construct the target code sequences automatically and the chore of each individual instruction translation largely occurs at the
compilation time, instead of at the runtime.

To log all system call events, VMscope leverages and extends this binary translation
capability to intercept all system call instructions, namely *int $0x80* and *sysenter/sysexit*.
More specifically, before a system call instruction is executed, a VMscope-provided
callback routine will be invoked to collect the associated context information (Section
4.2). In addition, right after the system call is completed, another callback routine will
be invoked to obtain the return value, which essentially requires the interception of the
instruction immediately following the system call instruction (simplified as the *post-
syscall* instruction). Considering the fact that the actual execution of a system call instruction will trigger the transition from the user mode to the kernel mode, we need to
keep a local copy of the location of the post-syscall instruction. [3] Once the post-syscall
instruction is being translated, the interpretation code should be invoked again to collect
the return value(s) of the previous system call instruction.

Intuitively, we can have a single VM-wide variable to hold that location. Unfortunately, the multitasking support in modern OS kernels makes it more complicated. Considering the following scenario: process A is opening a local file with the system call
sys_open. Before this system call returns, a context switch occurs and another process

---

[3] The local copy is not needed for the system call instruction pair *sysenter/sysexit* as the instruction *sysexit* can uniquely identify itself.

B is chosen for execution, which leads to the return from a previous *sys_read* system call (of process B). To correctly interpret this return value, we need to correlate it with the corresponding system call from the same process. As such, we need to maintain a per-process memory area at the VMM layer to keep this syscall context information, which essentially requires the capability of VMM to keep track of the lifetime of running processes.

It is interesting to point out that our initial prototype avoids this problem by exploiting the way how the kernel-level process stack is organized and utilized. Specifically, for each process, Linux consolidates two different data structures – the process descriptor *thread_info*[4] and kernel-level process stack – in a single per-process memory area called *thread_union* (defined in the *include/linux/sched.h*).

```
union thread_union {
    struct thread_info thread_info;
    unsigned long stack[2048]; /* 1024 for 4KB stacks */
};
```

The length of this memory area is usually two page frames (8, 192 bytes or 8K), which, for efficiency reasons, are stored consecutively with the first page frame aligned to a multiple of 2^{13}. Based on the observations that the current kernel-level stack pointer is maintained in the ESP register and the size of $8K$ contains enough space for the stack and the *thread_info* data structure, we could choose to store the location of the post-syscall instruction right after the *thread_info* data structure. This approach does bring two advantages: (1) Firstly, it avoids the need to keep track of the lifetime of an internal process; (2) Secondly, we can efficiently access the post-syscall location value[5] through the ESP register, i.e., $ESP\&(8192-1)+sizeof(struct\ thread_info)$. However, considering that the variable is stored inside the guest OS kernel and therefore could be potentially manipulated by attackers, our current prototype maintains them in the per-process memory area at the VMM layer, which is outside of the VM.

4.2 Interpretation

The correct interpretation of intercepted system call events requires the understanding of the calling convention on how to invoke a system call. On Linux, it will pass system call arguments mainly through registers. For example, the system call number is kept in the EAX register and, for system calls with no more than 6 arguments, the arguments are passed in EBX, ECX, EDX, ESI, EDI, and EBP registers, respectively. For system calls with more than 6 arguments, they are simply pushed on the stack and a pointer to the block of arguments is passed in the EBX register. After the system call is completed, the result will be returned in the EAX register. Note that the placement of VMscope allows us to observe the content of these registers.

---

[4] For Linux kernel 2.4 versions, the process control block structure *task_struct* is packed together with the kernel level stack into the per-process memory area.

[5] For Linux kernel 2.4 versions, the post-syscall location value can be calculated as $ESP\&(8192-1)+sizeof(struct\ task_struct)$.

```
Process ID (   Process Name)[System Call   #]:    System Call Arguments
    PID 675 (           httpd)[sys_accept 102]: socket 3
    PID 675 (           httpd)[          102]: 12                                    [syscall return]
    PID 675 (           httpd)[sys_getskna 102]: socket 12
    PID 675 (           httpd)[          102]: 0 family  2; 192.168.1.2:80           [syscall return]
    ...
    PID 675 (           httpd)[sys_poll   168]: nfd 1; timeout 300000;  fds[0].fd 12 (events 1);
    ...
    PID 675 (           httpd)[          168]: 1(nfds 1) fds[0].fd 12 (revents 1);   [syscall return]
    PID 675 (           httpd)[sys_read     3]: 12
    PID 675 (           httpd)[            3]: (GET /12345.html HTTP/1.1 Host ...)440 [syscall return]
    PID 675 (           httpd)[sys_stat64 195]: /var/www/html/12345.html
    PID 675 (           httpd)[          195]: 0                                     [syscall return]
    PID 675 (           httpd)[sys_open     5]: /var/www/html/12345.html; flags 0
    PID 675 (           httpd)[            5]: 13                                    [syscall return]
    ...
    PID 675 (           httpd)[sys_writev 146]: fd 12; iov[0].base 0x08223f58 len 277; iov[0] (HTTP/1.1 200 OK..)
    PID 675 (           httpd)[          146]: 277                                   [syscall return]
    PID 675 (           httpd)[sys_sendfil 187]: out-fd 12; in-fd 13
    PID 675 (           httpd)[          146]: 1627                                  [syscall return]
    ...
    PID 675 (           httpd)[sys_shutdow 102]: socket 12 (SHUT_WR)
```

Fig. 2. VMscope log excerpt showing how the Apache web server (Redhat 8.0) responses to an incoming request for the /var/www/html/12345.html

In addition to reading the numerical values of these registers, VMscope will also correlate them with run-time information to identify the associated semantic meaning. As an example, for a *sys_open* system call event, the EBX register contains the memory address pointing to the file name that is intended to open. As mentioned earlier, this memory address is a virtual address and it is specific to the internal monitored process. As such, after obtaining the EBX content, VMscope further needs to traverse the page table related to the internal process to find the actual file name. Since VMscope is running outside the VM, the actual traversal requires a slightly different memory addressing scheme. We accomplish this by externally traversing the page table related to the internal process responsible for the intercepted system call. Note that the page table base address can be located through the CR3 control register. To protect the virtual memory process space from each other, each process will have its own, unique page directory and Linux loads the CR3 register for the new process that is switched in for execution on every context switch.

As a concrete example, Figure 2 shows the log excerpt collected when the Apache web server (version 2.0.40) serves an incoming request that asks for a web file named *12345.html*. The collection of these system call events enables the understanding on the dynamics of the Apache web server. More specifically, the *sys_accept*[6] system call is used to accept the incoming TCP 3-way handshake request and the *sys_poll* is used to wait for actual HTTP request content. The arrival of the HTTP request will be followed by a *sys_read* system call and the payload is then interpreted to find out the intent of the client. In this case, it is requesting for the *12345.html* file through the HTTP/1.1 protocol. The web server checks the existence of the requested file (via *sys_stat64*) and then opens it (via *sys_open*). Instead of directly reading the file content (via *sys_read*) and writing the content back to the client (via *sys_write*), the server directly uses the

---

[6] There exists a top-level network-related system call, i.e., *sys_socketcall*, which supports a number of sub-commands such as *socket, bind, connect, listen, accept, getsockname, getpeername, socketpair, send, recv, sendto, recvfrom, shutdown, setsockopt, getsockopt, sendmsg,* and *recvmsg* etc.

sys_sendfile to send the file content. Finally, the connection with the client is shut down (via *sys_shutdown*).

Our current prototype supports 259 system calls (with 2835 lines of code implementation) and will interpret the semantic meaning of their arguments and return values. Note that the way to interpret the return value is the same as the way in interpreting the system call under the context of the corresponding system call. As pointed out earlier, it is complicated by the multitasking support in modern OS kernels because potential context switches require VMscope to remember these context information. Similar to the way in handling the post-syscall instruction, we store the associated system call context information (e.g., EBX, ECX, etc) in the per-process memory area at the VMM layer when processing the system call instructions. Once the system call is returned, VMscope can conveniently examine its context information from the per-process memory area and then interpret the return value accordingly. As shown in Figure 2, VMscope is able to print out the client request payload (e.g., *GET /12345.html HTTP/1.1 Host...*) that is not contained in the system call return value – the EAX register. Also notice that for each intercepted system call event, VMscope will collect the associated process information such as PID and process name. Note that these information are kept in the *task_struct* data structure, which can be deducted from the first member of the *thread_info* data structure.

5   Evaluation

In this section, we evaluate the effectiveness and efficiency of VMscope. In particular, we conduct two sets of experiments (Section 5.1) to show: (1) How advanced intrusions that successfully evade internal logging can still be captured by VMscope; and (2) Whether the collected log by VMscope is sufficient in practice to reconstruct detailed attackers' behavior. We present performance measurement results in Section 5.2 and discuss possible limitations in Section 5.3.

5.1   Effectiveness

Experiments with NoSEBrEaK. VMscope advances existing honeypot monitoring techniques by eliminating the need of installing logging sensors inside the honeypots while maintaining the same deep inspection capability as traditional internal honeypot monitoring tools. To demonstrate this capability, we perform a number of experiments to compare the effectiveness of VMscope and Sebek, which is the de-facto honeypot monitoring tool, *especially under advanced attacks*. More specifically, we choose a recent development of NoSEBrEaK that is able to maintain its tight control on a compromised honeypot system while all of its commands can circumvent the logging by Sebek.

We prepare a Linux-based honeypot with Sebek 3.2.0*b* installed to monitor the system dynamics. Similar to the NoSEBrEaK attack outlined in [35], we introduce a vulnerable CGI program that will be exploited to load and execute a binary from the network. During the attack, a binary consisting of the Python runtime environment as well as a specialized *kebes*[35] server program is launched after the exploitation. In this experiment, we simply start the server program and use the corresponding client to

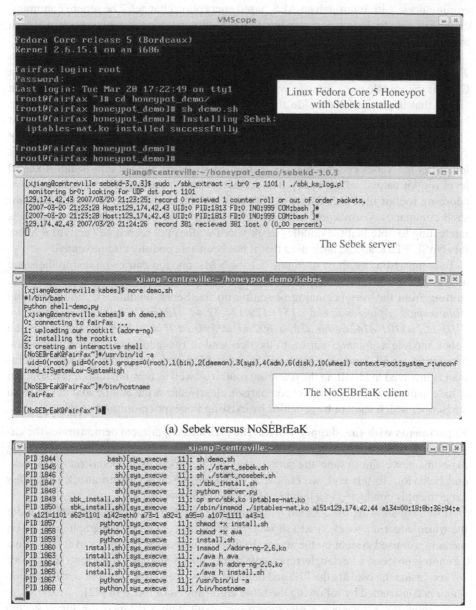

(a) Sebek versus NoSEBrEaK

(b) VMscope versus NoSEBrEaK

Fig. 3. The comparison of honeypot monitoring results from Sebek and VMscope when under the NoSEBrEaK attack: the VMscope log shows related *sys_execve* events

communicate with it through an AES-based encryption channel. The secure communication is set up by following a standard Diffie-Hellman key exchange procedure, which avoids the need of pre-shared secrets between the client and the server.

Figure 5.1 shows the screenshot of the experiment, which has three *xterm* windows. The top window (with the black background color) is a Linux honeypot running Fedora Core 5; the middle one (with the white background color) shows the log output from Sebek that is pre-installed inside the honeypot; the bottom one (also with the white background color) is the NoSEBrEaK-based attack window after launching the *kebes* client, which communicates with the server program and gains access to the honeypot system. As shown in the bottom window of Figure 5.1, the NoSEBrEaK-based attack leverages the kebes communication channel to stealthily upload and install a kernel level rootkit named *adore-ng* [7]. The rootkit is used to hide the existence of related adore-ng rootkit files or processes. After that, an interactive shell is created and two shell commands – */usr/bin/id -a* and */bin/hostname* – are subsequently executed. It is interesting to note that the middle Sebek window does not record any activities about this NoSEBrEaK attack, indicating that it has been successfully circumvented.

In comparison, we show in Figure 5.1 the VMscope log entries related to the same attack. The result shows that VMscope successfully records every command executed, starting from the very beginning of setting up the Sebek module, i.e., the command */sbin/insmod ./iptables-nat.ko a151=129.174.42.44 a134=00:18:8b:36:94:e0 a121= 1101 a62=1101 a142=eth0 a73=1 a92=1 a95=0 a107=1111 a43=1* that hides the Sebek module as *iptables-nat.ko*, to the very end of two additional shell commands – */usr/bin/id -a* and */bin/hostname*. In the middle of Figure 5.1, it also records those commands involved in installing the *adore-ng* rootkit as well as how the rootkit is instructed to hide malicious files. This direct comparison clearly shows the unique advantages from VMscope, which can not be provided by existing honeypot monitoring tools.

Experiments with the Slapper worm. The previous experiment demonstrates the capability of VMscope to reliably record stealthy attackers' behavior. In the following experiment, we aim to show the sufficiency of VMscope logs in reconstructing attackers' behavior. To this end, we choose a well-known Slapper worm attack [51]. This experiment is conducted in a local isolated lab environment.

Instead of showing the detailed VMscope log (> 190, 000 system call events) about the worm infection, we choose to show in Figure 4 the contamination graph inflicted on the compromised system by the worm. In the contamination graph, an oval represents a running process, a rectangle represents a file, and a diamond represents a network socket. Inside the oval are the PID and name of the process. Note that the contamination graph is constructed by following the same algorithm as outlined in [42].

To show the sufficiency, we compare our result with a detailed log file collected by an internal (open-source) system call tracking tool called syscalltrack [5] as well as another detailed Slapper worm analysis [51] and confirm that Figure 4 reveals all contaminations by the Slapper worm. Specifically, our log shows that the Slapper worm infection mainly involves three steps:

Step 1: It first exploits a buffer overflow vulnerability [51] in an httpd worker process (PID:1691 in this experiment) to obtain system access to the vulnerable system. As

Step 1: Exploiting the Apache web
server vulnerability

1691: httpd

/bin/bash –i

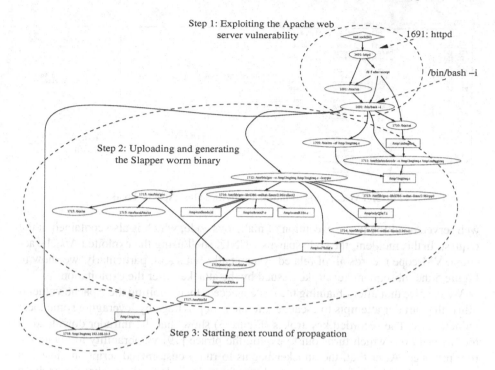

Step 2: Uploading and generating
the Slapper worm binary

Step 3: Starting next round of propagation

Fig. 4. Slapper worm infection reconstructed from VMscope log

indicated by the execution of the command (*/bin/bash -i*), the exploitation is successful and it leads to the creation of a remote shell.

Step 2: From the spawned remote shell, it further uploads a uuencoded[13] version of the worm source code to the compromised system and then decodes it (*/usr/bin/uudecode -o /tmp/.bugtraq.c /tmp/.uubugtraq*), locally compiles (*/usr/bin/gcc -o /tmp/.bugtraq /tmp/ . bugtraq.c -lcrypto*) it to generate the worm binary code.

Step 3: After that, the binary code is launched (*/tmp/.bugtraq 192.168.10.5*) to start next-round of propagation. Further investigation shows that the Slapper worm is rather sophisticated in creating a customized peer-to-peer attack network from these compromised machines. The IP address involved in this step is the one that infected this vulnerable machine, not the victim IP address chosen for next-round of infection.

Experiments with honeypots. We also deployed a number of honeypots in the wild to demonstrate the effectiveness of VMscope in monitoring real-world attacks. In the following, we choose one representative incident and describe how VMscope effectively reveal the detailed attack behavior.

This honeypot incident is related to an OpenSSL vulnerability [18] in the Apache web server (version 1.3). It was deployed at 23:00pm, Jan. 26th, 2007 and then compromised 3 hours later. From the collected log, a TCP connection heading for port 443 is firstly established. The connection is used by the attacker to send a specially-crafted chunk-encoded HTTP request. The request will cause a buffer overflow in the Apache

```
Process ID (    Process Name)[System Call   #]:    System Call Arguments      - - - - - - - - - -
  PID 1562 (              sh)[sys_execve  11]: bash -i
  ...                                                                         1. Gaining a regular
  PID 1572 (            bash)[sys_execve  11]: uname -a                          account: apache
  PID 1573 (            bash)[sys_execve  11]: id
  PID 1574 (            bash)[sys_execve  11]: w                               - - - - - - - - - -
  ...
  PID 1632 (            bash)[sys_execve  11]: ls
  PID 1633 (            bash)[sys_execve  11]: wget xxxxxxxx.xx.ro/soft/expl   2. Escalating to the
  PID 1634 (            bash)[sys_execve  11]: chmod +x expl                      root privilege
  PID 1635 (            bash)[sys_execve  11]: ./expl
  ...                                                                         - - - - - - - - - -
  PID 1674 (              sh)[sys_execve  11]: wget xxxxxxxx.xx.ro/soft/naky.tgz
  PID 1676 (              sh)[sys_execve  11]: tar -zxvf naky.tgz             3. Installing a set
  PID 1679 (              sh)[sys_execve  11]: chmod +x *                        of backdoors
  PID 1680 (              sh)[sys_execve  11]: ./install
  ...                                                                         - - - - - - - - - -
  PID 1882 (            bash)[sys_execve  11]: mkdir '. '
  PID 1883 (            bash)[sys_execve  11]: wget www.xxxxxxxxx.org/vulturul/bnc.tgz
  PID 1886 (            bash)[sys_execve  11]: tar xvfz bnc.tgz               4. Installing an IRC
  PID 1888 (            bash)[sys_execve  11]: rm -rf bnc.tgz                    bot runnable even
  PID 1889 (            bash)[sys_execve  11]: mv psybnc crond                   after reboot
  PID 1892 (            bash)[sys_execve  11]: crond
  PID 1894 (            bash)[sys_execve  11]: pico /etc/rc.d/rc.local        - - - - - - - - - -
  ...
```

Fig. 5. VMscope log of intruder activities after Apache break-in

web server, resulting in the execution of malicious code, which is also contained in the request. In this incident, the code spawns a UNIX shell using the exploited Apache account. VMscope records all of related system call events and, particularly, we show in Figure 5 the subsequent keystrokes issued by the attacker after the exploitation.

We observe that after obtaining the system access by exploiting the Apache vulnerability, the intruder attempts to escalate into the root privilege by leveraging some local vulnerability. The recorded keystrokes (Figure 5) show that the intruder downloads a tool named *expl*, which turns out to exploit the ptrace [19] vulnerability to obtain the root privilege. After that, the attacker begins to run a customized script and install a pre-packaged package named *naky.tgz*. Later forensic analysis shows that the package contains a trojaned ssh daemon, two infamous kernel-level rootkits – adore and knark, and a log cleaner. The trojaned ssh daemon will directly give the intruder a root shell after authentication. After executing the customized script, the intruder also downloads a software package *bnc.tgz*, which contains a bot software named *psybnc*. The attacker renames the bot software as *crond* and modifies a system-wide configuration file, i.e., */etc/rc.d/rc.local*, so that the trojan service will be restarted even after machine reboot.

5.2   Performance

We evaluate the performance of VMscope with a number of benchmarks, including real applications and standard micro-benchmarks. Our testing platform was a Dell PowerEdge server with a 3.73GHz Intel Xeon processor and 4GB of RAM. Table 1 shows the configuration details for each benchmark test. For each benchmark, we run 10 experiments and record the average results. Each result has been normalized with respect to the speed of the unmodified QEMU system, which is referred to as the BASE measurement.

Five benchmarks that we consider to be a reasonable assessment of the system's performance can be found in Figure 6. First, the Apache [8] web server was run in the Worker MPM mode to serve a 32k-size web page. The ApacheBench program was then run on another machine in the same Ethernet to determine the request throughput of the system as a whole. VMscope achieved 96.4% of the BASE throughput. Next, the nbench [3] suite was used to show the performance under a set of primarily computation based tests. The slowest test (LU DECOMPOSITION [3]) in the nbench system came in at 92.1% of fullspeed. Third, gzip was used to compress a 256 megabyte file, and the

Table 1. Configuration information used for performance evaluation

Item	Version	Configuration
RedHat	Fedora Core 5	Run a customized Linux kernel 2.6.15-1
Apache	2.2.0-5.1.2	Default configuration in the Apache Worker MPM mode
ApacheBench	0.63	./ApacheBench -n 100 -c 10 <url/file>
Nbench	2.2.2	Default configuration
Gzip	1.3.3	Compress a 256 MB file
Make	3.8.0	Compile Linux kernel 2.6.15-1
Unixbench	4.1.0	Default configuration

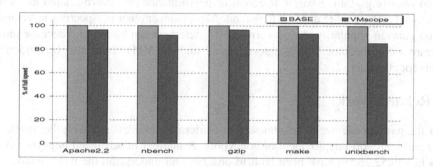

Fig. 6. Normalized performance for applications and benchmarks

operation was timed. The VMscope-monitored system was found to run at 96.6% of fullspeed. Fourth, make was used to compile the Linux kernel 2.6.15-1 source code and the VMscope achieves the 93.4% of fullspeed. Finally, the Unixbench [12] unix benchmarking suite was used as a microbenchmark to test various aspects of the system's performance at tasks such as process creation, pipe throughput, filesystem throughput, etc. The overall score indicates that the monitored system ran at 85.6% of normal speed. As a result, the overall performance of VMscope is reasonable with no less than 85% of the BASE system.

5.3 Limitations

There are a few limitations to our approach. Firstly, VMscope assumes a trustworthy virtualization-based substrate layer to host high-interaction honeypots. In other words, though attackers might compromise the vulnerable system arbitrarily, we assume that they cannot break out of the VM environment and compromise the underlying VMM. VMscope itself should also be considered as a part of the trusted computing base (TCB) of the system, which would result in a slightly larger TCB base. For example, when interpreting the observed system call events, current prototype would add 2835 lines of code (LOCs) to the TCB.

Secondly, to properly interpret system call events, VMscope requires the knowledge of system calls and system call convention. As such, it is possible that an attacker might choose to remap the system calls or system call convention in a non-standard way to mislead or escape VMscope. However, the syscall remapping requires the modification of either interrupt descriptor table (IDT) or the system call hander routine and the unauthorized modification on these important kernel objects could be detected and prevented with security-enhanced VMMs [61]. Note that it still remains a challenge to accurately identify those dynamic kernel objects (e.g., the VFS dispatch table).

Finally, the VMscope-based VM environment can be potentially fingerprinted and detected by attackers. In fact, a number of recent malware are able to check whether they are running inside VM environments and, if so, choose to exhibit different behavior [1]. As a counter-measure, we can improve the fidelity of VM implementation to mitigate some of existing detection schemes [49]. However, there are more fundamental ones (e.g., timing-based detection or performance slowdown-related methods [37,57,45]) that are more difficult to defend. Also, from another perspective, as virtualization gains in popularity, the concern on VM detection can be reduced because most malware would become VMM-agnostic again and the VMs could also be attractive targets for attackers.

6 Related Work

Over the past decade, we have witnessed considerable progress made on the development and real-world deployment of honeypots. A number of advanced honeypot systems [26,39,52,58,59] have been built to observe and understand the new means and methods by attackers. Particularly, the recent advancement on virtualization technology has created unique capability and tremendous convenience in deploying and managing honeypots. Our system, along with other research efforts [25,53], complements and strengthens these efforts by providing the desirable capability of transparently observing, intercepting, and recording interested system events about monitored VMs.

Our work is mainly motivated by the NoSEBrEaK system [35] that has successfully demonstrated the possibility of circumventing the widely used honeypot monitoring tool – Sebek – while still maintaining its tight control on compromised systems. Note that in addition to our work, a number of other systems [25,40,47,53] were also proposed to enable better honeypot monitoring. For example, both Xebek [53] and VMM-based sensors [25] take the approach of extending the para-virtualization-based VMMs (either Xen[27] or User Mode Linux [34]) to aim for invisible honeypot monitoring. However, as pointed out in Section 1, para-virtualization based VMMs need to access and modify guest OS source code and the modification on guest OS still creates internal "presence" within the VM. We argue that any internal presence of logging sensors would lead to the possibility of being misused or subverted once the attacker takes the full control of the honeypot. As such, a more tamper-resistant honeypot monitoring system should require its entirety being deployed "out-of-the-box" from the monitored VMs. In fact, this is one main design decision made when developing the VMscope system (Section 1).

Besides system monitoring, researchers also leverage virtual machines to detect intrusions [38,41,23], analyze intrusions [36,46] or malware [28], diagnose system problems [43,60], and isolate services [30,50]. These services leverage the desirable properties (e.g., isolation and encapsulation) provided by virtual machines to enhance the security of systems without relying on the correctness of the guest OS and other application-level programs. Particularly, Livewire [38] and IntroVirt [41] apply the general methodology of virtual machine introspection to detect intrusions on the monitored VMs and the detection is based on the knowledge of specific vulnerabilities being exploited or certain kernel objects (e.g., the system call table) that should not be modified. VMscope has a different goal for honeypot monitoring but utilizes the same VMI methodology when interpreting the observed system call events. It is worth mentioning that, leveraging the very same virtualization techniques, researchers also demonstrated possible threats in implementing stealthy "undetectable" malware [44,54,62]. We believe that these emerging threats could be mitigated or even defeated with recent efforts on building secure hypervisors (e.g., sHype [55] and TRANGO [11]) and enabling trusted booting [24].

7 Conclusion

We have presented VMscope, a virtualization-based honeypot monitoring system that is capable of inspecting and interpreting system internal events from outside the VM-based honeypot. Such an out-of-the-box monitoring system provides the desirable transparency and tramper-resistance in monitoring honeypots. In the meantime, it still retains the same deep inspection capability as traditional honeypot internal sensors (e.g. Sebek [4]). We have built a proof-of-concept prototype and our experimental results with real-word deployment as well as the comparison with existing de-facto honeypot monitoring tools have successfully demonstrated its robustness and effectiveness.

References

1. Agobot, http://www.f-secure.com/v-descs/agobot.shtml
2. Ethereal: A Network Protocol Analyzer, http://www.ethereal.com
3. Linux/unix nbench, http://www.tux.org/mayer/linux/bmark.html
4. Sebek, http://www.honeynet.org/tools/sebek/
5. Syscalltrack: http://syscalltrack.sourceforge.net/
6. Tcpdump, http://www.tcpdump.org
7. The adore-ng Rootkit, http://stealth.openwall.net/rootkits/
8. The Apache HTTP Server Project, http://httpd.apache.org
9. The Honeynet Project, http://www.honeynet.org
10. The Strange Decline of Computer Worms, http://www.theregister.co.uk/2005/03/17/f-secure_websec/print.html
11. TRANGO, the Real-Time Embedded Hypervisor, http://www.trango-systems.com/
12. Unixbench, http://www.tux.org/pub/tux/benchmarks/System/unixbench
13. Uuencoding, http://en.wikipedia.org/wiki/Uuencode
14. VirtualBox, http://www.virtualbox.org/
15. Virus Writers Get Stealthy, http://news.zdnet.co.uk/internet/security/0,39020375,39191840,00.htm
16. VMware, http://www.vmware.com/
17. CERT Advisory CA-2001-31 Buffer Overflow in CDE Subprocess Control Service (January 2002), http://www.cert.org/advisories/CA-2001-31.html

18. CERT Advisory CA-2002-17 Apache Web Server Chunk Handling Vulnerability (March 2003), http://www.cert.org/advisories/CA-2002-17.html
19. Linux Kernel Ptrace Privilege Escalation Vulnerability (March 2003),http://www.secunia.com/advisories/8337/
20. Windows WMF Zero-Day Attack (December 2005), http://www.counterpane.com/alert-cis-ra-0030-01.html
21. Windows PowerPoint Zero-Day Attack, http://www.eweek.com/article2/0,1895,1988874,00.asp
22. Windows Word Zero-Day Attack, http://www.eweek.com/article2/0,1895,1965042,00.asp
23. Anagnostakis, K.G., Sidiroglou, S., Akritidis, P., Xinidis, K., Markatos, E., Keromytis, A.D.: Detecting Targeted Attacks Using Shadow Honeypots. In: Proc. of the 14th USENIX Security Symposium (August 2005)
24. Arbaugh, W.A., Farbert, D,J., Smith, J.M.: A Secure and Reliable Bootstrap Architecture. In: Proc. of the 1997 IEEE Symposium on Security and Privacy, IEEE Computer Society Press, Los Alamitos (1997)
25. Asrigo, K., Litty, L., Lie, D.: Using VMM-Based Sensors to Monitor Honeypots. In: Proc. of the 2nd VEE (June 2006)
26. Baecher, P., Koetter, M., Holz, T., Dornseif, M., Freiling, F.: The Nepenthes Platform: An Efficient Approach to Collect Malware. In: Zamboni, D., Kruegel, C. (eds.) RAID 2006. LNCS, vol. 4219, Springer, Heidelberg (2006)
27. Barham, P., Dragovic, B., Fraser, K., Hand, S., Harris, T., Neugebauer, R., Ho, A., Pratt, I., Warfield, A.: Xen and the Art of Virtualization. In: Proc. of the 2003 SOSP (October 2003)
28. Bayer, U., Kruegel, C., Kirda, E.: TTAnalyze: A Tool for Analyzing Malware. In: Proc. of the 15th European Institute for Computer Antivirus Research Annual Conference (April 2006)
29. Bellard, F.: QEMU, a Fast and Portable Dynamic Translator. In: Proc. of USENIX Annual Technical Conference 2005 (FREENIX Track) (July 2005)
30. Bryant, E., Early, J., Gopalakrishna, R., Roth, G., Spafford, E.H., Watson, K., Williams, P., Yost, S.: Poly2 Paradigm: A Secure Network Service Architecture. In: Proc. of the 19th ACSAC (December 2003)
31. Chen, P.M., Noble, B.D.: When Virtual is Better Than Real. HotOS VIII (2001)
32. Corey, J.: Local Honeypot Identification. Phrack 62 07(15) (July 2004)
33. Dagon, D., Qin, X., Gu, G., Lee, W., Grizzard, J., Levine, J., Owen, H.: HoneyStat: Local Worm Detection Using Honeypots. In: Jonsson, E., Valdes, A., Almgren, M. (eds.) RAID 2004. LNCS, vol. 3224, Springer, Heidelberg (2004)
34. Dike, J.: User Mode Linux, http://user-mode-linux.sourceforge.net
35. Dornseif, M., Holz, T., Klein, C.: NoSEBrEaK - Attacking Honeynets. In: Proc. of the 5th Annual IEEE Information Assurance Workshop, Westpoint, June 2004, IEEE Computer Society Press, Los Alamitos (2004)
36. Dunlap, G.W., King, S.T., Cinar, S., Basrai, M.A., Chen, P.M.: ReVirt: Enabling Intrusion Analysis Through Virtual-Machine Logging and Replay. In: Proc. of the 2002 OSDI (December 2002)
37. Franklin, J., Luk, M., McCune, J.M., Seshadri, A., Perrig, A., van Doorn, L.: Remote Detection of Virtual Machine Monitors with Fuzzy Benchmarking. Technical Report, CMU-CyLab-07-001 (January 2007)
38. Garfinkel, T., Rosenblum, M.: A Virtual Machine Introspection Based Architecture for Intrusion Detection. In: Proc. of the 2003 NDSS (February 2003)
39. Jiang, X., Xu, D.: Collapsar: A VM-Based Architecture for Network Attack Detention Center. In: Proc. of the 13th USENIX Security Symposium (August 2004)

40. Jones, S.T., Arpaci-Dusseau, A.C., Arpaci-Dusseau, R.H.: Antfarm: Tracking Processes in a Virtual Machine Environment. In: Proc. of the 2006 USENIX Annual Technical Conference (March 2006)
41. Joshi, A., King, S.T., Dunlap, G.W., Chen, P.M.: Detecting Past and Present Intrusions through Vulnerability-specific Predicates. In: Proc. of the 2005 Symposium on Operating Systems Principles (SOSP) (October 2005)
42. King, S.T., Chen, P.M.: Backtracking Intrusions. In: Proc. of the 19th ACM Symposium on Operating Systems Principles, October 2003, ACM Press, New York (2003)
43. King, S.T., Dunlap, G.W., Chen, P.M.: Debugging Operating Systems with Time-Traveling Virtual Machines. In: Proc. of the 2005 Annual USENIX Technical Conference (2005)
44. King, S.T., Chen, P.M., Wang, Y.-M., Verbowski, C., Wang, H.J., Lorch, J.R.: SubVirt: Implementing Malware with Virtual Machines. In: Proc. of the 2006 IEEE Symposium on Security and Privacy, IEEE Computer Society Press, Los Alamitos (2006)
45. Kohno, T., Broido, A., claffy, k.: Remote Physical Device Fingerprinting. In: Proc. of the 2005 IEEE Symposium on Security and Privacy, May 2005, IEEE Computer Society Press, Los Alamitos (2005)
46. Koju, T., Takada, S., Doi, N.: An Efficient and Generic Reversible Debugger using the Virtual Machine based Approach. In: Proc. of the 1st ACM/USENIX International Conference on Virtual Execution Environments, June 2005, ACM Press, New York (2005)
47. Kourai, K., Chiba, S.: HyperSpector: Virtual Distributed Monitoring Environments for Secure Intrusion Detection. In: Proc. of the 1st ACM/USENIX International Conference on Virtual Execution Environments, June 2005, ACM Press, New York (2005)
48. Leita, C., Dacier, M., Massicotte, F.: Automatic Handling of Protocol Dependencies and Reaction to 0-day Attacks with ScriptGen based Honeypots. In: Zamboni, D., Kruegel, C. (eds.) RAID 2006. LNCS, vol. 4219, Springer, Heidelberg (2006)
49. Liston, T.: On the Cutting Edge: Thwarting Virtual Machine Detection (Invited Talk at NDSS'07), http://handlers.sans.org/tliston/ThwartingVMDetection_Liston_Skoudis.pdf
50. Meushaw, R., Simard, D.: NetTop: Commercial Technology in High Assurance Applications. Tech Trend Notes: Preview of Tomorrow's Information Technologies (2000)
51. Perriot, F., Szor, P.: An Analysis of the Slapper Worm Exploit. Symantec White Paper, http://securityresponse.symantec.com/avcenter/reference/analysis.slapper.wor m.pdf
52. Provos, N.: A Virtual Honeypot Framework. In: Proc. of the 13th USENIX Security Symposium (August 2004)
53. Quynh, N.A.: Xebek: A Next Generation Honeypot Monitoring System (February 2006), http://www.eusecwest.com/esw06/esw06-nguyen.ppt
54. Rutkowska, J.: Subverting Vista Kernel For Fun And Profit. Blackhat (2006)
55. Sailer, R., Valdez, E., Jaeger, T., Perez, R., van Doorn, L., Griffin, J.L., Berger, S.: sHype: Secure Hypervisor Approach to Trusted Virtualized Systems. IBM Research Report RC23511 (February 2005)
56. sd: Linux on-the-fly kernel patching without LKM. Phrack, 11(58), article 7 of 15 (2001)
57. Seshadri, A., Luk, M., Shi, E., Perrig, A., van Doorn, L., Khosla, P.: Pioneer: Verifying Integrity and Guaranteeing Execution of Code on Legacy Platforms. In: Proc. of the 2005 SOSP (October 2005)
58. Vrable, M., Ma, J., Chen, J., Moore, D., Vandekieft, E., Snoeren, A.C., Voelker, G.M., Savage, S.: Scalability, Fidelity and Containment in the Potemkin Virtual Honeyfarm. In: Proc. of the 20th ACM Symposium on Operating Systems Principles, October 2005, ACM Press, New York (2005)

59. Wang, Y.-M., Beck, D., Jiang, X., Roussev, R., Verbowski, C., Chen, S., King, S.: Automated Web Patrol with Strider HoneyMonkeys: Finding Web Sites That Exploit Browser Vulnerabilities. In: Proc. of the 2006 NDSS (February 2006)
60. Whitaker, A., Cox, R.S., Gribble, S.D.: Using Time Travel to Diagnose Computer Problems. In: Proc. of the 11th SIGOPS European Workshop (September 2004)
61. Xu, M., Jiang, X., Sandhu, R., Zhang, X.: Towards a VMM-based Usage Control Framework for OS Kernel Integrity Protection. In: Proc. of the 12th ACM Symposium on Access Control Models and Technologies, June 2007, ACM Press, New York (2007)
62. Zovi, D.D.: Hardware Virtualization Based Rootkits. Blackhat 2006 (August 2006)

A Forced Sampled Execution Approach to Kernel Rootkit Identification

Jeffrey Wilhelm and Tzi-cker Chiueh

Core Research Group
Symantec Research Laboratories
{jeffrey_wilhelm,tzi-cker_chiueh}@symantec.com

Abstract. Kernel rootkits are considered one of the most dangerous forms of malware because they reside inside the kernel and can perform the most privileged operations on the compromised machine. Most existing kernel rootkit detection techniques attempt to detect the existence of kernel rootkits, but cannot do much about removing them, other than booting the victim machine from a clean operating system image and configuration. This paper describes the design, implementation and evaluation of a kernel rootkit identification system for the Windows platform called Limbo, which prevents kernel rootkits from entering the kernel by checking the legitimacy of every kernel driver before it is loaded into the operating system. Limbo determines whether a kernel driver is a kernel rootkit based on its binary contents and run-time behavior. To expose the execution behavior of a kernel driver under test, Limbo features a **forced sampled execution** approach to traverse the driver's control flow graph. Through a comprehensive characterization study of current kernel rootkits, we derive a set of run-time features that can best distinguish between legitimate and malicious kernel drivers. Applying a Naive Bayes classification algorithm on this chosen feature set, the first Limbo prototype is able to achieve 96.2% accuracy for a test set of 754 kernel drivers, 311 of which are kernel rootkits.

Keywords: rootkit detection, X86 ISA emulation, dynamic malware analysis, Bayes classifier, and intrusion prevention.

1 Introduction

A kernel rootkit [13,1,12,11,4] is a piece of binary code that a computer intruder, after breaking into a machine, installs into the victim's operating system to perform various malicious functions, including data gathering, hiding processes and files, sending out spam emails, mounting DoS attacks against a chosen target, etc. The majority of kernel rootkits are installed by a separate user-level process, which creeps into the victim machine by exploiting browser weaknesses or application vulnerabilities. In addition, they are mostly installed into the kernel through a well-defined application program interface (API) that allows legitimate kernel modules to be loaded into the kernel's address space.

C. Kruegel, R. Lippmann, and A. Clark (Eds.): RAID 2007, LNCS 4637, pp. 219–235, 2007.
© Springer-Verlag Berlin Heidelberg 2007

Recent threat trend analysis [9] reports that malware authors are increasingly turning to rootkits to establish a permanent, undetectable presence on the systems they compromise. Although it is possible to detect existence of kernel rootkits through in-depth scanning of the kernel address space, this approach is less than ideal because it is extremely difficult to remove kernel rootkits, which can reside anywhere inside the kernel and run at the same privilege level as the security software and operating system. The goal of the Limbo project is develop a real-time kernel rootkit identification system that can pro-actively prevent kernel rootkits from being loaded into Microsoft's Windows operating system.

In contrast to existing kernel rootkit detection systems and products [30,2,7,18,6,17,28,22,19], which mostly detect rootkits after they are loaded into the kernel, Limbo takes a *preventive* approach in that it checks whether a kernel driver is a rootkit or not before it is loaded into the kernel, and prohibits the driver from being loaded if that is the case. Because Limbo is required to make this determination in real time, the time budget for this check is quite limited, which makes the kernel rootkit identification problem even more challenging.

Limbo bases its decision on the static attributes and dynamic behaviors of the kernel driver under test. That is, it needs to actually run the kernel driver and monitor its execution. Applying the run-time monitoring approach to kernel rootkit identification involves three technical challenges. First, how to build an emulation environment that can both run arbitrary kernel modules successfully and provide flexible interfaces for recording interesting events? Second, how to collect as many run-time behaviors as possible from a kernel driver without trying all possible inputs or exploring all possible execution paths through the driver? Third, how to extract effective features from a kernel driver's run-time behaviors and use them as the basis for training a classifier that could distinguish between legitimate kernel drivers and malicious kernel rootkits?

Limbo is built on top of PAM32, which is an instruction set architecture emulator designed to run user-level X86 or IA32 binaries. The original PAM32 does not provide an adequate emulation of the Windows kernel for kernel module execution because it does not support kernel-mode instructions, accesses to kernel data structures, or calls to Windows OS's kernel functions. Limbo adds a sufficient amount of kernel emulation into PAM32 so that it can successfully execute a total of over 270 kernel drivers used in the development of this project. Even if a kernel driver can successfully run on an emulator, there is no guarantee that the emulator can extract all the interesting run-time behaviors from the kernel driver, because each execution run most likely only exercises a particular portion of the driver's binary. Limbo solves this problem by *flood emulation* or *forced sampled execution*, which forces a kernel driver's control towards particular paths and strives to exercise each of the driver's basic blocks at least a certain number of times. To solve the final problem, we manually perform a comprehensive characterization of a set of kernel rootkits and legitimate kernel drivers, use the analysis results to derive a set of distinguishing features based on their binary attributes and run-time behaviors, and then feed them as inputs to a Naive Bayes classifier training tool. Through these three techniques, Limbo is able to correctly identify kernel rootkits and legitimate kernel drivers 96% of the time for a test suite of 754 kernel drivers, while keeping the additional performance overhead under 500 msec.

The rest of this paper is organized as follows. Section 2 reviews previous works related to kernel rootkit detection and identification. Section 3 summarizes the result of our manual behavioral characterization study of kernel rootkits. Section 4 describes the design and implementation of the Limbo kernel rootkit identification system. Section 5 presents the efficiency and effectiveness result of a quantitative performance evaluation study of the first Limbo prototype. Section 6 concludes this paper with a summary of the main research contributions of this work, and directions for future work.

2   Related Work

The fundamental problem underlying kernel rootkit identification is how to determine if a piece of binary code is malicious or not. A simpler version of this problem is how to determine if a program is a semantically equivalent variant of a known malicious program. There are several approaches to this problem. The simplest approach is string comparison as used in anti-virus file scanning products [7,8], which aims to detect known malware using byte-level signatures extracted from the malware. A slightly more sophisticated approach is to parse binaries into instructions, then extract instruction-level features such as n-gram or n-set [29,14] and apply standard training algorithms to derive a classifier that can distinguish between benign and malicious binaries based on these features. The third approach is to apply program analysis techniques to binary programs to compute their control-flow graph representation, and determine if a given binary is a variant of a known malware by computing their graph isomorphic distance [27,10]. For example, Microsoft's Strider Gatekeeper [31] monitors the auto-start extensibility points (ASEPs) to determine if any suspicious software is installed in the machine start-up script. Christodorescu et al. [5] characterize variations of worms in terms of semantically equivalent operations in these malware variants. Kruegel [16] took the same approach to analyze kernel rootkit samples, derived equivalent instruction sequence patterns with the same execution semantics, and used them as the basis to statically identify kernel rootkits. The same group [15] also applied a similar technique to statically analyze a particular class of spyware, Browser Helper Object(BHO)-based spyware that leak information, to detect possible information leaking behavior, essentially a form of binary information flow analysis.

The fourth approach is to run the given binary program, monitor its run-time behavior, and raise an alert if the behavior exhibits a different pattern than those associated with known good code. The is approach potentially can catch an entire class of malware without analyzing the underlying binary code. In general, this approach may be a good fit for user-level rootkit/spyware detection, but is less effective for kernel rootkit detection because it may lead to corruption of the kernel address space.

Finally, one can determine if a kernel rootkit exists inside the operating system based on its side effects. For example, if the results returned by two different interfaces inside the kernel to the same query (e.g. list of files in this directory) differ, there must be a kernel rootkit that hides processes/files sitting in between these two interfaces [30,24]. This approach, however, cannot detect kernel root kits that do not hide processes/files. As another example, if certain critical kernel data structures such as the system call dispatch table, interrupt vector table, or the list of active processes are modified, there is a good chance that a kernel rootkit already sneaked into the kernel. Many existing kernel rootkit detection systems/products [21,6,7,18,19] take the last approach together with signature matching.

The above approaches can be taxonomized according to the type of features they use and the detection algorithms applied to these features. More concretely, features used in rootkit detection or identification can be information statically extracted from the binary code, run-time interaction patterns, or side effects left in the kernel address space, whereas algorithms used to reach a detection or identification decision can be based on similarity match to known malware, finding deviation from known benign code, or data-driven classifier that is trained to distinguish between known malware and known benign code.

The kernel rootkit identification system described in this paper, Limbo, is unique in that it applies a data-driven classifier to run-time behavioral features. Because collecting run-time behaviors of kernel drivers is difficult, no known rootkit detection systems take this approach. Limbo solves this problem by developing a user-level emulator that can effectively stress every part of the input kernel driver. This emulator makes it possible to extract a given kernel driver's run-time behavior without running it inside the kernel, thus preventing kernel rootkits from corrupting the kernel address space.

Moser et al. [20] proposed a malware analysis system that attempts to explore as many execution paths of a piece of malware as possible by computing the inputs required to force the malware's control to take a particular path. Although this technique is more accurate than Limbo's forced sampled execution approach because it ensures that the program state along an execution path is always consistent, its implementation complexity is much higher. Moreover, because Limbo is designed to determine if a kernel driver is legitimate or not in real time, this multi-path exploration technique is too slow to be feasible for Limbo.

3   Behavioral Characterization of Kernel Rootkits

To distinguish legitimate kernel drivers from kernel rootkits, we assembled a set of 73 kernel rootkits, which are collected by Symantec's Security Response between November 2005 and May 2006, and a set of legitimate kernel drivers, which includes 234 kernel drivers installed on a standard Symantec corporate machine and 27 kernel drivers used in several commercial security software products. For each kernel driver and rootkit, we disassembled and manually reverse-engineered it, and then ran it through Limbo's emulator in such a way that every basic block of its binary code is exercised for a certain number of times. Then we manually analyzed the static attributes and dynamic behaviors of these drivers, and derived a set of features that can best distinguish between legitimate kernel drivers and kernel rootkits. The following presents the set of features resulting from this analysis.

The features are classified into the following seven categories, the first two of which are static attributes derived from a driver's binary whereas the last five are dynamic attributes derived from a driver's run-time behavior. Each member in the feature set represents either a logical flag or an integer count.

3.1   Portable Executable (PE) File Features

– The majority of legitimate kernel drivers contain debug information such as the symbol table, whereas kernel rootkits mostly don't.
– Use of Microsoft's StackGuard buffer overflow protection technology is quite prevalent among legitimate kernel drivers, but is relatively rare among kernel rootkits.

3.2   Import Object Features

– Kernel rootkits tend to have a fewer number of objects in the import table than legitimate kernel drivers. For example, the kernel rootkit, `Apropos.C`, does not have any entries in the import table and imports all the objects it needs at run time rather than at load time.
– Certain import objects occur infrequently in legitimate kernel drivers, but other imports, such as those that manipulate actual hardware, are quite common in legitimate kernel drivers.
– Certain libraries are almost never used in kernel rootkits.
– The number of dynamic imports, i.e., those resolved by `MmGetSystemRoutine Address`, is higher in kernel rootkits than in legitimate kernel driver. This count does NOT include imports that are dynamically resolved by directly parsing a PE binary's headers within memory.

3.3   Device-Related Features

– Legitimate kernel drivers tend to create fewer virtual devices than kernel rootkits.
– It is more likely for kernel rootkits than for legitimate kernel drivers to create virtual devices that can only be opened exclusively, because kernel rootkits want to ensure that once they open a virtual device, the virtual device cannot be accessed by other entities.
– Each kernel driver is typically attached to a virtual device. It is more likely for a kernel rootkit to attach itself to a critical virtual device, such as the TCP or UDP stack, in order to filter or log data passing through the virtual device.
– When a kernel driver opens the keyboard virtual device, it is more likely to be a kernel rootkit, because this is the common behavior of a kernel-mode key logger.

3.4   Data Structure Access Features

- A Memory Descriptor List (MDL) contains the physical page layout for a contiguous range of the kernel virtual address space. It is more likely for kernel rootkits than for legitimate kernel drivers to allocate an MDL that contains memory allocated to some kernel data structures such as the system service descriptor table (SSDT), and modify these data structures that are normally write-protected.
- It is more likely for kernel rootkits than for legitimate kernel drivers to directly read or write an opaque kernel data structure such as the EPROCESS structure. Legitimate kernel drivers rarely access EPROCESS, but kernel rootkits modify EPROCESS to hide processes, using a technique known as DKOM (Direct Kernel Object Modification) [25].
- To intercept the control transfer of execution paths in the kernel, it is more likely for kernel rootkits than for legitimate kernel drivers to modify various function pointer tables in the kernel, such as the system service descriptor table (SSDT).
- Some kernel rootkits modify the first few bytes of the functions in one of the kernel import libraries (in particular, ntoskrnl.exe, HAL.dll, and ndis.sys) in order to intercept the kernel's control transfer. This technique is known as *in-line hooking*.

3.5   Descriptor Table Features

- Some kernel rootkits use the store IDT (SIDT) instruction to read the interrupt descriptor table address in order to tell if they are running under the control of a virtual machine monitor. This technique is popularized by Joanna Rutkowska [23].
- Some kernel rootkits use the load IDT (LIDT) instruction to modify the base address of the interrupt descriptor table (IDT), and redirect hardware interrupts to a completely different set of interrupt service routines.
- Some kernel rootkits use the store GDT (SGDT) instruction to read the global descriptor table's base address, or use the load GDT (LGDT) instruction to set the global descriptor table's base address.

3.6   Miscellaneous Features

- Some kernel rootkits modify the IA32_SYSENTER_EIP model specific register, which contains the address of the user to kernel mode system call handler on newer x86 hardware. No legitimate kernel drivers modify this register.
- Kernel rootkits often open themselves or their user-mode components in *exclusive* mode so as to prevent security software from accessing these files.
- Kernel rootkits are more likely to obfuscate their code than legitimate kernel drivers, which almost never use any obfuscation.

4 Design and Implementation of Limbo

4.1 X86 and Windows Kernel Emulator

To successfully execute kernel drivers, Limbo needs an emulator that can interpret all X86 instructions and support library and kernel functions that these drivers are likely to call. PAM32 is an X86 ISA emulator for user-level Windows applications. We chose PAM32 because it is a proven tool that has been used for years inside Symantec for a wide variety of projects ranging from malware reverse engineering to threat signature creation, and comes with a set of useful utilities for deriving static/dynamic characteristics of Windows binary programs. PAM32 interprets each instruction in a Windows binary one by one, and enables collection of various run-time statistics, such as instruction frequency histogram and counting of devious instruction sequences such as "return to a return instruction", depending on the configuration parameter setting when it is launched. Unfortunately the original version of PAM32 does not support calls to internal kernel functions, and therefore cannot execute kernel drivers that do make such calls. To support kernel driver execution, we make the following modifications to PAM32:

- Support for privileged instructions such as I/O instructions and modifications to control registers.
- Emulation for over 90 Windows kernel functions that our test kernel drivers rely on for correct functioning.
- Support for accesses to kernel data structures, such as KeServiceDescriptorTable, including their creation, initialization and emulation.
- Support for flooded emulation, which is designed to discover as many run-time behaviors of the kernel driver under test as possible by forcing the driver's control along both arms of every encountered conditional branch.
- Collection of 32 run-time features, each of which corresponds to a binary attribute or an execution behavior that potentially can distinguish kernel rootkits from legitimate kernel drivers, as described in Section 3.

Although the original PAM32 engine is compiled as C++, the actual code is written entirely in C. For ease in prototyping, the extensions to PAM32 have been written as C++ classes. In addition, we make use of STL container classes to hold critical data.

Currently PAM32 emulates only a subset of kernel functions in the Windows operating system because the emulation routines are developed manually. An open research question is whether it is possible to automate the process of adding kernel function emulation to emulators such as PAM32. To emulate a new kernel function, we fist identify the missing kernel function and the associated DLL, e.g., `PsSetLoadImageNotifyRoutine` in `ntoskrnl.exe`. Then we look up in the Microsoft DDK to identify the input arguments, the return value, and the calling convention of the missing kernel function. Next, we add the missing function to the export list, which is used to resolve the import table of a kernel driver when it is loaded into Limbo's emulator. The most challenging part in emulating a kernel function is to implement the logic underlying the emulated kernel function. Inside the emulator, each emulated kernel function is implemented as a case statement that is labeled with the name of the emulated kernel function. Each such statement consists of three components: reading input arguments, setting the return variable with a value of proper type, and clearing up the stack according to the function's call convention. The following example shows how the kernel function `NTOSPsSetLoadImageNotifyRoutine` is emulated in Limbo's emulator:

```
case NTOSPsSetLoadImageNotifyRoutine:
{
    // Read arguments
    DWORD loadImageRoutine =
            PAM32ReadStack(hLocal, 4);

    .......

    // Set the return value
    SET_RETURN_VAL(NTSTATUS_SUCCESS);

    // Clean the stack
    ReturnFromApi(hLocal, 4);
    break;
}
```

4.2   Forced Sampled Execution

Because Limbo tests a kernel driver's legitimacy based on its run-time behavior, it is essential that it explore as many execution paths through the driver as possible. In theory, to derive proper inputs that force a particular execution path of a binary code requires solving a system of constraints derived from the code's logic. Therefore, to truly explore all possible paths of a kernel driver requires solving a potentially exponential number of systems of constraints, and is thus computationally infeasible for Limbo given its real-time constraint. To "force out" a binary code's execution behavior without incurring expensive constraint solving computation, Limbo applies a technique called *flood emulation*, which was originally developed to detect heuristically detect virus.

Flood emulation is an example of *forced sampled execution*, and makes two approximations to the ideal of fully exploring a program's all possible paths. First, instead of computing inputs that can drive a program's control along a particular path, flood emulation simply forces the program counter (PC) of the emulator to a certain value so that the program's control can go to a specific location. Note that this change of PC value is not part of the program's underlying logic, and may actually result in an impossible path, i.e., an execution path through a program that should never take place according to the program's logic. Second, to avoid exploring an exponential number of execution paths of a kernel driver under test, flood emulation uses a context-independent sampling approach to traverse the control flow graph of the kernel driver under test.

As Limbo's emulator interprets the kernel driver under test instruction by instruction, it breaks the driver code into a series of basic blocks, and ensures that each encountered basic block is executed at least once, but no more than N times, where N is a configurable parameter. Whenever Limbo's emulator encounters a conditional branch instruction, it uses the following algorithm to determine how to proceed next:

- If the actual destination block of the conditional branch, which could be its target or fall-through arm, has not yet reached its execution iteration limit (N), the emulator continues with the destination block. In addition, if the non-destination arm has never been discovered, the emulator saves the CPU state, the current stack and the entry point of the non-target block in a special stack called the *branch stack* for later exploration.
- If the actual destination arm of the conditional branch has reached its execution iteration limit and the non-destination arm has NEVER been discovered, the emulator forces the driver's control to the non-destination arm by setting the PC accordingly.
- Otherwise, Limbo's emulator pops the top-most item on the branch stack, restores the emulator state accordingly and starts executing the associated block of instructions.

Essentially flood emulation traverses the program's control flow graph in a depth-first fashion, back-tracking the traversal only when the last block's execution iteration limit is exceeded. In addition to per-block execution iteration limits, Limbo's emulator also limits the total number of instructions emulated to ensure that the total driver legitimacy test time is bounded. This limit is on the order of millions of instructions in the current Limbo prototype. Under this traversal algorithm, the main reason that flood emulation may fail to exercise a test program's basic block is that the emulator never has a chance to discover the basic block before the total instruction count limit is reached. In practice, this does not appear to be a problem because the product of the number of basic blocks in a program and the per-block execution iteration limit is typically smaller than the total instruction count limit.

The depth-first traversal scheme may fail to expose interesting behaviors of a basic block because it never has a chance to be executed at all or because it never has a chance to be executed under a context in which interesting behaviors occur. For example, for a function involved in a recursive function call chain, it is possible that the execution iteration limits of this function's basic blocks are used up in the beginning of the emulation run; as a result the function never has a chance to be executed in a context where it is called from another function, which will pass an interesting function pointer as an input argument. To address this problem, the sampled execution strategy should spend the execution iteration limit of each basic block more intelligently, so that it can exercise each basic block in as many distinct contexts as possible. One way to sample the control flow graph is to limit the number of times at which a basic block is executed when it is under the same sequence of last K stack frames. The current Limbo prototype, however, uses the simplest sampling strategy: execute every encountered basic block as many times as reaching its execution iteration limit.

The other limitation of the current Limbo emulator is that it restores only the CPU and stack state when back-tracking a previous basic block. When Limbo's emulator forces the control to go to a particular arm of a conditional branch, it does not attempt to adjust the values of the associated control variables so that their values are consistent with the fact that the control goes to the chosen arm. Neither does it "undo" side effects left by another arm. Consequently, in many cases, the Limbo emulator is actually executing impossible paths in the test program. Although this seemingly simplistic approach may appear illogical at first sight, it actually could effectively expose a test binary's instruction-level behaviors that are useful for malware identification, as demonstrated by the empirical results shown in Section 5. The reason is that our interest here is to get a glimpse of the test binary's run-time behavior rather than to faithfully trace the binary's control flow.

When a kernel driver under test is loaded into Limbo's emulator, the emulator initializes driver-specific variables, the emulator state, the feature set, and the state of emulated kernel structures. During loading, the emulator maps the driver's PE sections to the emulated memory space, and resolves its import objects. If the driver has an import that is not yet supported by the emulator, it will still be resolved with a dummy address. The emulator executes the driver by decoding and executing each instruction in software, and leaving results of the instruction on the emulated CPU and memory state. If the instruction pointer refers to an emulated kernel function, the emulator emulates the function call and returns a result back to the driver. During an emulation run, the emulator continuously records features, the extraction of which could be triggered by specific instructions, specific kernel function calls, accesses to certain kernel memory areas, or other conditions. An emulation run terminates when the total instruction count limit is reached, when the control returns from the main entry point of the driver under test, or when the branch stack used in flood emulation becomes empty. After an emulation run is completed, the emulator extracts several additional features via post-processing, and cleans up the emulator state.

4.3 Classifier Training

The current Limbo prototype uses a total of 32 features in its kernel rootkit detection algorithm. The majority of them correspond to the static and dynamic attributes that we associate with kernel rootkits in the behavioral characterization study, as described in Section 3. Each of these features is either a binary flag that indicates whether a particular attribute is present or a counter of the number of certain dynamic events that are characteristic of existing kernel rootkits. The set of kernel drivers used in classifier training is the same as those used in the manual characterization study discussed in Section 3. It consists of 73 kernel rootkits and 261 legitimate kernel drivers. We call this set the *training* kernel driver set.

We used a Naive Bayes classifier [32] training tool to output a binary classifier that can determine if an unknown kernel driver is a kernel rootkit or not based on the 32 features extracted from an emulation run of the driver. More concretely, this classifier training algorithm assumes that the 32 features are independent of one another, and computes from the training set the conditional probability that a particular feature assumes a certain value when the underlying binary is a kernel rootkit or a legitimate kernel driver. With these conditional probability distributions, the resulting classifier can determine an unknown kernel driver's legitimacy by computing the probability that it is a kernel rootkit or a legitimate kernel driver, and rendering the final verdict with the classification with a higher probability.

5   Effectiveness and Efficiency Evaluation

To evaluate the effectiveness of Limbo's forced sample execution approach to kernel rootkit identification, we run each driver in the *training* kernel driver set through Limbo's PAM32 emulator to collect the corresponding feature set, and feed these feature sets into a standard Naive Bayes classifier training tool. While running samples in this training set, we make sure each of them runs to the total instruction count limit by adding emulation support for whatever kernel functions, kernel data structures and privilege instructions these samples happen to need. After iteratively hand-tuning the training parameters, the classifier training tool produces a 2-category classifier that maximizes the margin between the two categories.

To confirm the validity of Limbo's approach to real-time kernel rootkit identification, we first applied the classifier derived from the training kernel driver set back to the same kernel driver set. The classification results under 10-fold cross validation are shown in Table 1. Because a smaller false positive rate is more important than a smaller false negative rate, the classifier is hand-tuned to reduce the false positive rate (1.9%) even at the expense of false negative rate (9.6%). A false negative means that the classifier mistakes a kernel rootkit for a legitimate kernel driver. Despite the relatively high false negative rate, the overall accuracy of the resulting classifier is high at 96.4%, which means that 96.4% of the kernel drivers tested are correctly classified.

Table 1. The classification accuracy of applying the Naive Bayes classifier trained with the *training* kernel driver set on the same kernel driver set

Outcome	Accuracy
True Positive	90.4% (66/73)
False Negative	9.6% (7/73)
True Negative	98.1% (256/261)
False Positive	1.9% (5/261)
Overall Accuracy	96.4% (322/334)

Table 2. The classification accuracy of applying the classifier trained with the *training* kernel driver set on the *evaluation* kernel driver set

Outcome	Accuracy
True Positive	92.6% (288/311)
False Negative	7.3% (23/311)
True Negative	98.6% (437/443)
False Positive	1.4% (6/443)
Overall Accuracy	96.2% (725/754)

Because Limbo's emulator is carefully tuned to run each sample in the first kernel driver set successfully, the feature sets extracted are more complete. However, when used in the field, there is no guarantee that Limbo's emulator can run each kernel driver under test to its total instruction count limit. To gauge the effects of incomplete emulation and the effectiveness of Limbo's classifier, we collect a second set of kernel drivers for which Limbo's emulator and classifier have not been specifically tuned. In this set, called the *evaluation* kernel driver set, the known kernel rootkits are those collected by Symantec Security Response between January 2005 and May 2006, for a total of 311 samples; the known legitimate kernel drivers are taken from 5 desktop machines in Symantec Research Labs and the same 27 Symantec's own kernel drivers in the training set, for a total of 443 samples.

Again, we ran each kernel driver in the *evaluation* kernel driver set through Limbo's emulator to completion or termination, and calculated the corresponding set of static/dynamic features. The results of applying the classifier derived from the *training* kernel driver set to the *evaluation* kernel driver set under 10-fold cross validation are shown in Table 2. Surprisingly, the overall accuracy only degraded slightly, from 96.4% to 96.2%. After examining the detailed breakdown, we found that both the false negative rate and the false positive rate are actually decreased, a strong indication that Limbo's approach is relatively robust. The fact that the overall classification accuracy remains practically the same suggests that Limbo's ability to sample execution behaviors, choice of features, and classification algorithm make a promising base for building future kernel rootkit detection technology.

To evaluate the trade-off between sensitivity and specificity, we plot the receiver operating characteristics (ROC) curve of Limbo's classifier when varying threshold values used in the classifier training process, The ROC curve for the *evaluation* kernel driver set, as shown in Figure 1 shows the trade-off between the classifier's true positive rate and false positive rate. It allows us to interactively hand-tune the resulting classifier until it strikes the most desirable tradeoff between these two metrics.

Finally, to further gauge how well Limbo is able to cope with rootkits appearing in the future, which might use new techniques to evade the emulator or to perform more similarly to legitimate kernel drivers, we collected a third kernel driver set, which corresponds to malicious kernel rootkits submitted to Symantec during June 2006 (a total of 69 instances). These drivers were then classified

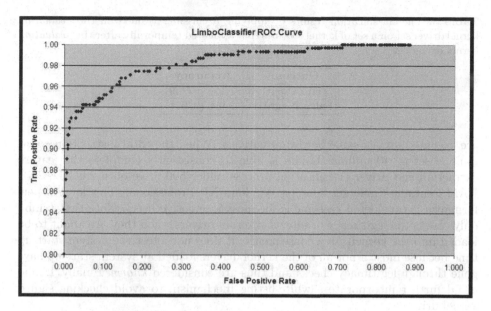

Fig. 1. The receiver operating characteristics curve of the Limbo classifier under the *evaluation* kernel driver set

using a classifier that is trained on the *evaluation* kernel driver set described above (which contained drivers up to May 2006). The classification results are shown in Table 3. Again, these results suggest that Limbo has the potential to catch entirely new threats without requiring frequent retraining or additional tuning.

False positives and negatives could arise either because Limbo's feature set is not perfect in distinguishing between legitimate kernel drivers and malicious kernel rootkits, or because Limbo cannot always extract the required features from the test kernel drivers. An in-depth analysis of the false positives and negatives from the above experiments reveals that their root cause is Limbo's limited feature extraction capability. For example, we added to Limbo's emulator the emulation of five more kernel functions in order to extract all dynamic features from the two kernel rootkits in Table 3 that Limbo previously mis-classified. After successfully extracting their features, Limbo could indeed correctly recognize them as kernel rootkits without any retraining, i.e., zero false negative! In addition, we applied the new emulator to the false positives and negatives in Table 2 to re-extract their features, re-ran the same classifier on these features, and improved the total accuracy rate from 96.2% to 98.5%.

Because Limbo checks each kernel driver before it is to be loaded into the operating system, it introduces additional delay in the driver loading process. The time taken to determine if a new kernel driver is legitimate or not mostly depends on the total instruction count limit, because most of the time goes to extraction of the driver's feature set by executing it in the emulator. The current Limbo emulator executes instructions about 100 times slower than when they

Table 3. The classification results of applying a classifier trained on the *evaluation* kernel driver set on a set of kernel rootkits that appeared temporally after the *evaluation* kernel driver set

Outcome	Accuracy
True Positive	97.1% (67/69)
False Negative	2.9% (2/69)

are executed on the same hardware natively. When the total instruction count limit is set to 10 million, Limbo is able to consistently complete the feature extraction and driver classification process under 500 msec on a 2.4GHz, 2GB RAM Pentium-4 machine running Windows XP Professional. This level of performance is considered reasonable for most interactive users. Note that Limbo only checks the legitimacy of *unknown* kernel drivers when they are about to be loaded into the kernel. As a consequence, it does not affect the system start-up time because most if not all of the kernel drivers loaded at system start-up have gone through legitimacy checks and thus are considered *known*. Finally, Limbo could further incorporate a white-listing mechanism to avoid checking signed kernel drivers.

6   Attack Analysis

The current Limbo prototype has several limitations, most of which are related to its emulation fidelity. As with all emulators, it is impossible to emulate all features of an operating system, processor, and runtime environment. For example, different processors have different instruction sets. Different machines have different hardware configurations. The inability to completely emulate these items enables attackers to evade an emulation-based system. However, we believe evasion techniques that exploit holes in emulators will become less effective as system emulation technologies improve and techniques that detect evasion attempts advance.

Traditional binary obfuscation techniques designed to defeat signature-based AV scanning software are less effective against Limbo, because Limbo relies more on run-time behaviors than on static instruction sequences. Behavior-level obfuscation also seems difficult, because the run-time behaviors of most legitimate kernel drivers follow well-defined patterns and show little variety. Despite this, we recommend re-training Limbo's classifier periodically so that it can upgrade its distinguishing features in accordance to emerging kernel drivers and rootkits.

7   Conclusion and Future Work

Rootkit identification is challenging because fundamentally it requires one to solve the problem of determining if a given piece of binary code is malicious or not based on its static attributes and/or dynamic behaviors. Kernel rootkit identification is a more difficult problem because reliably extracting a kernel driver's run-time behavior is a significant technical challenge. The goal of the Limbo project is even more formidable: perform kernel rootkit identification in real time, before each kernel driver is to be loaded into the Windows operating system. This paper describes the design, implementation and evaluation of the first known real-time kernel rootkit identification system that achieves high identification accuracy for the current generation of kernel rootkits active in the wild. The Limbo technology, as described in this paper, is scheduled to go into all of Symantec's Norton Security products. More concretely, the research contributions of this work include

- The first comprehensive characterization of the run-time behaviors of the current generation of kernel rootkits, and a set of rootkit identification features based on these behaviors,
- A forced sampled execution approach to extract the run-time behaviors of kernel rootkits that is simple and effective, and
- A fully operational prototype that successfully demonstrates its ability to pro-actively identify kernel rootkits before they are loaded into the kernel in real time.

There are several directions we plan to pursue to further improve the identification accuracy of the Limbo system. First, future kernel rootkits are likely to follow the foot steps of computer viruses by incorporating logic to break emulators. To address this problem, we plan to leverage virtual machine technology to improve the emulation fidelity of Limbo's emulator, particularly in kernel function calls, kernel data structure accesses and privileged instruction execution. Second, the way the current Limbo prototype samples the control flow graph of the kernel driver under test does not make the best use of the per-block execution iteration limit, in the sense that it does not attempt to cover as many contexts for a given basic block as possible. We are working on a more intelligent sampled execution strategy so as to expose more varieties of run-time behaviors from the driver under test. Third, we plan to classify kernel rootkits into categories according to their functionalities and run-time behaviors, and apply this high-level category information to the training of the classification algorithm to further improve the accuracy of kernel rootkit identification. Finally, it will be interesting to apply the same methodology to user-level rootkit or spyware identification and see how effective it is. This requires a separate behavioral characterization effort to deduce a set of features that can best distinguish between legitimate and malicious binaries. Because the number of possible behaviors is significantly larger, the amount of effort that such a characterization study requires is expected to be much higher.

References

1. Altholz, N., Stevenson, L.: Rootkits for Dummies. John Wiley and Sons Ltd., Chichester (2006)
2. Avira: Avira rootkit detection, http://www.antirootkit.com/software/Avira-Rootkit-Detection.htm

3. Butler, J.: Vice - catch the hookers! In: Conference Proceedings of Black Hat 2004 (July 2004)
4. Butler, J., Sparks, S.: Raising the bar for windows rootkit detection. Phrack 63 (July 2005)
5. Christodorescu, M., Jha, S., Seshia, S., Song, D., Bryant, R.: Semantics-Aware Malware Detection. In: Proceedings of IEEE Symposium on Security and Privacy (Oakland), IEEE Computer Society Press, Los Alamitos (2005)
6. Cogswell, B., Russinovich, M.: Rootkitrevealer v1.71 (November 2006), http://www.microsoft.com/technet/sysinternals/utilities/RootkitRevealer.mspx
7. Corporation, F.-S.: F-secure blacklight rootkit elimination technology, http://securityticker.blogspot.com/2006/05/f-secure-backlight.html
8. Corporation, S.: Norton antivirus, http://www.symantec.com/home_homeoffice/products/overview.jsp?pcid=is&p vid=nav2006
9. Corporation, S.: Internet security threat report (September 2006), http://www.symantec.com/enterprise/threatreport/index.jsp
10. Flake, H.: Automated reverse engineering. In: Proceedings of Black Hat 2004 (July 2004)
11. Fuzen: Fu rootkit, http://www.rootkit.com/project.php?id=12
12. Hoglund, G., Butler, J.: The companion website of the rootkit book, http://www.rootkit.com
13. Hoglund, G., Butler, J.: Rootkits: Subverting the Windows Kernel. Addison-Wesley Professional, Reading (2005)
14. Karim, M., Walenstein, A., Lakhotia, A., Parida, L.: Malware phylogeny generation using permutations of code. European Research Journal of Computer Virology (2005)
15. Kirda, E., Kruegel, C., Banks, G., Vigna, G., Kemmerer, R.: Behavior-based spyware detection1. In: Proceedings of Usenix Security Symposium (2006)
16. Kruegel, C., Robertson, W., Vigna, G.: Detecting kernel-level rootkits through binary analysis. In: Yew, P.-C., Xue, J. (eds.) ACSAC 2004. LNCS, vol. 3189, Springer, Heidelberg (2004)
17. Labs, M.A.: Rootkit detective, http://vil.nai.com/vil/stinger/
18. Livingston, B.: Icesword author speaks out on rootkits, http://itmanagement.earthweb.com/columns/executive_tech/article.php/3512621
19. Micro, T.: Rootkitbuster, http://www.trendmicro.com/download/rbuster.asp
20. Moser, A., Kruegel, C., Kirda, E.: Exploring Multiple Execution Paths for Malware Analysis. In: Proceedings of 2007 IEEE Symposium on Security and Privacy, IEEE Computer Society Press, Los Alamitos (2007)
21. Petroni, N., Fraser, T., Molina, J., Arbaugh, W.: Copilot - a coprocessor-based kernel runtime integrity monitor. In: Proceedings of Usenix Security Symposium (August 2004)
22. Research, P.: Rootkit cleaner, http://research.pandasoftware.com/blogs/research/archive/2006/12/14/Rootkit-cleaner.aspx
23. Rutkowska, J.: Red pill... or how to detect vmm using (almost) one cpu instruction, http://www.invisiblethings.org/papers/redpill.html
24. Rutkowska, J.: Thoughts about cross-view based rootkit detection (June 2005), http://www.invisiblethings.org/papers/crossview_detection_thoughts.pdf
25. Rutkowska, J.: Rootkits detection on windows systems. In: Proceedings of ITUnderground Conference 2004 (October 2004)
26. Rutkowska, J.: System virginity verifier: Defining the roadmap for malware detection on windows systems (September 2005),http://www.invisiblethings.org/papers/hitb05_virginity_verifier.ppt

27. Sabin, T.: Comparing binaries with graph isomorphisms, http://www.bindview.com/Services/Razor/Papers/2004/comparing_binaries.cfm
28. Sophos: Sophos anti-rootkit, http://www.sophos.com/products/free-tools/sophos-anti-rootkit.html
29. Stamp, M., Wong, W.: Hunting for metamorphic engines. Journal in Computer Virology 2(3) (December 2006)
30. Wang, Y., Beck, D., Roussev, R., Verbowski, C.: Detecting stealth software with strider ghostbuster. In: Proc. Int. Conf. on Dependable Systems and Networks (DSN-DCCS) (June 2005)
31. Wang, Y., Roussev, R., Verbowski, C., Johnson, A., Wu, M., Huang, Y., Kuo, S.: Gatekeeper: Monitoring auto-start extensibility points (aseps) for spyware management. In: Proceedings of Usenix Large Installation System Administration Conference (LISA) (2004)
32. Wikipedia: Naive bayes classifier, http://en.wikipedia.org/wiki/Naive_Bayes_classifier

Advanced Allergy Attacks:
Does a Corpus Really Help?

Simon P. Chung and Aloysius K. Mok*

Department of Computer Sciences,
University of Texas at Austin, Austin TX 78712, USA
{phchung,mok}@cs.utexas.edu

Abstract. As research in automatic signature generators (ASGs) receives more attention, various attacks against these systems are being identified. One of these attacks is the "allergy attack" which induces the target ASG into generating harmful signatures to filter out normal traffic at the perimeter defense, resulting in a DoS against the protected network. It is tempting to attribute the success of allergy attacks to a failure in not checking the generated signatures against a corpus of known "normal" traffic, as suggested by some researchers. In this paper, we argue that the problem is more fundamental in nature; the alleged "solution" is not effective against allergy attacks as long as the normal traffic exhibits certain characteristics that are commonly found in reality. We have come up with two advanced allergy attacks that cannot be stopped by a corpus-based defense. We also propose a page-rank-based metric for quantifying the damage caused by an allergy attack. Both the analysis based on the proposed metric and our experiments with Polygraph and Hamsa show that the advanced attacks presented will block out 10% to 100% of HTTP requests to the three websites studied: CNN.com, Amazon.com and Google.com.

Keywords: Automatic Signature Generation, Intrusion Prevention Systems, Allergy Attacks.

1 Introduction

The use of automatic signature generators (ASGs) as a defense against fast propagating, zero-day worms has received a lot of attention lately, and various attacks against these systems are also being discovered. Allergy attack is one of these attacks, and was defined in [2] as follows:

> An allergy attack is a denial of service (DoS) attack achieved through inducing ASG systems into generating signatures that match normal traffic. Thus, when the signatures generated are applied to the perimeter defense, the target normal traffic will be blocked and result in the desired DoS.

* The research reported here is supported partially by a grant from the Office of Naval Research under contract number N00014-03-1-0705.

C. Kruegel, R. Lippmann, and A. Clark (Eds.): RAID 2007, LNCS 4637, pp. 236–255, 2007.

It might appear that there are simple counter-measures to allergy attacks; the simplest "solution" is to perform a manual inspection of the generated signatures before they are deployed. This is, however, a non-solution inasmuch as it defeats the very purpose of having an ASG: to automate the defense against fast attacks. Other ASGs employ some form of corpus-based mechanisms to retrofit for a low false positive rate. In these ASGs, a new signature will only be deployed if it matches a sufficiently small portion of past normal traffic stored in a corpus that is commonly called the "innocuous pool"; for brevity we shall use the term corpus when there is no confusion.

In this paper, we shall show that corpus-based mechanisms are not a general solution against allergy attacks. In particular, we will identify two major weaknesses of a corpus-based defense, and present advanced allergy attacks that exploit them. The first type of attacks exploits the inability of a static corpus to capture how normal traffic evolves over time. As a result, the type II allergy attacks, which induces the ASG into generating signatures that match traffic pattern specific to future traffic, cannot be stopped by a corpus-based mechanism. The second type of attacks, the type III allergy attack employs a divide-and-conquer strategy; it induces the ASG into generating a set of allergic signatures, each only blocking a small portion of normal traffic, but together can create a significant amount of damage. As we will argue, this appears to be an inevitable consequence of the natural diversity in normal traffic.

The rest of this paper is organized as follows: in Sect. 2, we will survey related work and in Sect. 3, we will present a metric for quantifying the damages caused by an allergy attack that blocks out only part of a target website. In Sect. 4 and 5, we will demonstrate the feasibility and effectiveness of the type II and type III allergy attack, and study some popular websites, including CNN.com, Amazon.com and Google.com. Our discussion in Sect. 4 and 5 assumes that the attacker can induce the ASG into generating any allergic signature with a sufficiently low false positive rate when evaluated against the ASG's corpus, and focus on showing that these signatures can still cause a significant level of damage. In Sect. 6, we will validate our assumption by presenting our experience in inducing Polygraph and Hamsa into generating the signatures studied in Sect. 4 and 5. Finally, we will conclude in Sect. 7.

We emphasize that even though our discussions focus on attack against HTTP requests, the type II and type III attacks are not limited to HTTP traffic. The underlying weaknesses of a corpus-based defense exploited by these attacks, namely the static nature of the corpus, and the diversity in normal traffic exists for all kinds of real traffic. We focus on HTTP only because it is probably the most tempting target for allergy attacks and is the major focus of many existing ASGs. A compromised ASG that filters out normal HTTP requests means inconvenience to Internet users and worse, direct business loss to site owners.

2   Related Work

2.1   Automatic Signature Generators

In most published ASGs (like [6,17,5]), suspicious traffic is identified by some network-based monitoring mechanisms. The signature generation process will then extract *properties that are prevalent among suspicious traffic*, and construct signatures to filter packets with such properties. Usually, the signature generated is simply a byte sequence, and any packet containing that byte sequence will be dropped by the perimeter defense.

Recent advances in ASGs introduced the use of host-based mechanisms (e.g., STEM in [9] and taint analysis in [14,3]) to identify attack traffic and to capture information about how the target host processes them. The use of information from host-based systems in signature generation leads to the development of new signature formats. In [3,1], signatures are no longer byte sequences to be matched against incoming traffic, but are basically "programs" that takes a packet as input, and determines whether it will lead to the same control/data flow needed in exploiting a known vulnerability. Other new signature formats have also been proposed. For example, the approaches in [12,8] generate signatures to match packets that contain sets/sequences of "tokens" (byte sequences), while [7] outputs signatures that identify bytes corresponding to certain control structures commonly found in suspicious traffic.

2.2   Attacks Against ASGs

Worm Polymorphism. From the early research in ASGs, worm polymorphism is a well recognized problem. This is particularly true for systems that generate signatures to identify "invariant" bytes in the attack traffic. As argued in [12], exploits against certain vulnerabilities simply do not have any single contiguous byte sequence that can be used to identify all instances of the attack while keeping the false positive low. In other words, it is impossible for some traditional ASGs to generate one effective signature for all exploitations of certain vulnerabilities. As a solution to this problem, [12] proposed the use of signatures that identify multiple byte sequences in the observed traffic, instead of only a single byte sequence. However, as shown in [16,13], even this approach can be evaded by specially crafted polymorphic worms.

Allergy Attack. In contrast to worm polymorphism, allergy attack against ASGs is a much less recognized problem. Although many published ASGs are vulnerable to the allergy attack, this threat is mentioned only very briefly in three published work, as cited in the survey in [2]. Unlike worm polymorphism that can lead to high false negatives, allergy attacks aim to introduce false positives. While false negatives denote failure of the defense to protect the targeted host but incur no additional damage, false positives can actually incur unanticipated penalty to the targeted host due to the deployment of the defense mechanism itself. Hence, allergy attacks are at least as important a problem facing ASGs as polymorphism.

As noted in [2], the root cause of the problem with allergy attack is the use of semantic-free signature generation which extracts bytes from suspicious traffic without considering how those bytes correspond to the observed malicious/worm behavior. In other words, all parts of the worm are considered the same by the signature generation process, and it is possible to extract as signatures bytes that are totally irrelevant to any attack. Most traditional approach that extract byte sequences (or features of packets) prevalent in suspicious traffic but uncommon in normal traffic can be considered semantic-free. Purely network-based mechanisms for identifying suspicious traffic also facilitate allergy attacks; they allow attackers to easily pretend to be "suspicious", and have their traffic used in signature generation. These mechanisms also give the attackers complete freedom in what they send in for signature generation.

We should note that newer ASGs that are not semantic-free, such as [3,1] are less vulnerable to allergy attacks. However, these ASGs are necessarily host-based and come at a cost. The signature generation process is usually more complicated and thus takes longer time than in traditional ASGs. The use of host-based detection also leads to higher management cost and lower portability. Many host-based mechanisms used in these new ASGs are quite heavy-weighted, and may not be suitable for all legacy systems. Also, ASGs that employ host-based detection require a separate detector for each type of host. For example, if both Windows and Linux machines are to be protected, then at least two host-based detectors are needed by the ASG.

2.3   Handling False Positives in Traditional ASGs

Even though the threats from false positives artificially introduced by allergy attacks have been largely ignored, traditional ASGs employ various mechanisms to reduce "naturally occurring false positives". For example, both [17,5] use a blacklisting mechanism to avoid generating signatures for normal traffic that the ASGs are known to misclassify. In [12,8], a normal traffic corpus is used to evaluate the expected false positive rates of candidate signatures, and those that match a significant portion of the normal traffic will be discarded. However, these mechanisms against "naturally occurring" false positives are ineffective against maliciously crafted traffic from an allergy attack. As shown in [2], the blacklisting mechanism in [5] cannot stop an allergy attack even if the target traffic is partly blacklisted. The use of a normal traffic corpus is also not an effective defense against allergy attacks, as we shall demonstrate in Sect. 4 and 5.

A related problem with a corpus-based mechanism is that the attackers may contaminate the corpus with traffic similar to an imminent attack, so that signatures generated for that attack will be dropped when evaluated against the corpus. This technique is mentioned in [12,8,13], and is called "innocuous/normal pool poisoning". In order to solve this problem, the authors of [12,13] proposed to "collect the innocuous pool using a sliding window, always using a pool that is relatively old (perhaps one month)", while [8] suggested to "collect the samples for the normal pool at random over a larger period of time". However, as we'll see, both solutions may significantly increase the power of type II attacks.

3   Quantifying the Power of Allergy Attacks

Before we present the advanced allergy attacks, we will introduce our metric for quantifying the damages they produce. Our metric is specific for attacks that make particular pages under the target web site unavailable. We use a localized version of page rank in [15] (under a localized version of their random surfer model) to measure the importance of individual pages, and derive the amount of damages caused by an attack from the importance of the pages blocked.

3.1   Localized Random Surfer Model

The major difference between the original random surfer model in [15] and our localized version is that we only consider pages at the site of interest, due to the lack in resources for the Internet-wide web crawling in [15]. In particular, we assume visits to the site concerned always starts with a fixed "root page". The surfer in our model randomly follows links on the currently visited page with a probability d (we assume d to be 0.85, which is the same value used in [15] and all subsequent studies of the Pagerank algorithm), or "get bored" with probability 1-d, just as in [15]. However, when the surfer gets bored, he/she simply leaves, instead of jumping to any other page in the site.

3.2   Localized Page Rank

Under our localized random surfer model, the metric for measuring the importance of a page is called the "localized page rank", which measures the expected number of times a page will be visited in a user session, i.e. between the time when a user first visits the root page, to the time he/she leaves.

The computation of the localized page rank is the same as in [15], except that we do not normalize the page rank, and we initialize the page rank of the root to 1. We do not perform normalization because we are more interested in the actual number of times that a page will be visited, instead of its relative importance among all other pages. The initial page rank of the root represents the visit to the root page that occurs at the beginning of each user session.

Finally, we note that our modifications to the original random surfer model may lead to underestimation of the importance of pages. In particular, a user session may start at a non-root page, and the user may jump to some random page in the studied site when he/she gets bored. However, observe that visitors usually don't know the URLs of many non-root pages, and most external links point to the root page of a site. As a result, visitors don't have much choice but to start their visits at the root page, and cannot jump to many pages when they get bored. In other words, inaccuracy in the computed page ranks due to deviation from our surfer model should be minimal.

3.3   The Broken Link Probability

We are now ready to quantify the damage caused by an allergy attack to a website. We call our metric the "broken link probability" (BLP), which is defined as the probability that a user will click on a link to any unreachable page before the end of the user session. The BLP is intended to measure the degree of frustration (or inconvenience) caused by an allergy attack.

To calculate the BLP, we first recompute the localized page rank for the website under attack. However, during this computation, pages made unavailable by the attack have a localized page rank of zero, though they are still counted as "children" of pages that link to them (without knowing which pages are blocked by an attack, visitors will behave as if there's no attack, and have equal chance of clicking on any link, broken or not). With the new set of localized page ranks, the BLP can be obtained by the following formula:

$$BLP = \sum_{p_i \in UR} d \sum_{p_j \in M(p_i)} \frac{PR(p_j)}{L(p_j)}. \tag{1}$$

where UR is the set of pages made unreachable by the attack, $M(p_i)$ is the set of pages that have links to page p_i, $PR(p_i)$ is the localized page rank of the page p_i, and $L(p_i)$ is the number of pages pointed to by p_i. From the above formula, we see that the BLP is effectively the sum of page ranks that the blocked pages inherit from pages that remain available under the attack. Note that while the localized page rank of a page is an overcount for the probability of visiting that page if it links to other pages to form a loop, it is not a problem for the BLP computation. This is because the user session ends on the first attempt to visit an unavailable page; i.e. an unreachable page can only be reached at most once in a user session. This also means visits to various unreachable pages in a user session are mutually exclusive. Thus, we can compute the BLP by simply adding up the localized page rank of the unreachable pages.

Finally, note that there is a close resemblance between a user session and a TCP flow. This makes the BLP a good estimate of the false positive rate expected when the allergic signatures are evaluated against a normal traffic corpus. In particular, any TCP flow that is filtered by some allergic signature will correspond to the same user session under our model: the one that visits the same pages as in the flow until the first unreachable page is accessed.

4   Type II Allergy Attack

The term "type II allergy attack" was coined in [2] as a specific type of allergy attack, though the idea first appeared in [17] as a threat against their blacklisting mechanism, quoted as follows:

> However, even this approach may fall short against a sophisticated attacker with prior knowledge of an unreleased document. In this scenario an attacker might coerce Earlybird into blocking the documents released by simulating a worm containing substrings unique only to the unreleased document.

In other words, the type II allergy attack targets future traffic and induces the ASG into generating signatures to match patterns that appear in future traffic, but not those at present. As a result, the generated signatures will be deemed acceptable when matched against the blacklist in [17,5], or any static corpus which cannot predict what future traffic will be like. In order to prevent type II attacks, the defender must identify all traffic components that evolve over time (and avoid generating signatures for those components), or the signatures must be constantly re-evaluated.[1]

A point worth noting is that it is not always necessary to predict how traffic will evolve in order to launch a type II attack. The discussions in [17,2] assume that the corpus is always "fresh" and captures all the normal traffic at the time of the attack. However, it may not always be feasible to keep an up-to-date corpus; in addition to the possibly prohibitive cost of constantly updating the corpus, as mentioned in Sect. 2, a relatively old corpus may also be needed as a defense against innocuous pool poisoning. In other words, instead of targeting "future" traffic only, we should consider a type II allergy attack as one that induces the ASG into generating signatures to filter traffic that appears only after the corpus is generated. As we will see, this significantly increases the power of the type II allergy attacks, and allows the attack to have instant effect.

In the following, we will show how some components common in HTTP requests can be exploited by a type II attack, and analyze the amount of damages that these attacks can cause on some example web sites.

4.1   Dates in URLs

The first common component in HTTP requests that can be utilized by a type II allergy attack is the date encoded in URLs. Websites that constantly put up new materials while keeping old ones available usually have the creation date of a page encoded somewhere in its URL. This provides a very handy way of organizing materials created at different time. Examples of websites that organize their pages in this manner include CNN.com, whitehouse.gov, yahoo.com and symantec.com. In the following, we will take CNN.com as an example for our study of type II attacks targeting dates encoded in URLs.

We start our study of CNN.com by finding out URLs of pages under CNN.com, as well as how they link to one another. For this purpose, we employ a simple web crawler based on [10]. Our web crawler starts at www.cnn.com, the "root page" under the localized random surfer model. Because of resource limitation, we only focus on pages that are reachable within 5 clicks from the root page. Furthermore, at any visited page, the crawler will only expand its exploration to pages that either reside in the same directory as the current page, or are in a direct subdirectory of the one holding the current page. However, due to the redirection of some URLs under CNN.com to other sites, our web crawler also collects information of pages under Time.com, EW.com and Money.cnn.com. We performed our experiments from 16th Feb to 9th Mar, 2007, and crawled the target site at 9am and 12 noon every day. In all our experiments, the web crawler retrieved more than 5000 URLs in total, and more than 1000 of the

---

[1] There are simply too many events that can change normal traffic to practically enumerate them and perform the checking only when these events occurs.

URLs are under the server CNN.com. We note the above restrictions may result in undercounted BLP for some allergic signatures. However, since pages that are more than 5 clicks away from the root usually have very low page rank, and pages under CNN.com usually link to other pages that are either in the same directory or a subdirectory, we believe the inaccuracy caused by the restrictions on the web crawler should be minimal.

With the information collected, we studied how the BLP of 5 signatures that encode the date of 24th to 28th Feb evolve from 5 days before to 4 days after the designated day (e.g. for the signature "/02/24/", we measured its BLP for each of the two data sets collected from 19th to the 28th of Feb). As mentioned before, we use the BLP as both a measure of the damage caused by the allergic signature and an estimate of the false positive caused when the it is evaluated against traffic collected on a particular day. Finally, in the following discussion, we will call the day designated by the "date-encoding" signature "day 0", the day that's one day before will be denoted as "day -1", that which is one day after "day 1", and so on. The results of our experiments are shown in Fig. 1a.

As we see from Fig. 1a, all 5 tested signatures produce a zero BLP before the corresponding day 0. We have experimented with other allergic signatures which encode the dates ranging from 16th Feb to 9th Mar, and they all show a similar pattern. Though in some cases, the tested allergic signatures appear before the corresponding day 0. This is usually caused by URLs that point to pages created in the previous years (e.g. we find the string "/02/21/" in two URLs that point to the 21st Feb, 2005 issue of the Money magazine). Nonetheless, the BLP of all the tested signatures remain below $1.5 * 10^{-6}$ before day 0. Thus, any allergic signature encoding a date after the corpus is generated will

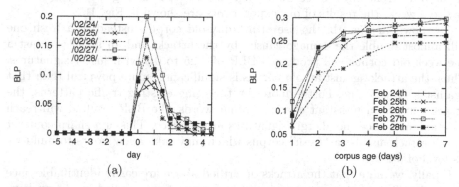

(a)   (b)

Fig. 1. Fig. 1a on the left shows how the BLP of 5 different date-encoded signatures changes from 5 days before to 4 days after the designated date (with the designated date denoted by day 0, days before that denoted by day -1, day -2 and so forth, days after are denoted day 1, day 2, etc). The BLP of the tested signature at 9am of day n is denoted by the point directly above the mark "n" on the x-axis, while the BLP at 12noon is denoted by the point between "n" and "n+1" on the x-axis. Fig. 1b on the right shows the effectiveness of type II attacks that target dates in URL when used against corpus of different age and launched on 5 different days (24th - 28th Feb).

have a false positive below $1.5 * 10^{-4}\%$ when evaluated against the corpus[2]. In other words, the type II allergy attack that employ "date-encoding" signatures will evade even corpus-based defenses with a very low false positive threshold (both [16,8] suggested a 1% threshold, while the lowest threshold used in [12] is 0.001%).

Now let's consider the power of the described attack against an up-to-date corpus. Assuming that any allergic signature will be removed within a day since it start filtering normal traffic, it appears the attacker should induce the ASG into generating one single allergic signature for some future day (extra signatures will take effect on a different day, and thus cannot add to the damages at day 0). From Fig. 1a, we see that this attack will create a more than 6% chance for visitors to CNN.com to reach an unavailable page if the allergic signature is not removed by 9am. Also, note that the two days with the lowest BLP, 24th and 25th Feb, are both weekend days. In other words, the amount of damage for the type II allergy attack studied above can be far greater if it targets a weekday; the BLP created can be as high as 0.12 at 9am, and up to 0.2 if the attack is not stopped by noon. Finally, we'd like to point out that the attack against an up-to-date corpus requires a certain "build-up" time to reach the level of damage predicted. In other words, the figures given above only apply if the attack is not detected until 9am or 12noon; if the allergic signature is removed in the first few hours of day 0, the damage caused will be much smaller.

On the other hand, if the corpus is n-day old, with the same notation used above, the attacker can induce the ASG to generate signatures for the date of day 0 to day -(n-1). For example, the attack on 16th Feb against a 3-day-old corpus will involve the signatures "/02/16", "/02/15/" and "/02/14/". We have experimented with the effectiveness of this attack when it is launched at noon of the 5 different days tested above, against a corpus of "age" ranging from 1 day to a week, the results of our experiments are shown in Fig. 1b.

As shown in Fig. 1b, the use of a 2-day-old corpus instead of a fresh one will almost double the damage caused by the attack, and an attack against a one-week old corpus will produce a BLP of 0.25 to 0.3 with just 7 signatures. Thus, the attack against an old corpus is significantly more powerful than that against a "fresh" one. Furthermore, by targeting existing traffic patterns, the attack can produce instant effect; in other words, the BLP resulted will reach its maximum once the allergic signatures are in place. This is a sharp contrast to the attack against a "fresh" corpus which may take a few hours to build up its level of damage.

Finally, we note that the attacks described above are easily identifiable once the broken links are reported and human intervention is called in. As we have already noted, human intervention defeats the purpose of ASGs, and the attacks can make some important parts of the target site temporarily unavailable.

---

[2] We believe it is highly unlikely that the studied signatures will match some other parts of an HTTP requests, since dates in other fields are represented differently, and the use of "/" outside the URL is very uncommon.

4.2   Timestamp in Cookies

Another component in HTTP traffic that can be utilized by a type II attack is the timestamp in web cookies. Web cookies are employed by many sites to keep track of user preferences. New visitors to these websites will receive a set of web cookies together with the content of the first page requested. The cookies will be stored in the user's machine, and will be sent with all further HTTP requests to the site. Also, an expiration date is associated with each cookie sent to the user, and when the date is reached, a new cookie will be issued.

We find that some sites use cookies to record the time for various user events. For example, cookies from Amazon.com contains an 11-digit "session-id-time" which expires in a week and records the day where the user's last session started. Another example of these timestamp cookies are the "TM" and "LM" cookies from Google.com, where the former stores the time when the user first visited the site, while the latter records when the user last modifies his/her preferences. The time recorded in "TM" and "LM" are accurate up to one second, and will not expire until year 2038. In other words, the "TM" value for any existing user will remain the same, while the "LM" value only changes infrequently.

A type II allergy attack can exploit these timestamp cookies by inducing the ASG into generating signatures that match future values taken by these cookies (or their prefixes). To avoid the signatures from unintendedly matching other parts of HTTP requests, the name of the cookies should be included, e.g. signatures targeting the "session-id-time" cookie should be of the form "session-id-time=xxxx". With this signature format and a value for "xxxx" that is only used after the corpus is generated, the signatures should be deemed usable by the ASG.

As for the effectiveness of the attack, let's assume the corpus used is up-to-date. The attack against Amazon.com will then employ a signature that filters the value taken by the "session-id-time" cookie on a particular future day 0, and will make all pages under Amazon.com inaccessible to any user who has the corresponding cookie expires on or before day 0; their session-id-time cookie will be updated to the value targeted by the attack after the first request, resulting in all subsequent requests being filtered. Similarly, the attack against the "TM" and "LM" will target the values taken by these cookies on a particular future day, and will make all pages under Google.com unavailable to any user that either modifies their preference or first visit the site on the designated day. Even though the attacked sites will be virtually unreachable to any affected users, we note that this may only be a small portion of the user population.

On the other hand, if the ASG employs an old corpus, the attack can target all values that the timestamp cookies can take after the corpus is generated, and create more significant damages. Note that virtually all HTTP requests to Amazon.com will contain a "session-id-time" cookie that is generated between day 0 and day -6; any other timestamp cookies will have expired, and will be updated after the first request. As a result, if the corpus used is more than one week old, the attacker can induce the ASG into generating signatures for all valid values of the "session-id-time" cookie, and effectively make all pages under

Amazon.com unavailable. As for the attack against Google.com, an old corpus means the attacker can deny the access to the site for all users that first visited Google.com or modified their preference after the corpus is generated.

In conclusion, an up-to-date corpus is very effective in limiting the power of a type II attack. However, using a "fresh" corpus also makes it easier for worms to evade the ASG through innocuous poisoning. The use of a corpus with traffic collected over a long period of time (which is a solution to "innocuous pool poisoning" proposed in [8]) may have the same effect as using an old corpus. Let's consider the encoded-date attack in Sect. 4.1 against a corpus with traffic collected over a month (i.e. from day 0 to day -30). At 12noon of day 0, we can assume that the allergic signature encoding the date for day 0 to appear in 20% of the traffic for that day, but appears in close to 0% in the remaining 30 days of traffic in the corpus. Similarly, the byte sequence that encodes the date for day -1 will appear in 20% and 10% of traffic on day -1 and day 0 respectively, and never appear for the other days. As a result, both signatures will match less than 1% of all the traffic in the corpus, and can be used in a type II attack to create a BLP of 0.15 to 0.2. Further analysis shows that the sum of the BLP at noon from day 0 to day 4 is at most 0.36 for the 5 signatures tested in Sect. 4.1. Thus, a corpus with over 40 days' traffic will probably allow allergic signatures for the date of day 0 to day -7 to be used to create the same level of damage as when the type II attack is launched against a one-week-old corpus.

5   Type III Allergy Attack

A more nuanced weakness of a corpus-based defense is the diversity in normal traffic, which is exploited in a type III allergy attack. We define a type III attack as follows:

> A type III allergy attack is an attack that induces the target ASG into generating a set of signatures, such that each will have a false positive low enough to be acceptable to the ASG, but as a whole, the set will block a significant portion of normal traffic and amount to a non-trivial DoS against the target network.

The main difference between the type II and the type III attack is that signatures generated by the former have their false positives increase significantly over time, while false positive rates for signatures from the latter stay at a low level. In other words, the type III attack takes a more "brute-force" approach, and requires more signatures than the type II attack. On the other hand, the type III attack is much more flexible, and is much easier to design.

We can also see the type III attack as a divide-and-conquer strategy; it "divides" the target traffic into small pieces, and "conquer" each with an allergic signature specific for that piece. With signatures specific for small pieces of traffic, we can guarantee that each signature will have a sufficiently low false positive. However, the success of this strategy depends on the following conditions:

1. The ASG must tolerate signatures that cause some minimal false positives.
2. There must be sufficient diversity in the normal traffic for the attacker to "divide" them into small pieces, each distinguished by the signature that matches only that piece but nothing else. In other words, if there is very little variation among normal traffic, any allergic signature will have a very high false positive, and it would be impossible to launch a type III attack.

Our literature survey shows that the first condition should be met by any reasonable ASG. In fact, in order for the ASG to be of any use, it must tolerate a certain degree of false positives in the signatures. This is because the corpus may contain anomalous traffic, even after all instances of known attacks have been removed. In fact, the studies in [16] found that 0.007% of traffic in their corpus matches the signature for the true invariant bytes of the worm they've tested. The author of [16] also reported a similar 0.008% of anomalous traffic in the innocuous pool used in [12]. In other words, if the ASG were to be effective against the worm tested in [16], it must accept signatures that match as much as 0.08% of flows in the normal traffic corpus. For our discussions below, we assume the ASG will accept any signature that matches less than 1% of the traffic in the corpus[3]. Next, let us consider how the attacker can "divide" the normal traffic and satisfy the second condition.

5.1 Diversity in Pages Visited

For any website of reasonable size, the BLP of a page may drop very quickly with the number of clicks required to reach that page from the root. In other words, pages that are only reachable after 2 or 3 clicks from the root page may well have BLP far below 0.01, our false positive threshold. This is especially true for sites like CNN.com where pages tend to have a large number of links (e.g. the root page alone points to more than 100 pages). Thus, the mere size of the target site may provide the diversity needed for a type III allergy attack; all but the most popular pages under these sites are requested only in a very small portion of user sessions. As a result, an allergic signature that targets requests for any particular page is very likely to evade a corpus-based defense, and a significant amount of damage can be caused by a large number of such signatures, each matching requests for different pages. To evaluate the effectiveness of this attack, we once again experimented with the data collected about CNN.com.

We construct our type III attack against CNN.com with a very generic method that can be applied to any other website. In particular, we search over all pages under our target site, starting with the root page, and consider pages reachable with fewer clicks from the root first. For any page examined, we compute the BLP expected if that page is blocked. If the BLP is lower than the threshold, we mark that page as a target, otherwise, we "expand" the search from that page (i.e. examining all pages pointed to by the current page later). For each target page, we extract random 10-byte subsequences from the "path" part of its URL, and use the first one with BLP below the threshold as the allergic signature for

---

[3] Both [8,16] use a false positive threshold of 1%.

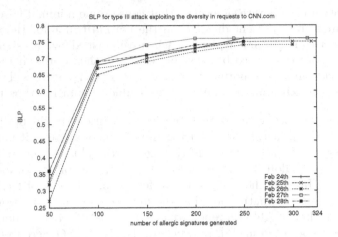

Fig. 2. BLP caused by different number of allergic signatures from the type III attack targeting the "not-so-popular" pages under CNN.com

that page. Finally, we sort the signatures in descending order of their BLP, and compute the total BLP resulted when different number of these signatures are applied. We have repeated this experiment for the five data sets collected at 9am of 24th to 28th Feb, and the results are shown in Fig. 2.

As we can see, the first 50 allergic signatures always create a BLP of more than 0.25, and an additional 50 signatures will bring the BLP up to 0.6. Also note that the algorithm presented is not optimized for finding the smallest set of signatures that creates the maximum BLP; instead, it is only intended as a simple proof-of-concept. Thus, it is entirely possible for a type III attack to produce the same level of damage predicted in Fig. 2 with fewer signatures.

5.2   Diversity in Search Terms

The diversity of keywords queried at different search engines like Google.com can also be exploited in a type III attack. We conjecture that the queries from different users are so diverse that even the most frequently searched keywords are involved in a very small portion of flows, and the data from Hitwise [4] seems to support this conjecture. By collecting network data from various ISPs, Hitwise provides various statistics concerning the use of search terms at various search engines. According to Hitwise, the top 10 search terms "that successfully drove traffic to websites in the Hitwise All Categories category for the 4 weeks ending February 24, 2007, based on US Internet usage" are as shown in Table 1.

As we can see, even the most popular keyword, "myspace" accounted for only 1.07% of all observed searches. Furthermore, the volume of searches received drops quickly with a search term's ranking. Even though it is not clear how Hitwise come up with their ranking, the data above seems to suggest that

Table 1. Top 10 search terms for the 4 weeks ending 24th Feb, 2007, with the percentage of searches that each term accounts for

Rank	Search Term	Volume
1	myspace	1.07%
2	myspace.com	0.64%
3	ebay	0.41%
4	www.myspace.com	0.35%
5	yahoo	0.21%
6	mapquest	0.18%
7	myspace layouts	0.18%
8	youtube	0.18%
9	craigslist	0.14%
10	yahoo.com	0.14%

all but the most popular search terms will appear in a far less than 1% of traffic. Thus, an allergic signature targeting queries for a specific search term will most likely have a false positive low enough to evade any corpus-based defense.

Even though it is hard to evaluate the power of an allergic signature that blocks out all queries for a particular search term, we argue that the damage caused by such attacks can be non-trivial and many-folded. First of all, this may mean direct business loss to the search engine. Let's take Google.com as an example. Under Google's advertising program, Google AdWords, each advertisement is associated with a set of search terms, and it only appears when a user searches for one of those terms. Furthermore, Google only charges an advertiser when a user clicks on his/her advertisement. As a result, a type III attack that blocks out all queries for search terms associated with an advertisement will make that advertisement completely non-profitable for Google.

The type III attack described above will also affect parties whose websites will be listed when somebody queries on the targeted keywords. The most obvious example victims are the advertisers on Google AdWord whose advertisements will never reach their customers. Damages can also come in other flavors. For example, according to [18], the following search terms: "BARACK OBAMA", "HILLARY CLINTON" and "JOHN EWARDS" (three politicians running for the president of the US) all accounts for less than 0.01% of all searches observed by Hitwise between Sep 2006 and Jan 2007. In other words, it is entirely feasible to have a type III attack that blocks out all searches for a particular candidate, which may create non-trivial damage to his/her campaign.

5.3 Cookies Revisited

In addition to recording time, web cookies are sometimes used to distinguish different users/user sessions. For example, the cookies from Google.com include a 16-digit hexadecimal value called "PREF-ID", which uniquely identifies a user.

Similarly, both Yahoo.com and Amazon.com include an ID for either the user or the corresponding user session in their cookies. The uniqueness of these "ID cookies" are introducing the diversity necessary for type III attacks into normal traffic, and can be exploited as follows: suppose the target cookie can taken values in each byte/digit, we will generate one allergic signature to match each of the possible values taken by the first k bytes/digits of the cookie, with k being the smallest integer such that n^k is below the false positive threshold. To make sure that each signature only matches the beginning of the cookie value as intended, we will include the name of the target cookie as well.

For all the "ID cookies" we have seen, their values remain the same throughout a user session. Thus, each flow in the corpus will match exactly one of the allergic signatures. Furthermore, the values of these "ID cookies" are usually assigned such that the portion of cookies starting with a certain byte sequence is the same as the portion with any other prefix. As a result, each of the above allergic signatures will have a false positive very close to n^k, and thus will evade the corpus-based defense. Finally, since the allergic signatures cover all possible prefix of the target cookie, they will filter out almost all traffic to the target site.

We have experimented with the above attack by collecting 10 sets of cookies from Google.com, with 100,000 cookies in every set. We measured the distribution of the values for the first two bytes of the "PREF-ID" cookie, and find that each two-byte prefix of "PREF-ID" appears in 0.47% to 0.33% of cookies in each data set. In other words, the described type III attack allows us to evade a corpus-based defense with a threshold of far less than 1%, and virtually block all traffic to Google.com with 256 signatures.

We note that the type III attacks will be much less effective if a lower false positive threshold is used. For example, if the threshold is lowered to 0.01% (which appears the lowest possible value according to [16]), we find that the attack against CNN.com described in Sect. 5.1 will require more than 1000 signatures to achieve a BLP of less than 0.02. The attack based on the diversity in search terms may be less affected by a lower false positive threshold, since the figures from Hitwise seem to suggest that there are plenty of search terms that appear in less than 0.01% of traffic, and a significantly larger set of signatures may be required for the attack in Sect. 5.3 to block out all traffic to Google.com. However, a lower false positive threshold will also reduce the cost of evading the ASG through innocuous pool poisoning: the attackers now need a much smaller volume of bogus traffic to make a real signature against their attack dropped by the corpus-based mechanism. In other words, the tradeoff between defending against allergy attacks and innocuous pool poisoning manifests itself once again. Finally, the (possibly) large number of signatures involved in a type III attack is not necessarily a shortcoming. It gives the attack certain stealthiness: it would be hard to manually remove all the allergic signatures involved. A slow type III attack may also mean a constant influx of allergic signatures, each causing minor damages, which makes stopping the attack serious nuisances.

6   Experimenting with Polygraph and Hamsa

In this section, we will present our experience in launching the attacks described in Sect. 4.1, 5.1 and 5.3 (which target encoded dates and requests for less popular pages under CNN.com, and the identification cookie used by Google.com respectively) against Polygraph [12] and Hamsa [8]. We choose to experiment with these two ASGs because they are two of the most advanced network-based ASGs that limit their false positives with a corpus-based mechanism. Our focus on network-based ASGs is based on the belief that they have certain practical advantages over systems that employ host-based components. We based our experiments on a slightly modified version of Polygraph provided by the authors of [16], and our own implementation of Hamsa. Our implementation of Hamsa deviates from that presented in [8] slightly: we do not require a token to appear in 15% or more of the worm flows in order to be used in the signature generation. We believe this requirement allows the attackers to evade the ASG easily, given that the attacker can always introduce noise as in [16], and some of the "invariant" parts of a worm may actually vary (e.g. in a stack buffer overflow, the return address can be over written with many different values). We note that the tested attacks should also be effective against the original Hamsa; we only need to carry them out in multiple rounds, each generating 6 allergic signatures.

We have experimented with launching the two attacks against CNN.com on the same 5 days as studied in Sect. 4.1 and 5.1 (24th - 28th Feb). For the experiments on the type II attack, we generate a 7-day-old corpus by simulating 50,000 user sessions[4] with the data collected 7 days before the corresponding day 0 (e.g. the experiment on the attack on 24th Feb uses a corpus generated from data collected on 17th Feb). For the type III attack, we assume a "fresh" corpus with 50,000 simulated user sessions based on the data collected at 9am of day 0. For our experiments on Hamsa and the conjunction/token-subsequence signature generator of Polygraph, we construct the worm pool to contain 3 copies of each allergic signature we want the ASG to generate. After that, we invoke the tested signature generation process once. We then evaluate the false positive caused by the generated signatures with 150,000 simulated user sessions generated using the data collected at 9am of the tested day 0. We find that the measured false positives from the type II attack is always within 1% of the computed BLP value. As for the type III attack, the false positives measured in the experiments are lower than predicted, but the difference is always below 6.2%.

The setup for the experiments on the Bayes signature generator in Polygraph is a little different, since the Bayes signature generation algorithm effectively generates one signature to cover all traffic in the worm pool, and guarantees that this "combined" signature has a false positive rate below the threshold. As a result, we may need to invoke the signature generation process multiple times to achieve the level of damages expected. Our experiments show that one invocation is sufficient for the tested type II attack, since the byte sequences involved in the attack rarely appear in the corpus. On the other hand, the type

---

[4] [12] used a training set and testing set of 45,111 and 125,301 flows respectively.

III attack requires multiple invocation of the Bayes signature generation process. Thus, we modify our experiment as follows: in each round of the experiment, we construct the worm pool with 5 of the target byte sequences that are not yet covered, 3 copies for each. We find that a little less than 100 rounds is needed to have all the target byte sequences filtered. As before, we evaluated the signatures generated for the two attacks with 150,000 simulated user sessions, and find the false positives obtained from the experiments are within 2% range of that predicted by our BLP analysis.

The discrepancy between the measured false positive and that predicted by the BLP analysis may be explained by the randomness in the generation of the corpus and the test traffic pool. The former may result in some target signatures matching more flows in the corpus than allowed, and prevent their inclusion in the final set of signatures. We believe this is the main reason why the measured false positives of the attacks against Hamsa and the conjunction/token-subsequence signature generation in Polygraph is 5% lower than expected. On the other hand, the fluctuation in the generation of the testing traffic pool affects the measured false positive rate of the generated signatures, which may account for the smaller differences seen in the other experiments.

For the type III attack targeting identification cookies from Google.com, we repeat the experiment 5 times. In each experiment, we construct the corpus used by the ASGs with a different set of 50,000 cookies. The rest of the experimental set up is the same as above; i.e. we invoke the signature generator once with the worm pool containing all the target byte sequence for the experiments with Hamsa and the conjunction/token-subsequence generator of Polygraph, and perform the experiment in multiple rounds, each with 5 remaining target byte sequences for the Bayes signature generation. The generated signatures are then evaluated with 5 different sets of 100,000 cookies. The signatures generated result in a 100% false positive against the tested sets of cookies as expected. Once again, the attack against Hamsa and the conjunction/token-subsequence generator of Polygraph needs only one invocation of the signature generation process. On the other hand, the attack against the Bayes signature generation requires around 130 rounds to finish.

Obviously, the possible need to invoke the signature generator multiple times is a drawback of the type III attacks in general. Depending on the frequency at which the signature generation process can be invoked, the attack can take a long time to complete. Nonetheless, in order to contain fast propagating worms, the maximum time between two invocations cannot be too long; in [5], this is given as "on the order of ten minutes". Now, let's assume the signature generation can be invoked every 10 mins[5]; it will then take around 8 hours to generate the top

---

[5] According to [11], if content filtering is deployed under the "top 100 ISPs" scenario, a reaction time of 10 mins is necessary to protect 90% of vulnerable hosts against a worm capable of making 40 probes/sec, and the probe rate of Code-Red v2 is assumed to be 10/sec. Also note is that an invocation of the signature generation process every 10 mins is certainly insufficient in stopping SQL Slammer, which infected 90% of vulnerable hosts in 10 mins.

Table 2. A summary of the four most powerful attacks discussed

Attack Name	Type II/III?	Target Site	Target traffic component	Number of signatures	Damage caused
Encoded-Date Attack	Type II	CNN.com	Dates encoded in URLs	7 sigs	BLP of more than 0.25 (when the corpus is 7 days or older).
Timestamp-cookie Attack	Type II	Amazon.com	Timestamps in cookies	7 sigs	Block all traffic to Amazon.com if the corpus is 7 days or older.
Infrequent-requests Attack	Type III	CNN.com	Requests to pages other than the most popular ones	100 sigs	BLP of more than 0.6
ID-cookie Attack	Type III	Google.com	Identification cookies	256 sigs	Block all traffic to Google.com

50 allergic signatures in the type III attack against CNN.com (which will result in a BLP of more than 0.25).

7 Conclusions

In this paper, we argued that testing signatures generated by a vulnerable ASG against a static corpus of normal traffic before their deployment cannot prevent the high false positives caused by an allergy attack. In particular, we have identified two advanced attacks that can evade such corpus-based defense. The first attack, called the type II allergy attack, exploits the difficulty of capturing the evolution of normal traffic with a static corpus; as a result, allergic signatures targeting traffic patterns that emerge after the generation of the corpus will go undetected. The second attack, called the type III allergy attack, employs a more brute-force, divide-and-conquer approach; it simply induces the target ASGs into generating a set of signatures, each with a sufficiently low false positive to go pass the corpus-based defense, but as a whole will block out a significant portion of normal traffic. This attack is possible due to the natural diversity occurring in normal traffic, which provides a way to "divide" them into small pieces, each matched by a different allergic signature.

We have provided multiple examples of both type II and type III attacks against popular sites like CNN.com, Amazon.com and Google.com. In order to analyze the amount of damages caused by some of these attacks, we proposed a metric called the "broken link probability", which measures the probability that a surfer will try to access pages made unavailable by the attack during his/her visit to the target site. The BLP is also a good estimate of the portion of flows in a corpus that will be filtered by a candidate allergic signature, which is necessary in designing type II and type III attacks. With the BLP and some other techniques, we have analyzed the effectiveness of all the proposed attacks. A summary of the most powerful ones is given in Table 2.

Even though there are various mitigations that can limit (but not completely stop) the damages caused by a type II/III allergy attack, it is important to note that most of them come at a cost of accentuating the threat from innocuous pool poisoning. For example, the power of a type II attack can be significantly reduced by keeping the corpus up-to-date which can be costly if not problematical. More importantly, a fresh corpus allows instant effect for innocuous pool poisoning; the attacker can launch the intended attack immediately after sending out the bogus traffic. The same applies for defending against type III attack by setting a lower threshold for allowable false positives in new signatures; a successful innocuous pool poisoning will require a much smaller volume of bogus traffic. Another possible defense against the type III attack is to check the total false positives caused by all the signatures generated in each invocation of the signature generation process, just as the Bayes signature generation algorithm in Polygraph does. This will have the effect of reducing the number of allergic signatures generated in each "round" of the attack, and thus increase the time to complete a type III attack. Without being able to determine which signature is bogus and which filters real worm traffic, such defense can run into the same problem faced by the Bayes signature generator as demonstrated in [16]: it is impossible to be effective against real attacks while keeping the false positive low. An attacker can exploit this fundamental weakness by, say, mounting both an allergy attack and an innocuous pool poisoning attack simultaneously.

Finally, we emphasize that even though our discussion focused on attacks against HTTP requests, type II and type III attacks can be used against other kinds of traffic too. This is especially true for type III attacks. In fact, we find that many important protocols contain fields that uniquely identify a particular user/communication session (e.g. the protocol for DNS and MSN), and diversity in requested services is also commonly found in many types of traffic (e.g. domain name to be resolved, recipient email address). All these can be seen as opportunities for type III attacks against non-HTTP traffic as is being validated in ongoing work.

References

1. Brumley, D., Newsome, J., Song, D., Wang, H., Jha, S.: Towards Automatic Generation of Vulnerability-Based Signatures. In: Proceedings of The 2006 IEEE Symposium on Security and Privacy, Oakland, May 2006, IEEE Computer Society Press, Los Alamitos (2006)

2. Chung, S.P., Mok, A.K.: Allergy attack against automatic signature generation. In: Zamboni, D., Kruegel, C. (eds.) RAID 2006. LNCS, vol. 4219, Springer, Heidelberg (2006)

3. Costa, M., Crowcroft, J., Castro, M., Rowstron, A., Zhou, L., Zhang, L., Barham, P.: Vigilante: End-to-end containment of internet worms. In: Proceedings of 20th ACM Symposium on Operating Systems Principles, Brighton, October 2005, ACM Press, New York (2005)

4. H.http://www.hitwise.com

5. Kim, H., Karp, B.: Autograph: Toward automated, distributed worm signature detection. In: Proceedings of 13th USENIX Security Symposium, California (August 2004)
6. Kreibich, C., Crowcroft, J.: Honeycomb - Creating Intrusion Detection Signatures Using Honeypots. In: Proceedings of the Second Workshop on Hot Topics in Networks (Hotnets II), Boston (November 2003)
7. Krugel, C., Kirda, E., Mutz, D., Robertson, W., Vigna, G.: Polymorphic worm detection using structural information of executables. In: Valdes, A., Zamboni, D. (eds.) RAID 2005. LNCS, vol. 3858, Springer, Heidelberg (2006)
8. Li, Z., Sanghi, M., Chen, Y., Kao, M., Chavez, B.: Hamsa: fast signature generation for zero-day polymorphic worms with provable attack resilience. In: Proceedings of The 2006 IEEE Symposium on Security and Privacy, Oakland, May 2006, IEEE Computer Society Press, Los Alamitos (2006)
9. Locasto, M.E., Wang, K., Keromytis, A.D., Stolfo, S.J.: Flips: Hybrid adaptive intrusion prevention. In: Valdes, A., Zamboni, D. (eds.) RAID 2005. LNCS, vol. 3858, Springer, Heidelberg (2006)
10. Miller, R.C., Bharat, K.: SPHINX: A Framework for Creating Personal, Site-Specific Web Crawlers. In: Proceedings of 7th World Wide Web Conference, Brisbane (April 1998)
11. Moore, D., Shannon, C., Voelker, G.M., Savage, S.: Internet quarantine: Requirements for containing self-propagating code. In: Proceedings of The 22nd Annual Joint Conference of the IEEE Computer and Communications Societies (INFO-COM 2003), San Francisco, April 2003, IEEE Computer Society Press, Los Alamitos (2003)
12. Newsome, J., Karp, B., Song, D.: Polygraph: Automatically generating signatures for polymorphic worms. In: Proceedings of The 2005 IEEE Symposium on Security and Privacy, Oakland, May 2005, IEEE Computer Society Press, Los Alamitos (2005)
13. Newsome, J., Karp, B., Song, D.: Paragraph: Thwarting signature learning by training maliciously. In: Zamboni, D., Kruegel, C. (eds.) RAID 2006. LNCS, vol. 4219, Springer, Heidelberg (2006)
14. Newsome, J., Song, D.: Dynamic taint analysis for automatic detection, analysis, and signature generation of exploits on commodity software. In: Proceedings of 12th Annual Network and Distributed System Security Symposium (NDSS 05) (February 2005)
15. Page, L., Brin, S., Motwani, R., Winograd, T.: The pagerank citation ranking: Bringing order to the web. Technical report, Stanford Digital Library Technologies Project (1998)
16. Perdisci, R., Dagon, D., Lee, W., Fogla, P., Sharif, M.: Misleading Worm Signature Generators Using Deliberate Noise Injection. In: Proceedings of The 2006 IEEE Symposium on Security and Privacy, Oakland, May 2006, IEEE Computer Society Press, Los Alamitos (2006)
17. Singh, S., Estan, C., Varghese, G., Savage, S.: Automated worm fingerprinting. In: Proceedings of 5th Symposium on Operating Systems Design and Implementation, California (December 2004)
18. Tancer, B.: Obama clinton chart updated with edwards (January 2007), http://www.hitwise.com/datacenter/industrysearchterms/all-categories.php

Alert Verification Evasion Through Server Response Forging

Adam D. Todd, Richard A. Raines, Rusty O. Baldwin, Barry E. Mullins,
and Steven K. Rogers

Center for Cyberspace Research,
Air Force Institute of Technology, Department of Electrical and Computer Engineering,
2950 Hobson Way, Bldg 642, Wright-Patterson AFB, OH 45433-7765
richard.raines@afit.edu
Sensors Directorate, Air Force Research Laboratory,
Wright-Patterson AFB, OH 45433-7765

Abstract. Intrusion Detection Systems (IDSs) are necessary components in the defense of any computer network. Network administrators rely on IDSs to detect attacks, but ultimately it is their responsibility to investigate IDS alerts and determine the damage done. With the number of alerts increasing, IDS analysts have turned to automated methods to help with alert verification. This research investigates this next step of the intrusion detection process. Some alert verification mechanisms attempt to identify successful intrusion attempts based on server responses and protocol analysis. This research examines the server responses generated by four different exploits across four different Linux distributions. Next, three techniques capable of forging server responses on Linux operating systems are developed and implemented. This research shows that these new alert verification evasion methods can make attacks appear unsuccessful even though the exploitation occurs. This type of attack ignores detection and tries to evade the verification process.

Keywords: Network Intrusion Detection, Alert Verification, Evasion, Exploits.

1 Introduction

Intrusion Detection Systems (IDSs) have become essential components in the defense of any computer network. Both government agencies and private corporations use IDSs to detect a variety of attacks which cannot be detected or prevented by a conventional firewall. The proliferation of IDSs has resulted in attackers developing many different evasion techniques. Network administrators and computer security professionals must remain apprised of current evasion techniques and IDS protections or risk leaving their computer networks vulnerable to attack.

The intrusion detection process identifies abnormal activity which is often an attempt to compromise a system or consume a resource which denies others access [1]. IDSs generate alerts which draw the administrator's attention to possible malicious activity. Hackers modify their attacks to incorporate methods attempting to bypass these IDSs. Most evasion techniques focus on modifying the attacks to circumvent the IDSs entirely. Some older attacks exploit flaws in network protocols [2], while newer evasion strategies focus on the application layer (e.g., URL

C. Kruegel, R. Lippmann, and A. Clark (Eds.): RAID 2007, LNCS 4637, pp. 256–275, 2007.

obfuscation) [3]. As intrusion detection becomes more sophisticated, so do the IDS evasion techniques.

Research in this field primarily focuses on adapting intrusion detection strategies to identify new attacks. While researchers and analysts can modify the rules and detection schemes of IDSs to recognize new evasion methods, the entire process ultimately relies on verification to determine the success or failure of an attack. With the number of alerts increasing, the human analyst is looking for automated approaches of verifying and analyzing these alerts. This research looks at exploiting the last step in the intrusion detection process—verification. The IDS may detect all attacks but the final responsibility is to determine whether or not the intrusion was successful. By modifying the behavior of a compromised server, it is possible to evade verification by making a successful attack appear unsuccessful.

2 Background

2.1 Intrusion Detection

Intrusion Detection is the process of detecting inappropriate, incorrect, or anomalous activity. Such actions are often an attempt to comprise a system by violating confidentiality, breaching integrity or denying the availability of a resource. Intrusion detection can either be performed manually or automatically. Manual intrusion detection usually consists of an experienced network administrator examining logs. However, this process is usually automated by using an Intrusion Detection Systems [1].

When an automated IDS detects a probable intrusion or attack, it logs relevant information and alerts an administrator. Determining if the event was an actual intrusion, the success of the attack, and any consequent action to take is usually outside the scope of most IDSs. Another automated system, an Intrusion Prevention System (IPS), attempts to detect and stop any attack before it can be successful [1]. While IPSs can be effective, most network administrators still use IDSs.

IDSs come in one of two forms: host-based IDS (HIDS) and network-based IDS (NIDS). A HIDS monitors a single host and examines system calls and logs, and sometimes even specific port activity. A NIDS monitors the flow of network packets from multiple hosts. Some modern IDSs are a combination of these approaches. The focus of this research will be on NIDSs.

2.2 Detection Techniques

NIDSs use a variety of different detection techniques to observe network information and determine if a flow is an attack or intrusion. Some NIDSs identify patterns of traffic and then match them to signatures of known malicious activity. This process is known as misuse detection. Anomaly detection systems compare network traffic against a baseline of "normal" activity. Each technique is valid and comes with its own strengths and weaknesses [4].

In misuse detection, the intrusion detection decision is made based on a set of predefined rules. These detection rules are simple in the sense that they define expected behavior observed during an attack or intrusion. When a NIDS observes a traffic pattern matching one of these rules, it gathers information and generates an alert. While this approach seems simple, these rules must be very strict if a NIDS is to have an acceptable detection and false alarm rate [5]. Misuse detection can be accomplished by a variety of implementations. The simplest intrusion detection method uses basic string matching. Expert systems determine the security state of the system given a more complex set of rules and then examine network traffic for specific signs of intrusion or invalid transitions between states [5, 6]. Contextual signatures extend the traditional form of string-based signatures by including additional information about the context of the network traffic being analyzed which can help reduce the number of false positives significantly [7].

An anomaly-based IDS detects intrusions by monitoring network activity and classifying it as either normal or anomalous based on heuristics rather than patterns or signatures. The goal is to detect any traffic that falls outside of normal system operation. This differs from misuse detection systems which can only detect attacks with known signatures. In order to determine what constitutes a possible attack, the system must be taught what "normal" behavior is. This can be accomplished in many ways including self-learning via artificial intelligence techniques, mathematical modeling of normal activity and data-mining [1, 8, 9].

2.3 IDS Analysis

While IDSs help a network administrator detect attacks, it is the responsibility of the expert analyst to determine if an intrusion actually did any damage. In this area, IDSs have not met the expectations of network security administrators [10]. Rather, IDSs are known for creating a large number of alerts that are either false alarms or represent an unsuccessful attack. It is left up to the analyst to sort through this chaos. Context-based IDSs use a real-time network awareness which provides extra information, but even this capability falls short of solving the problem.

Data correlation is one method for aiding with all the alerts. Correlation recognizes and associates related network activity to get a better understanding of intrusions and attacks [11]. Correlating associated alerts can reduce the number of alerts the analyst has to review.

Another method is alert verification which is an automated approach for confirming successful attacks. Many analysts look to automated methods to help process the volume of alerts generated [10]. One technique compares the target system with the configuration required for an attack to be successful. Another alert verification method compares the outcome of the suspected attack with the expected outcome of a successful attack [12]. This verification method examines server responses and performs protocol analysis.

Verification methods may be active or passive. Active verification mechanisms gather information after an alert occurs, while passive mechanisms gather initial configuration data so checks can be made before an attack occurs. The most important characteristic of alert verification mechanisms is accuracy. Accurate mechanisms keep the number of false negatives and false positives low. Automated alert verification mechanisms seem to be a solution to the overwhelming volume of alert messages generated; however, they also offer another device to exploit and attack.

2.4 Evasion Techniques

With the prevalence of IDSs, many attackers have devised evasion techniques. While hackers designed these evasion techniques to bypass security systems, researchers may examine these attacks to determine how these systems can be improved. There are many classic examples of evasion techniques that have been incorporated into the protection models of IDSs.

Low and Slow. The "low and slow" method tries to avoid detection by extending the attack over time and/or space [4].

Obfuscation. Obfuscation is a technique which manipulates the attack data so the actual data packet will not match the IDS signature [3, 13].

Protocol Problems. Protocol ambiguities can lead to many different attack vectors [2, 14].

Denial of Service. The denial of service (DoS) evasion technique simply tries to overload the NIDS [3, 14].

Mimicry Attacks. Mimicry attacks attempt to avoid detection by crafting the attack code and data streams to resemble valid applications and network traffic [15].

Verification Evasion. Most evasion techniques to date are designed to elude the automated aspects of intrusion detection while ignoring the verification process [16]. This technique attempts to avoid a thorough investigation by fooling the verification process. It is a form of mimicry attack in the sense that it creates responses which resemble those of failed attacks. If the analyst or verification process recognizes these characteristics as corresponding to an unsuccessful attack, then there will probably be no follow-up investigation.

Server response forging is one of the more successful attacks because verification techniques often rely on server responses to determine the outcome of an attack [12]. Typically, server responses are seen as a trusted method for determining the success of an attack. Most systems will respond with an error message if the attack is unsuccessful. However, if the attack is successful then typically no response is issued because the injected attack code is running instead of the server application itself. Attackers can modify the exploit code to include issuing a response that the automated verification mechanism associates with failed attacks, and then simply wait before connecting to the backdoor or remote shell. While the attack still triggers an alert, this evasion method attempts to convince IDS analysts that nothing is wrong by eluding the verification process.

3 Methodology

3.1 Experimental Design

To facilitate the conduct of this research, a network test bed was established. Two computers are connected via Category 5 network cables and a 10/100 network switch. One computer is the attacking system. It sends the exploits and captures the server responses. The second computer acts as a host to a variety of virtual, victim machines.

The attacking computer is an Intel x86-based system running Fedora Core 5 as its operating system [17]. Fedora Core 5 was selected due to its ease of use and prevalence as one of the top Linux distributions [18]. The attacking system is also configured to use Metasploit 2.7 [19]. Metasploit is a framework which facilitates the development and delivery of exploits. Ethereal 0.10.14 is installed on the attacking computer to capture network traffic [20].

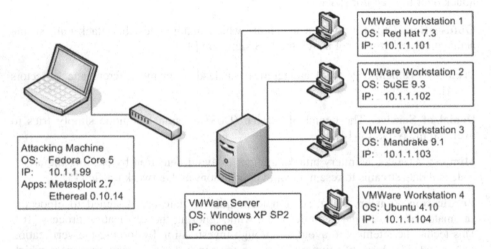

Fig. 1. Testing Network Architecture

The host computer runs Windows XP Service Pack 2 and uses VMWare Workstation 5.5 to host the victim machines [21]. Each of these virtual machines emulates hardware but runs on the host's underlying architecture (Intel x86). The victim machines run a variety of Linux distributions as shown in Figure 1. These versions of Linux correspond to the top four Linux distributions in use today [18]. In some instances older versions of the distributions are used to facilitate exploits (e.g., Red Hat 7.3 instead of Fedora Core 6 and Mandrake 9.1 instead of Mandriva 2007).

The simulated network is isolated and assigned private IP addresses. Figure 1 shows the network architecture. The host computer does not have a valid private IP address so t is unable to send or receive traffic in this simulation. Random network traffic is not generated because the goal of this research focuses on the responses of servers and the ability to forge these responses which should not be affected by additional traffic.

The virtual machines are installed with default configurations and any subsequent system or application level patches are installed following the instructions included with the patches. Additional software listed in Table 1 is installed to provide network services with vulnerabilities available for testing. All applications were installed with default settings following the install instructions included with the source files.

Vulnerabilities are chosen based on their prevalence and exploit code availability. In particular, vulnerabilities with available Metasploit exploits were chosen because these exploits are highly configurable and have been proven reliable for testing and research. If a Metasploit exploit is not available for a vulnerability, a public exploit is used. Table 2 lists the vulnerabilities and Table 3 lists the corresponding exploits.

Table 1. Victim Applications

Application	Service	Vulnerable Ver.	Patched Ver.
Samba	SMB (file share)	2.2.5	3.0.23
GNU Mailutils	IMAP (mail)	0.6	1.1
PoPToP	PPTP (VPN)	1.1.3	1.3.0

Table 2. Vulnerabilities

Vulnerability	CVE ID	Description
Samba Fragment Reassembly Overflow	2003-0085	There is a remote buffer overflow in Samba. The service fails to check a field length inside of the request before using this length in a memcpy() operation, resulting in a buffer overflow [22].
GNU Mailutils imap4d Server Client Command Format String	2005-1523	Mailutils contains a flaw that allows a malicious user to execute arbitrary code. The issue is triggered when format specifiers are sent as part of user-supplied commands, and are unchecked by the imap4d server [23].
PoPToP PPTP Negative Read Overflow	2003-0213	The PoPToP PPTP Server contains a flaw that allows a malicious user to execute arbitrary code. The issue is triggered when the server receives a malicious packet with the length field set to either zero or one. This causes a read operation to use a negative value, allowing sensitive memory regions to be overwritten with user-supplied data [24].
Samba call_trans2open() Function Overflow	2003-0201	Samba contains a flaw that allows a remote attack to execute arbitrary code. The issue is due to a flaw in trans2.c in which the call_trans2open() function user input is not properly sanitized [25].

Table 3. Exploits

Exploit	Type	Version	Corresponding CVE
samba_nttrans	Metasploit	Rev 3818	2003-0085
gnu_mailutils_imap4d	Metasploit	Rev 3818	2005-1523
poptop_negative_read	Metasploit	Rev 3818	2003-0213
trans2root.pl	Public	N/A	2003-0201

3.2 Performance Metrics

This research focuses on server response forging; thus, server response is the only metric. A server response is the packet or packets sent in response to a message received from a client. The client message can be a legitimate request in which case the server responds accordingly or the client message may be erroneous in which case the server typically responds with an error message. The request may also be a malicious exploit in which case the server's response is uncertain. If the exploit is successful, the server may not send a server response.

This research considers only the server response packets, or lack thereof, after the exploit has been sent. This investigation only focuses on the stream of server packets after the exploit is received. This stream of server packets is comparable to the information a NIDS logs for the verification process. It is this server response, when forged, which may allow intrusion detection evasion by fooling the verification mechanism and therefore the analyst.

3.3 Test Design

Two research goals, evaluate the server response to exploits and develop a method for forging server responses on Linux systems, are pursued through the development of testing methodologies described below.

Server Response Test Design. The Metasploit Framework console was used to configure the chosen exploits (cf., Table 3). The linux_ia32_exec payload is used in each test. This payload executes a command specified by the "CMD" variable on the target machine. During these tests, the payload command is set to ping the attacking system once ("ping −c 1 10.1.1.99"). Each vulnerable and patched server is tested and the remote host ("RHOST") is set to the corresponding IP address in each test. Public exploits are executed with the required arguments (e.g., local host and remote host). Public exploits lack the robustness of the Metasploit Framework, so there is no opportunity to select the payload. After each trial, the tested server is restored to its original state using VMWare's "Revert to Snapshot" feature.

The server responses are captured using Ethereal. The capture starts before the exploit is sent and is subsequently terminated after all server response packets have been captured. Server responses are generally completed within a couple seconds. However, some exploits use a brute force technique for determining the return address and therefore make thousands of requests. The network captures containing the server responses are saved in the libpcap format after each test [26]. After all trials are completed, the server responses are compared to determine the possibility of server forging.

Response Forging Design. Previous research investigated Windows implementations and the effectiveness of such an attack; however, this is the first known research extending this ability to the Linux environment [16]. In general, forging a server response may provide misleading information that may cause an attack to be falsely classified as unsuccessful. This new form of attack requires the exploit to carry a shellcode capable of creating and sending a forged server response.

Shellcode Development. The first challenge of a shellcode which can send a response is finding a way to send the message. The shellcode needs a socket on which to send the message. Obtaining a socket can be accomplished in two ways: by creating a new socket specifically for the purpose of forging a response or finding an existing socket which can be reused.

The first method is fairly straightforward. The shellcode simply creates a new socket by making one call to an operating system library, and then sends out the forged response by modifying the IP and TCP header information and including the server response message.

The second method requires the shellcode to reuse a socket. Reusing a socket has several benefits including not needing to forge much of the header information. Reusing an existing connection also keeps the forgery from being noticed by a firewall or NIDS looking for new TCP connections. Two techniques are available to find an existing socket: findsock and findrecv.

Findsock finds the socket based on the remote host's TCP port number [27, 28]. Basically, the shellcode iterates through every open socket file descriptor and compares the remote connections port number with the number specified by the attacker. When the socket with the corresponding port number is found, the shellcode returns the file descriptor which can be used to send messages back to the attacking computer.

Findrecv locates the established socket by looking for a secondary message sent to that socket by the attacker [27, 29]. In this approach, the exploit sends the shellcode in one message and then sends an additional "tag" message. The shellcode loops through all the sockets and attempts to receive the tag. If the tag is found and matches the one sent by the attacker, then the established socket is found and the shellcode returns the file descriptor.

The second challenge of the shellcode is creating the forged response. To deceive the NIDS and the analyst, the response must appear to be legitimate. Even the smallest things like the message's header information must be correct or the response may get flagged. The actual message contents must be determined ahead of time and will vary depending on the service attacked, the version number, and possibly the operating system.

Testing Implementation. Our research tests the developed exploits and shellcodes using an experimental client-server application written in C. The server process listens for client connections on port 8080. After establishing a connection, the client sends a request to the server. The server receives this message and copies it to another buffer using strcpy(), and then it echoes back the request assuming nothing has gone awry.

The receive buffer is 760 bytes while the destination buffer is only 740 bytes. By using strcpy() with a larger source buffer than destination buffer, the server is vulnerable to a buffer overflow attack. These buffer sizes represent a typical buffer overflow size. The Metasploit Framework contains 13 Linux exploits, and the average available payload size was 737 bytes. A buffer overflow attack occurs when the return memory address is overwritten. At the end of execution, the function attempts to return to where it was called, but during a buffer overflow attack the return address is usually overwritten to point back into the attacker specified buffer. Once control flow has jumped back into the exploit message, it falls through until it reaches the shellcode. The shellcode must be passed into the buffer as machine byte-code so that it can be interpreted as instructions and executed. However, before a shellcode can be sent to a vulnerable application, "bad" characters must be removed (c.f., Section 3.5). To alleviate these problems, the Metasploit encoder was used to remove all the problematic characters. It works by using a specified encoding scheme to encrypt the real shellcode, and then attaches a decoding algorithm to the front of the exploit to decrypt the rest of the shellcode once it begins to execute.

In this scenario, the client is responsible for generating and sending the exploit. The testing client has several shellcodes to choose from and each has already been encoded with the default Metasploit encoder. After selecting the shellcode to use with this exploit, the client fills the request with a NOP sled. Next, the encoded shellcode is placed in the buffer, and then the remaining space is filled with a new return address which will overwrite the handler's return address on the server. Once the complete exploit is created, the client sends the request to the server and waits for the response.

4 Analysis

4.1 Server Responses

The analysis begins with a description of the server responses of the vulnerable applications followed by the patched application responses. These responses are compared to determine if response forging is a viable attack. Consistent differences between the two responses along with consistency amongst patched server responses are key elements in determining the possibility of forging. This section also compares the differences in responses between operating systems to determine if they affect the universality of server response forging. Finally, general observations and requirements for successful server response forging are discussed.

Responses to samba_nttrans. This experiment captures the server responses generated by using the samba_nttrans exploit against the vulnerable Samba version 2.25 and the patched version 3.0.23. The application was only found to be vulnerable on seven of the ten Linux distributions (cf., Table 4).

All four Linux distributions tested in this research were vulnerable to this exploit, and all shared similar server responses. This exploit starts by establishing an SMB session and connecting to the SMB file tree. After this session has been created, the exploit sends a malformed NT Trans request which contains a buffer overflow. The Samba service fails to check the length field inside the NT Trans request before using this value as the buffer's length in a memcpy() operation [22]. After exploitation, the Samba server executes the shellcode, but the service does not crash nor does it send back any response. After the shellcode has been executed, the process simply sends back a FIN-ACK to close the connection.

After installing Samba 3.0.23, the buffer overflow was unsuccessful. When the service received a malformed NT Trans request, it replied with an SMB error message stating that the command was unknown and closed the connection.

Responses to gnu_mailutils_imap4d. This experiment captured the server responses generated by using the gnu_mailutils_imap4d exploit against the vulnerable GNU Mailutils version 0.6 and the patched version 1.1. The application was found to be exploitable on only three of the ten distributions (cf., Table 4).

Of the four Linux distributions tested, three were vulnerable to this exploit. All three vulnerable distributions shared similar server responses. This exploit connects to the server and determines the correct parameters for a buffer overflow attack. The server runs an Internet Message Access Protocol (IMAP) server which is used for sending and receiving email. After an IMAP session has been established, a malicious request is sent. In all three vulnerable test scenarios, the application was exploited and responded with a normal IMAP response message followed by several IMAP response messages filled with spaces.

On the patched version 1.1 of GNU Mailutils, the exploit could not determine the information necessary to successfully execute the buffer overflow attack. When presented with erroneous requests, the server sent an IMAP response and then closed the connection. When attempting to exploit the patched Mailutils on the SuSE 9.3, the application also responded with a bad arguments IMAP message. This is the same response given by the Ubuntu 4.10 system, which was the only configuration not vulnerable to this exploit.

Responses to poptop_negative_read. This experiment captured the server responses when the poptop_negative_read exploit was used against the vulnerable PoPToP PPTP daemon version 1.1.3 and the patched version 1.3.0. The application was found to be vulnerable on three of the ten distributions (cf., Table 4).

Three of the four Linux distributions tested were vulnerable to this exploit. The exploit is contained within one 408-byte packet. The overflow occurs in a malicious "Start Control Connection Request". The PPTP length field is set to 1, and the return address is overwritten. The new return address points back into the user-supplied request which contains the shellcode. After the server is exploited, the connection is immediately closed with a FIN-ACK packet, and then the shellcode is executed. This server response was shared amongst the vulnerable configurations.

SuSE 9.3 was not vulnerable to the PoPToP negative read exploit and neither were the other operating systems after installing PoPToP version 1.3.0. In both cases, the PPTP server responded to these malformed requests by simply resetting the connection with a TCP RST packet.

Responses to trans2root. The trans2root exploit is included in the Metasploit framework (samba_trans2open); however, this experiment used the public exploit because the Metasploit exploit was unsuccessful in prior trials. This exploit takes advantage of the

Samba call_trans2open() function overflow vulnerability. This experiment captured the server responses generated by using the trans2root exploit against the vulnerable Samba version 2.25 and the patched version 3.0.23. The application was found to be able to exploit only five of the ten distributions (cf., Table 4).

All four of the configurations were initially vulnerable to the trans2root exploit. This exploit establishes an SMB session, connects to the SMB file tree, and sends a buffer overflow. Since this is a public exploit, it has a hardcoded shellcode which establishes a shell back to the attacking computer. Besides the packets establishing the remote shell, the exploited server responded with a simple acknowledgment and closed the connection with a FIN-ACK packet.

The configurations running the patched Samba version 3.0.23 responded to the malicious Trans2 requests with an SMB error message. After replying with an error message, the service closed the connection with a RST-ACK packet.

Operating System Differences. This set of experiments tested the server responses generated by different operating systems to the same exploit. Each operating system was tested while installed with the vulnerable version of the application and then again after the patched version of the service was installed. A forged server response attack is much more useful if it can be used against a variety of operating systems instead of being target specific. In these tests, patched server responses seemed to be uniform in every case except the GNU Mailutils exploit. Two of the servers responded with additional error messages that the others did not. Ultimately, it seems that the server responses remain consistent across Linux distributions, and this is probably because these are third-party applications designed to run on any Linux system and therefore are not inherently implementation specific.

Not only was this experiment designed to determine the differences in server responses between vulnerable and patched servers, but also designed to establish the universality of these responses and therefore the applicability of the server response forging attack. All tested exploits targeted vulnerabilities in applications compiled and installed separately after the initial operating system installation; however, even though all operating systems were running the same applications, they were not all susceptible to the exploit. Table 4 shows the variety of Linux distributions and versions tested and their corresponding vulnerability to the four exploits.

Table 4. Operating System Vulnerability (Y = vulnerable, N = not vulnerable)

O.S.	Samba (nttrans)	Mailutils	PoPToP	Samba (trans2open)
Red Hat 7.3	Y	Y	Y	Y
Fedora Core 2	N	N	N	N
SuSE 9.3	Y	Y	N	Y
Mandrake 9.1	Y	Y	Y	Y
Mandrake 10.2	N	N	N	N
Ubuntu 4.10	Y	N	Y	Y
Ubuntu 5.04	Y	N	N	N
Ubuntu 6.06	N	N	N	N
Debian 3.0	Y	N	N	N
Debian 3.1	Y	N	N	Y

The differences in vulnerability may be explained by different memory management techniques or advances in buffer overflow protection. Buffer overflow attacks rely on overwriting the return address with an address pointing back into the buffer on the stack. This type of attack may fail when the buffer is stored in a different memory location because it makes the buffer address on the stack harder to guess. It could be the exploits are only designed to brute-force the memory locations where specific operating systems typically place the buffer on the stack. Another possibility is the push for more secure operating systems which have incorporated protections against buffer overflow attacks. There are several buffer overflow prevention mechanisms for operating systems including making stacks non-executable and replacing some library calls with safe versions of the same calls [30].

Server Response Summary. Server response forging is a valuable attack against an overwhelmed NIDS analyst using an automated verification mechanism to determine the success of an attack. As noted previously, verification systems sometimes resolve alerts by simply looking for the appropriate server response, typically generated by patched servers. This technique opens up the possibility of forging. Successful forging requires: 1) the messages generated by a patched server must be different than that of a vulnerable server, otherwise, the two events would be indistinguishable and the analyst would not rely on the server response as a method for determining the success of an exploit; 2) the response from a patched server must be constant or predictable. This condition enables the correct and expected server response to be passed along with the exploit; and 3) successful forging requires that a vulnerable server does not provide extra information indicating it has been exploited (e.g., automatically sending a RST of FIN packet to close the connection). While a server response may still be forged, this contradicting evidence may be enough to cause an analyst to investigate further.

With the above guidelines in mind, server response forging seems to be a potential attack against two of the four exploits. The two Samba exploits meet all the requirements: the vulnerable and patched server responses are different, the server response is constant, and, finally, the vulnerable server does not respond with any uncontrollable information which indicates that the server has been exploited. To forge a patched server response, the samba_nttrans exploit must generate an SMB error message and then close the connection with a RST packet. The trans2root exploit would similarly need to send an SMB error message and close the connection with using a RST packet instead of a normal FIN-ACK response.

The other two exploits, Mailutils and PoPToP, are not good candidates for the forged server response attack. After a vulnerable server is compromised using the mailutils exploit, it returns several erroneous IMAP responses. In the test cases above, these IMAP responses occurred before the ping request which means they were automatically generated before the shellcode executed and spawned the ping request. If these messages are automatically generated by a vulnerable server, then an automated verification mechanism will see these messages and investigate the system despite the fact that it sees the appropriate response later. The PoPToP exploit faces a similar problem. Immediately after the server is exploited, it closes the connection using a FIN-ACK packet. The exploit then executes the shellcode, but this does not leave the shellcode with the opportunity to generate the appropriate patched server response which is closing the connection using a RST. Again the verification mechanism will see the vulnerable server response and most likely alert the analyst to investigate the intrusion.

Server response testing is necessary to determine if an exploit can be used with this type of forgery attack. The conditions must be just right, but as this experimentation shows, it is not an impossible set of requirements to meet. Half of the tested exploits appear to be compatible with server response forging, and this research did not consider web vulnerabilities which have been shown to be very susceptible to forged server responses [16]. With testing for the applicability of this attack complete and successful, the next step is developing forging techniques.

4.2 Server Response Forging

The previous section presented the requirements for forging a packet. This section examines the details and implementations of three different forging methods developed during the research and experimentation phases.

Raw Socket. The first method for forging a packet begins by creating a new socket. To send a message, the shellcode must have a socket file descriptor on which to send out the message. A simple way to obtain this socket file descriptor is by creating one. The Linux kernel contains a socket library which has a simple socket constructor. This constructor creates a raw socket capable of sending out raw datagrams. This is an important feature because the shellcode must create a custom datagram capable of forging the server response.

Network packets consist of header information and a payload. The payload is the message to be sent which in this case is a forged response. Packets subdivide the header information between the different protocol layers. Typical internet traffic consists of an Ethernet header, IP protocol header and, in most cases, a TCP protocol header. The most important header is the TCP header which contains packet flags, the acknowledgement number, the sequence number, and the destination and source ports. Some of the port numbers should be known ahead of time and the checksum can be calculated, but the other information is much harder to determine. A TCP session is usually initialized with a random sequence number to make session hijacking more difficult; however, if the attacker knows the initial numbers, subsequent numbers are predictable. If the forged server response uses an inaccurate sequence or acknowledgement number, the IDS or firewall may flag or drop the packet. Therefore, the attacker must either determine the sequence numbers from the first few packets of the exploit and estimate the correct sequence and acknowledgement numbers during runtime or make some risky assumptions ahead of time.

Creating a raw datagram and modifying the header information requires additional Linux libraries which offer direct access to these data structures. The ability to forge a server response using raw sockets is enabled by using the C programming language. The shellcode will generate a forged message from one host to another. The source and destination address including port numbers are dynamic along with the forged message. This particular example generates a shellcode of over 900 bytes; however, the length could be shortened drastically if it were implemented in assembly language and optimized.

The raw socket method of forging a server response has advantages and disadvantages. One benefit is that it does not require a currently established network connection. This shellcode does not require a connection to be open, but it may be difficult to calculate the sequence number, and it may appear strange that a server response was sent after the connection was closed. The raw socket creation also allows the modification of TCP header information. This is quite useful when the server response is a TCP packet with the RST flag. The primary drawback of this method is the overall size of the payload. The extra function calls and header modification increase the total shellcode length, which can be extremely burdensome if more than one packet is required to forge the server response. In the end, this approach has its advantages but the increased size might be too much of a hindrance, especially with buffer overflow exploits that have limited space for the overflow.

Findport. The second method for forging a server response reuses a previously existing socket. Reusing a socket means that the shellcode saves time and space by not creating one. While some exploits cause a network connection to close immediately, other exploits cause the connection to remain open until the shellcode has executed. With the exploit leaving the current network connection open, the shellcode should be able to find this open socket file descriptor and reuse it to send back information to the client machine.

The findsock shellcode locates the current connection by looping through all the socket file descriptors and analyzing the peer associated with each socket by calling getpeername(). Each socket has an associated peer which is represented as an address structure. This structure contains the IP address along with the port number. In this instance, the shellcode examines each peer and compares the port associated with each address to a hardcoded port determined by the attacker ahead of time.

The shellcode uses an interrupt to access the system call table instead of making function calls which require libraries to be included. The code increments through each socket, compares the port number in each address structure to the hardcoded port of the attacker, and finally returns the corresponding socket file descriptor to be used later when forging the response.

The message string is created by using a calling scheme which pushes the next address onto the stack. Usually this is the address of the next instruction, but in this case it is the address of the forged message string. Next, the function parameters of send are pushed onto the stack and then the stack pointer is moved to the third parameter to the system call table interrupt. Again, the shellcode uses interrupts instead of library function calls to send the packet. The final step pushes the index corresponding to a socket call and then causes an interrupt to trigger the system call table.

This technique was implemented using assembly language as this allows for the highest degree of optimization. The final shellcode has a payload of 54 bytes plus the length of the forged message. However, a payload must be encoded before it is used in an exploit. This process adds additional bytes causing a payload forging a message of 8 bytes to be 86 bytes instead of the original size of 62 bytes. The byte code generated from the original shellcode was converted into a new payload for the Metasploit framework.

The findport technique for forging is fairly simple and has a relatively small payload size. It reuses an existing network connection which may allow it to pass through firewalls unnoticed. Firewalls can be triggered when new outbound connections are created. It can also send more than one response quite easily. Once the socket descriptor is located, sending messages is relatively simple and does not require much space beyond that of the additional message. One of the drawbacks to this technique is that it requires the network connection to remain open. Another disadvantage of this method is that it will not work with network address translation, proxies, or any other devices the obscure the port of the original client. A final weakness is the inability to set TCP flags which is a necessity for some of the server responses. Nevertheless, this approach works well when size is a factor or there is a need to send back multiple messages.

Findtag. The second technique to find and reuse a socket is known in the Metasploit Framework as findrecv. This method attempts to find the current connection associated with the exploit by reading from the receive buffer of every socket. For this technique to work, the attacker must send an additional packet after the exploit. This packet contains a tag and helps the shellcode find the correct socket.

This findtag strategy loops through all the socket file descriptors and uses the socket function recv() to determine if there are any more bytes to read from the network buffer. If so, the payload reads them in and compares them to the predetermined tag. If the tag matches, the correct socket is found and can be reused to send back the forged server response.

The shellcode stores the socket descriptor and increments through all the possible sockets. The receive function is called using a system interrupt and the result is stored on the stack. If the first 4 bytes of this string match the hardcoded tag, then the correct socket file descriptor has been found. After the shellcode has a socket to use, it creates a message and sends it out.

Again, this technique was implemented using assembly language. The resulting shellcode is 57 bytes in addition to the length of the forged server response. Again, the byte code must be encoded before it can be sent as the payload of an exploit. Using the default encoder of the Metasploit Framework, a payload with an 8 byte server response is 90 bytes. The shellcode was converted to byte code and transformed into a new Metasploit framework payload.

This server response forging technique is similar to findport. It shares some of the same advantages and disadvantages, but there are also differences. It remains a relatively simple and small payload. It still can pass through firewalls relatively unnoticed because it does not create a new socket but uses a pre-established connection instead. Findtag can send multiple messages without a significant increase in size. In addition to these advantages, this shellcode can also find the correct network connection even through proxies and network address translation. It can accomplish this because it is not concerned with the peer information which is obscured. This approach, however, still requires an open socket and still cannot modify TCP header flags. The findtag approach also depends on the correct socket having the correct information remaining in the network buffer. This requirement presents a couple problems. First, there is a timing issue. The attacker must send the information long enough after the original exploit so it is not read in along with the exploit, but it must also be sent before the shellcode attempts to read the network buffer. Another concern is that the shellcode loop might read in data from other sockets which could cause errors or faults elsewhere in the system.

Response Forging Summary. Response forging must be accomplished through socket creation or reuse. The previous section discussed the implementation of socket creation and two forms of socket reuse. Other methods were considered, but those methods were only slight variations of the already proposed ideas. Each of the three implementations was shown to be effective, and each had its own set of advantages and disadvantages.

Findport and findtag have a relatively small size, but are incapable of modifying TCP headers. This means that neither of these techniques can generate a RST packet required to forge some server responses. Findport and findtag are not effective against the two exploits shown to be susceptible to server response forging in these experiments: samba_nttrans and trans2root.

The raw socket method was rather large, but allows for greater control over the server response including the ability to set the TCP flags. This means that it can create an RST packet which is part of the forged server response for both samba_nttrans and trans2root. However, both of these exploits require an SMB error message to be sent before closing the connection with a RST. This additional message means that the raw socket payload will be very large; possibly too large. The samba_nttrans has a maximum payload size of 1024 bytes, while the trans2root exploit is limited to 734 bytes [31].

4.3 Intrusion Detection Enhancement

This new form of IDS evasion brings with it complications for the current method of intrusion detection and alert verification. In the past, IDS improvements have focused on adjusting rules and implementations to detect new attacks and evasion techniques. This new evasion tactic is not concerned with detection. The goal of this attack is to fool the verification process into believing the attack was unsuccessful and make the forged server responses indistinguishable from those of actual patched servers. This section examines several adaptations that can be made to the current intrusion detection process which may allow detection of these new attacks.

Payload Analysis. The first method analyzes the payload of the attack. Every attack can be divided into the exploit and payload, and every payload can be broken down into a NOP sled, shellcode and return address. This new evasion technique includes additional shellcode which forges a server response. These modifications may be enough for an automated process to detect this attack.

If an IDS can extract the payload, then it might be possible to analyze the payload and determine its behavior; however, several factors stand in the way of analyzing a payload. Attackers encode payloads before sending them, so before an IDS can examine the original payload, it must be decoded and the shellcode must be separated from the NOP sled and return addresses. The next pitfall when interpreting the effects of a specific shellcode is obfuscation. Modern attacks use code obfuscation and polymorphism to make reverse engineering and signature analysis nearly impossible [32]. There are techniques for dealing with obfuscated code, but these take considerable time and expertise. All of these requirements make decoding a payload burdensome and impractical.

Payload size analysis is an alternative measure which IDSs may undertake to determine the effects of a payload. Previous research has shown that anomalous behavior may be determined by simply inspecting the size of packets [33]. Subsequent research suggests identifying the type of attack based on payload size [16]. This research has found that only payloads with a certain size are capable of generating a forged response; however, it is more accurate to say that only shellcodes of a sufficient size can generate forged responses. In this experiment, the size of the buffer overflow payloads were unaffected by the type of shellcode used. The payloads were a constant size determined by the constraints of the specific buffer overflow exploit. The shellcodes capable of forging server responses are larger than most simple shellcodes; however, this only means that there are fewer NOPs at the beginning of the payload. Therefore, payload size analysis really becomes shellcode size analysis and faces similar, decoding hurdles as payload code analysis discussed above.

Catalog Vulnerabilities and Responses. Another possible solution to this attack involves cataloging vulnerabilities and their responses. While this research examined a small subset of the Linux vulnerabilities, general patterns still emerged. Three characteristics necessary for a vulnerability to be susceptible to server response forging were outlined above. This included a constant patched-server response which differs from a vulnerable-server response and a lack of evidence suggesting an exploit has occurred. The process of analyzing every vulnerability to determine if it meets the criteria for this attack would be time consuming, but it may also provide the verification process with valuable information.

Analyst Awareness. This type of evasion attack exemplifies the importance of analysis and verification in the overall intrusion detection process. Improved analyst awareness may be the most effective defense against such an attack. Automated alert verification may alleviate some of the burden for the analyst, but it also incurs new vulnerabilities. Increasing the contextual awareness of these devices may help. System configurations and patch levels must be collected and monitored on all networked machines. This data collection will be time consuming and difficult for large organizations; however, NIDSs would then be able to compare the vulnerability information with the detected attack to determine the success of the intrusion.

Ultimately, the responsibility for network security and intrusion detection comes down to the person behind the systems. Automated alert verification may help with handling the overwhelming task of sorting through alerts, but it is most likely not the "holy grail" of intrusion detection. System administrators and security personnel must be aware of new attacks and stay current on their training. The field of intrusion detection is extremely important and constantly changing, and the people behind the machines must remain aware of new advances and make sure their systems are not at risk.

5   Conclusions

This research examined the final step in intrusion detection, alert verification, as a source of vulnerability. Previous studies concluded that alert verification relies on server responses to determine the success of an attack, and this research has shown that these server responses may be forged within the Linux environment. This type of attack ignores the technical aspect of detection and simply tries to evade the analysis and verification process. Server responses cannot be used as a trusted method for analyzing attacks. Analysis is an important part of intrusion detection and the security of corporate and government networks. These new evasion techniques mean current network defense strategies and IDSs must be reevaluated and improved.

6 Future Work

This research has exposed a vulnerability in the intrusion detection process. Now evasion techniques not only target the technical aspects of intrusion detection but also the verification part. Research experiments have shown two of four vulnerabilities to be susceptible and provided shellcodes capable of exploiting these weaknesses. This work has opened some avenues for future work including:

1. Increasing the scope of tested exploits and Linux distributions.
2. Generating a catalog of all the server responses to aid in forging and/or detection.
3. Identifying other flaws in the intrusion detection process, possibly also involving the human analyst.
4. Adapting current intrusion detection methodology to account for these attacks and other weaknesses in the analysis portion of the process.

Acknowledgments

The authors wish to express their gratitude to the RAID reviewers for their insightful comments to strengthen the paper. Special thanks to Andreas Wespi for quick turn responses and "shepherding" our efforts. This work was sponsored by the Sensors Directorate of the United States Air Force Research Laboratory.

References

1. Intrusion-detection System: Wikipedia: The Free Encyclopedia (2006), http://en.wikipedia.org/wiki/Intrusion_Detection_System
2. Ptacek, T.H., Newsham, T.N.: Insertion, evasion, and denial of service: Eluding network intrusion detection. Secure Networks, Inc. (January 1998)
3. Del Carlo, C., et al.: Intrusion detection evasion (2003)
4. Snort Documentation (2006), http://www.snort.org/docs/
5. Axelsson, S.: Intrusion detection systems: A survey and taxonomy. Chalmers University (March 2000)
6. Lindqvist, U., Porras, P.A.: Detecting computer and network misuse through the Production-Based Expert System Toolset(P-BEST). Doktorsavhandlingar vid Chalmers Tekniska Hogskola, pp. 161-189 (1999)
7. Sommer, R., Paxson, V.: Enhancing byte-level network intrusion detection signatures with context. In: Proceedings of the 10th ACM conference on Computer and communication security, pp. 262–271. ACM Press, New York (2003)

8. Zanero, S., Savaresi, S.M.: Unsupervised learning techniques for an intrusion detection system. In: Proceedings of the 2004 ACM symposium on Applied computing, pp. 412–419. ACM Press, New York (2004)
9. Chebrolu, S., Abraham, A., Thomas, J.: Feature Deduction and Ensemble Design of Intrusion Detection Systems. Computers and Security, Elsevier Science (2005)
10. Kruegel, C., Robertson, W.: Alert Verification: Determining the Success of Intrusion Attempts. In: Proc. First Workshop the Detection of Intrusions and Malware and Vulnerability Assessment (DIMVA 2004) (July 2004)
11. Valeur, F., et al.: Comprehensive approach to intrusion detection alert correlation. IEEE Transactions on Dependable and Secure Computing 1(3), 146–169 (2004)
12. Zhou, J., Carlson, A.J., Bishop, M.: Verify Results of Network Intrusion Alerts Using Lightweight Protocol Analysis. In: Computer Security Applications Conference, 21st Annual, pp. 117–126 (2005)
13. Kruegel, C., et al.: Polymorphic worm detection using structural information of executables. In: Valdes, A., Zamboni, D. (eds.) RAID 2005. LNCS, vol. 3858, Springer, Heidelberg (2006)
14. Timm, K.: IDS Evasion Techniques and Tactics. SecurityFocus (Infocus) 7 (2002)
15. Wagner, D., Soto, P.: Mimicry attacks on host-based intrusion detection systems. In: Proceedings of the 9th ACM conference on Computer and communications security, pp. 255–264. ACM Press, New York (2002)
16. Chaboya, D.J., Raines, R.A., Baldwin, R.O., Mullins, B.E.: Network Intrusion Detection Systems Evasion Techniques and Solutions. IEEE Security and Privacy 4(6), 36–43 (2006)
17. Fedora User Documentation (2006), http://fedora.redhat.com/docs/
18. The Top Ten Distributions: A Beginner's Guide to Choosing a (Linux) Distribution (2006), http://distrowatch.com/dwres.php?resource=major
19. Metasploit Framework User Guide (2005), http://www.metasploit.com/projects/Framework/docs/userguide.pdf
20. Lamping, U., Sharpe, R., Warnicke, E.: Ethereal User's Guide (2005), http://www.ethereal.com/docs/eug_html_chunked/
21. Workstation 5: Powerful Virtual Machine Software for the Technical Professional (2006), http://www.vmware.com/pdf/ws55_manual.pdf
22. Samba Fragment Reassembly Overflow: Open Source Vulnerability Database (2004), http://www.osvdb.org/6323
23. GNU Mailutils imap4d Server Client Command Format String: Open Source Vulnerability Database (2005), http://www.osvdb.org/16857
24. PoPToP PPTP Negative Read Overflow: Open Source Vulnerability Database (2005), http://www.osvdb.org/3293
25. Samba call_trans2open() Function Overflow: Open Source Vulnerability Database (2005), http://www.osvdb.org/4469
26. Jacobson, V., Leres, C., McCanne, S.: PCAP (2003), http://www.tcpdump.org/pcap/pcap.html
27. Linux Shellcode (2007), http://www.metasploit.com/shellcode_linux.html
28. UNIX Assembly Codes Development for Vulnerabilities Illustration Purposes (2001), http://lsd-pl.net/projects/asmcodes.zip
29. Chong, S.K.: History and Advances in Windows Shellcode. Phrack (2004)
30. Kuperman, B.A., et al.: "Detection and prevention of stack buffer overflow attacks. Communications of the ACM 48(11), 50–56 (2005)
31. Current Exploits (2007), http://metasploit.com/projects/Framework/exploits.html

32. Polychronakis, M., Anagnostakis, K.G., Markatos, E.P.: Network-Level Polymorphic Shellcode Detection Using Emulation. In: Büschkes, R., Laskov, P. (eds.) DIMVA 2006. LNCS, vol. 4064, Springer, Heidelberg (2006)
33. Mahoney, M.: Network Traffic Anomaly Detection Based on Packet Bytes. In: Proc. ACM-SAC, pp. 346–350 (2003)

Hit-List Worm Detection and Bot Identification in Large Networks Using Protocol Graphs

M. Patrick Collins[1] and Michael K. Reiter[2]

[1] CERT/Network Situational Awareness, Software Engineering Institute,
Carnegie Mellon University
mcollins@cert.org
[2] Department of Computer Science, University of North Carolina
at Chapel Hill
reiter@cs.unc.edu

Abstract. We present a novel method for detecting hit-list worms using *protocol graphs*. In a protocol graph, a vertex represents a single IP address, and an edge represents communications between those addresses using a specific protocol (e.g., HTTP). We show that the protocol graphs of four diverse and representative protocols (HTTP, FTP, SMTP, and Oracle), as constructed from monitoring for fixed durations on a large intercontinental network, exhibit stable graph sizes and largest connected component sizes. Moreover, we demonstrate that worm propagations, even of a sophisticated hit-list variety in which the attacker has advance knowledge of his targets and always connects successfully, perturb these properties. We demonstrate that these properties can be monitored very efficiently even in very large networks, giving rise to a viable and novel approach for worm detection. We also demonstrate extensions by which the attacking hosts (bots) can be identified with high accuracy.

Keywords: Graph analysis, Anomaly detection, Large networks.

1 Introduction

Large numbers of Internet worms have prompted researchers to develop a variety of anomaly-based approaches to detect these attacks. Examples include monitoring the number of failed connection attempts by a host (e.g., [5,16,27]), or the connection rate of a host to new targets (e.g., [24,19,17]). These systems are designed to detect abnormally frequent connections and often rely on evidence of connection failure, such as half-open TCP connections. To avoid detection by these systems, an attacker can use a *hit list* [20] generated previous to the attack or generated by another party [3]. An attacker using an accurate hit list contacts only targets known to be running an accessible server, and therefore will not trigger an alarm predicated on connection failure. By constraining the number of attack connections initiated by each attacker-controlled *bot*, the attacker could compromise targets while evading detection by most (if not all) techniques that monitor the behavior of individual hosts or rely on connection failures.

C. Kruegel, R. Lippmann, and A. Clark (Eds.): RAID 2007, LNCS 4637, pp. 276–295, 2007.

In this paper, we propose a new detection method, based on monitoring *protocol graphs*. A protocol graph is a representation of a traffic log for a single protocol. In this graph, the vertices represent the IP addresses used as clients or servers for a particular protocol (e.g., FTP), and the edges represent communication between those addresses. We expect that a protocol graph will have properties that derive from its underlying protocol's design and use. For example, we expect that since Oracle communications require password authentication and HTTP interactions do not, a protocol graph representing Oracle will have more connected components than a protocol graph representing HTTP, though the HTTP graph's connected components will likely be larger.

Our detection approach focuses on two graph properties: the number of vertices comprising the graph ("graph size") and the number of vertices in the largest connected component of the graph ("largest component size") for traffic logs collected in a fixed duration. We hypothesize that while an attacker may have a hit list identifying servers within a network, he will not have accurate information about the activity or audience for those servers. As a consequence, a hit-list attack will either artificially inflate the number of vertices in a protocol graph, or it will connect disjoint components, resulting in a greater than expected largest component size.

To test this, we examine protocol graphs generated from traffic of several common protocols as observed in a large (larger than a /8) network. Specifically, we examine HTTP, SMTP, Oracle and FTP. Using this data, we confirm that protocol graphs for these protocols have predictable graph and largest component sizes. We then inject synthetic hit-list attacks into the network, launched from one or more attacker-controlled bots, to determine if these attacks detectably modify either graph size or largest component size of the observed protocol graphs. The results of our study indicate that monitoring graph size and particularly largest component size is an effective means of hit-list worm detection for a wide range of attack parameters and protocols. For example, if tuned to yield one false alarm per day, our techniques reliably detect aggressive hit-list attacks and detect even moderate hit-list attacks with regularity, whether from one or many attacker-controlled bots.

Once an alarm is raised, an important component of diagnosis is determining which of the vertices in the graph represent bots. We show how to use protocol graphs to achieve this by measuring the *number* of connected components resulting from the removal of high-degree vertices in the graph. We demonstrate through extensions to our analysis that we can identify bots with a high degree of accuracy for FTP, SMTP and HTTP, and with somewhat less (though still useful) accuracy for Oracle. We also show that our bot identification accuracy exceeds what can be achieved by examining vertex degree alone.

While there are many conceivable measures of a protocol graph that might be useful for detecting worms, any such measure must be efficient to monitor if detection is to occur in near-real-time. The graph size and largest component size are very advantageous in this respect, in that they admit very efficient computation via well-known *union-find* algorithms (see [7]). A union-find algorithm implements a collection of disjoint sets of elements supporting two operations: two sets in the collection can be merged (union), and the set containing a particular element can be located (find). In our application, the elements of sets are IP addresses, and the sets are the connected components of the protocol graph. As such, when a new communication record is observed, the set containing each endpoint is located (two find operations) and, if these two sets are distinct, they can be merged (a union operation). Using well-known techniques, communication records can be processed in amortized time that is effectively a small constant per communication record, and in space proportional to the number of IP addresses observed. By comparison, detection approaches that track connection rates to new targets (e.g., [24,17]) require space proportional to the number of unique connections observed, which can far exceed the number of unique IP addresses observed. While our attacker identification that is performed following an alarm incurs costs similar to these prior techniques, we emphasize that it can be proceed simultaneously with reactive defenses being deployed and so need not be as time-critical as detection itself.

To summarize, the contributions of our paper include (i) defining protocol graphs and detailing their use as a hit-list attack detection technique; (ii) demonstrating through trace-driven analysis on a large network that this technique is effective for detecting hit-list attacks; (iii) extending protocol graph analysis to infer the locations of bots when hit-list worms are detected; and (iv) describing efficient algorithms by which worm detection and bot identification can be performed, in particular with detection being even more efficient than techniques that focus on localized behavior of hosts.

Our paper proceeds as follows. Section 2 summarizes previous relevant work. Section 3 describes protocol graphs and the data we use in our analysis. Section 4 examines the size of graphs and their largest components under normal circumstances, and introduces our anomaly detection technique. In Section 5, we test our technique through simulated hit-list attacks. We extend our approach to identify attackers in Section 6. Section 7 addresses implementation issues. Section 8 summarizes our results and discusses ongoing and future research.

2   Previous Work

Several intrusion-detection and protocol-identification systems have used graph-based communication models. Numerous visualization tools (e.g., [12,26,25]) present various attributes of communication graphs for visual inspection. Staniford et al.'s GrIDS system [21] generates graphs describing communications between IP addresses or more abstract entities within a network, such as the computers comprising a department. A more recent implementation of this approach by Ellis et al. [6] has been used for worm detection. Karagiannis at al. [9] develop a graphical traffic profiling system called BLINC for identifying applications from their traffic. Stolfo et al.'s [22] Email Mining Toolkit develops graphical representations of email communications and uses them to detect email viruses and worms.

In all of these cases, the systems detect (or pesent data to a human to detect) phenomena of interest based primarily on localized (e.g., per-vertex or vertex neighborhood) properties of the graph. GrIDS generates rules describing how internal departments or organizations communicate, and can develop threshold rules (e.g., "trigger an alarm if the vertex has degree more than 20"). Ellis' approach uses combinations of *link predicates* to identify a host's behavior. Karagiannis' approach expresses these same communications using subgraph models called *graphlets*. Stolfo et al.'s approach identifies *cliques* per user, to whom the user has been observed sending the same email, and flags emails that span multiple cliques as potentially containing a virus or worm. In comparison to these efforts, our work focuses on aggregate graph behavior (graph size and largest component size) as opposed to localized properties of the graph or individual vertices. Moreover, some of these approaches utilize more protocol semantics (e.g., the event of sending an email to multiple users [22], or the expected communication patters of an application [9]) that we do not consider here in the interest of both generality and efficiency.

Several empirical studies have attempted to map out the structure of application networks. Such studies of which we are aware have been conducted by actively crawling the application network in a depth- or breadth-first manner, starting from some seed set of known participants. For example, Broder et al. [4] studied web interconnectivity by characterizing the links between pages. Ripeanu et al. [14] and Saroiu et al. [15] similarly conducted such studies of Gnutella and BitTorrent, respectively. Pouwelse et al. [13] use a similar probe and crawl approach to identify BitTorrent networks over an 8-month period. Our work differs from these in that our techniques are purely passive and are assembled (and evaluated) for the purpose of worm detection.

Our protocol graphs are more closely related to the *call graphs* studied by Aiello et al. [2] in the context of the AT&T voice network. In a call graph, each vertex represents a phone number and each (directed) edge denotes a call placed from one vertex to another. Aiello et al. observe that the size of the largest connected component of observed call graphs is $\Theta(|V|)$, where V denotes the vertices of the graph. These call graphs are similar to our protocol graphs, the primary differences being that call graphs are directed (the protocol graphs we study are undirected) and that they are used to characterize a different domain (telephony, versus data networks here). However, Aiello et al. studied call graphs to understand their basic structure, but not with attention to worm detection (and in fact we are unaware of worms in that domain).

3   Preliminaries

In this section, we investigate the construction and composition of protocol graphs. Protocol graphs are generated from traffic logs; our analyses use CISCO Netflow, but graphs can also be constructed using `tcpdump` data or server logs.

This section is structured as follows. Section 3.1 describes the construction of protocol graphs and our notation for describing them and their properties. Section 3.2 describes our source data.

3.1 Protocol Graphs

We consider a log file (set) $\Lambda = \{\lambda_1, \ldots, \lambda_n\}$ of traffic records. Each record λ has fields for IP addresses, namely source address λ.sip and destination address λ.dip. In addition, λ.server denotes the address of the server in the protocol interaction (λ.server $\in \{\lambda.\text{sip}, \lambda.\text{dip}\}$), though we emphasize that we require λ.server only for evaluation purposes; it is not used in our detection or attacker identification mechanisms.

Given Λ, we define an undirected graph $G(\Lambda) = \langle V(\Lambda), E(\Lambda) \rangle$, where

$$V(\Lambda) = \bigcup_{\lambda \in \Lambda} \{\lambda.\text{sip}, \lambda.\text{dip}\} \qquad E(\Lambda) = \bigcup_{\lambda \in \Lambda} \{(\lambda.\text{sip}, \lambda.\text{dip})\}$$

The largest connected component of a graph $G(\Lambda)$ is denoted $C(\Lambda) \subseteq V(\Lambda)$. Note that by construction, $G(\Lambda)$ has no connected component of size one (i.e., an isolated vertex); all components are of size two or greater.[1]

We denote by Λ_π a log file that is recorded during the interval $\pi \subseteq [00{:}00\text{GMT},$ $23{:}59\text{GMT}]$ on some specified date. We define $\mathcal{V}_\Pi^{\text{dur}}$ and $\mathcal{C}_\Pi^{\text{dur}}$ to be random variables of which $|V(\Lambda_\pi)|$ and $|C(\Lambda_\pi)|$, for logs Λ_π collected in dur-length time intervals $\pi \subseteq \Pi$, are observations. For example, in the following sections we will focus on $\Pi = [00{:}00\text{GMT}, 11{:}59\text{GMT}]$ (denoted am) and $\Pi = [12{:}00\text{GMT},$ $23{:}59\text{GMT}]$ (denoted pm), and take $|V(\Lambda_\pi)|$ and $|C(\Lambda_\pi)|$ with $\pi \subseteq$ am of length 60 seconds (s) as an observation of $\mathcal{V}_{\text{am}}^{60\text{s}}$ and $\mathcal{C}_{\text{am}}^{60\text{s}}$, respectively. We denote the mean and standard deviation of $\mathcal{V}_\Pi^{\text{dur}}$ by $\mu(\mathcal{V}_\Pi^{\text{dur}})$ and $\sigma(\mathcal{V}_\Pi^{\text{dur}})$, respectively, and similarly for $\mathcal{C}_\Pi^{\text{dur}}$.

3.2 Data Set

The source data for these analyses are CISCO Netflow traffic summaries collected on a large (larger than a /8) ISP network. We use collectors at the border of the network's autonomous intranets in order to record the internal and cross border network activity. Therefore, all protocol participants that communicate between intranets or with the Internet are observed. Netflow reports flow logs, where a flow is a sequence of packets with the same addressing information that are closely related in time. Flow data is a compact summary of network traffic and therefore useful for maintaining records of traffic across large networks.

Flow data does not include payload information, and as a result we identify protocol traffic by using port numbers. Given a flow record, we convert it to a log record λ of the type we need by setting λ.server to the IP address that has the corresponding service port; e.g., in a flow involving ports 80 and 3946, the

---

[1] It is possible for various logging mechanisms, under specific circumstances, to record a flow from a host to itself. We eliminate those records for this work.

protocol is assumed to be HTTP and the server is the IP address using port 80. Protocol graphs constructed using log files with payload could look for banners within the payload to identify services.

The protocols used for analysis are listed below.

- HTTP: The HTTP dataset consists of traffic where the source or destination port is port 80 and the other port is ephemeral (≥ 1024). HTTP is the most active protocol on the monitored network, comprising approximately 50% of the total number of bytes crossing the network during the workday.
- SMTP: SMTP consists of TCP traffic where the source or destination port is port 25 and the other port is ephemeral. After HTTP, SMTP is the most active protocol on the monitored network, comprising approximately 30% of the total number of bytes.
- Oracle: The Oracle dataset consists of traffic where one port is 1521 and the other port is ephemeral. While Oracle traffic is a fraction of HTTP and SMTP traffic, it is a business-critical application. More importantly, Oracle connections are password-protected and we expect that as a consequence any single user will have access to a limited number of Oracle servers.
- FTP: The FTP dataset consists of records where one port is either 20 or 21, and the other port is ephemeral. While FTP provides password-based authentication, public FTP servers are still available.

We study these protocols due to their diversity in patterns of activity; e.g., we expect an individual web client to contact multiple web servers, but we expect an individual Oracle client to contact far fewer Oracle servers. That said, this list does not include all protocols that we would like to analyze. A notable omission is peer-to-peer file sharing protocols; we omit these since the monitored network blocks all ports commonly associated with peer-to-peer file-sharing applications (BitTorrent, eDonkey, Kazaa, etc.).

4   Building a Hit-List Worm Detector

In this section we describe the general behavior of protocol graphs over time, and show that the distributions of V_{Π}^{dur} and C_{Π}^{dur} can be satisfactorily modeled as normal for appropriate choices of Π and dur (Section 4.1). The parameters of these distributions change as a function of the protocol (HTTP, SMTP, FTP, Oracle), the interval in which logging occurs (Π), and the duration of log collection (dur). Nevertheless, in all cases the graph and largest component sizes are normally distributed, which enables us to postulate a detection mechanism for hit-list worms and estimate the false alarm rate for any detection threshold (Section 4.2).

4.1   Graph Behavior over Time

Figure 1 is a plot of the observed values of $|V(\Lambda_{\pi})|$ and $|C(\Lambda_{\pi})|$ for Oracle traffic on the monitored network for Monday, March 5th, 2007. Each logging interval

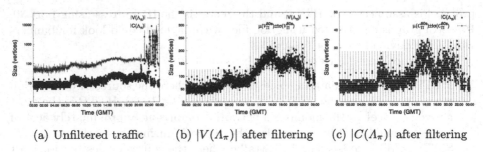

(a) Unfiltered traffic   (b) $|V(\Lambda_\pi)|$ after filtering   (c) $|C(\Lambda_\pi)|$ after filtering

Fig. 1. Oracle traffic on March 5, 2007; start time of π is on x-axis; dur = 60s

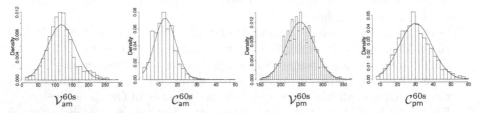

Fig. 2. Distributions for Oracle over March 12–16, 2007, fitted to normal distributions

π begins at a time indicated on the x-axis, and continues for dur = 60s. Traffic between servers internal to the monitored network and their clients (internal or external to the monitored network) was recorded. Plots including external servers show the same business-cycle dependencies and stability. However, we ignore external servers because the vantage point of our monitored network will not allow us to see an external attack on an external server.

Figure 1(a) is plotted logarithmically due to the anomalous activity visible after 18:00GMT. At this time, multiple bots scanned the monitored network for Oracle servers. These types of disruptive events are common to all the training data; we identify and eliminate these scans using Jung et al.'s sequential hypothesis testing method [8]. In this method, scanners are identified when they attempt to connect to servers that are not present within the targeted network. This method will not succeed against hit-list attackers, as a hit-list attacker will only communicate with servers that are present on the network. Figure 1(b)–(c) is a plot of the same activity after the scan events are removed: Figure 1(b) plots $|V(\Lambda_\pi)|$, while Figure 1(c) plots $|C(\Lambda_\pi)|$.

Once scans are removed from the traffic logs, the distribution of traffic can be satisfactorily modeled with normal distributions. More precisely, we divide the day into two intervals, namely am = [00:00GMT, 11:59GMT] and pm = [12:00GMT, 23:59GMT]. For each protocol we consider, we define random variables $\mathcal{V}_{am}^{60s}$ and $\mathcal{V}_{pm}^{60s}$, of which the points on the left and right halves of Figure 1(b) are observations for Oracle, respectively. Similarly, we define random variables $\mathcal{C}_{am}^{60s}$ and $\mathcal{C}_{pm}^{60s}$, of which the points on the left and right halves of Figure 1(c) are observations, respectively. By taking such observations from all of March 12–16, 2007 for each of $\mathcal{V}_{am}^{60s}$, $\mathcal{V}_{pm}^{60s}$, $\mathcal{C}_{am}^{60s}$ and $\mathcal{C}_{pm}^{60s}$, we fit a normal distribution to each effectively; see Figure 2.[2] On the left half of Figure 1(b), we plot $\mu(V_{am}^{60s})$ as a horizontal line and $t\ \sigma(V_{am}^{60s})$ as error bars with $t = 3.5$. We do similarly with $\mu(V_{pm}^{60s})$ and $t\ \sigma(V_{pm}^{60s})$ on the right half, and with $\mu(C_{am}^{60s})$ and $t\ \sigma(C_{am}^{60s})$ and $\mu(C_{pm}^{60s})$ and $t\ \sigma(C_{pm}^{60s})$ on the left and right halves of Figure 1(c), respectively. The choice of $t = 3.5$ will be justified below.

In exactly the same way, we additionally fit normal distributions to V_{am}^{30s}, C_{am}^{30s}, V_{pm}^{30s}, and C_{pm}^{30s} for each protocol, with equally good results. And, of course, we could have selected finer-granularity intervals than half-days (am and pm), resulting in more precise means and standard deviations on, e.g., an hourly basis. Indeed, the tails on the distributions of V_{am}^{60s} and C_{am}^{60s} in Figure 2 are a result of the coarse granularity of our chosen intervals, owing to the increase in activity at 07:00GMT (see Figure 1(b)). We elect to not refine our am and pm intervals here, however, for presentational convenience.

4.2 Detection and the False Alarm Rate

Our detection system is a simple hypothesis testing system; the null hypothesis is that an observed log file Λ does not include a worm propagation. Recall from Section 4.1 that for a fixed interval $\Pi \in \{am, pm\}$, graph size V_{Π}^{dur} and largest component size C_{Π}^{dur} normally distributed with mean and standard deviation $\mu(V_{\Pi}^{dur})$ and $\sigma(C_{\Pi}^{dur})$, respectively. As such, for a dur-length period $\pi \subseteq \Pi$, we raise an alarm for a protocol graph $G(\Lambda_\pi) = \langle V(\Lambda_\pi), E(\Lambda_\pi) \rangle$ if either of the following conditions holds:

$$|V(\Lambda_\pi)| > \mu(V_{\Pi}^{dur}) + t\ \sigma(V_{\Pi}^{dur}) \tag{1}$$

$$|C(\Lambda_\pi)| > \mu(C_{\Pi}^{dur}) + t\ \sigma(C_{\Pi}^{dur}) \tag{2}$$

Recall that for a normally distributed random variable $\mathcal{X}$ with mean $\mu(\mathcal{X})$ and standard deviation $\sigma(\mathcal{X})$,

$$\Pr[\mathcal{X} \leq x] = \frac{1}{2}\left[1 + \operatorname{erf}\left(\frac{x - \mu(\mathcal{X})}{\sigma(\mathcal{X})\sqrt{2}}\right)\right]$$

where $\operatorname{erf}(\cdot)$ is the "error function" [10]. This enables us to compute the contribution of condition (1) to the false rejection (alarm) rate frr for a given threshold t as $1 - \Pr[V_{\Pi}^{dur} \leq \mu(V_{\Pi}^{dur}) + t\ \sigma(V_{\Pi}^{dur})]$, and similarly for the contribution of condition (2) to frr. Conversely, since $\operatorname{erf}^{-1}(\cdot)$ exists, given a desired frr we can compute a threshold t so that our frr is not exceeded:

$$t = \sqrt{2}\ \operatorname{erf}^{-1}\left(\frac{1}{2} - \frac{frr}{2}\right) \tag{3}$$

Note that the use of $\frac{frr}{2}$ in (3) ensures that each of conditions (1) and (2) contribute at most half of the target frr and consequently that both conditions combined will yield at most the target frr.

---

[2] For all protocols, the observed Shapiro-Wilk statistic is in excess of 0.94.

Finally, recall that each Λ_π represents one dur-length time period π, and frr is expressed as a fraction of the log files, or equivalently, dur-length time intervals, in which a false alarm occurs. We can obviously extrapolate this frr to see its implications for false alarms over longer periods of time. For the remainder of this paper, we will take as our goal a false alarm frequency of one per day (with dur = 60s), yielding a threshold of $t = 3.5$. This threshold is chosen simply as a representative value for analysis, and can be adjusted to achieve other false alarm frequencies.

This estimate depends on accurate calculations for $\mu(V_\Pi^{\mathsf{dur}})$, $\mu(C_\Pi^{\mathsf{dur}})$, $\sigma(V_\Pi^{\mathsf{dur}})$, and $\sigma(C_\Pi^{\mathsf{dur}})$ for the time interval Π in which the monitoring occurs. In the remainder of this paper, we will compute these values based on data collected on March 12–16, 2007.

5   Protocol Graph Change During Attack

We showed in Section 4 that, for the protocols examined, $C_{\mathsf{am}}^{\mathsf{dur}}$, $V_{\mathsf{am}}^{\mathsf{dur}}$, $C_{\mathsf{pm}}^{\mathsf{dur}}$ and $V_{\mathsf{pm}}^{\mathsf{dur}}$ are normally distributed (Section 4.1), leading to a method for computing the false alarm rate for any given detection threshold (Section 4.2). In this section, we test the effectiveness of this detection mechanism against simulated hit-list attacks. Section 5.1 describes the model of attack used. Section 5.2 describes the experiment and our evaluation criteria. The detection results of our simulations are discussed in Section 5.3.

5.1   Attack and Defense Model

We simulate hit-list attacks, as described by Staniford et al. [20]. A *hit list* is a list of target servers identified before the actual attack. An apparent example of a

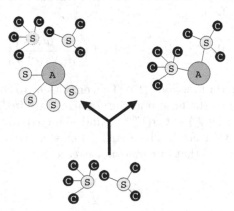

Fig. 3. Illustration of attacks, where "C", "S" and "A" denote a client, server and attacker-controlled bot, respectively. Attack on left affects total graph size ($|V(\Lambda_\pi)|$), and so depicts graph inflation. Attack on right affects largest component size ($|C(\Lambda_\pi)|$), and so depicts component inflation.

hit-list worm is the Witty worm: reports by Shannon and Moore [18] hypothesized that Witty initially spread via a hit list. Further analyses by Kumar et al. [11] identified Witty's "patient zero" and demonstrated that this host behaved in a distinctly different fashion from subsequently-infected Witty hosts, lending support to the theory that patient zero used a hit list to infect targets.

We hypothesize that an attacker who has a hit list for a targeted network will be detectable by examining $|C(\Lambda_\pi)|$ and $|V(\Lambda_\pi)|$ where Λ_π is a log file recorded during a time interval π in which a hit-list worm propagated. We assume that the attacker has the hit list but no knowledge of the targeted servers' current activity or audience. If this is the case, the attacker contacting his hit list will alter the observed protocol graph through *graph inflation* or *component inflation*.

Figure 3 shows how these attacks impact protocol graphs. Graph inflation occurs when an attacker communicates with servers that are not active during the observation period π. When this occurs, the attacker artificially inflates the number of vertices in the graph, resulting in a value of $|V(\Lambda_\pi)|$ that is detectably large. The vertices of a protocol graph include both clients and servers, while the attacker's hit list will be composed exclusively of servers. As a result, we expect that graph inflation will require communicating with many of the hit-list elements (roughly $t\, \sigma(V_\Pi^{\mathsf{dur}})$ for dur-length $\pi \subseteq \Pi$) to trigger condition (1).

Component inflation occurs when the attacker communicates with servers already present in Λ_π during the observation period π. When this occurs, the attacker might merge components in the graph, and $|C(\Lambda_\pi)|$ will then be detectably large. In comparison to graph inflation, component inflation can happen very rapidly; e.g., it may trigger condition (2) if an attacker communicates with only two servers. However, if the graph already has a small number of components (as is the case with SMTP), or the attacker uses multiple bots to attack, then the attack may not be noticed.

5.2   Experiment Construction

The training period for our experiments was March 12–16, 2007. We considered two different values for dur, namely 30s and 60s. Table 1 contains the means and standard deviations for $V_{\mathsf{am}}^{\mathsf{dur}}$, $C_{\mathsf{am}}^{\mathsf{dur}}$, $V_{\mathsf{pm}}^{\mathsf{dur}}$ and $C_{\mathsf{pm}}^{\mathsf{dur}}$ for the training period and for each choice of dur, which are needed to evaluate conditions (1) and (2). As shown in Table 1, the largest components for HTTP and SMTP were close to the total sizes of the protocol graphs on average.

An important point illustrated in Table 1 is that the graph sizes can differ by orders of magnitude depending on the protocol. This demonstrates the primary argument for generating per-protocol graphs: the *standard deviations* in graph size and largest component size for HTTP and SMTP are larger than the mean sizes for Oracle and FTP.

For testing, we model our attack as follows. During a period π, we collect a log ctrl_π of normal traffic. In parallel, the attacker uses a hit-list set HitList to generate its own traffic log attk. This log is merged with ctrl_π to create a new log $\Lambda_\pi = \mathsf{ctrl}_\pi \cup \mathsf{attk}$. We then examine conditions (1) and (2) for interval $\Pi \in \{\mathsf{am}, \mathsf{pm}\}$ such that $\pi \subseteq \Pi$; if either condition is true, then we raise an

Table 1. Means and standard deviations (to three significant digits on standard deviation) for V_{am}^{dur}, C_{am}^{dur}, V_{pm}^{dur} and C_{pm}^{dur} for dur $\in \{30s, 60s\}$ on March 12–16, 2007

r.v.	HTTP		SMTP		Oracle		FTP	
	μ	σ	μ	σ	μ	σ	μ	σ
V_{am}^{30s}	10263	878	2653	357	65.3	18.7	291.9	57.0
C_{am}^{30s}	9502	851	2100	367	17.52	4.00	65.30	8.10
V_{pm}^{30s}	16460	2540	3859	336	128.7	32.4	359.8	67.1
C_{pm}^{30s}	15420	2420	3454	570	30.60	6.28	80.02	8.23
V_{am}^{60s}	14760	1210	4520	634	111.8	28.1	467.4	76.9
C_{am}^{60s}	13940	1180	4069	650	12.92	4.24	37.3	11.3
V_{pm}^{60s}	23280	3480	6540	935	240.3	31.7	555.5	94.8
C_{pm}^{60s}	22140	3320	6200	937	28.84	8.44	45.9	12.2

Table 2. Count of servers observed between 12:00GMT and 13:00GMT on each of March 12–16, 2007

Protocol	Servers
SMTP	2818
HTTP	8145
Oracle	262
FTP	1409

alarm. In our tests, we select periods π of length dur from March 19, 2007, i.e., the next business day after the training period.

To generate the HitList sets, we intersect the sets of servers which are observed as active on each of March 12–16, 2007 between 12:00GMT and 13:00GMT. The numbers of servers so observed are shown in Table 2. The attacker attacks the network over a protocol by selecting hitListPerc percentage of these servers (for the corresponding protocol) at random to form HitList. The attacker (or rather, his bots) then contacts each element of HitList to generate the log file attk.

More precisely, we allow the attacker to use multiple bots in the attack; let bots denote the bots used by the attacker. bots do not appear in the log $ctrl_\pi$, so as to decrease chances of triggering condition (2). Each bot $bot_i \in$ bots is assigned a hit list $HitList_i$ consisting of a random $\frac{|HitList|}{|bots|}$ fraction of HitList. Each bot's hit list is drawn randomly from HitList, but hit lists do not intersect. That is, $\bigcup_i HitList_i =$ HitList and for $i \neq j$, $HitList_i \cap HitList_j = \emptyset$. By employing hit lists that do not intersect, we again decrease the chances of triggering condition (2). attk is generated by creating synthetic attack records from each bot_i to all members of $HitList_i$. In our simulations, members of $HitList_i$ do not participate in the attack after being contacted by bot_i; i.e., each $\lambda \in$ attk is initiated by a member of bots. That said, this restriction is largely irrelevant to our results, since neither $|V(\Lambda_\pi)|$ nor $|C(\Lambda_\pi)|$ is sensitive to whether a member of $HitList_i$ is contacted by another member of $HitList_i$ (after it is "infected") or by bot_i itself.

5.3   True Alarms

Table 3 shows the effectiveness of the detection mechanism as a function of dur for different hitListPerc values. hitListPerc varies between 25% and 100%. The value in each cell is the percentage of attacks that were detected by the system.

Table 3 sheds light on the effectiveness of our approach. The most aggressive worms we considered, namely those that contacted hitListPerc $\geq$ 75% of known servers (see Table 2) within dur = 30s, were easily detected: our tests detected these worms more than 90% of the time for all protocols and all numbers of |bots|, and at least 95% of the time except in one case.

The table also sheds light on approaches an adversary might take to make his worm more stealthy. First, the adversary might decrease hitListPerc. While this does impact detection, our detection capability is still useful: e.g., as hitListPerc is decreased to 50% in dur = 30s, the true detection rates drop, but remain 80% or higher for all protocols except SMTP. Second, the adversary might increase dur. If the adversary keeps hitListPerc $\geq$ 75%, then increasing dur from 30s to 60s appears to have no detrimental effect on the true alarm rate of the detector for HTTP, Oracle or FTP, and it remains at 60% or higher for SMTP, as well.

Third, the adversary might increase |bots|. Note that whereas the previous two attempts to evade detection necessarily slow the worm propagation, increasing |bots| while keeping hitListPerc and dur fixed need not—though it obviously requires the adversary to have compromised more hosts prior to launching his hit-list worm. Intuitively, increasing |bots| might decrease the likelihood of detection by our technique by reducing the probability that one bot_i will merge components of the graph and thereby trigger condition (2). (Recall that bots' individual hit lists do not intersect.) However, Table 3 suggests that in many cases this is ineffective unless the adversary simultaneously decreases hitListPerc: with hitListPerc $\geq$ 75%, all true detection rates with |bots| = 5 remain above 92% with the exception of SMTP (at 60% for dur = 60s). The effects of increasing |bots| may become more pronounced with larger numbers, though if |bots| approaches $t\, \sigma(\mathcal{V}_{II}^{dur})$ then the attacker risks being detected by condition (1) immediately.

Table 3. True alarm percentages for combined detector (conditions (1) and (2))

		HTTP				SMTP				Oracle				FTP			
		hitListPerc =				hitListPerc =				hitListPerc =				hitListPerc =			
dur	bots	25	50	75	100	25	50	75	100	25	50	75	100	25	50	75	100
30s	1	73	80	95	100	28	74	100	100	100	100	100	100	100	100	100	100
	3	72	80	95	100	25	50	97	100	33	95	100	100	100	100	100	100
	5	60	80	92	100	23	45	98	100	16	87	99	100	100	100	100	100
60s	1	68	80	100	100	20	50	70	80	100	100	100	100	100	100	100	100
	3	65	68	100	100	10	35	65	70	28	100	100	100	100	100	100	100
	5	65	63	100	100	5	30	60	55	12	100	100	100	100	100	100	100

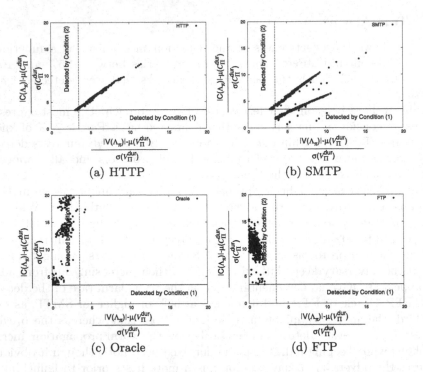

Fig. 4. Contributions of conditions (1) and (2) to true alarms in Table 3. For clarity, only true alarms where $\frac{|V(\Lambda_\pi)| - \mu(\mathcal{V}_\Pi^{dur})}{\sigma(\mathcal{V}_\Pi^{dur})} \leq 20$ or $\frac{|C(\Lambda_\pi)| - \mu(\mathcal{C}_\Pi^{dur})}{\sigma(\mathcal{C}_\Pi^{dur})} \leq 20$ are plotted.

Figure 4 compares the effectiveness of conditions (1) and (2) for each of the test protocols. Each plot in this figure is a scatter plot comparing the deviation of $|C(\Lambda_\pi)|$ against the deviation of $|V(\Lambda_\pi)|$ during attacks. Specifically, values on the horizontal axis are $(|V(\Lambda_\pi)| - \mu(\mathcal{V}_\Pi^{dur}))/\sigma(\mathcal{V}_\Pi^{dur})$, and values on the vertical axis are $(|C(\Lambda_\pi)| - \mu(\mathcal{C}_\Pi^{dur}))/\sigma(\mathcal{C}_\Pi^{dur})$, for $\Pi \supseteq \pi$. The points on the scatter plot represent the true alarms summarized in Table 3, though for presentational convenience only those true alarms where $(|V(\Lambda_\pi)| - \mu(\mathcal{V}_\Pi^{dur}))/\sigma(\mathcal{V}_\Pi^{dur}) \leq 20$ or $(|C(\Lambda_\pi)| - \mu(\mathcal{C}_\Pi^{dur}))/\sigma(\mathcal{C}_\Pi^{dur}) \leq 20$ are shown. Each plot has reference lines at $t = 3.5$ on the horizontal and vertical axes to indicate the trigger point for each detection mechanism. That is, a "•" above the horizontal $t = 3.5$ line indicates a test in which condition (2) was met, and a "•" to the right of the vertical $t = 3.5$ line indicates a test in which condition (1) was met.

We would expect that if both conditions were effectively equivalent, then every "•" would be in the upper right "quadrant" of each graph. HTTP (Figure 4(a)) shows this behavior, owing to the fact that in HTTP, the largest component size and graph size are nearly the same in average and in standard deviation; see Table 1. As such, each bot contacts only the largest component with high probability, and so adds to the largest component all nodes that it also adds to the graph. A similar phenomenon occurs with SMTP (Figure 4(b)), though with different scales in am and pm, yielding the two distinct patterns shown

there. However, the other graphs demonstrate different behaviors. Figure 4(c)
and (d) shows that the growth of $|C(\Lambda_\pi)|$ is an effective mechanism for detecting
disruptions in both Oracle and FTP networks. The only protocol where graph
inflation appears to be a more potent indicator than component inflation is
SMTP. From this, we conclude that component inflation (condition (2)) is a
more potent detector than graph inflation (condition (1)) when the protocol's
graph structure is disjoint, but that each test has a role to play in detecting
attacks.

6   Bot Identification

Once an attack is detected, individual attackers (bots) are identifiable by how
they deform the protocol graph. As discussed in Section 5.1, we expect a bot to
impact the graph's structure by connecting otherwise disjoint components. We
therefore expect that removing a bot from a graph $G(\Lambda)$ will separate components and so the number of connected components will increase.

To test this hypothesis, we consider the effect of removing all records λ involving an individual IP address from Λ. Specifically, for a log file Λ and an IP
address v, define:

$$\Lambda^{\neg v} = \{\lambda \in \Lambda : \lambda.\text{sip} \neq v \wedge \lambda.\text{dip} \neq v\}$$

As such, $G(\Lambda)$ differs from $G(\Lambda^{\neg v})$ in that the latter includes neither v nor any
$v' \in V(\Lambda)$ of degree one that is adjacent only to v in $G(\Lambda)$.

In order to detect a bot, we are primarily interested in comparing $G(\Lambda)$ and
$G(\Lambda^{\neg v})$ for vertices v of high degree in $G(\Lambda)$, based on the intuition that bots
should have high degree. Figure 5 examines the impact of eliminating each of
the ten highest-degree vertices v in $G(\Lambda)$ from each log file Λ for FTP discussed
in Section 5 that resulted in a true alarm. Specifically:

- Figure 5(a) represents $|V(\Lambda^{\neg v})| - |V(\Lambda)|$, i.e., the difference in the number
  of vertices due to eliminating v and all isolated neighbors, which will be
  negative;
- Figure 5(b) represents $|C(\Lambda^{\neg v})| - |C(\Lambda)|$, i.e., the difference in the size of the
  largest connected component due to eliminating v and all isolated neighbors,
  which can be negative or zero; and
- Figure 5(c) represents $|K(\Lambda^{\neg v})| - |K(\Lambda)|$, i.e., the difference in the number
  of connected components due to eliminating v and all isolated neighbors,
  which can be positive, zero, or -1 if eliminating v and its isolated neighbors
  eliminates an entire connected component.

Each boxplot separates the cases in which v is a bot (right) or is not a bot
(left). In each case, five horizontal lines from bottom to top mark the minimum, first quartile, median, third quartile and maximum values, with the lines
for the first and third quartiles making a "box" that includes the median line.
The five horizontal lines and the box are evident, e.g., in the "bot" boxplot in

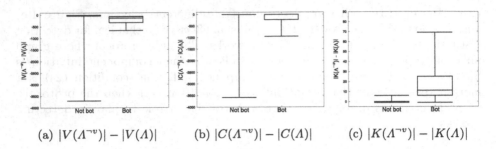

(a) $|V(\Lambda^{\neg v})| - |V(\Lambda)|$ (b) $|C(\Lambda^{\neg v})| - |C(\Lambda)|$ (c) $|K(\Lambda^{\neg v})| - |K(\Lambda)|$

Fig. 5. Effects of eliminating high degree vertices v from FTP attack traffic logs Λ

Figure 5(c). However, because some horizontal lines are on top of one another in other boxplots, the five lines or the box is not evident in all cases.

This figure shows a strong dichotomy between the two graph parameters used for detection (graph size and largest component size) and the number of components. As shown in Figures 5(a) and 5(b), the impact of eliminating bots and the impact of eliminating other vertices largely overlap, for either graph size or largest component size. In comparison, eliminating bots has a radically different effect on the number of components, as shown in Figure 5(c): when a non-bot vertex is eliminated, the number of components increases a small amount, or sometimes decreases. In contrast, when a bot is eliminated, the number of components *increases* strongly.

Also of note is that the change in the total number of components (Figure 5(c)) is relatively small, and small enough to add little power for attack *detection*. For example, if we were to define a random variable $\mathcal{K}_{pm}^{dur}$ analogous to $\mathcal{V}_{pm}^{dur}$ and $\mathcal{C}_{pm}^{dur}$, and then formulate a worm detection rule analogous to (1) and (2) for component count—i.e., raise an alarm for log file Λ_π where $\pi \in$ pm had duration dur, if $|K(\Lambda_\pi)| > \mu(\mathcal{K}_{pm}^{dur}) + t \; \sigma(\mathcal{K}_{pm}^{dur})$—then roughly 80% of our hit-list attacks within FTP would go undetected by this check. This is because of the large standard deviation of this measure: $\sigma(\mathcal{K}_{pm}^{60s}) \approx 12.5$.

Despite the fact that the number of components does not offer additional power for attack detection, Figure 5(c) suggests that removing a high-degree vertex v from a graph $G(\Lambda)$ on which an alarm has been raised, and checking the number of connected components that result, can provide an effective test to determine whether v is a bot. More specifically, we define the following bot identification test:

$$\mathsf{isbot}_{\Lambda,\theta}(v) = \begin{cases} 1 & \text{if } |K(\Lambda^{\neg v})| - |K(\Lambda)| > \theta \\ 0 & \text{otherwise} \end{cases} \qquad (4)$$

We characterize the quality of this test using ROC curves. Each curve in Figure 6 is a plot of true positive (i.e., bot identification) rate versus false positive rate for one of the protocols we consider and for the simulated hit-list worm attacks discussed in Section 5 that yielded a true alarm with $|\text{bots}| = 5$ (the hardest case in which to find the bots) and hitListPerc $\in \{25\%, 50\%, 75\%\}$. Each

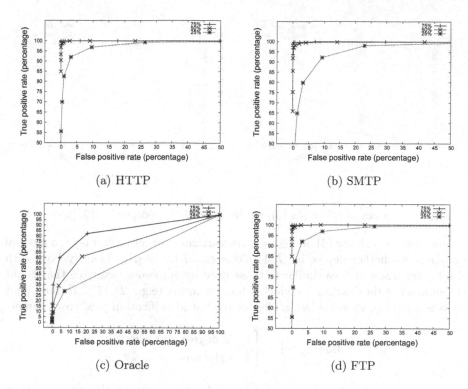

Fig. 6. Attacker identification accuracy of (4); hitListPerc $\in \{25\%, 50\%, 75\%\}$, $|\text{hidegree}| = 10$, $|\text{bots}| = 5$

point on a curve shows the true and false positive rates for a particular setting of θ. More specifically, if hidegree $\subseteq V(\Lambda)$ is a set of highest-degree vertices in $G(\Lambda)$, and if hidegreebots $\subseteq$ hidegree denotes the bots in hidegree, then any point in Figure 6 is defined by

$$\text{true positive rate} = \frac{\sum_{v \in \text{hidegreebots}} \text{isbot}_{\Lambda,\theta}(v)}{|\text{hidegreebots}|}$$

$$\text{false positive rate} = \frac{\sum_{v \in \text{hidegree} \setminus \text{hidegreebots}} \text{isbot}_{\Lambda,\theta}(v)}{|\text{hidegree} \setminus \text{hidegreebots}|}$$

As Figure 6 shows, a more aggressive worm (i.e., as hitListPerc grows) exposes its bots with a greater degree of accuracy in this test, not surprisingly, and the absolute detection accuracy for the most aggressive worms we consider is very good for HTTP, SMTP and FTP. Moreover, while the curves in Figure 6 were calculated with $|\text{hidegree}| = 10$, we have found that the accuracy is very robust to increasing $|\text{hidegree}|$ as high as 100. As such, when identifying bots, it does not appear important to the accuracy of the test that the investigator first accurately estimate the number of bots involved in the attack. We are more thoroughly exploring the sensitivity of (4) to $|\text{hidegree}|$ in ongoing work, however.

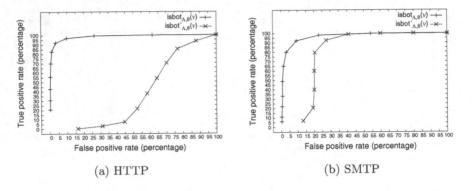

(a) HTTP   (b) SMTP

Fig. 7. Accuracy of (4) versus (5); hitListPerc $= 25\%$, $|\text{hidegree}| = 10$, $|\text{bots}| = 5$

Because we evaluate (4) on high-degree vertices in order to find bots, a natural question is whether degree in $G(\Lambda)$ alone could be used to identify bots with similar accuracy, an idea similar to those used by numerous detectors that count the number of destinations to which a host connects (e.g., [24,17]). To shed light on this question, we consider an alternative bot identification predicate, namely

$$\text{isbot}'_{\Lambda,\theta}(v) = \begin{cases} 1 & \text{if } \text{degree}_\Lambda(v) > \theta \\ 0 & \text{otherwise} \end{cases} \tag{5}$$

where $\text{degree}_\Lambda(v)$ is the degree of v in $G(\Lambda)$, and compare this test to (4) in Figure 7. As this figure shows, using (5) offers much less accurate results in some circumstances, lending support to the notion that our proposal (4) for bot identification is more effective than this alternative.

7   Implementation

Any worm detection system must be efficient to keep up with the high pace of flows observed in some protocols. A strength of our detection approach based on conditions (1) and (2) in Section 4 is that it admits very efficient implementation by well-known *union-find* algorithms [7]. Such an algorithm maintains a collection of disjoint sets, and supports three types of operations on that collection: a `makeset` operation creates a new singleton set containing its argument; a `find` operation locates the set containing its argument; and a `union` operation merges the two sets named in its arguments into one set. The size of each set in the collection can be maintained easily because each set in the collection is disjoint: a new set created by `makeset` has size one, and the set resulting from a `union` is of size the sum of the sizes of the merged sets.

The implementation of a worm detection system using a union-find algorithm is straightforward: for each $\lambda \in \Lambda$, the sets containing λ.sip and λ.dip are located by `find` operations (or created via `makeset` if the address has not yet been observed in Λ), and if these sets are distinct, they are merged by a `union` operation. $|C(\Lambda)|$ is simply the size of the largest set, and $|V(\Lambda)|$ is the sum of the sizes of the sets.

The efficiency of this implementation derives from the use of classic techniques (see [7]). A famous result by Tarjan (see [23]) shows that with these techniques, a log file Λ can be processed in time $O(|\Lambda|\alpha(|V(\Lambda)|))$, where $\alpha(\cdot)$ is the inverse of Ackermann's function $A(\cdot)$, i.e., $\alpha(n) = \arg\min_k : A(k) \geq n$. Due to the rapid growth of $A(k)$ as a function of k (see [1,23]), $\alpha(n) \leq 5$ for any practical value of $|V(\Lambda)|$. So, practically speaking, this algorithm enables the processing of flows with computation only a small constant per flow. Perhaps as importantly, this can be achieved in space $O(|V(\Lambda)|)$. In contrast, accurately tracking the number of unique destinations to which each vertex connects—a component of several other worm detection systems (e.g., [24,17])—requires $\Omega(|E(\Lambda)|)$ space, a potentially much greater cost for large networks. Hence our approach is strikingly efficient while also being an effective detection technique.

Once an alarm is raised for a graph $G(\Lambda) = \langle V(\Lambda), E(\Lambda) \rangle$ due to it violating condition (1) or (2), identifying the bots via the technique of Section 6 requires that we find the high-degree vertices in $V(\Lambda)$, i.e., the vertices that have the most unique neighbors. To our knowledge, the most efficient method to do this amounts to simply building the graph explicitly and counting each vertex's neighbors, which does involve additional overhead, namely $O(|E(\Lambda)|)$ space and $O(|\Lambda| \log(|E(\Lambda)|))$ time in the best algorithm of which we are aware. However, this additional cost must be incurred only after a detection and so can proceed in parallel with other reactive measures, presumably in a somewhat less time-critical fashion or on a more resource-rich platform than detection itself.

8   Conclusion

In this paper, we introduced a novel form of network monitoring technique based on protocol graphs. We demonstrated using logs collected from a very large intercontinental network that the graph and largest component sizes of protocol graphs for representative protocols are stable over time (Section 4.1). We used this observation to postulate tests to detect hit-list worms, and showed how these tests can be tuned to limit false alarms to any desired level (Section 4.2). We also showed that our tests are an effective approach to detecting a range of hit-list attacks (Section 5).

We also examined the problem of identifying the attacker's bots once a detection occurs (Section 6). We demonstrated that the change in the number of connected components caused by removing a vertex from the graph can be an accurate indicator of whether this vertex represents a bot, and specifically can be more accurate than examining merely vertex degrees.

Finally, we examined algorithms for implementing both hit-list worm detection and bot identification using our techniques (Section 7). We found that hit-list worm detection, in particular, can be implemented using more efficient algorithms than many other worm detection approaches, using classic union-find algorithms. For networks of the size we have considered here, such efficiencies are not merely of theoretical interest, but can make the difference between what is practical and what is not. Our bot identification algorithms are of similar performance complexity to prior techniques, but need not be executed on the critical path of detection.

Since a protocol graph captures only the traffic of a single protocol, our detector could be circumvented by a worm that propagates within a variety of different protocols. A natural extension of our techniques for detecting such a worm would be to consider graphs that involve multiple protocols at once, though we have not evaluated this possibility and leave this for future work.

Acknowledgements

We are grateful to Dawn Song for initial discussions on topics related to this paper, and to the anonymous reviewers for comments that helped to improve the paper. This work was supported in part by NSF grant CNS-0433540.

References

1. Aho, A.V., Hopcroft, J.E., Ullman, J.D.: The Design and Analysis of Computer Algorithms. Addison-Wesley, Reading (1975)
2. Aiello, W., Chung, F., Lu, L.: A random graph model for massive graphs. In: Proceedings of the 32nd ACM Symposium on Theory of Computing, pp. 171–180. ACM Press, New York (2000)
3. Antonatos, S., Akritidis, P., Markatos, E.P., Anagnostakis, K.G.: Defending against hitlist worms using network address space randomization. In: WORM '05: Proceedings of the 2005 ACM Workshop on Rapid Malcode, New York, NY, USA, pp. 30–40. ACM Press, New York (2005)
4. Broder, A., Kumar, R., Maghoul, F., Raghavan, P., Rajagopalan, S., Stata, R., Tomkins, A., Wiener, J.: Graph structure in the web. In: Proc. of the WWW9 Conference, Amsterdam, Holland, pp. 309–320 (2000)
5. Chen, S., Tang, Y.: Slowing down Internet worms. In: Proceedings of the 24th International Conference on Distributed Computing Systems, Tokyo, Japan, March 2004, pp. 312–319 (2004)
6. Ellis, D., Aiken, J., McLeod, A., Keppler, D., Amman, P.: Graph-based worm detection on operational enterprise networks. Technical Report MTR-06W0000035, MITRE Corporation (April 2006)
7. Galil, Z., Italiano, G.F.: Data structures and algorithms for disjoint set union problems. ACM Computing Surveys 23, 319–344 (1991)
8. Jung, J., Paxson, V., Berger, A.W., Balakrishnan, H.: Fast portscan detection using sequential hypothesis testing. In: Proceedings of the 2004 IEEE Symposium on Security and Privacy, May 2004, IEEE Computer Society Press, Los Alamitos (2004)
9. Karagiannis, T., Papagiannaki, K., Faloutsos, M.: BLINC: multilevel traffic classification in the dark. In: Proceedings of ACM SIGCOMM '05, New York, NY, USA, pp. 229–240. ACM Press, New York (2005)
10. Kreyszig, E.: Advanced Engineering Mathematics, 9th edn. J. Wiley and Sons, Chichester (2005)

11. Kumar, A., Paxson, V., Weaver, N.: Exploiting underlying structure for detailed reconstruction of an Internet scale event. In: Proceedings of the ACM Internet Measurement Conference, New Orleans, LA, USA, October 2005, ACM Press, New York (2005)
12. Lakkaraju, K., Yurcik, W., Lee, A.: NVisionIP: NetFlow visualizations of system state for security situational awareness. In: Proceedings of the 2004 Workshop on Visualization for Computer Security (October 2006)
13. Pouwelse, J., Garbacki, P., Epema, D., Sips, H.: A measurement study of the BitTorrent peer-to-peer file-sharing system. Technical Report PDS-2004-007, Delft University of Technology (April 2004)
14. Ripeanu, M., Foster, I., Iamnitchi, A.: Mapping the gnutella network: Properties of large-scale peer-to-peer systems and implications for system design. IEEE Internet Computing 6(1) (2002)
15. Saroiu, S., Gummadi, P.K., Gribble, S.D.: A measurement study of peer-to-peer file sharing systems. In: Proceedings of Multimedia Computing and Networking 2002, San Jose, CA, USA (2002)
16. Schechter, S., Jung, J., Berger, A.: Fast detection of scanning worm infections. In: Jonsson, E., Valdes, A., Almgren, M. (eds.) RAID 2004. LNCS, vol. 3224, Springer, Heidelberg (2004)
17. Sekar, V., Xie, Y., Reiter, M.K., Zhang, H.: A multi-resolution approach to worm detection and containment. In: Proceedings of the 2006 International Conference on Dependable Systems and Networks, June 2006, pp. 189–198 (2006)
18. Shannon, C., Moore, D.: The spread of the Witty worm. IEEE Security and Privacy 2(4), 46–50 (2004)
19. Singh, S., Estan, C., Varghese, G., Savage, S.: Automated worm fingerprinting. In: Proceedings of the ACM/USENIX Symposium on Operating System Design and Implementation, December 2005, ACM Press, New York (2005)
20. Staniford, S., Paxson, V., Weaver, N.: How to 0wn the Internet in your spare time. In: Proceedings of the 11th USENIX Security Symposium, August 2002, pp. 149–167 (2002)
21. Staniford-Chen, S., Cheung, S., Crawford, R., Dilger, M., Frank, J., Hoagland, J., Levitt, K., Wee, C., Yip, R., Zerkle, D.: GrIDS – A graph-based intrusion detection system for large networks. In: Proceedings of the 19th National Information Systems Security Conference, pp. 361–370 (1996)
22. Stolfo, S.J., Hershkop, S., Hu, C., Li, W., Nimeskern, O., Wang, K.: Behavior-based modeling and its application to email analysis. ACM Transactions on Internet Technology 6(2), 187–221 (2006)
23. Tarjan, R.E.: Data Structures in Network Algorithms. Regional Conference Series in Applied Mathematics, Society for Industrial and Applied Mathematics, vol. 44 (1983)
24. Twycross, J., Williamson, M.W.: Implementing and testing a virus throttle. In: Proceedings of the 12th USENIX Security Symposium, August 2003, pp. 285–294 (2003)
25. Wright, C., Monrose, F., Masson, G.: Using visual motifs to classify encrypted traffic. In: Proceedings of the 2006 Workshop on Visualization for Computer Security (November 2006)
26. Yin, X., Yurcik, W., Treaster, M.: VisFlowConnect: NetFlow visualizations of link relationships for security situational awareness. In: Proceedings of the 2004 Workshop on Visualization for Computer Security (October 2006)
27. Zou, C., Gao, L., Gong, W., Towsley, D.: Monitoring and early warning for Internet worms. In: Proceedings of the 10th ACM Conference on Computer and Communications Security, New York, NY, USA, pp. 190–199. ACM Press, New York (2003)

SpyShield: Preserving Privacy from Spy Add-Ons

Zhuowei Li, XiaoFeng Wang, and Jong Youl Choi

School of Informatics, Indiana University at Bloomington, USA
{zholi,xw7,jychoi}@indiana.edu

Abstract. Spyware infections are becoming extremely pervasive, posing a grave threat to Internet users' privacy. Control of such an epidemic is increasingly difficult for the existing defense mechanisms, which in many cases rely on detection alone. In this paper, we propose SpyShield, a new *containment* technique, to add another layer of defense against spyware. Our technique can automatically block the visions of untrusted programs in the presence of sensitive information, which preserves users' privacy even after spyware has managed to evade detection. It also enables users to avoid the risks of using free software which could be bundled with surveillance code. As a first step, our design of SpyShield offers general protection against spy add-ons, an important type of spyware. This is achieved through enforcing a set of security policies to the channels an add-on can use to monitor its host application, such as COM interfaces and shared memory, so as to block unauthorized leakage of sensitive information. We prototyped SpyShield under Windows XP to protect Internet Explorer and also evaluated it using real plug-ins. Our experimental study shows that the technique can effectively disrupt spyware surveillance in accordance with security policies and introduce only a small overhead.

1 Introduction

Spyware is rapidly becoming one of the most dangerous threats to the nation's critical information infrastructure. Webroot estimated that about 89 percent of consumer computers are riddled with spyware in this country with an average of 30 pieces per machine [4]. A recent study [19] further shows that a large portion of spyware infections are in the form of add-ons to common software such as Internet Explorer (IE). These add-ons seriously threaten the safety of personal identity information, as they can be used to stealthily collect from users sensitive data such as passwords, credit card numbers and social security numbers.

Add-ons are optional software modules which complement or enhance a software application they are attached to (called a *host application* or simply a *host*). Examples of these modules include Microsoft's plug-ins [1] and Mozilla's extensions [3]. Software manufacturers usually offer standard interfaces for third parties to develop their own add-ons, which we call *add-on interfaces*. Through such interfaces, a spy add-on may acquire sensitive information from the host application or even control it.

The threat posed by spy add-ons is recognized as an important security concern and has recently received great research attentions [19,15]. Existing defense against such spyware heavily relies on detection techniques. Specifically, spyware scanners are used to search binary executables for the presence of binary-pattern signatures which appear

C. Kruegel, R. Lippmann, and A. Clark (Eds.): RAID 2007, LNCS 4637, pp. 296–316, 2007.

in a spyware database. Signature-based detection can be evaded by metamorphic and polymorphic spyware which transforms its code for every new infection. An alternative is behavior-based detection [19] which employs dynamic analysis or static analysis to capture spyware's surveillance activities. Although this technique is more resilient to metamorphism, it could still be got around by the spyware which exhibits unconventional behaviors, for example, direct reading of sensitive data from process memory.

Since no detection techniques are absolutely reliable, we have to consider an in-depth defense strategy: in case a piece of spyware penetrates other layers of defense, protection must still be there to save important information from being stolen. In addition, since surveillance code could be bundled with useful and often free software, it becomes highly desired to enable users to use such software while avoiding the potential risk it brings about. Serving these purposes is the technique of *spyware containment*, which strives to preserve clients' privacy in the presence of malicious surveillance. Existing research on this subject is limited to the techniques which provide a trusted input path for passwords [21,17]. These techniques are inadequate to contain spy add-ons which can also snoop on other important data, for example, the account balance displayed in a browser.

In this paper, we present the first spyware-containment technique which offers general protection against the surveillance from spy add-ons. Our approach, called *SpyShield*, can automatically block the view of an untrusted add-on whenever sensitive data are being accessed by its host application. This is achieved through a proxy which enforces security policies to add-on interfaces. For example, our approach ensures that whenever an IE browser is visiting citi.com, no data can flow through a COM interface into an untrusted plug-in. While it is impossible to get the privacy via COM interfaces, spy add-ons could bypass the proxy through direct memory access. SpyShield addresses the concerns by separating untrusted add-ons from their host's process.

We prototyped SpyShield on Windows XP and evaluated it using known spyware. Our implementation effectively blocked their surveillance attempts in accordance with a set of security policies. We also demonstrate that our technique introduces small performance overheads. We believe that SpyShield advances the state-of-the-art of spyware defense in following perspectives:

- **General protection against spy add-ons.** SpyShield offers the first general avenue to protect sensitive information from untrusted add-ons. Our design works for different add-on interfaces, such as COM and XPCOM [7], and therefore can be used in the applications adopting these interfaces, such as Internet Explorer, Microsoft Outlook, Mozilla Firefox.
- **Fine-grained access control.** We propose a new policy model, called *sensitive zone*. An application enters a sensitive zone whenever it starts processing sensitive data. Inside that zone, our approach allows defining and enforcing fine-grained access policies. For example, we may grant untrusted plug-ins free access to unimportant data on a web page such as advertisements, but forbid them to read and write sensitive data such as passwords.
- **Resilience to attacks.** SpyShield can protect itself from being attacked. It utilizes a lightweight kernel driver to prevent unauthorized modification of the proxy's code

and data, and any attempts to load untrusted code into the kernel of an operating system (OS).
- **Small overheads.** Our research further shows that the overhead of SpyShield, which is mainly caused by cross-process communications, may not be significant enough to be perceived by the user, as it could be overshadowed by the delay for accomplishing an add-on's normal mission.
- **Ease of use.** SpyShield does not require modifying host applications and OS settings. Users do not need to change their behaviors when using it, though they can choose to modify default security polices through a secure and user-friendly interface. SpyShield can also be easily turned off and on.

The rest of the paper is organized as follows. Section 2 presents the design of SpyShield. Section 3 describes our implementation of a prototype system. Section 4 reports the evaluations of our technique. Section 5 discusses its limitations. Section 6 reviews the related approaches and compares them with SpyShield. Section 7 concludes the paper and envisions the future research.

2 Design

SpyShield inserts an access-control proxy between untrusted add-ons and their host application to control their communications according to a set of security policies. Based on the method how to interpose communications, SpyShield can be implemented in two ways: either one-process or two-process solution. While in one-process solution add-ons and the host application coexist inside a same process, SpyShield can separate them into two different processes so that we can put a process barrier to inhibit untrusted add-ons from accessing the memory space of the host application to obtain any sensitive information. Figure 1 illustrates an example using Internet Explorer (IE) as the host application. The proxy in the Figure consists of two components, a *reference controller* in the form of an IE plug-in, and an *add-on manager* serving as an independent process which handles a set of untrusted plug-ins. To these plug-ins, the add-on manager plays the role of an IE browser, which automatically loads them into memory and offers standard COM interfaces to enable them to subscribe to events and ask for information of their interest. Actual invocation of COM interface [31], however, is delegated to the

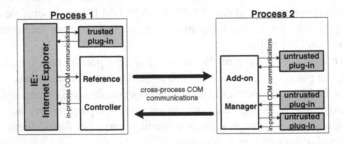

Fig. 1. A containment mechanism for untrusted plug-ins (e.g., BHO, toolbar) in Internet Explorer

reference controller by transporting add-ons' requests through a cross-process communication channel. Upon receiving each request from plug-ins, the reference controller will make a decision regarding whether to forward the request to the browser. The decisions will be based on a set of security policies pre-defined by a user. IE's event or responses should go through the security policy enforced by the reference controller. With this approach, we can prevent a spy plug-in from stealing information through either the COM interfaces or direct access to the browser's memory. An end user, on the other hand, will have more controls of her information by adjusting security policies.

To defeat any attempts from thwarting the access-control proxy, the proxy can be overseen by a kernel driver, called *proxy guardian*, which prevents unauthorized attempts to temper with the proxy's data and code. Although we use IE as an example here, the architecture is general enough to work on other add-on interfaces such as XP-COM [7] and other applications such as Mozilla Firefox.

2.1 Access-Control Proxy

The objective of the access-control proxy is to permit or deny add-ons' access to their host application's data based on security policies. This is achieved through collaborations between the reference controller in the form of an application's add-on, and the add-on manager which hosts untrusted add-ons. After an untrusted add-on is loaded, its request to subscribe to an event is intercepted and recorded by the add-on manager which informs the reference controller to register that event using an event-handling function (called a *callback* function). The occurrence of the event first triggers that function which then decides whether to invoke the add-on and pass to it the parameters received from the application.

Though most spyware add-ons are event-driven, there are exceptions: for example, UCMore [9] toolbar can poll the COM interfaces of an IE browser for the URLs and the web pages visited recently. To contain such spyware, an access-control proxy needs to interpose on all add-on interfaces. In the above example, the add-on manager can implement IWebBrowser2, a COM interface which offers add-ons methods such as get_LocationURL and get_Document for accessing URLs and web pages. This allows the reference controller to block all undesired invocations of these methods.

An add-on may attempt to directly interact with its host application, without going through an add-on interface. For example, a Windows toolbar may requests from a COM interface a handle of a browser's window for directly retrieving its content. In this case, the add-on manager needs to create that window's substitute for the toolbar and selectively copy data to it according to security policies.

An important design issue is the choice between the solution which keeps a host application, the proxy and add-ons inside the same process, and the alternative which separates the add-on manager and untrusted add-ons from the host and the reference controller. The one-process solution gives good performance, which avoids expensive cross-process communications. However, it leaves the door open for the attacks using direct memory access. The two-process solution separates the untrusted add-ons from their host application's process, and therefore eliminates the threat originated from direct memory access. This approach also protects a host application from the add-ons containing security flaws which may crash the application or be exploited by attackers.

Its weakness is performance, which suffers from cross-process communications (CPC). SpyShield allows trusted add-ons to communicate with a host application directly, which serves to limit performance degradation to untrusted add-ons. Selection of right CPC techniques can also reduce such overheads. For example, communication through shared memory is much faster than through pipes.

An important question is how to identify untrusted add-ons. SpyShield offers an automatic mechanism which classifies add-ons according to their hash values. The mechanism includes a database of hash values for trusted add-ons which are computed using a secure hash function such as SHA-256. An add-on is deemed untrusted if its hash cannot be found from the database. The content of the database can be maintained automatically using some heuristic rules: for example, the add-ons directly installed from a CD or signed by a trusted vendor such as Adobe Acrobat are considered to be trusted, while those downloaded from untrusted websites are untrusted. In order to prevent spyware from adding itself into the database, the database is also protected by a kernel driver called *proxy guardian* (Section 2.3). An authorized user is allowed to add in other trusted add-ons after being authenticated by her password and passing a CAPTCHA test [27] which tells humans and programs apart.

2.2 Security Policies

We developed a simple access control model for SpyShield, called *sensitive zone*. An application is said to enter a sensitive zone if it starts to process sensitive data. Within that zone, security policies are used to specify the resources to which an untrusted add-on's access is allowed or denied. If denied, the privacy information within the resources is preserved in the sensitive zone.

Sensitive data can be automatically identified with the metadata generated from users' inputs. For example, the URLs or IP addresses of sensitive websites such as banks are used to indicate the presence of confidential data like passwords and account balances. Other examples include names and directory paths of sensitive documents, email addresses and subjects of sensitive messages and keywords such as "password" within a data record. SpyShield can offer default settings of such metadata, which includes, for example, all banks' URLs. Authorized users are allowed to modify them.

Data imported by a host application are first checked by the reference controller against the metadata to determine whether a sensitive zone has been entered. An affirmative answer triggers the enforcement of a set of policies to restrict untrusted add-ons' access to such data. A security policy can be defined over add-on interfaces, their methods and input parameters to these methods. Table 1 gives example rules, which have controlled malicious IE plug-ins successfully in our expriements.

The security policies of a sensitive zone are applied to all the members in that zone. For example, if we include all banks' URLs in the same zone, the access control proxy will enforce the same set of rules whenever a browser visits any one of them. Flexibility and fine-grained controls can be achieved through multiple zones, which users are allowed to define. SpyShield offers a friendly and application-specific interface for authorized users to define sensitive zones and describe security policies. We present an example in Figure 2.

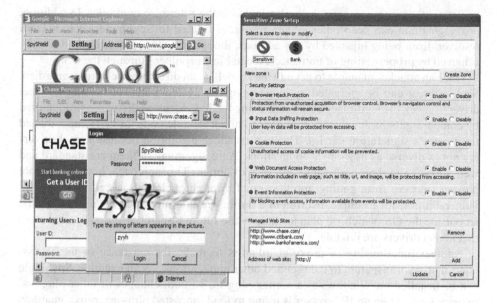

Fig. 2. The SpyShield toolbar

Table 1. Examples of Security Policies

Name	Policy	Comments
Browser rule	IDispatch→Invoke(Event) ↦→decline	Block an IE browser's attempt to trigger untrusted plug-ins through calling the invoke functions of their IDispatch interfaces.
Plug-in rule	IWebBrowser2→get_LocationURL| IWebBrowser2→get_Document| IWebBrowser2→navigate| IWebBrowser2→navigate2 ↦→decline	Block untrusted plug-ins' attempts to access current URLs and documents through calling the member functions get_LocationURL, get_Document, navigate and navigate2 of IWebBrowser2 interface.

2.3 Proxy Guardian

Without proper protection, the access-control proxy is subject to a variety of attacks. For example, a spy add-on may tamper with the proxy's code and data, in particular sensitive zones and the hash database for trusted add-ons. Under some operating systems (OS) such as Windows, an add-on may also be able to read and write the virtual memory of its host application's process through API calls even when it is running inside another process [20]. To defeat these attacks, we developed *proxy guardian*, a kernel monitor to provide kernel-level protection to SpyShield components.

Proxy guardian interposes on the system calls related to file systems (e.g., NtWrite File), auto-start extensibility points (ASEP) [29] such as registry keys (e.g., NtSet ValueKey) and processes (e.g., NtWriteVirtualMemory), which enables it to block the attempts to access the proxy. Specifically, it ensures that only a dedicated uninstaller can remove the proxy's executables and data, and the ASEP for loading it to the memory. The uninstaller itself is also under the protection and can only be activated through both password authentication and a CAPTCHA test. Only the proxy is allowed to change its data. User-mode processes are prevented from accessing a host application's process image which also includes the reference controller. In addition, proxy guardian can keep other system resources related to SpyShield, such as DNS resolver, from being hijacked by spy add-ons, though the same protection can also be achieved by proper setting of untrusted executables' privileges through the OS.

Once an attacker manages to get into the kernel, it can directly attack proxy guardian. Such a threat can be mitigated by intercepting the system calls for loading a kernel driver to check the legitimacy of the code being loaded. A trusted driver can be identified by comparing its hash values with those of known reliable code, or verifying a trusted third party's signature it carries. This is a reasonable solution because kernel drivers are not as diverse as user-mode applications. Actually, many of them are standard and well-known, and their hash values are easy to obtain. This approach, however, cannot prevent spyware from getting into the kernel through exploiting a legitimate driver's vulnerabilities, for example, overrun of a buffer. Countermeasures to this attack must sit outside the OS, which we plan to study in the future research. Here, we just assume that kernel drivers are reliable.

Another functionality of proxy guardian is to make the existence of the access-control proxy transparent to the user and other applications. As an example, SpyShield can be installed on Windows as a normal plug-in, without changes of other plug-ins' registry keys; when an IE browser is trying to load untrusted plug-ins, proxy guardian blocks its system calls and lets the plug-in manager load them instead. This also allows an authorized user to easily turn off the proxy by leaving the loading procedure unchanged. We can further apply the techniques used by kernel-mode rootkits to manipulate the interactions between untrusted add-ons and the OS so as to hide the proxy's process, which protects it from being detected by spyware.

3   Implementation

To study the effectiveness of SpyShield, we implemented a prototype for Internet Explorer under Windows XP using C++. The choice of IE as the host application is due to the fact that the vast majority of known spy add-ons are in the form of IE plug-ins. However, our design is general, which also works for other applications such as Mozilla Firefox. In this section, we first present the technical backgrounds of COM and IE plug-ins, and then describe the details of our implementation.

3.1   IE Plug-in Architecture

COM Interfaces. The Component Object Model (COM) [31] is an extensible object software architecture for building applications and systems from the modular objects supplied by different software vendors. An object is a piece of compiled binary code that exposes some predefined services to COM *clients*, the service recipients. These services are offered through a set of COM interfaces, each of which is a strongly-typed contract between software objects to provide a collection of functions (aka., methods).

COM supports transparent cross-process interoperability which allows a client to communicate with an object regardless of where it is running. This is achieved through a system object encapsulating all the "legwork" associated with finding and launching objects, and managing the communication between them. When a client is accessing an object outside its process, COM creates a "`proxy`" which implements the object's interfaces. The "`proxy`" acts as the object's deputy by forwarding all the function calls from the client, marshalling all parameters if necessary and delivering the outcomes of the calls to the client. The remote process also accommodates a "`stub`" to mediate the communications between the "`proxy`" and the object.

Browser Helper Object and Toolbar. A browser helper object (BHO) is a COM object designed to expand the functionality of IE as a plug-in. A BHO object is required to implement the `IUnknown` interface, `IObjectWithSite` and `IDispatch` if it needs to subscribe to IE events during runtime. A toolbar is also a COM object serving as an IE plug-in. Compared with a BHO, it implements more interfaces to provide more functionalities which include graphics, usually in the form of a tool band, for a richer display and control for user interactions. A toolbar must carry four interfaces, `IUnknown`, `IObjectWithSite`, `IPersistStream` and `IDeskBand`, and may also involve several other interfaces such as `IInputObject` for focus changes of a user input object and `IDispatch` for event subscription and processing.

3.2 The Access-Control Proxy

We implemented SpyShield as an access control proxy for IE plug-ins. The proxy includes a reference controller (RC) and an add-on manager (AM), two proxy components for managing BHOs and toolbars. The reference controller is a special plug-in which serves as both BHO and toolbar. It also contains an access control module to identify the sensitive zone being entered and thus to permit or block function calls originated from the browser and the add-on manager in accordance with security policies. The add-on manager acts on the behalf of the IE browser to provide COM interfaces to the untrusted plug-ins and mediate their communications. During the initialization stage, the browser loads trusted plug-ins and the reference controller only, leaving the task to import untrusted plug-ins to the add-on manager. This is achieved transparently through a kernel driver, which we describe in the next subsection. We implemented both one-process and two-process solutions, though here we only elaborate the second approach in which the add-on manager is running as a separate process.

Each proxy component contains three COM objects, *proxy BHO*, *proxy toolbar* and *proxy browser*. Proxy BHO/toolbar exports the COM interfaces on the plug-in's side to IE browsers and the reference controller. Proxy browser exports the COM interfaces on the browser's side to the add-on manager and untrusted plug-ins. These COM objects work in a collaborative way: for example, if one of them acquires the access to the `IUnknown` interface of an external object such as an IE browser, it passes the pointer of the interface on to the other objects, which enables them to directly interact with that external object. The reference controller uses its proxy BHO/toolbar as the delegate of untrusted plug-ins to interact with browsers, and the add-on manager employs its proxy browser as a substitute for the browsers to communicate with untrusted plug-ins. The other COM objects only serve to exchange parameters and requests with their counterparts in the other proxy object, and therefore are not used in our implementation of the one-process solution.

In the follow-up subsections, we elaborate our implementation of proxy interfaces, cross-process communication and access control mechanism.

Proxy Interfaces. Proxy browser implements a set of COM interfaces that an IE browser uses to accommodate BHOs and toolbars, and proxy BHO/toolbar adopts the interfaces on the plug-in's side. These interfaces 'wrap' their counterparts so as to put access control in place. For example, IE first triggers `Invoke()` within our proxy's `IDispatch` interface in response to the occurrence of an event, which allows it to decide whether to contact the same interface of untrusted plug-ins to activate their callback functions. Another example is an attempt from a plug-in to read the HTML files downloaded by IE, which must go through the proxy's `IWebBrowser2` interface and is therefore subject to its control. The COM objects within our proxy can also simulate the behaviors of the objects they substitute. As an example, our proxy follows IE's handling of the `QueryInterface()` call which does not return to the caller the interface reference of `IInputObjectSite`.

A technical challenge to enforcing access control comes from COM functions' capability to pass interface pointers. Without a proper design, an untrusted plug-in may acquire through our proxy a pointer to an IE browser's interface for directly interacting with that interface, which bypasses access control. Our solution is to detect such an attempt within the proxy's interface functions and returns to the plug-ins the pointers to the substitutes of the requested IE interfaces. This was implemented in the following functions: `QueryInterface()` in Interface `IUnknown`, `QueryService()` in `IServiceProvider`, `get_Document()` in `IWebBrowser2`, and `Invoke()` in `IDispatch`. `QueryInterface()` is the first function queried by plug-ins about other interfaces. `QueryService()` can be used to get the interface pointers of `IWebBrowser2`, `IOleWindow` and `ITravelLogStg`. Of particular interest is `get_Document()`, which returns a pointer to a COM object inside IE containing the documents being downloaded. Our prototype creates a substitute of that object and selectively copies to it the content of documents in conformation with access rules. `Invoke()` adds to the complication by taking an interface pointer of IE's `IDispatch` as part of the input parameters for a plug-in's callback function. Our proxy parses such parameters and modifies the pointer to a local substitute.

Table 2 describes the interfaces that we implemented for the access-control proxy.

Cross-process Communications. As we introduced in Section 3.1, COM provides a mechanism which allows a client to request and receive services from an object running in another process through the interactions between the object's "`proxy`" in the client process and "`stub`" in its own process. This was employed by our implementation of

Table 2. Interfaces implemented in our prototype

COMPONENTS	INTERFACES
Proxy Browser	`IUnknown,` `IWebBrowser2,` `IServiceProvider,` `IOleCommandTarget,` `IInputObjectSite, IOleWindow, IConnectionPointContainer, IConnectionPoint,` `IWebBrowser2, IOleWindow, ITravelLogStg,` `IHTMLDocument2,` `IOleObject,` `IConnectionPointContainer,` `IOleContainer,` `IMarkupServices, ICustomDoc, IOleWindow,`
Proxy BHO	`IUnknown, IObjectWithSite, IDispatch,` `IWebBrowser2,`
Proxy toolbar	`IUnknown,` `IObjectWithSite,` `IDispatch,` `IDeskBand,` `IPersistStream,` `IOleCommandTarget, IInputObject,` `IWebBrowser2`

the two-process solution to achieve cross-process communications (CPC). IE 6 offers the "proxy" and "stub" objects for all interfaces in Table 2 except IInputObject and IInputObjectSite. The problem has been fixed by IE 7 which provides iepro xy.dll to support CPC for both interfaces. Interestingly, we found this DLL can also be used in IE 6. Therefore, our prototype works under both IE versions.

Our two-process solution makes the add-on manager an independent process to accommodate untrusted plug-ins. This design, supported by COM's multi-threaded CPC, helps reduce the overheads of our approach in terms of memory usage: no matter how many IE processes have been launched, the add-on manager always stays in a single process. This is because COM automatically directs a new IE process's request to the existing add-on process which forks a new thread to serve it.

Access Control. The access control component was implemented in the reference controller. Whenever an IE browser visits a new website, the component acquires its URL from the parameters of invoke triggered by the event DISPID_BEFORENAVIGATE2 and compares it with those defining sensitive zones. If the browser is found to be in one of the zones, corresponding security policies are applied. Otherwise, the proxy still needs to check the validity of the URL through a DNS query, as an invalid URL must also be protected to defeat error-page hijacking. Our prototype sets a default zone with the security rules in Table 1. To enforce the browser rule, the access-control proxy blocks IE's calls to untrusted plug-ins' invoke function. The plug-in rule was achieved by blocking the calls to get_LocationURL, get_Document, Navigate and Navigate2 from the add-on manager. In addition, our kernel driver also intercepts and blocks the attempts to directly read or write the browser's virtual memory from another process.

Our prototype allows an authorized party to easily define a new sensitive zone and set security policies. It includes an IE toolbar to indicate the sensitivity of the current website and provide an entrance to policy settings. Through that toolbar, an authorized user can access a friendly user interface (Figure 2) to view and modify existing sensitive zones and their policies, as well as add new ones. The simplest way to define a new zone is just to specify the URL of a sensitive website. The default security policies for a new zone decline all the requests from an untrusted plug-in whenever the browser is visiting that URL. To enable the user to set the policies with finer granularity, the interface offers the options to regulate a variety of channels through which a plug-in can access or even control the browser. For example, if 'Browser Hijack Protection' is enabled, the plug-in will not be allowed to invoke Navigate2 which can be used to hijack the browser; if 'Cookie Protection' is set, the plug-in will be prevented from calling the COM functions such as get_cookie (in IHTMLDocument2) to acquire the cookie(s) associated with the website being visited.

To prevent spyware from tampering with the security policies, our prototype enforces a strict authentication which involves both password and a CAPTCHA. Figure 2 presents a screen snapshot of this mechanism. Such an authentication mechanism will only be invoked for customizing security policies, which is not supposed to happen frequently and therefore should not significantly increase users' burden. The chance for the setting change could be further reduced through careful construction of default zones, which can include the URLs of the sensitive websites, such as online banks.

3.3 Kernel Driver

We implemented proxy guardian as a kernel driver for Windows XP, which is used to prevent the add-on process from directly accessing the IE process, protect access-control data such as security policies and the database for trusted plug-ins from being sabotaged by spyware, and initialize the proxy transparently to avoid changes to IE and the Windows registry. This was achieved using an API hooking technique [26]. Table 3 lists the system calls hooked in our kernel driver.

Table 3. System calls hooked in our kernel driver

CATEGORY	SYSTEM CALL
File system	NtWriteFile, NtDeleteFile, NtSetInformationFile
Registry keys and valuekeys	NtDeleteKey, NtRenameKey, NtReplaceKey, NtRestoreKey, SetInformationKey, NtSetValueKey, NtDeleteValueKey, NtQueryValueKey
Process, thread	NtTerminateProcess, NtTerminateThread
Virtual memory	NtAllocateVirtualMemory, NtReadVirtualMemory, NtWriteVirtualMemory

The kernel driver can block the calls from the add-on process which operates on IE and the reference controller's virtual memory. System calls to modify the proxy's data are permitted only if they come from the proxy's process. The executables and the registry entry of the proxy can only be deleted and changed by an uninstaller, a program which is also protected by the kernel driver and allowed to run by authorized users only. Such users can revise the setting of the kernel driver, for example, specifying which files and processes should be under protection. We did not implement the mechanism to check the drivers to be loaded into the kernel, which can be done by interposing on other system calls.

The kernel driver can also insert our proxy between IE and untrusted plug-ins without altering any OS settings. It classifies the BHOs and toolbars recorded in registry entries[1] according to their hash values to compile a list of CLSIDs for trusted plug-ins. When an IE browser attempts to retrieve a plug-in's registry key, the driver intercepts its system call NtQueryValueKey and extracts the related CLSID. If it is not on the list, the driver removes it from the output of the call and notifies the add-on manager to load the plug-in instead.

4 Evaluations

We evaluated SpyShield using our prototype. Our purpose is to understand the effectiveness of our technique in containing spy add-ons and its overheads. All experiments were conducted on a desktop with Intel Pentium 3.2GHz CPU and 1GB memory. Its software includes Windows XP professional, Internet Explorer 7.0 and a vmware workstation. The effectiveness tests happened inside the virtual machine with a guest OS of

---

[1] Specifically, the registry key for BHOs' CLSIDs is \HKLM\SOFTWARE\Microsoft\Windows\CurrentVersion\Explorer\Browser Helper Objects, two registry keys for toolbars' CLSIDs are \HKLM\SOFTWARE\Microsoft\Internet Explorer\Toolbar and \HKCU\Software\Microsoft\Internet Explorer\Toolbar\WebBrowser

Windows XP professional, and Internet Explorer 6.0. The performance of our prototype was evaluated in the host OS. We elaborate this study in the follow-up subsections.

4.1 Effectiveness

The effectiveness study aims at understanding SpyShield's ability to withstand spyware surveillance, which was achieved from the following perspectives. We first compared spy add-ons' networking behaviors in an unprotected browser with those under our prototype. Such behaviors usually constitute spyware's calling-home activities and contribute to the delivery of stolen data to the perpetrator. Therefore, this study reveals the effectiveness of our technique in preventing leakage of sensitive information. Then, we identified the COM events and calls being blocked by our access-control proxy. This further demonstrates the role SpyShield played in disrupting spyware surveillance, as these events and calls were used by spy add-ons to access sensitive data within an IE.

We evaluated our prototype using nine real BHOs and toolbars which are listed in Table 4. Five of them are spy plug-ins and the rest are legitimate. Under SpyShield, these plug-ins worked properly outside a sensitive zone. This demonstrates that our design does not disrupt plug-ins' legitimate operations. In the experiment, we first installed them to the unprotected IE inside the vmware station, and navigated the IE to access six websites listed in Table 5. In the host OS, we ran Wireshark [5] (aka. Ethereal), a traffic analysis tool, to record all network traffic from the virtual machine. Then, we activated SpyShield and repeated the above experiment.

To identify the network traffic caused by a plug-in, we recorded *baseline*, the network traffic observed while surfing these six websites without any plug-in. We also developed an analysis tool to capture the packets generated by a BHO or a toolbar. This tool classifies packets according to their destination IP addresses: any address outside baseline was deemed as coming from a plug-in. Effective suppression of such traffic within a sensitive zone offers the evidence to the efficacy of our technique.

A problem is that multiple visits of the website with dynamic contents might yield different network traffic. This could mislead our approach into including legitimate packets. We tackled this problem through cleaning the output of the tool against a manually compiled list of legitimate destination IP addresses. On the list were 25 addresses, most of which were from `msn` and `chase`.

We also recorded to a log file all the function calls intercepted by proxy interfaces, which told the story about plug-ins' activities. For example, `Browser Accelerator`

Table 4. BHOs and Toolbars used in our experiments

INDEX	PLUG-IN	TOOLBAR	BHO	TYPE
1	AvenueMedia/Internet Optimizer	No	Yes	Spyware
2	Browser Accelerator	Yes	Yes	Adware
3	eXactSearch Toolbar	Yes	Yes	Adware
4	Mirar Toolbar	Yes	Yes	Adware
5	UCmore	Yes	No	Adware
6	Google Toolbar	Yes	Yes	Normal
7	LostGoggles	No	Yes	Normal
8	Security Software Search Bar 1.01	Yes	Yes	Normal
9	Yahoo! Toolbar	Yes	Yes	Normal

Table 5. Websites used in our experiments. [†]We visited "`http://www.google.com`" to retrieve "*money + saving + account*", keywords interesting to spyware, so as to elicit their networking behaviors. [‡]We also included "`http://an.invalid.url`" in a sensitive zone because it leads to the DNS error page which is intensively used by spy plug-ins to hijack an IE browser.

Alias	URL	Sensitive Zone?
bbc	`http://www.bbc.co.uk`	NO
msn	`http://www.msn.com`	NO
google	`http://www.google.com`	NO[†]
chase	`http://www.chase.com`	YES
citi	`http://www.citi.com`	YES
invalid	`http://an.invalid.url`	YES[‡]

calls `get_Document` to retrieve an HTML document as soon as a browser downloads it; this call was blocked by our proxy when the browser was inside a sensitive zone.

Traffic Differential Analysis. We present in Table 6 and Table 7 the results of our differential analysis of plug-ins' networking behaviors, which demonstrates the effectiveness of SpyShield in suppressing leakage of sensitive information. Both tables report plug-ins' network traffic when an IE browser visiting the URLs in Table 5, with Table 6 for an unprotect IE browser and Table 7 for the browser protected by SpyShield. Among these URLs, the first three were not in a sensitive zone and the rest were.

The tables show that most spy plug-ins produced network traffic while visiting some URLs. In the experiment, we observed that the occurrence of such traffic was contingent on the availability of the information flows from the browser to the plug-ins. Through examining the content of the traffic, we further discovered that in many cases such traffic carried the URLs of the websites being visited. Our prototype controlled the plug-ins' interactions with the browser, which contributed to curbing such traffic inside the sensitive zone. Outside the sensitive zone, the traffic recorded in both tables is identical, which suggests that our prototype did not disrupt the plug-ins' operations. We elaborate our analysis of individual plug-ins' behaviors below.

Table 6. Network traffic from BHOs and toolbars in an unprotected IE browser

Index	Plug-in	bbc	msn	google	Sensitive Zone chase	citi	invalid
1	AvenueMedia/Internet Optimizer	-	-	-	-	-	Exist
2	Browser Accelerator	Exist	Exist	Exist	Exist	Exist	Exist
3	eXactSearch Toolbar	-	-	-	-	-	Exist
4	Mirar Toolbar	Exist	Exist	Exist	Exist	Exist	Exist
5	UCmore	Exist	Exist	Exist	Exist	Exist	Exist

Table 7. Network traffic from BHO/Toolbars under SpyShield. *Only part of the traffic in Table 6 was observed, which is irrelevant to the sensitive websites visited.

Index	Plug-in	bbc	msn	google	Sensitive Zone chase	citi	invalid
1	AvenueMedia/Internet Optimizer	-	-	-	-	-	-
2	Browser Accelerator	Exist	Exist	Exist	Exist*	Exist*	Exist*
3	eXactSearch Toolbar	-	-	-	-	-	-
4	Mirar Toolbar	Exist	Exist	Exist	-	-	-
5	UCmore	Exist	Exist	Exist	-	-	-

Legitimate Plug-ins. Legitimate BHOs and toolbars do not collect information without users' consent. Therefore, they should not produce network traffic without being explicitly invoked, unless there is an agreement between the company distributing these plug-ins and the customers. In our experiment, we did not observe any networking behaviors from all four legitimate plug-ins (Plug-ins with indices 6,7,8,9 in Table 4).

Spyware Plug-ins. Our implementation blocked all events and function calls related to untrusted plug-ins when the browser was visiting a sensitive website like 'http://www.chase.com'. This could also affect spy plug-ins' communication which serves to deliver the information stolen to the perpetrator. In our experiment, we did observe the change of their networking behaviors, which are discussed as follows.

- AvenueMedia/Internet Optimizer is a BHO which can hijack a browser by redirecting it to an advertisement website whenever an invalid URL http://invalid.url is encountered. The same technique could also be used to stealthily place a malicious site between the user and a sensitive website for eavesdropping on their communication. The BHO employs a special technique to detect an invalid URL: it subscribes to an event DISPID_BEFORENAVIGATE2 occurring when a website is to be accessed, and can therefore use a DNS query to determine the validity of the URL even before the browser does. Such a trick does not work on SpyShield, as our approach also hooked that event to identify sensitive zones. In our experiment, we found that the BHO's network traffic in response to an invalid link disappeared under our prototype.

- Browser Accelerator extracts the information from the web page loaded in a browser and sends it to data.browseraccelerator.com. Under SpyShield, the packets responsible for such behaviors could not be observed once the browser was inside the sensitive zone. However, we still detected some packets destined to client.browseraccelerat or.com which our approach did not eliminate. We studied the contents of these packets and found them having little bearing on the sensitive website. Moreover, the same packets were also recorded when the browser was outside the sensitive zone. This leads us to believe they did not contain any sensitive information.

- eXactSearchBar also intends to hijack the invalid link. It redirects the browser to an advertisement site http://www.bestoftheweb.cc/errorpage/?src=4040&url=an.invalid&url once an error page was loaded. Packets related to such behaviors did not show up in the sensitive zone when the browser was protected by SpyShield. Previous research [28] also reported other networking activities of the spyware, which however were not observed in our experiments. This might be due to the change of the spyware's behaviors.

- Mirar collects data from the web page downloaded by a browser and displays advertisements related to its contents. It also encrypts its network traffic using SSL. In our experiment, we found its networking behaviors disappeared within the sensitive zone when SpyShield was running.

- UCmore is a toolbar which forwards the URLs of websites being visited and other information such as time and cache data of the local host to users.ucmore.com. This activity was stopped by SpyShield when sensitive websites were being surfed.

Control of Sensitive Events and Malicious Calls. Within a sensitive zone, SpyShield is designed to block event notifications and function calls in accordance with security policies. This was evaluated in our experiment through analyzing the log exported by our prototype which recorded the dangerous behaviors of spy plug-ins being prevented by the access-control proxy. Here we elaborate this study.

All spy add-ons in our experiment took IE's IWebBrowser2 interface as an entrance to other interfaces, and also made intensive use of it to retrieve a browser's sensitive data. In addition, most of them subscribed to certain events to trigger the calls for accomplishing their missions. As an example, we list in Table 8 the COM function calls of Browser Accelerator invoked by the event DISPID_DOCUMENTCOMPLETE which indicates the completion of downloading a web page to a browser. Another example is AvenueMedia/Internet Optimizer which took advantage of the event DISPID_BEFORENAVIGATE2 to identify an invalid link, and then called stop() and Navigate2to redirect a browser to another website.

Table 8. Function Calls of Browser Accelerator triggered by Event DISPID_DOCUMENTCOMPLETE

Interface	Function Call	Description
IWebBrowser2	get_Document()	Retrieve the interface pointer of IDispatch in an IE object for the active HTML document.
IDispatch	QueryInterface()	Query the interface pointer of IHTMLDocument2.
IHTMLDocument2	get_parentWindow()	Retrieve the interface pointer of IHTMLWindow2 in an IE object which accommodates the active HTML document.
IHTMLDocument2	QueryInterface()	Query the interface pointer of IOleObject.
IOleObject	GetClientSite()	Get the pointer of an interface which maintains the information regarding the display location of an embedded object in an active HTML document.
IHTMLDocument2	QueryInterface()	Query the interface pointer of ICustomDoc.
ICustomDoc	SetUIHandler()	Set the pointer of a customized interface.
IWebBrowser2	get_LocationURL()	Retrieve the URL of the web page that IE is currently displaying.

SpyShield prevented these plug-ins' malicious activities within a sensitive zone through blocking all event notifications issued by IE. Without such notifications, function calls driven by these events disappeared. For example, our prototype intercepted and denied access to invoke() for 104 events subscribed by UCmore when visiting the website http://www.chase.com, which stopped 6 calls used to collect information from the site. Though most spy plug-ins were event-driven, we also found two exceptions which were capable of collecting data from a browser without being triggered by any event. Specifically, both Mirar and UCmore spawned threads once initialized and used them to periodically poll the function get_LocationURL() for the URL to be visited. This malicious behavior was blocked by our prototype with the plug-in rule in Table 1.

4.2   Overheads

We also studied the overheads introduced by SpyShield through experimentally evaluating the performance of plug-ins under our implementation (including the prototypes for both one-process and two-process solutions) against those running inside unprotected IE. Our research intends to understand the performance impacts of SpyShield from the following perspectives: (1) the overheads of cross-process communications, (2) the delay of COM function calls through the access-control proxy, (3) the waiting time of web navigation, a major feature of most IE plug-ins and (4) memory usage of the proxy. To this end, we conducted multiple experiments and also implemented a BHO which collaborated with our prototype proxy to record timing information.

Cross-process Communications. In this experiment, we measured the performance of cross-process communications and compared it with that of in-process communications. Our experiment involved emitting a message from our proxy through the COM interface to the BHO which bounced back a response. The round-trip delay during this process was halved and recorded by the proxy. This experiment was repeated for 1000 times each for the one-process setting in which the BHO and the proxy were inside the same process, and the two-process setting where the BHO ran in a separate process and the communication went through CPC. The results are the averages of the delays recorded in these experiments.

The average latency of CPC observed in the experiments is 177.3μs, almost 1327 times as much as that of in-process communication which is merely 0.1336μs. This result was echoed by a previous study [6]. Apparently, such a huge overhead could greatly affect the performance of the plug-ins running in a separate process, and therefore put the practicality of our approach in doubt. A close look at the time necessary for a plug-in to accomplish its missions, however, reveals that communication only plays a very small role. This suggests that the CPC overhead introduced by SpyShield could be overshadowed by plug-ins' other delays, which is confirmed by our studies on cross-process function calls and web navigation.

Cross-process Function Calls. We evaluated the performance of COM function calls both within a process and across the process boundary. Our experiments involved five COM functions extensively used by BHOs and toolbars, which include `Invoke` and `SetSite` on the plug-ins' side, and `get_LocationURL`, `get_LocationName`, `get_Document` and `Navigate2` on the browser's side. We used our proxy as a substitute for IE to invoke a BHO's function, so as to measure the time for completing that call. The delays of the calls on the reverse direction, from a plug-in to IE, were tracked by the BHO. Our experiments were conducted under both the one-process setting for in-process function calls and the two-process setting for cross-process calls. Figure 3.(A) describes the experimental results which were averaged over 10 experiments.

From the figure, we can see that the overheads of cross-process calls are not terrible: the processing time of most of them was between 21.5% and 35.8% longer than that of their in-process counterparts. The exceptions are `SetSite` and `get_Document`. `SetSite` sends the `IUnknown` pointer to a plug-in, which involves few other activities than communicating through the COM interface. Therefore, it is subject to the strong influence of CPC. Fortunately, the function is only invoked once during a plug-in's initialization and does not affect its runtime performance. Instead of CPC, the overhead for calling `get_Document` mainly comes from the delay for creating a substitute for an IE object in the proxy (Section 3.2). It is also one-time cost in most cases, as our proxy can re-use the substitute for subsequent calls to the function.

Web Navigation. The overhead of SpyShield is usually perceived by the user from the delay in receiving services from plug-ins. Most of such services require retrieving

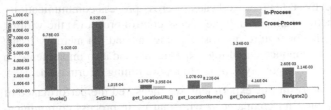
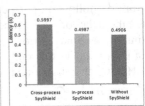

(A) The processing time of function calls in SpyShield   (B) The latency of webpage navigation

Fig. 3. The overheads of function calls and web navigation

documents from the Internet. As an example, our study shows that web navigation is involved in at least 80% features of Google Toolbar and 8 out of 9 features of Yahoo! Toolbar. Therefore, it is important to measure the latency of such a web activity in order to understand the performance of SpyShield.

In our research, we studied the delay caused by web navigation. Our experiment was carried out under the following three settings: (1) the BHO directly attached to an IE browser, (2) the BHO connected to the proxy within the browser's process and (3) the BHO and the add-on manager running in a separate process. In all these settings, the BHO directed the browser to the website http://www.bbc.co.uk by calling the function Navigate2, and recorded the time between the invocation of that function and the occurrence of the event DISPID_DOCUMENTCOMPLETE which indicates the completion of the navigation (i.e., all documents in the webpage have been downloaded). We repeated the experiment for 6 times under each setting to get the average latencies reported in Figure 3.(B): the navigation overhead was only 1.65% for the one-process solution and 22.25% for the two process solution. We believe such overheads are reasonable given the protection provided by our approach.

Memory Overheads. We also measured the memory overhead introduced by the two-process solution. The reference controller increased an IE browser's memory usage by 1MB. The size of the memory allocated to the add-on manager varied with different plug-ins, which was around 18MB for the google toolbar and 14MB for the Yahoo! toolbar. On the other hand, we found that a google toolbar directly attached to IE added 4.8MB to a browser's process memory. This became 3.3MB for the Yahoo! toolbar. Therefore, the memory overhead of our prototype ranged from 11MB to 15MB.

Such an overhead is for a single browser window. As we discussed in Section 3.2, the add-on manager running in a separate process can provide services to multiple browser windows by spawning service threads. In our experiment, we observed that launching a new IE window only cost the add-on manager 0.1 to 0.5MB, depending on the plug-in being requested. This is much lower than the memory cost of creating a new plug-in instance, which is necessary if the plug-in is directly attached to IE instead of the proxy.

5 Discussions

In this section, we discuss the limitations of the current design and implementation of SpyShield, and the potential improvement.

Limitations of Design. The current design of SpyShield is specific to the containment of spy add-ons. The user's interactions with sensitive data are still subject to the surveillance of keyloggers which intercept keystroke inputs, and screen grabbers which snoop on screen outputs. To defeat these attacks, we need to extend SpyShield to include system-wide security policies and an enforcement mechanism which prevents sensitive information from flowing into untrusted objects. Development of such a technique is part of our future research.

Although SpyShield can prevent spyware from being loaded into the kernel through system calls, it is unable to fend off the attacks through a kernel driver's vulnerabilities, for example, buffer overrun. When this happens, we rely on other techniques [16] to protect the kernel.

Limitations of Implementation. The current implementation of SpyShield applies the same security policies to the whole window object. This becomes problematic when a frame object is displaying multiple web pages in different zones within one window. A quick solution is to enforce the strictest policies of these zones. A better approach, however, should work on individual web page and treat them differently. Such functionality is expected in the future improvement of the prototype.

For simplicity, we only wrapped the COM interfaces requested by all the toolbars and BHOs used in our experiments. A thorough implementation needs to create all documented interfaces both in the reference controller and the add-on manager to accommodate different kinds of plug-ins.

6 Related Work

Existing defense against spyware infections mainly relies on detection techniques. These techniques are either based on signatures or behaviors, which we survey as follows.

Signature-based approaches analyze binary executables to identify spyware components or scan network traffics to detect spyware's communications with the perpetrator [2,10,23]. These approaches are fast, but can only detect known spyware. They can also be easily evaded [24]. Behavior-based approaches detect spyware according to its behaviors. Siren [13] and NetSpy [28] analyze the difference between the network traffic from an infected system and that of a clean system to identify spyware's networking activities. Web Tap [12] runs an network-based anomaly detector to capture spyware's network traffic. Gatekeeper [29] monitors the changes of Windows auto-start extensibility points for detecting spyware. GhostBuster [30] exposes rootkits by comparing a view of a clean system with that of an infected system. Recently, Kirda, et al proposed a technique [19] which applies dynamic analysis to detect suspicious communications between an IE browser and its plug-ins, and then analyzes the binaries of suspicious plug-ins to identify the library calls which may lead to leakage of sensitive information. SpyShield complements these techniques by adding an additional layer of defense which protects the user's privacy even after the detection mechanisms have been compromised.

Most of the existing proposals for spyware containment have been limited to protecting confidential inputs such as passwords from keyloggers. Bump in the Ether [21] offers a mechanism which bypasses common avenues of attack through a trusted tunnel implemented using a mobile device. SpyBlock [17] evades the surveillance of the keyloggers inside a virtual machine by directly injecting users' passwords into the network traffic intercepted by the host. These approaches are not very effective to spyware add-ons which are already part of their host application and can not only directly access its sensitive inputs but also snoop on its sensitive outputs such as the bank account displayed in a browser. In addition, they need either additional hardware (mobile device) or heavyweight software (a virtual machine). Microsoft's Next-Generation Secure Computing Base proposes encrypting keyboard, mouse input, and video output [8]. Though a promising approach, it significantly modifies current operating systems and its practicality is yet to see. By comparison, SpyShield is fully compatible with existing systems and can be easily installed and removed.

Similar to the two-process solution of SpyShield, *privilege separation* [25] partitions a program into a *monitor* to handle privileged operations, and a *slave* to perform unprivileged operations. Program partition is traditionally done manually over source code. Recent research, however, has made an impressive progress on automating this step [14]. While apparently assuming the same architecture, SpyShield actually aims at a different goal, inhibiting sensitive information from flowing into untrusted add-ons. To this end, it needs not only to segregate the privileged part of the program from the unprivileged part, but also to enforce security policies to their communication channel, the add-on interfaces, so as to regulate the information exchange between them. In addition, SpyShield separates a binary executable from its binary add-ons along their interfaces while privilege separation usually works on source code.

Another proposal which also employs the two-process architecture for privacy protection is *data sandboxing* [18]. The approach partitions a program into a private part which is allowed to access local files but forbidden to make network connections, and a public part which is permitted to perform networking activities but disallowed to read local data. Such a policy is enforced through system-call interposition [18]. In contrast, SpyShield aims at control of the communications through add-on interfaces, a task which system calls may not have sufficient granularity to handle.

Information flow analysis started with the famous Bell-LaPadula model which controls the interactions between processes and files [11]. More recent work [22,32] focused on tracing data flows within a program. By comparison, SpyShield does not work on such instruction-level tracing, which incurs large performance overheads in absence of source code, and instead manages the information flows across the boundary between add-ons and their host application.

7   Conclusions and Future Work

In this paper, we propose SpyShield, a novel spyware *containment* technique, which can automatically block the visions of untrusted programs in the presence of sensitive information. Such a technique can also defeat the surveillance of new strains of spyware. As a first step, our approach offers general protection against spy add-ons which constitute a significant portion of existing spyware infections. SpyShield enforces security policies to add-on interfaces and other channels used by add-ons to interact with their host applications, so as to prevent sensitive information from flowing into untrusted add-ons.

It can also defend itself against a variety of attacks. We implemented a prototype for protecting Internet Explorer and empirically evaluated its efficacy. Our experimental studies show that this technique can effectively mitigate the threats of spyware surveillance and also introduces a small overhead.

References

1. Browser extensions, http://msdn.microsoft.com/workshop/browser/ext/extensions. asp
2. The home of spybot search & destroy, http://www.safer-networking.org/
3. Mozillazine: Extension development,
   http://kb.mozillazine.org/Dev_:_Extensions
4. State of Spyware Q2 2006: Consumer Report,
   http://www.webroot.com/resources/stateofspyware/excerpt.html
5. Wireshark, http://www.wireshark.org/
6. DCOM technical overview (1996),
   http://msdn2.microsoft.com/en-us/library/ms809340.aspx
7. XPCOM Part 1: An introduction to XPCOM (1996), http://www-128.ibm.com/developerworks/webservices/library/co-xpcom.html
8. Microsoft Next-Generation Secure Computing Base - Technical FAQ (July 2003), http://www.microsoft.com/technet/archive/security/news/ngscb.mspx?mfr=true
9. Ucmore toolbar, the search accelerator (2007), http://www.ucmore.com/
10. Snort developed by sourcefire (January 2006), http://www.snort.org/
11. Bell, D.E., LaPadula, L.J.: Secure computer systems: Unified exposition and multics interpretation. MTR-2997, available as NTIS AD-A023 588, MITRE Corporation (1976)
12. Borders, K., Prakash, A.: Web tap: detecting covert web traffic. In: Proceedings of the 11th ACM conference on Computer and communications security, pp. 110–120. ACM Press, New York (2004)
13. Borders, K., Zhao, X., Prakash, A.: Siren: Catching evasive malware (short paper). In: IEEE S&P, pp. 78–85. IEEE Computer Society Press, Los Alamitos (2006)
14. Brumley, D., Song, D.X.: Privtrans: Automatically partitioning programs for privilege separation. In: USENIX Security Symposium, pp. 57–72 (2004)
15. Egele, M., Kruegel, C., Kirda, E., Yin, H., Song, D.: Dynamic Spyware Analysis. In: Usenix Annual Technical Conference, USA (June 2007)
16. Garfinkel, T., Rosenblum, M.: A virtual machine introspection based architecture for intrusion detection. In: NDSS (2003)
17. Jackson, C., Boneh, D., Mitchell, J.C.: Stronger password authentication using virtual machines. Stanford University (submission, 2006)
18. Khatiwala, T., Swaminathan, R., Venkatakrishnan, V.: Data sandboxing: A technique for enforcing confidentiality policies. In: ACSAC (December 2006)
19. Kirda, E., Kruegel, C., Banks, G., Vigna, G., Kemmerer, R.: Behavior-based spyware detection. In: Proceedings of 15th USENIX Security Symposium (August 2006)
20. Mani, V.: Cross Process Subclassing (2003),
    http://www.codeproject.com/dll/subhook.asp
21. McCune, J.M., Perrig, A., Reiter, M.K.: Bump in the ether: A framework for securing sensitive user input. In: Proceedings of the USENIX Annual Technical Conference, June 2006, pp. 185–198 (2006)
22. Newsome, J., Song, D.X.: Dynamic taint analysis for automatic detection, analysis, and signature generation of exploits on commodity software. In: NDSS (2005)

23. Paxson, V.: Bro: a system for detecting network intruders in real-time. Computer Networks 31(23-24), 2435–2463 (1999)
24. Rubin, S., Jha, S., Miller, B.P.: Automatic generation and analysis of nids attacks. In: ACSAC, pp. 28–38 (2004)
25. Saltzer, J.H.: Protection and the control of information sharing in miltics. Communications of the ACM 17(7), 388–402 (1974)
26. Schreiber, S.B.: Undocumented Windows 2000 Secret: a programmers cookbook, May 2001. Addison-Wesley, Reading (2001)
27. von Ahn, L., Blum, M., Hopper, N.J., Langford, J.: CAPTCHA: Using Hard AI Problems for Security. In: Biham, E. (ed.) Advances in Cryptology – EUROCRPYT 2003. LNCS, vol. 2656, pp. 294–311. Springer, Heidelberg (2003)
28. Wang, H., Jha, S., Ganapathy, V.: NetSpy: Automatic Generation of Spyware Signatures for NIDS. In: Jesshope, C., Egan, C. (eds.) ACSAC 2006. LNCS, vol. 4186, Springer, Heidelberg (2006)
29. Wang, Y.-M., Roussev, R., Verbowski, C., Johnson, A., Wu, M.-W., Huang, Y., Kuo, S.-Y.: Gatekeeper: Monitoring Auto-Start Extensibility Points (ASEPs) for Spyware Management. In: USENIX LISA 2004 (2004)
30. Wang, Y.-M., Vo, B., Roussev, R., Verbowski, C., Johnson, A.: Strider ghostbuster: Why it's a bad idea for stealth software to hide files. Technical Report MSR-TR-2004-71, Microsoft Research (2004)
31. Willliams, S., Kindel, C.: The component object model: A technical overview (October 1994), http://msdn2.microsoft.com/en-us/library/ms809980.aspx
32. Xu, W., Bhatkar, S., Sekar, R.: Taint-enhanced policy enforcement: A practical approach to defeat a wide range of attacks. In: Proceedings of the 15th USENIX Security Symposium, Vancouver, BC, Canada (August 2006)

Vortex: Enabling Cooperative Selective Wormholing for Network Security Systems

John R. Lange, Peter A. Dinda, and Fabián E. Bustamante

Northwestern University, Evanston IL 60208, USA
{jarusl,pdinda,fabianb}@cs.northwestern.edu

Abstract. We present a novel approach to remote traffic aggregation for Network Intrusion Detection Systems (NIDS) called *Cooperative Selective Wormholing* (CSW). Our approach works by selectively aggregating traffic bound for unused network ports on a volunteer's commodity PC. CSW could enable NIDS operators to cheaply and efficiently monitor large distributed portions of the Internet, something they are currently incapable of. Based on a study of several hundred hosts in a university network, we posit that there is sufficient heterogeneity in hosts' network service configurations to achieve a high degree of network coverage by re-using *unused port space* on client machines. We demonstrate *Vortex*, a proof-of-concept CSW implementation that runs on a wide range of commodity PCs (Unix and Windows). Our experiments show that Vortex can selectively aggregate traffic to a virtual machine backend, effectively allowing two machines to share the same IP address transparently. We close with a discussion of the basic requirements for a large-scale CSW deployment.

Keywords: wormholes, honeynets, honeypots, volunteer systems.

1 Introduction

We present *Cooperative Selective Wormholing (CSW)*, a novel approach to providing traffic for use in network intrusion detection systems (NIDS). Our approach adopts a cooperative model [8,11,23,24] in which volunteers contribute their hosts' unused network ports and a portion of their bandwidth. NIDS operators selectively aggregate the traffic bound for these ports in order to effectively monitor large distributed portions of the Internet.

Collecting and analyzing network traffic to detect new methods of attack has long been recognized as a necessity by the security community, and numerous systems have been developed to provide such a service. While the design and functionality of these systems are vastly different, nearly all of them operate by aggregating network traffic from some source. CSW is such a source, one whose volunteer nature presents the potential for dramatically improved coverage of the Internet.

CSW is inspired by the wormholing model of Weaver, et al. [30], in which a dedicated, low-cost hardware frontend device is attached to a network of interest

C. Kruegel, R. Lippmann, and A. Clark (Eds.): RAID 2007, LNCS 4637, pp. 317–336, 2007.

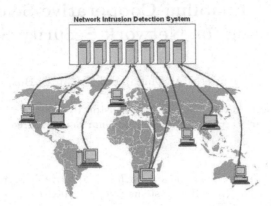

Fig. 1. Cooperative Selective Wormholing provides distributed traffic aggregation for NIDS through volunteer PCs

to forward traffic for a range of IP addresses to a backend honeypot. CSW also uses a frontend/backend distinction, but it does not require any hardware deployment and allows individual machine owners to participate. CSW enables the aggregation of traffic bound to specific unused ports, thus allowing the wormhole to transparently coexist on a volunteer machine. Figure 1 illustrates CSW at a high level.

Network telescopes are the currently preferred method of traffic aggregation in the security community [17]. By providing access to portions of the routed IP address spaces on which little or no legitimate traffic exists, network telescopes make possible the monitoring of unexpected network events such as network scanning or some forms of flooding DoS attacks. Perhaps the main drawback of the telescope approach is that it inherently restricts access to network traffic to well-connected or well-funded individuals or groups capable of convincing an organization to redirect its traffic to a remote location.

While it has been shown that accommodations for network telescopes can be made, the model creates barriers for unaffiliated and unconnected investigators. In contrast, CSW makes it possible for *any* researcher to deploy a large scale distributed traffic aggregation infrastructure, solely by finding *individual* volunteers. It has clearly been shown that it is possible to convince individuals to volunteer resources for a research effort, often on a massive scale [8,11,23,24]. CSW is similar to such efforts, except that individuals volunteer *unused ports and bandwidth*.

CSW wormholes capture traffic destined for unused ports on the volunteer's machine and tunnel it to generic backend NIDS that are stood up by researchers and others. The sender of the traffic is ideally completely unaware that he is in fact interacting with a backend instead of with the volunteer's machine. Furthermore, the wormhole only runs on unused ports, none of the volunteer's own traffic is disclosed to the backend, alleviating privacy concerns.

As a first step to realizing the CSW vision, we have developed *Vortex*, a prototype tool that enables volunteers to instantiate cooperative selective wormholes on their machines. Vortex was developed based on our experience with network virtualization and high performance grid computing. It is implemented using VTL and VNET, two toolsets we have presented previously [10,25]. Vortex runs on both Unix and Windows environments without interfering with any local activity. Our evaluation of Vortex helps to establish the feasibility of CSW and acts as a corner stone to its implementation.

We now elaborate on the three central issues of CSW:

- Coverage: Does the Internet possess enough diversity in open network port configurations to provide acceptable amounts of traffic for CSW?
- Invisibility to clients: Can CSW systems be designed in such a way as to not inconvenience the user running them?
- Invisibility to attackers: Will attackers be able to detect the presence of a CSW on a volunteer's machine?

We will also present the design, implementation, and evaluation of Vortex, our CSW proof-of-concept tool.

2   Coverage

The principal issue with any traffic aggregation technique is the degree of coverage it can obtain over the network. We define coverage as the distribution of traffic aggregators over a sample space. For instance, a network telescope gives very fine-grained coverage over a very small area, so it can very accurately capture behavior inside a subnet, but it cannot accurately describe the Internet at large. Until now the distribution of monitored *addresses*, the *horizontal coverage*, was the only coverage that needed to be considered. CSW improves *horizontal coverage* by allowing cheap access to more widely distributed addresses, however CSW has its own coverage issue: can a CSW system cover a relevant sample of network ports? We use *vertical coverage* to denote coverage of network ports.

2.1   Horizontal Coverage

The largest advantage of CSW systems is the possibility of gaining a large degree of random coverage over the entire Internet address space. Telescopes inherently sample at a very low resolution, on the order of large subnets, and are difficult to deploy remotely, so their localized observations may not be representative of the actual activity taking place across the entire Internet. On the other hand, CSW systems could provide a *random sample* of the Internet address space, thus ensuring more widely applicable analyses. Note that the utility of using volunteer hosts to gain a distributed presence has already been established [21].

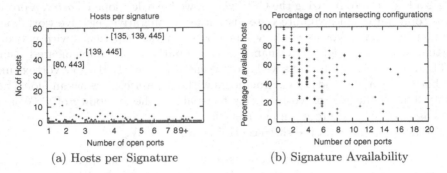

| (a) Hosts per Signature | (b) Signature Availability |

Fig. 2. Signature prevalence and intersections from random sample of university hosts

2.2   Vertical Coverage

While CSW systems have the potential to provide superior resolution at the address level, they inherently restrict port coverage. The issue of this *vertical coverage* is specific to CSW, since the resolution possible is dependent on the heterogeneity of the available ports, and their combinations, present in the Internet. This heterogeneity corresponds to both the prevalence of operating systems as well as the diversity of services active on volunteer hosts.

A CSW system would ideally be able to stand up port configurations in the same proportion that those configurations are present in the actual Internet. If some percentage of machines run a web server then the wormholed traffic would ideally represent that same percentage. Thus CSW loses its appeal when too many potential volunteer clients share the same open port configuration.

To gain an idea of the port distribution in the Internet we conducted a study of the Northwestern University network. We scanned the first 1024 TCP ports over 1000 machines randomly selected from the university network. We then culled invalid devices (network switches, printers, etc) from the results, and analyzed the remaining scans to identify the distribution of open ports. We refer to the set of open ports on a machine as the *port signature* or simply the *signature* of that host.

We positively identified 401 of the 1000 addresses as capable of operating as a Vortex sensor (general purpose computers running a Vortex-compatible OS) using the OS fingerprinting functionality of nmap. An additional 253 of the 1000 hosts had no open ports, suggesting either an unknown OS, or (more likely) a firewalled/secured OS configurations. It is reasonable to believe that many of these additional hosts are also Vortex-compatible. Nonetheless, we focus on the (worst case) 401 machines, from which we detected 123 distinct port signatures.

Configuration Diversity. We analyzed the number of hosts running each signature, to determine if there were any obviously prevalent signatures. The results are are shown in Figure 2(a), which plots the number of relevant hosts as a function of the size of the port signature. There are three non-surprising prevalent signatures, which we label. The most popular signature includes three ports associated with standard Windows services commonly present on machines acting as Windows file servers. The second most popular signature contains a subset of the Windows file server ports, consistent with a standard Windows desktop machine. Finally, the third most popular signature consists of ports used by web servers (http and https). Taken together these signatures are present on 138 (34%)of the 401 hosts we scanned. The figure also shows that there are 81 hosts (20%) with signatures that are unique to our data set, suggesting that there is a significant degree of diversity in port signatures. The remaining 45% of hosts exhibited a diverse range of signatures.

Configuration Separation or Non-Intersection. If a selection of signatures all included a common subset of ports, the effectiveness of CSW in that selection would be greatly diminished. We define any host whose port signature does not intersect a given configuration that we want to monitor as an available host for that configuration. To analyze the degree of separation present in various signatures, and the availability implications, we used three approaches.

Entire Signatures. We first determined the amount of intersection among the signatures themselves. We considered each signature in turn and determined the number of hosts in the set that did not intersect with the selected signature. These non-intersecting hosts would be available for a CSW of the prospective signature. The results are shown in Figure 2(b). We can see that the signatures with the fewest open ports are also the signatures with the highest degree of availability. This is especially notable when considered with the previous observation that the most prevalent signatures had only a small number (2 or 3) ports. The *minimum* availabilities of 2 and 3 port signatures are 50% and 20% respectively. More importantly, as the number of open ports increases the number of available hosts does not decrease to zero. The worst availability is 7.98% (32 hosts). The typical availability is much higher. Also, we are likely underestimating availability as we are not counting hosts that have no open ports.

Port Combinations. We also measured the separation of the signatures by considering subsets of the ports included in each signature. We considered each unique signature and looked at the combinations possible when selecting a given number of ports from the signature. Figure 3 shows the availability of combinatorial results obtained from choosing different numbers of ports ranging from 1 to 5. When choosing a single port (Figure 3(a)), the availability is simply 100% minus the percentage of hosts using that port. The top line represents the availability of the single port while the bottom line shows the percentage of hosts containing that port in their signature. In the rest of graphs we retain the bottom line showing the percentage of hosts containing the port combination in their signature, but use a scatter plot to show the availability. Each point represents one of the possible port subsets of the given size. The results are sorted by port combination popularity, with the most common port combinations to the left.

While our previous results on the availability of entire signatures lets us estimate an upper limit for each signature, the combinatorial analysis we describe here is trying to isolate common port combinations present in the trace, letting us estimate a lower limit. Figure 2(a) shows that there are three popular small

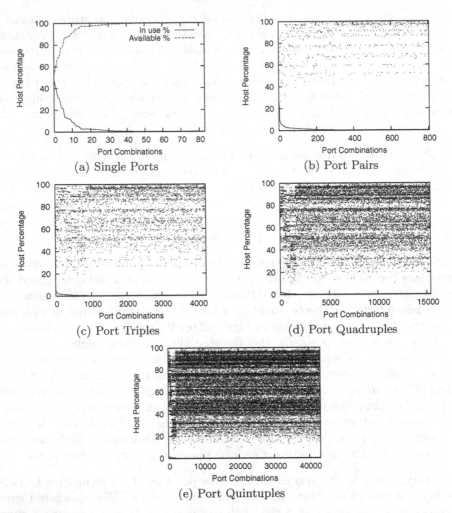

Fig. 3. Probabilities that a given port combination is available in the set of hosts gathered from the randomized port scan. Port combinations are calculated from the signatures present in the scan results, and sorted by decreasing popularity.

port signatures, however combinations including those popular ports are likely more common. For instance, if a given machine M has the port signature <80, 139, 443, 445> then it would *not* be included in the host count for either the <80, 443> or <139, 445> signature, even though it would not be available for either signature. By analyzing port combinations we can treat machine M as belonging to both the <80, 443> and <139, 445> signatures.

Interestingly the graphs for the four higher order combinations (Figure 3(b)-(e)) exhibit a common structure. Each contains bands of availability in roughly the same locations, as well as a common dip in availability for combinations of medium popularity. The other notable aspect of the graphs is that there is a

Tag	MachineClass	Signature (Open Ports)
EXG	Exchange Server	25, 80, 110, 135, 137, 139, 143, 443, 445, 593, 691, 993, 995
LHS	Linux Hosting Service	22, 25, 80, 443, 993, 995
WIN	Windows Desktop	139, 445
WFS	Windows File Server	135, 137, 139, 445
LMS	Linux Mail Server	22, 25, 119, 515, 635, 993
LWS	Linux Web Server	22, 25, 80, 443
WDC	Windows PDC	53, 88, 135, 139, 389, 445, 464, 593, 636
SMB	Linux Mail + SMB	22, 25, 119, 137, 138, 139, 445, 515, 631, 993

Fig. 4. Partial list of Common Machine Configurations and their Signatures

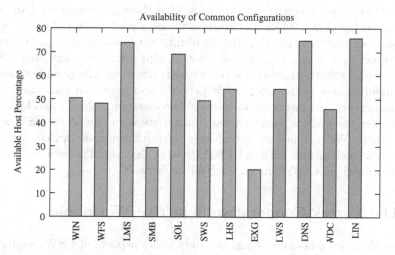

Fig. 5. Host availability for selective wormholing of several common signatures. Availability is measured as the percentage of hosts in the host set returned from a randomized scan that are available for a signature.

more concentrated collection of availability bands towards the top, indicating that there is substantial availability for a large subset of port combinations.

The upshot of this analysis is that it provides considerable confidence that even with a restrictive definition for port signature intersection, very popular port signatures are likely to be available on a substantial number of Internet hosts.

Signatures of Common Machine Configurations. We next consider the availability of port signatures found on currently common machine configurations. Figure 4 contains a subset of the configurations and signatures we tested. We included common operating systems (including Windows, Linux, Solaris, and MacOS X), as well common configurations of those operating systems (such as web servers, email server, and domain controllers). We considered the signature for each common configuration and ran it against our host set to determine the availability of the configuration.

Figure 5 contains the results for the configurations we analyzed. Each machine configuration is shown along with its corresponding availability in our host set. The graph shows that the availability is quite good for most common configurations. The worst cases are machines configured as Windows Exchange servers as well as a Linux mail servers running Samba. This is to be expected since both of these signatures contain standard Windows ports as well as ports commonly found on Unix and server-class machines, effectively bridging the different machine configurations. Still, the results show that at least 20% of hosts will always be available for any of the given machine configurations.

2.3   Coverage Feasibility

The results from the analysis of our random sample of machines connected to the Northwestern University network show that there is a substantial amount of heterogeneity present. While our results may be somewhat limited to our specific environment, they indicate that the feasibility of obtaining vertical coverage in the Internet as a whole is likely substantial. Our results suggest that CSW is likely to be an effective method for collecting traffic from a large and statistically meaningful sample of the Internet. We should also note that our analysis does not take into account intermediate network devices such as NATs and firewalls. If such devices are present then they would interfere with any active CSW located behind them. We currently do not address these intermediate devices other than to say that mechanisms, such as UPNP, do exist that could possibly allow traffic to be delivered to a CSW through a NAT or firewall.

3   The Vortex Cooperative Selective Wormhole

To provide a proof-of-concept and to study other aspects of CSW, we have developed Vortex. Vortex interfaces with an overlay networking system to support connectivity with different backends. Vortex is an outgrowth of research into using virtual machines (VMs) for high performance distributed computing, and so is built using several tools developed in that work. While these tools provided a general and easy avenue for implementing a CSW they are by no means required. Vortex could, for example, be easily implemented as a firewall extension.

3.1   Design

Vortex functions by instantiating a CSW on a client machine and communicating with a VM running as the backend system. This configuration is what would typically be seen if Vortex was used as a traffic aggregator for a virtual honeypot system. Vortex was implemented using our VTL and VNET toolsets [10,25]. Although we evaluate Vortex with a VM backend, the generality of VNET allows a wide range of backend systems to be used, such as passive monitors, monitors that perform simple connection interaction, virtual honeypots, or even physical honeypots. The Vortex architecture is illustrated in Figure 6.

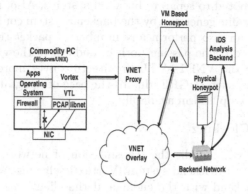

Fig. 6. Vortex Architecture. Vortex uses VTL to capture packets before they are dropped by the host firewall. The captured Ethernet frames are then sent to a VNET proxy which routes the traffic to an IDS backend system.

VTL is a framework designed to allow developers to rapidly develop transparent network services [10]. Primarily, it provides OS-independent methods for packet serialization, acquisition, and manipulation as well as state models used when working with stateful connections. VTL is built on top of Pcap [13,31] and libnet [12], thus providing a cross platform method for interacting with network traffic. Vortex uses VTL for both selective traffic capture as well as transmission of any outbound traffic from the VM backend. Vortex also relies on the VTL mechanisms for packet modification to ensure that traffic is accepted by all parties as legitimate.

VNET is an overlay network toolkit designed specifically for virtual machine-based environments. It provides a layer 2 abstraction for the VMs, tunneling complete Ethernet frames through an overlay whose topology and routing rules are globally controlled [25,26]. Vortex is designed to interface with VNET to provide connectivity to the virtual machine backend. At startup Vortex connects to a VNET proxy machine that routes all the traffic from the wormhole to a specific VNET-connected VM. Because VNET encapsulates entire Ethernet frames, traffic can move seamlessly between the overlay and a physical network interface. This allows VNET to connect to physical network devices as well as virtual network devices exposed by a VM.

The current version of Vortex has a very simple interaction model. A Vortex client instantiates wormholes on any number of unused ports and forwards all traffic to wormholed ports to a single VNET proxy. The VNET overlay is then configured to route all traffic from a given wormhole to a single VM. The VM is configured with the same IP address and routing table as the client machine, but has a separate MAC address. Any traffic that is generated by the backend VM on a wormholed port is tunneled back to the client where it is injected into the physical network. Despite the simplicity of the current interaction model, creation of more complicated use models is entirely possible within the VTL+VNET framework. For example, different wormholed ports on the same frontend could be routed to separate backend systems. Also, more stringent requirements on the traffic generated by the backend system could easily be added. The Vortex client can also perform any number of packet transformations, at layers 2 through 4, to traffic passing both in and out of the wormhole.

We chose to use the VNET+VTL architecture over more established tunnelling architectures, such as GRE, due to the ease of integration, packet access capabilities, and cross platform availability.

3.2   Wormhole Cloaking

While VTL and VNET handle the transmission of network packets from the volunteer machine to a backend system, Vortex itself must assure seamless integration of the backend with the client and the client's network. In order to transparently instantiate wormholes on a volunteer machine, Vortex must fool not only the outside world but also the local machine into handling packets as if they were generated locally. To operate transparently, any packets that are transmitted out of the wormhole must appear as if they were generated by the local machine. Also, if a particular port is being wormholed the local host must not reply to any traffic it receives on that port. Furthermore, in the case of a honeypot backend, traffic must be modified so that it is accepted by the honeypot. We now consider two key issues that must be addressed.

MAC Addresses. This issue only arises when a backend system wishes to interact with traffic that has been captured, that is it wants to send responses and receive replies. In this case any packets generated by the backend would need to share the same MAC address as the volunteer machine. It is feasible that the volunteer could report the MAC address of their machine and require the backend to configure itself to assume that address itself. However, this would require assumptions about the aggregation technique to be made by the backend, something we try to avoid. Also it would require volunteers to divulge information about themselves, which we also seek to avoid.

Instead of requiring the backend to handle this issue we instead have Vortex perform MAC address translation locally on the volunteer machine. Vortex first probes the local machine for its MAC and IP addresses, and then issues an ARP request through VNET to the backend for the local host's IP. The backend responds with an ARP reply containing its MAC address, which Vortex intercepts and stores. From that point onward Vortex rewrites incoming packets with the appropriate MAC address before forwarding them to either the backend or the local network. To ensure ARP table consistency all ARP requests and replies received by the local machine are captured by Vortex and sent to the backend, similarly any ARP packets generated by the backend are inserted into the clients local network.

Packet Suppression. The normal response of a TCP stack to a packet arriving on a closed port is for a host to send an RST packet to the source. However, in the case that the non-open port is being handled by Vortex, this behavior is unacceptable. The result would be a source host receiving both a RST packet

```
-A VORTEX_FW -p tcp –dport 6000:6050 -j ACCEPT
-A VORTEX_FW -p udp -m udp –dport 137 -j ACCEPT
-A VORTEX_FW -p udp -m udp –dport 138 -j ACCEPT
-A VORTEX_FW -m state –state ESTABLISHED,RELATED -j ACCEPT
-A VORTEX_FW -j DROP
```

Fig. 7. Example firewall (IPTables) rules to enable packet suppression

as well as whatever response was generated by the backend for every packet sent through the wormhole. The additional RST would not only likely interfere with the TCP connection, but it would also make Vortex's existence obvious if the source were an attacker. For Vortex to function correctly these RST packets must be suppressed.

To handle the TCP RST problem we use the local host firewalls included in most current OS environments, e.g. iptables and the Windows Firewall. These firewalls support configurations that simply drop packets destined for a port disallowed in the firewall rules, thus ensuring that packets to a closed port never reach the local TCP stack (this is the default behavior for the Windows Firewall). Figure 7 includes an example configuration for iptables. The example accepts TCP packets destined for local ports 6000-6050, udp packets for ports 137 and 138, and packets belonging to an established connection. All packets not included in the rules are dropped and never reach the local TCP stack. Because Vortex has no mechanism capable of blocking the local client from either receiving or transmitting packets, Vortex requires such firewall configurations to be in place in order to operate transparently. This requisite relationship between Vortex and local firewalls leads us to believe that CSW might be best implemented as a firewall extension.

4   Invisibility to Volunteers

A core requirement for Vortex is that it be able to function on a volunteer machine without any interference or impact on performance. While Section 3 discussed the mechanisms required to make Vortex traffic indistinguishable from normal host traffic, those are merely the basic requirements for CSW systems to function. In order for CSW systems to be effective they must also be invisible in more subtle ways, such as in their performance impacts or interference with applications the host machine is running. This requires that CSW systems implement mechanisms for detecting user behavior and reacting accordingly. The current experimental version of Vortex does not implement all of these mechanisms, but we envision incorporating them into a later version. To be truly invisible to a volunteer, a CSW must address the following issues.

4.1   Port Collisions

The most obvious form of interference from Vortex arises from port collisions. This occurs when a wormhole and a local application are simultaneously communicating on the same port number. This can happen when Vortex is launched or if Vortex has been configured on a specific port, when at some later point a local connection begins using that port. Because Vortex maintains transparency to the local machine, it must be able to detect these events on its own and close the wormhole if such an event occurs.

A client's list of open ports is readily available via the /**proc** directory on Linux and a win32 API call in Windows. Currently, Vortex employs active polling of the corresponding mechanism to acquire a list of open ports on the local machine and detect collisions with any active wormholes. If a collision is detected then Vortex closes the wormhole immediately. Polling is neither efficient nor responsive, so we plan on implementing a method for notification when the local host requests the use of a currently wormholed port. We plan on utilizing an NDIS driver hook for Windows environments and library interposition for Unix.

4.2 Performance Degradation

A CSW implementation must also ensure that performance does not significantly degrade on the client machine. This is especially critical for deployments relying on the use of volunteers, as no one will run a tool that slows their machine down noticeably. The performance impact can either be in the form of bandwidth usage or CPU utilization for packet processing.

To address this issue we are working on mechanisms that allow a user to specify the amount of resources they are willing to make available. This technique has been used successfully in many peer-to-peer applications as well as in cooperative computing initiatives. Our plans with Vortex include the implementation of a bandwidth rate limiter that is configurable by the user. This will allow a volunteer to determine the amount of bandwidth which they are willing to provide to Vortex. Another solution could include rulesets for when CSWs are allowed to be instantiated, for example only after a machine has been idle for a given amount time.

Network Overheads. We ran a series of experiments to quantify the performance of a CSW system (Vortex) as well as the possible performance impact on the client machine. Our experimental setup consisted of a Vortex client connected to a virtual machine backend located on the Northwestern University network. We ran two sets of experiments: first with the client located on a home network connected to the Internet via DSL, and a second with the client on the Northwestern network. In each case the traffic to the client was generated from machines on the Northwestern network. For each experiment we measured the raw bandwidth of both the client machine and the wormhole, as well as the available bandwidth of both when the other is being flooded with network traffic. We also used the Linux IProute2 implementation to test the impact of a bandwidth limiter.

Figures 8(a) and 8(c) illustrate the performance of a Vortex CSW. The graphs show the bandwidth through a wormhole under various conditions. Figure 8(a) shows the bandwidth of a Vortex CSW running on a client connected to the same LAN as the backend system, while Figure 8(c) shows the same for a client located on a DSL line. The *Raw* column shows the maximum available bandwidth

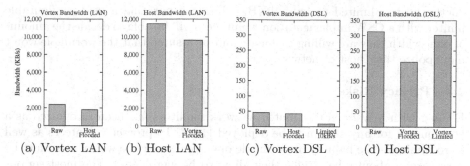

Fig. 8. Bandwidth measurements of clients hosted on DSL and LAN connections. (a) and (c) contain the performance results of a Vortex CSW, while (b) and (d) contain the performance results of the client machine. Measurements were taken under various traffic conditions and bandwidth is measured in kilobytes/second. Each figure shows the mean taken from 10 separate trials.

to a CSW when no other host traffic is present. Vortex is implemented in user space requiring two context switches for each packet received (One to receive the packet from PCAP or VNET, plus one to transmit the packet with libnet or VNET). While these context switches place a limit on the performance of the present version of Vortex, a more intelligent in-kernel design would be capable of performing much better. The figures also show the performance impact on the CSW when the client host is being flooded with traffic to a local service. In both cases Vortex is not starved of bandwidth and continues to function. Finally, for the DSL client we configured the kernel to limit the bandwidth from the client to the VNET proxy, which we will discuss later.

Figures 8(b) and 8(d) show the performance of the volunteer machine running a Vortex CSW. We performed the same experiments as described earlier. First we measured the *Raw* bandwidth of each client machine with Vortex not running and no other traffic present. We then performed the same test but with a Vortex CSW configured and being flooded with traffic. Both hosts show a drop of performance when Vortex is being used heavily, but our implementation is able to cushion the performance drop to roughly 15% due to its architecture. However, as we stated above, the performance of a CSW can be improved, and any improvement will adversely effect the performance of a host. There is clearly a tradeoff that the volunteer needs to make.

To demonstrate that constraints can be placed on a CSW system to prevent it from causing too large a drop in host performance, we ran the tests again with an external bandwidth limiter. For this experiment, we only measured the performance of the DSL host. In order to constrain Vortex we configured a network queue, using IPRoute2 in the Linux kernel, to limit any traffic to the VNET proxy to 10kB/s. We then measured the performance of both the Vortex CSW as well as the client machine. The results are included in the third column of figures 8(c) and 8(d). Figure 8(c) shows that the bandwidth of the CSW is indeed constrained to 10KB/s, while figure 8(d) shows that the performance degradation on the host is limited to only 10KB/s. By incorporating a user configurable limiter with a CSW implementation, volunteers will be able to decide the amount of bandwidth they are willing to donate and be assured that the wormhole won't monopolize their host or network.

4.3   Privacy Risks

Dealing with privacy in distributed network monitors has been recognized as a key concern for any system to be deployed [4,15]. To protect volunteers as well as to minimize the liability of wormhole operators, selective wormholes must be very careful about what traffic they allow to be aggregated. The most serious privacy issue that a CSW must deal with is ensuring that no private local traffic is mistakenly aggregated, but other smaller issues exist as well. For a CSW architecture to be successful it must alleviate any concerns that the volunteers might have.

There is no perfect way to address the problem of mistakenly aggregating private traffic. Ultimately the issue is tied to the behavior of the user and the other members of the users network. For instance, if a volunteer provides a Linux client on a corporate LAN, Vortex could be instructed to instantiate wormholes associated with windows file sharing services. If for some reason another user on the LAN decides to start trying to communicate with those ports, then traffic is being aggregated that might possibly be very sensitive in nature. In other words, a CSW system like Vortex can do nothing to prevent users from purposefully but mistakenly transmitting sensitive information through a wormhole. Vortex's method of preventing this is to allow a user to blacklist ports that they don't want Vortex to use, however this requires action by the user and does not prevent mistakes from being made.

The other privacy issue is the aggregation of sensitive information outside of aggregated network traffic. Vortex is specifically designed to require as little information from the user as possible. Currently the only information available to the Vortex backend system is the IP address of the machine as well as a list of in use network ports. If the user wishes, they are able to locally configure Vortex to only use a defined set of ports in case that they don't wish to disclose the port signature of their machine. Depending on the type of backend system in use, further steps can be taken to increase anonymity. For instance, non-interactive backend systems might not need to know the actual IP address of the volunteer machine, in which case Vortex could anonymize the IP and MAC addresses. Previous work has demonstrated anonymization of network data [16,32], and such techniques could easily be implemented in Vortex.

4.4   Security Exposure

Besides avoiding the exposure of private information, CSW systems must not create additional security vulnerabilities on the client machine or their network. The security issues themselves are shared with and have been explored in the context of other aggregation techniques, but the location of the aggregation nodes brings new aspects to the problem. There are two main new aspects to the security problem: exploitability of the wormhole implementation, and risks to the local resources resulting from a compromised backend system. Vortex currently minimizes the former, while leaving the latter as a policy decision for wormhole operators.

The current version of Vortex does minimal processing besides simply encapsulating Ethernet frames and tunneling them to a backend. The only processing performed by Vortex is on the Ethernet level headers themselves, which must first pass through network equipment and a pcap filter that only accepts packets with a valid format. However this might change if Vortex is implemented with additional packet processing capabilities such as anonymization, so such changes must be implemented with great care. Furthermore the packets captured by Vortex are never delivered to the local host, they are simply encapsulated and tunneled through Vortex.

The issue of transmitting traffic from the backend onto the volunteer's local network poses a complicated problem. While this issue is common to honeynets and other traffic aggregators, the fact that the potentially harmful traffic is being inserted onto a volunteer's network leads to a much more sensitive situation. Ultimately this is a policy decision that must be made by the wormhole operators themselves. Even though the current version of Vortex blindly writes all traffic from wormholed ports to the network, the capability to block all or some of the traffic is available through the VTL and VNET frameworks. VNET can be configured to only forward traffic from the wormhole but not to it, and VTL provides packet inspection mechanisms which would allow Vortex to make packet injection decisions based on rulesets run against the packet contents. Other CSW implementations could inject traffic at remote locations seperate from the client's network presence. This would allow full communication between the backend and attacker while not requiring the client to inject any traffic onto it's local network.

5   Invisibility to Attackers

To further evaluate the utility of CSW we investigated the degree to which the wormholes were detectable by an attacker. This section assumes that the CSW wormhole is connected to a honeypot or some other system that emulates an actual service. These systems depend on an attacker believing that their target is actually a legitimate machine, so it is important to understand whether CSW systems provide enough information to tip off an attacker. Furthermore, if an attacker discovers a wormhole then they can simply avoid it, or try to disrupt it [1,3].

The methods an attacker can use to detect the presence of wormholed port fall into two categories: First, because wormhole traffic is tunneled to a remote location, the packet latencies will be larger for wormhole traffic as opposed to traffic handled by the local machine. Second, because a honeypot will be configured differently from a client machine, often with a different OS, packet formats and network behavior will differ between the wormhole and local services. It is beyond the scope of this work to explore the possibility of transforming traffic formats to mimic different hosts, so we only focus on the issue of latency.

For CSWs to be hidden from an attacker, the added latency of the wormhole must fall within the variance of the latency for a local service. This means that the degree to which wormhole latency is masked depends on the connection quality and location of the wormhole host, the backend, and the attacker. Our experiments attempted to capture the different environments under which all three components might operate.

We conducted the experiments by installing Vortex wormholes at various network locations and connecting them to our VM backend located on the Northwestern University network. We then ran latency measurements from PlanetLab nodes located across North America. We measured latency by using tcpdump to time the durations of SYN/SYN-ACK sequences resulting from TCP connection setup requests. We chose to measure the SYN/SYN-ACK sequence because it is handled in kernel and so is independent of application behavior. The Vortex sensors were located on a home network with a DSL Internet connection, a home network with a cable Internet connection, and a Northwestern local area network. For each test we measured the SYN/SYN-ACK latency for a local service and a wormhole service.

The results are given in Figure 9. Each graph is for different client network (DSL, Cable, LAN). In a graph, paired bars compare the local service latency (left bar) with the wormhole latency (right bar). Bar pairs are given for each of the "attacker" PlanetLab sites. It is important to note that each bar represents an average, and standard deviation whiskers are also shown.

As expected the location of the various parties plays a large role in determining the average and standard deviation of the latency of a connection. Neither the DSL nor the cable networks exhibited enough latency variance to effectively mask the presence of a wormhole. Only the wormhole located on the LAN was able to disguise the presence of a wormhole. While somewhat discouraging, the tests do show that the latency is dependent only on the added latency between the wormhole client and the backend system, meaning that the wormhole implementation added minimal latency from packet processing. This suggests that intelligent and dynamic distribution of a backend system over a hosting service such as PlanetLab could help disguise the presence of a wormhole. That is, were the backend itself running on PlanetLab, it could move closer to the client. Furthermore, if the backend were a virtual machine, implementing such movement could be readily accomplished [22].

6   Related Work

Many different communities have sought to harness the unused resources of volunteer machines to perform large calculations or large scale measurements. The most well known of these projects uses donated CPU time to perform extremely large calculations. Projects such as SETI@home [24] and Folding@home [11] have demonstrated considerable success with such an approach, harnessing hundreds

Vortex: Enabling Cooperative Selective Wormholing   333

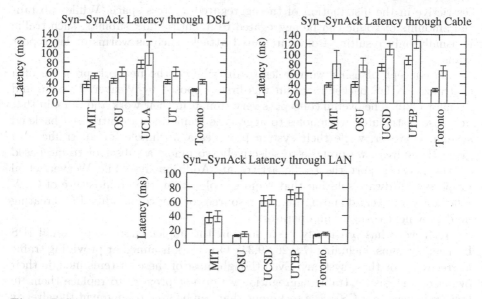

Fig. 9. Differences in latency between a local service and a CSW. Measurements were made by timing the Syn/SynACK sequence caused by the establishment of a TCP connection. Measurements were taken from various PlanetLab sites distributed across North America. For each site the latency of a local service is shown on the left side while the CSW latency is on the right.

of thousands of machines. The Internet measurement community has recently explored such a model, following the realization that widely distributed sensors were necessary to gain a relevant view of the network [8,23]. Measurement and computational clients can all be characterized as *active*, in that they compute or measure something and report the results. CSW clients, however, are *passive*, since they simply tunnel anything they receive back to a backend. While this difference might seem minor, it has serious implications for client privacy and security. Recent work in IDS systems has begun to move towards distributed monitoring as well [2,5,6,19,28], but these systems have yet to demonstrate a technique as readily deployable as a measurement system or computational engine.

To date traffic aggregation techniques have confined themselves to so called *dark address spaces* [14,18,27,33,34]. The idea is to aggregate traffic destined for unused IP addresses and reroute it into a given backend. This usually requires the reconfiguration of network equipment controlling large network domains. While this method of traffic aggregation, commonly referred to as a network telescope, is effective in collecting large amounts of candidate traffic, it has several drawbacks. First, it requires large segments of empty address space. This address space usually can only be found in large organizations such as universities. Accessing this address space requires the cooperation of network administrators for the entire period of aggregation. Furthermore, telescopes are inherently restrictive in the distribution of the aggregated address space. While substantial amounts of traffic can be aggregated from entire dark subnets, such traffic is usually only resulting from automated attacks such as worms or large port scans.

The concept of using wormholes to distributed the network presence of a centralized NIDS backend system was first proposed by Weaver, Paxson, and Staniford [30]. The overall concept is very similar in their work and ours, in that both use distributed wormholes to aggregate traffic into a centralized backend system. However, while their system provides a wormhole for all traffic to a given IP address, we propose to selectively wormhole a subset of traffic based on the network port the traffic arrives at. Additionally, while Weaver, et al propose a hardware solution that requires colocation, the architecture of CSW relies on volunteers donating unused resources of any commodity PC, creating no deployment costs for an operator.

Much work has previously been done in the implementation of actual IDS backend systems, including [7,9,20,29,34]. Our work is aimed at providing traffic aggregation for these systems. Even though most of these systems include their own mechanisms for traffic aggregation we do not propose to replace them, in fact we believe that CSW is a technique that can be used to augment the already present aggregation facilities these systems have in place.

7   Conclusion

In this paper we introduced the concept of *Cooperative Selective Wormholing (CSW)*, a new technique of traffic aggregation for intrusion detection systems. We demonstrated that there is room in the present Internet for CSW systems to achieve adequate address and port coverage, and examined the advantages and disadvantages of CSW compared to present traffic aggregration techniques. We presented a proof-of-concept CSW system, Vortex, and evaluated its performance, including its visibility to volunteers and attackers.

In the future we plan on expanding Vortex to provide a deployable selective wormhole architecture for use by security researchers. We are also looking for opportunities to integrate Vortex into existing honeynet architectures or other IDS analysis systems.

Acknowledgment

This work is in part supported by the NSF (awards ANI-0093221, ANI-0301108, and EIA-0224449), the DOE via ORNL, and by gifts from VMware, Dell, and Symantec.

References

1. Allman, M., Barford, P., Krishnamurthy, B., Wang, J.: Tracking the role of adversaries in measuring unwanted traffic. In: The 2nd Workshop on Steps to Reducing Unwanted Traffic on the Internet (2006)

2. Bailey, M., Cooke, E., Jahanian, F., Nazario, J., Watson, D.: The internet motion sensor: A distributed blackhole monitoring system. In: Proceedings of the 12th Annual Network and Distributed System Security Symposium (2005)
3. Bethencourt, J., Franklin, J., Vernon, M.: Mapping internet sensors with probe response attacks. In: Proceedings of the 14th USENIX Security Symposium (2005)
4. Claffy, K., Crovella, M., Friedman, T., Shannon, C., Spring, N.: Community-oriented network measurement infrastructure workshop report (2006)
5. Costa, M., Crowcroft, J., Castro, M., Rowstron, A., Zhou, L., Zhang, L., Barham, P.: Vigilante: End-to-end containment of internet worms. In: Proceedings of the twentieth ACM symposium on Operating systems principles, ACM Press, New York (2005)
6. Frincke, D.A., Tobin, D., McConnell, J.C., Marconi, J., Polla, D.: A framework for cooperative intrusion detection. In: Proc. 21st NIST-NCSC National Information Systems Security Conference, pp. 361–373 (1998)
7. Garfinkel, T., Rosenblum, M.: A virtual machine introspection based architecture for intrusion detection. In: Proc. Network and Distributed Systems Security Symposium (February 2003)
8. Grizzard, J.B., S Jr., C.R., Krasser, S., Owen, H.L., Riley, G.F.: Flow based observations from neti@home and honeynet data. In: Proceedings of the 2005 IEEE Workshop on Information Assurance and Security, IEEE Computer Society Press, Los Alamitos (2005)
9. Jiang, X., Xu, D.: Collapsar: A vm-based architecture for network attack detention center. In: Proceedings of the 13th USENIX Security Symposium (2004)
10. Lange, J.R., Dinda, P.A.: Transparent network services via a virtual traffic layer for virtual machines. In: Proceedings of the 16th IEEE International Symposium on High Performance Distributed Computing, IEEE Computer Society Press, Los Alamitos (to appear, 2007)
11. Larson, S.M., Snow, C.D., Shirts, M., Pande, V.S.: Folding@home and genome@home: Using distributed computing to tackle previously intractable problems in computational biology. In: Grant, R. (ed.) Computational Genomics, Horizon Press (2002)
12. Libnet, http://libnet.sourceforge.net/
13. Libpcap: Libpcap, http://sourceforge.net/projects/libpcap/
14. Liston, T.: The labrea tarpit, http://labrea.sourceforge.net/labrea-info.html
15. Lundin, E., Jonnson, E.: Privacy vs intrusion detection analysis. In: Proceedings of Recent Advances in Intrusion Detection (1999)
16. Minshall, G.: Tcpdpriv, http://ita.ee.lbl.gov/html/contrib/tcpdpriv.html
17. Moore, D., Shannon, C., Voelker, G., Savage, S.: Network telescopes: Technial report. Technical Report CS2004-0795, University of California, San Diego (2004)
18. Moore, D., Voelker, G.M., Savage, S.: Inferring internet Denial-of-Service activity. In: Prcoeedings of the 2001 USENIX Security Symposium (2001)
19. Pouget, F., Dacier, M., Pham, V.H.: Leurre.com: On the advantages of deploying a large scale distributed honeypot platform. In: Proceedings of ECCE'05, E-Crime and Computer Conference (2005)
20. Provos, N.: A virtual honeypot framework. In: Proceedings of the 13th USENIX Security Symposium (2004)
21. Rajab, M.A., Monrose, F., Terzis, A.: On the effectiveness of distributed worm monitoring. In: Proceedings of the 14th USENIX Security Symposium
22. Sapuntzakis, C., Chandra, R., Pfaff, B., Chow, J., Lam, M., Rosenblum, M.: Optimizing the migration of virtual computers. In: Proceedings of the 5th Symposium on Operating Systems Design and Implementation (December 2002)

23. Shavitt, Y., Shir, E.: Dimes: Let the internet measure itself. ACM SIGCOMM Computer Communication Review 35(5) (2005)
24. Sullivan, W.T., Werthimer, D., Bowyer, S., Cobb, J., Gedye, D., Anderson, D.: A new major seti project based on project serendip data and 100,000 personal computers. In: Cosmovici, C., Bowyer, S., Werthimer, D. (eds.) Proceedings of the Fifth International Conference on Bioastronomy. IAU Colloquim, vol. 161, Editrice Compositori, Bologna, Italy (1997)
25. Sundararaj, A.I., Dinda, P.A.: Towards virtual networks for virtual machine grid computing. In: Proceedings of the 3rd USENIX Virtual Machine Research and Technology Symposium (2004)
26. Sundararaj, A.I., Gupta, A., Dinda, P.A.: Increasing application performance in virtual environments through run-time inference and adaptation. In: Proceedings of the 14th IEEE International Symposium on High-Performance Distributed Computing, IEEE Computer Society Press, Los Alamitos (2005)
27. The Honeynet Project, http://project.honeynet.org
28. Vigna, G., Kemmerer, R.A., Blix, P.: Designing a web of highly-configurable intrusion detection sensors. In: Lee, W., Mé, L., Wespi, A. (eds.) RAID 2001. LNCS, vol. 2212, Springer, Heidelberg (2001)
29. Vrable, M., Ma, J., Chen, J., Moore, D., Vandekieft, E., Snoeren, A.C., Voelker, G., Savage, S.: Scalability, fidelity, and containment in the potemkin virtual honeyfarm. In: Proceedings of the 20th ACM symposium on Operating systems principles, ACM Press, New York (2005)
30. Weaver, N., Paxson, V., Staniford, S.: Wormholes and a honeyfarm: Automatically detecting novel worms. In: DIMACS Large Scale Attacks Workshop (2003)
31. WinPcap, http://www.winpcap.org/
32. Xu, J., Fan, J., Ammar, M., Moon, S.: Prefix-preserving ip address anonymization: Measurement-based security evaluation and a new cryptography-based scheme. In: Proceedings of the 10th IEEE International Conference on Network Protocols, IEEE Computer Society Press, Los Alamitos (2002)
33. Yegneswaran, V., Barford, P., Jha, S.: Global intrusion detection in the domino overlay system. In: Proceedings of Network and Distributed System Security Symposium (2004)
34. Yegneswaran, V., Barford, P., Plonka, D.: On the design and use of internet sinks for network abuse monitoring. In: Jonsson, E., Valdes, A., Almgren, M. (eds.) RAID 2004. LNCS, vol. 3224, Springer, Heidelberg (2004)

Author Index

Lecture Notes in Computer Science

For information about Vols. 1–4556

please contact your bookseller or Springer

Vol. 4603: F. Pfenning (Ed.), Automated Deduction – CADE-21. XII, 522 pages. 2007. (Sublibrary LNAI).

Vol. 4602: S. Barker, G.-J. Ahn (Eds.), Data and Applications Security XXI. X, 291 pages. 2007.

Vol. 4600: H. Comon-Lundh, C. Kirchner, H. Kirchner (Eds.), Rewriting, Computation and Proof. XVI, 273 pages. 2007.

Vol. 4599: S. Vassiliadis, M. Berekovic, T.D. Hämäläinen (Eds.), Embedded Computer Systems: Architectures, Modeling, and Simulation. XVIII, 466 pages. 2007.

Vol. 4598: G. Lin (Ed.), Computing and Combinatorics. XII, 570 pages. 2007.

Vol. 4597: P. Perner (Ed.), Advances in Data Mining. XI, 353 pages. 2007. (Sublibrary LNAI).

Vol. 4596: L. Arge, C. Cachin, T. Jurdziński, A. Tarlecki (Eds.), Automata, Languages and Programming. XVII, 953 pages. 2007.

Vol. 4595: D. Bošnački, S. Edelkamp (Eds.), Model Checking Software. X, 285 pages. 2007.

Vol. 4594: R. Bellazzi, A. Abu-Hanna, J. Hunter (Eds.), Artificial Intelligence in Medicine. XVI, 509 pages. 2007. (Sublibrary LNAI).

Vol. 4592: Z. Kedad, N. Lammari, E. Métais, F. Meziane, Y. Rezgui (Eds.), Natural Language Processing and Information Systems. XIV, 442 pages. 2007.

Vol. 4591: J. Davies, J. Gibbons (Eds.), Integrated Formal Methods. IX, 660 pages. 2007.

Vol. 4590: W. Damm, H. Hermanns (Eds.), Computer Aided Verification. XV, 562 pages. 2007.

Vol. 4589: J. Münch, P. Abrahamsson (Eds.), Product-Focused Software Process Improvement. XII, 414 pages. 2007.

Vol. 4588: T. Harju, J. Karhumäki, A. Lepistö (Eds.), Developments in Language Theory. XI, 423 pages. 2007.

Vol. 4587: R. Cooper, J. Kennedy (Eds.), Data Management. XIII, 259 pages. 2007.

Vol. 4586: J. Pieprzyk, H. Ghodosi, E. Dawson (Eds.), Information Security and Privacy. XIV, 476 pages. 2007.

Vol. 4585: M. Kryszkiewicz, J.F. Peters, H. Rybinski, A. Skowron (Eds.), Rough Sets and Intelligent Systems Paradigms. XIX, 836 pages. 2007. (Sublibrary LNAI).

Vol. 4584: N. Karssemeijer, B. Lelieveldt (Eds.), Information Processing in Medical Imaging. XX, 777 pages. 2007.

Vol. 4583: S.R. Della Rocca (Ed.), Typed Lambda Calculi and Applications. X, 397 pages. 2007.

Vol. 4582: J. Lopez, P. Samarati, J.L. Ferrer (Eds.), Public Key Infrastructure. XI, 375 pages. 2007.

Vol. 4581: A. Petrenko, M. Veanes, J. Tretmans, W. Grieskamp (Eds.), Testing of Software and Communicating Systems. XII, 379 pages. 2007.

Vol. 4580: B. Ma, K. Zhang (Eds.), Combinatorial Pattern Matching. XII, 366 pages. 2007.

Vol. 4579: B. M. Hämmerli, R. Sommer (Eds.), Detection of Intrusions and Malware, and Vulnerability Assessment. X, 251 pages. 2007.

Vol. 4578: F. Masulli, S. Mitra, G. Pasi (Eds.), Applications of Fuzzy Sets Theory. XVIII, 693 pages. 2007. (Sublibrary LNAI).

Vol. 4577: N. Sebe, Y. Liu, Y.-t. Zhuang, T.S. Huang (Eds.), Multimedia Content Analysis and Mining. XIII, 513 pages. 2007.

Vol. 4576: D. Leivant, R. de Queiroz (Eds.), Logic, Language, Information and Computation. X, 363 pages. 2007.

Vol. 4575: T. Takagi, T. Okamoto, E. Okamoto, T. Okamoto (Eds.), Pairing-Based Cryptography – Pairing 2007. XI, 408 pages. 2007.

Vol. 4574: J. Derrick, J. Vain (Eds.), Formal Techniques for Networked and Distributed Systems – FORTE 2007. XI, 375 pages. 2007.

Vol. 4573: M. Kauers, M. Kerber, R. Miner, W. Windsteiger (Eds.), Towards Mechanized Mathematical Assistants. XIII, 407 pages. 2007. (Sublibrary LNAI).

Vol. 4572: F. Stajano, C. Meadows, S. Capkun, T. Moore (Eds.), Security and Privacy in Ad-hoc and Sensor Networks. X, 247 pages. 2007.

Vol. 4571: P. Perner (Ed.), Machine Learning and Data Mining in Pattern Recognition. XIV, 913 pages. 2007. (Sublibrary LNAI).

Vol. 4570: H.G. Okuno, M. Ali (Eds.), New Trends in Applied Artificial Intelligence. XXI, 1194 pages. 2007. (Sublibrary LNAI).

Vol. 4569: A. Butz, B. Fisher, A. Krüger, P. Olivier, S. Owada (Eds.), Smart Graphics. IX, 237 pages. 2007.

Vol. 4568: T. Ishida, S. R. Fussell, P. T. J. M. Vossen (Eds.), Intercultural Collaboration. XIII, 395 pages. 2007.

Vol. 4566: M.J. Dainoff (Ed.), Ergonomics and Health Aspects of Work with Computers. XVIII, 390 pages. 2007.

Vol. 4565: D.D. Schmorrow, L.M. Reeves (Eds.), Foundations of Augmented Cognition. XIX, 450 pages. 2007. (Sublibrary LNAI).

Vol. 4564: D. Schuler (Ed.), Online Communities and Social Computing. XVII, 520 pages. 2007.

Vol. 4563: R. Shumaker (Ed.), Virtual Reality. XXII, 762 pages. 2007.

Vol. 4562: D. Harris (Ed.), Engineering Psychology and Cognitive Ergonomics. XXIII, 879 pages. 2007. (Sublibrary LNAI).

Vol. 4561: V.G. Duffy (Ed.), Digital Human Modeling. XXIII, 1068 pages. 2007.

Vol. 4560: N. Aykin (Ed.), Usability and Internationalization, Part II. XVIII, 576 pages. 2007.

Vol. 4559: N. Aykin (Ed.), Usability and Internationalization, Part I. XVIII, 661 pages. 2007.

Vol. 4558: M.J. Smith, G. Salvendy (Eds.), Human Interface and the Management of Information, Part II. XXIII, 1162 pages. 2007.

Vol. 4557: M.J. Smith, G. Salvendy (Eds.), Human Interface and the Management of Information, Part I. XXII, 1030 pages. 2007.